DATE DUE

5-31-96			
SE 2 4'98			

DEMCO 38-296

Arendt and Heidegger

Arendt and Heidegger

THE FATE OF THE POLITICAL

• *DANA R. VILLA* •

PRINCETON UNIVERSITY PRESS

PRINCETON, NEW JERSEY

Copyright © 1996 by Princeton University Press

William Street, Princeton, New Jersey 08540

niversity Press, Chichester, West Sussex

ts Reserved

iloging-in-Publication Data

na Richard.

Arendt and Heidegger : the fate of the political / Dana R. Villa.

p. cm.

Includes bibliographical references and index.

ISBN 0–691–04401–5 (CL : alk. paper).—ISBN 0–691–04400–7 (pbk. : alk. paper)

1. Arendt, Hannah—Contributions in political science.

2. Heidegger, Martin, 1889–1976—Contributions in political science.

3. Political science—Philosophy. I. Title.

JC251.A74V55   1995.

320′.092′2—dc20   95–13293

This book has been composed in Goudy

Princeton University Press books are printed on acid-free paper and meet the guidelines
for permanence and durability of the Committee on Production Guidelines for Book
Longevity of the Council on Library Resources

Printed in the United States of America by Princeton Academic Press

1   3   5   7   9   10   8   6   4   2

1   3   5   7   9   10   8   6   4   2
(pbk)

• CONTENTS •

THIS BOOK is about Hannah Arendt's theory of political action and its relation, both positive and negative, to the philosophy of Martin Heidegger. As such, its focus is at once narrow and broad. Narrow because I do not attempt to provide a comprehensive overview and critique of Arendt's political thought as a whole (readers anxious for such an overview would do well to consult George Kateb's study or Margaret Canovan's recent work). One unavoidable result of my focus on her theory of action is that important components of Arendt's thought are given summary treatment. Thus, to take but one example, *The Origins of Totalitarianism* receives relatively modest attention in what follows, as does *Eichmann in Jerusalem*. The danger of such a selective approach, as Canovan points out, is an underemphasis on the very experiences that drove Arendt to theorize about politics in the first place. Nevertheless, I feel that a focus on the radical and untraditional elements of her theory of action offers us a new and needed perspective on one of the most original political thinkers of the twentieth century. Indeed, it is my contention that the extent of Hannah Arendt's originality as a political thinker comes into view only through such sustained attention to her theory of political action and the way it breaks with the Western tradition of political thought.

The broadness of the project flows not simply from my using Heidegger to illuminate relatively neglected dimensions of Arendt's work and Arendt to criticize Heidegger's philosophical politics. To be sure, neither task is a small one. They are complicated, however, by the fact that so much of what is original in Arendt occurs as a critical response to our tradition of philosophy and political theory. Her theory of action performs what can only be called a depth critique of that tradition, right down to its Platonic-Aristotelian roots. She turns to Heidegger's deconstruction of Western philosophy in order to uncover the origins of this tradition's antipolitical prejudices. Arendt does not merely *repeat* Heidegger's "destructive" gesture: she pushes his interpretive violence in a direction he would not (and apparently did not) recognize. Thus, what is investigated here is not merely the complex relation of Arendt's political theory to Heidegger's philosophy but, perhaps more compellingly, Arendt's and Heidegger's critique of the tradition and their assessment of its contribution to contemporary pathologies.

The "and" in my title, then, hides the three-sided character of the discussion, a discussion that proceeds by juxtaposing Arendt and Heidegger to the foundationalist, authoritarian tradition they both attack. Needless to say, the Arendt who emerges in *this* context is a thinker at some distance from our everyday political concerns. Unlike some recent commentators, I have not attempted to "rethink" Arendt in order to make her more available to current political movements. All too often such "appropriative" readings have wound up either domesticating her thought or rejecting its central thematic concerns. Thus, for example, the all-important Arendtian distinction between public and private is often rejected by those who are critical of this distinction as it has been framed by liberal political theory. However, to want to hold onto Arendt's agonistic view of action while rejecting (or even failing to recognize) her concern for the peculiar reality of the public sphere is to leave Arendt behind. It is to make her guilty of holding *our* prejudices about how and why the line between public and private should be drawn, and then to chastise her for our projection. If one wants to criticize Arendt's public/private distinction, one should at least admit that it is *not* the same as that found in liberal theory, and that the motive behind it— namely, reminding us of the characteristics of a distinct yet historically variable phenomenological realm—has little to do with, say, Locke's demarcation of the boundaries of legitimate state power.

Reading Arendt with and against Heidegger is important, because it helps us to make sense of her fears about the dissipation of the public realm, a realm distinct from both the state and the economy. It also helps us to unravel the mystery of why she wanted to think of politics as a relatively pure, self-contained activity. Her fears and her response are thoughts out of season at a time when the blurring of boundaries is celebrated as the all-purpose cure for the deformations of the modern age.

Arendt's political theory, then, is important not solely for the resources it provides to current struggles (for greater equality, participation, and a healthier deliberative democracy). Its deeper value resides in the radically new perspective she offers on the *context* in which these struggles arise. Arendt attempts to "think what we are doing" in broad, world-historical terms. This project turns on making a distinction between politics, on the one hand, and "the political," on the other. This distinction draws attention to the large and unquestioned set of assumptions we currently bring to the understanding of political action, analysis, and judgment. Arendt deploys this distinction not in Platonist fashion, as a kind of transcendental measure of the *truly* political, but as a reminder of the limited and historically determined quality of *our* sense of the political. We will misconstrue this dimension of Arendt so long as our reading of her work is driven primarily by the political demands of our, or her, day. In my view, such readings constrict the horizons of her political thought, a thought fed equally by its encounter with the tradition and the conditions of contemporary existence, a thought whose urgency derives not so much from the imperative to act as from the need to understand.

• A C K N O W L E D G M E N T S •

Numerous individuals and institutions helped to make this book possible. I should like to thank the National Endowment for the Humanities for a timely grant; the Loeweinstein Fellowship at Amherst for additional funding; and the Trustees of Amherst College for their generous leaves policy. I should also like to thank the Center for European Studies at Harvard for providing a congenial home away from home during summers and my sabbatical. Finally, thanks to the staff at the Deutsches Literaturarchiv in Marbach for making available many of the manuscripts Heidegger sent Arendt. (The Arendt/Heidegger correspondence remains, as a general rule, off limits to scholars at the present time.)

I have benefited from conversation and argument with, amongst others, George Kateb, Seyla Benhabib, Richard Flathman, Bill Connolly, Bonnie Honig, Tracy Strong, Fred Dolan, Bob Gooding-Williams, Nathaniel Berman, Terry Aladjem, Patchen Markell, Shin Chiba, Nick Xenos, and (especially) Jeff Lomonaco. Parts of the book were presented at the Harvard and Princeton Political Philosophy Colloquiums: I wish to thank all who participated, especially Steve Macedo at Harvard. My colleague Austin Sarat proved a tireless reader of drafts and an indispensable source of much good advice. I first began reading Arendt seriously as a graduate student at Princeton, and I am grateful for the guidance Sheldon Wolin provided. I am also thankful to Richard Rorty, who afforded many of us at Princeton our first glimpse of a "disenchanted" Heidegger. As the book will attest, I have found disagreements with my teachers and colleagues to be the most instructive; I beg their indulgence.

Lurline Dowell word-processed the penultimate version of the entire book and was of great help throughout the composing process. Vicki Farrington bravely undertook the task of last-minute changes.

A special word of thanks to Cathy Ciepiela, Fred Dolan, and Tycho Manson for friendship over sometimes difficult years. The book is dedicated to my parents, whose support has been constant and unstinting. Finally, I should like to thank George Kateb, for the example provided by his dedication to the life of the mind, and Svetlana Boym, for teaching me about aesthetics and showing me that seriousness can take many forms, not all of them Germanic.

•

Parts of Chapter 3 originally appeared in *Political Theory*, vol. 20, no. 2, 274–308, © Sage Publications, reprinted by permission, Sage Publications, Inc.

As READERS of Arendt and Heidegger know, one aspect of the Western tradition they do not address critically is its gender bias. Both employ a philosophical/ theoretical vocabulary notable for its masculine pronouns and equation of "man" with humanity or human individuals. For the most part, I have chosen to leave their usage intact, rather than create the highly misleading impression of gender neutrality or gender sensitivity in their texts. Since much of my discussion concerns their response to Aristotle, Kant, Nietzsche, et al., the avoidance of anachronism with respect to these authors also required resisting the temptation to transmute their vocabulary into something more palatable from our perspective.

IN CITING works in the notes, short titles have generally been used. Works frequently cited throughout the book, as well as in the notes, have been identified by the following abbreviations. Full references can be found in the Bibliography.

BPF	Hannah Arendt, *Between Past and Future*
BT	Martin Heidegger, *Being and Time*
BW	Martin Heidegger, *Basic Writings*
CR	Hannah Arendt, *Crises of the Republic*
HAP	Philippe Lacoue-Labarthe, *Heidegger, Art and Politics*
HC	Hannah Arendt, *The Human Condition*
IM	Martin Heidegger, *An Introduction to Metaphysics*
Kant Lectures	Hannah Arendt, *Lectures on Kant's Political Philosophy*
LH	Martin Heidegger, "Letter on Humanism," in *Basic Writings*
LM	Hannah Arendt, *The Life of the Mind*
MDT	Hannah Arendt, *Men in Dark Times*
NE	Aristotle, *Nicomachean Ethics*
OR	Hannah Arendt, *On Revolution*
OT	Hannah Arendt, *The Origins of Totalitarianism*
OWA	Martin Heidegger, "The Origin of the Work of Art," in *Poetry, Language, Thought*
PDM	Jürgen Habermas, *The Philosophical Discourse of Modernity*
POB	Richard Wolin, *The Politics of Being*
QCT	Martin Heidegger, "The Question Concerning Technology," in *The Question Concerning Technology and Other Essays*
SZ	Martin Heidegger, *Sein und Zeit*

Arendt and Heidegger

The Problem of Action in Arendt

We are still far from thinking the essence of action
decisively enough.

—Heidegger, "Letter on Humanism"

HANNAH ARENDT's conception of political action is widely recognized as original, yet many regard it as so permeated by nostalgia that it is of questionable relevance to modern politics. Even the most sympathetic of her commentators accuse her of succumbing to the longing for Greece that has been the occupational hazard of German philosophy since Kant. Moreover, those readers point out, Arendt is not above abandoning the *polis* as paradigm and turning to a Homeric or Nietzschean glorification of the heroic dimension of action.[1] It would appear, then, that the resulting theory of political action requires substantial modification if it is to be relevant to our age.

Arendt's theory *is* acknowledged to be important and useful for the present insofar as it effects what Habermas has called "the systematic renewal of the Aristotelian concept of *praxis*."[2] This renewal has been important to a wide range of criticisms of the instrumentalization of action and the decline of the public realm in modern political theory and practice. Many who are in debt to Arendt on this score are nonetheless anxious to ignore those aspects of her theory that have not gained wide acceptance or defy easy synthesis. By means of a selective reading, Arendt's theory of political action can be "saved" from itself.

It is no coincidence, then, that political theorists sympathetic to her work have stressed its Aristotelian elements, to the point where Arendt's "Aristotelianism" is now a truism. Her theory of action is influential today as the most penetrating and original "recovery" of Aristotelian categories and distinctions for contemporary political theory. It has, for example, provided advocates of participatory democracy with an effective vocabulary for questioning liberalism's predominately instrumentalist conception of politics. In addition, it has been of fundamental importance to those working in the tradition of Critical Theory, enabling them to rethematize the intersubjective nature of political action, a dimension that had been obscured by categories inherited from Marx and Weber. Most recently, it has served to reintroduce an avowedly Aristotelian conception of community into debates between liberals and communitarians over the relative priority of "right" and "the good" in democratic politics.

Each of these appropriations originates in an essentially Aristotelian reading of Arendt's theory of political action. All have fully, sometimes brilliantly, exploited this side of her work. Yet such readings inevitably domesticate what is, in fact, the most radical rethinking of political action undertaken by a theorist in this century. As Nietzsche reminds us in *The Gay Science*, "seeing things as similar and making things the same is the sign of weak eyes."[3] Arendt's appropriators—her "friends"—are guilty of such hermeneutical myopia when they assert the primacy of the Aristotelian heritage in her work.

This is not to deny Aristotle's influence on Arendt's political theory. However, once we are clear as to the nature and ambition of the Arendtian project, the character of this influence becomes contestable. It is, in certain respects, more negative than positive. Arendt argues *against* Aristotle, and not merely against his philosophical prejudices. Her theory of action attempts a radical reconceptualization of action, one that proceeds, in part, through a critique and transformation of Aristotelian *praxis*. This fact is lost sight of in Habermas's insistence that Arendt's project is one of "renewal." More generally, if Arendt "recovers" elements of the Western tradition of political theory, she does so in order to better *overcome* that tradition. Her theory of action is a central moment in this project, insofar as it serves to highlight the very phenomenon which that tradition repeatedly condemns. So contextualized, Arendt's notion of action refers us less to Aristotle than it does to another overcomer of the tradition: her teacher, Martin Heidegger.

First, however, to the more familiar Arendt. No reader of *The Human Condition* can doubt the paradigmatic significance the Greek *polis* has for Arendt. She romanticizes Greek political life, but her depiction of the *polis* is no exercise in nostalgia. As theorists such as Sheldon Wolin and Benjamin Barber have helped us to see, Arendt's theory of action reformulates politics in terms of continuous and direct civic involvement.[4] She thereby challenges our most deeply rooted liberal preconceptions about the *nature* of politics. Following Aristotle, Arendt passionately asserts that the essence of politics is *action*. Laws and institutions, which to the liberal mind are the stuff of politics, for Arendt supply the framework for action. The activities of debate, deliberation, and participation in decision making come to occupy center stage. Moreover, since politics *is* action, we need to recast our notion of citizenship in a participatory mode: not to be active in the political affairs of one's community is to cease to be a genuine, full member of that community, as both Arendt and Aristotle point out.[5] No less important is Arendt's Aristotelian insistence that the public realm is a sphere unto itself, separated by a wide gulf from the interests and desires that make up civil society. By dramatically distinguishing the political realm from the economic, Arendt restores to politics an integrity and dignity that it is denied by the liberal tradition, a tradition that views politics as, in Barber's phrase, "the chambermaid of private interests."[6]

For proponents of participatory or decentralized democracy, the Arendtian "renewal of *praxis*" has far-reaching implications in both theory and practice. Her account of action made it possible to question standard procedural interpretations of democracy and the vocabulary of interests, preferences, and bargaining deployed by pluralist accounts. Best of all, it facilitated this critique in the name of *politics*, rather than more problematic notions such as social justice or community. By taking the Aristotelian idea of politics as an end in itself with the utmost seriousness, Arendt almost single-handedly transformed the debate about the nature, tasks, and possibilities of democratic politics. Her recovery of the Greek ideal of the *bios politikos* enabled participatory democrats to articulate a "strong" democratic politics, a politics grounded on an emphatic distinction between the public and private, one free of the "crass instrumentalism" that colors the liberal view of politics from Hobbes to the present.[7]

A very different, but equally influential, appropriation of Arendt has been performed by Jürgen Habermas and others working within the tradition of Critical Theory (e.g., Albrecht Wellmer, Richard Bernstein, and Seyla Benhabib).[8] These theorists, like their Frankfurt School predecessors, have been concerned with the threat posed by the universalization of technical rationality, in particular its extension to the political sphere. As ever-larger areas of social existence are subjected to the dictates of instrumental reason and to the prerogatives of rational administration, the space left for the exercise of citizenship gradually disappears. Enlightenment ideals of freedom, autonomy, and a rational, democratic political order are undermined and virtually extinguished by the process of economic and bureaucratic rationalization (Weber's "iron cage"). Indeed, in the opinion of an earlier generation of critical theorists (most notably Max Horkheimer and Theodor Adorno), the "dialectic of enlightenment" offered nothing but irony: the emancipatory potential of the Enlightenment was revealed as a mask for a reason whose essence was domination on a global scale.[9]

While agreeing with Horkheimer and Adorno (and, of course, Weber) that the process of rationalization has been far more ambiguous than Marx ever imagined, Habermas and others of his generation have been unable to accept their totalizing critique of reason with its accompanying retreat to the aesthetic realm. In reaction to Horkheimer and Adorno's negative dialectic (which terminates in yet another "night in which all cats are gray"), Habermas has struggled to show that "rationalization" does not inevitably mean domination. The imperialism of *zweckrationalität* (purposive rationality) needs to be combated on all fronts, to be sure, but this can be done effectively only in the name of an alternative rationality, one that aims at consensus rather than success or control. Habermas thinks that such a dialogical rationality is perhaps the central component of our identity as moderns.[10] And while this rationality may be covered over by technocratic doctrines of decisionism, it remains implicit in the very structure of communicative action.

For Habermas, then, the important thing is to bring to light the consensual rationality implicit in speech, to show the strides toward autonomy it has made throughout the modern period, and to remind us of the claim this rationality still exercises upon our political lives.[11] However, this project cannot even be formulated using only the conceptual resources of Marxism or Weberian social science. Marx's notion of labor as *praxis* conflates acting and making, blinding him to the specificity of the political realm and the peculiar structure of practical discourse. Weber's conception of rationalization explicitly denies the possibility of a "disenchanted," yet substantively rational, form of social action. Critical Theory thus found itself at an impasse, which it escaped, so the Habermasian story goes, thanks largely to Hannah Arendt.[12]

The rigorous Aristotelian distinction between *praxis* and *poiēsis* posed by Arendt's theory of action enabled Habermas to distinguish systematically between communicative and instrumental action and to identify the logics of rationalization appropriate to each.[13] Whereas rationalization in the economic sphere indeed connoted greater order, efficiency, and system coherence, the rationalization of communicative action pointed to increasing acceptance of the principle that validity claims be redeemed discursively, through a process of rational argumentation. Moreover, Arendt's sketches of the "general structures of unforced intersubjectivity" that are the preconditions of *praxis* supplied Habermas with a standard (the counterfactual "ideal speech situation") for ascertaining the conditions under which the "force of the better argument" could indeed carry the day.[14] Thanks to Arendt's theory of action, the way to a comprehensive theory of communicative rationality was opened.

Critical theorists rely on Arendt's "renewal of *praxis*" less for the conception of citizenship it implies than for the distinctions between types of action and rationality it makes possible. Her recovery of Aristotle becomes an important weapon in defending the "lifeworld" from the encroachments of the "system." Quite different in emphasis is the use to which her theory has been put by communitarian critics of liberal theories of justice. Michael Sandel, Charles Taylor, and Alasdair MacIntyre have all questioned the Enlightenment effort to derive principles of political right and practical judgment independent of any concrete, particular vision of the good.[15] In particular, they have been critical of the "point of origin" for all such deductions, the Kantian idea of an unsituated subject, a subject "unencumbered" by any and all constitutive attachments. Ultimately, they claim, the universalist aspirations of theorists like Kant and Rawls are self-defeating, in that the model of the self they presuppose fatally undercuts the real sources of our most deeply held principles and hopes, the traditions and communities that shape who we are. The result is a drift toward moral subjectivism and political anomie.

The primary culprit here, at least on Sandel's account, is a creature called "deontological liberalism." This breed of liberalism seeks to establish the absolute priority of right over the good, in order to ensure principles of justice that in no way interfere with individuals' freedom to choose and pursue their own idea of the good life. In other words, deontological liberalism presumes that rights can in fact "swing free" of any particular conception of the good, since the role of a *just* political society is "not to promote any particular ends" but rather to enable "its citizens to pursue their own ends consistent with a similar liberty for all."[16] The question deontological liberalism must answer before it proceeds with its deduction of principles is *how* this notion of "right" can be grounded. Both Kant and Rawls have used a hypothetical self to answer this question. While Kant's "transcendental ego" and Rawls "unencumbered self" are different from a methodological point of view (one metaphysical, the other not), they are similar in that they serve to isolate the rational, freely choosing self from the contingent desires, interests, strengths, and weaknesses that make up the concrete individual. By filtering out "the subject of all possible ends" from the empirical self, they ground right upon human freedom rather than that which is simply given.

According to communitarians, this vision of a sovereign chooser for whom justice precedes the good is an optical illusion. When pressed, liberal principles of justice reveal themselves to be derivative of *some* conception of the good; they are therefore "parasitic on a notion of community it [liberalism] officially rejects."[17] An "unencumbered self" would never choose Rawl's difference principle, for example, unless there was some "prior moral tie" to the other subjects in the "original position."[18] But if community in fact underlies justice, liberalism has effectively short-circuited the articulation of the constitutive attachments that make up our *public* selves. *Qua* citizens, we remain abstract, rights-bearing individuals, bereft of unifying purpose. Our intersubjective, "thickly constituted" selves find expression in the private sphere (in terms of family, religion, ethnic heritage), but we lack a political vocabulary and sense of membership that would be adequate to the expression of community purpose. For this reason, a politics of the common good has little claim on us.

If the communitarian critique of liberalism is at all cogent, then political theory would appear to be in dire need of a vocabulary that would help turn the "inverted world" of liberalism right side up. Such a vocabulary would recognize that the self is not and cannot be a *premise* of politics, but only the "precarious achievement" of a life lived in a political community animated by a strong sense of shared purpose and identity.[19] Such a vocabulary, some of the communitarians believe, is to be found in Arendt's theory of political action. Arendt's theory identifies freedom not with an individual's choice of life-style, but with "acting together" for the sake of the community.[20] Her account stresses how such acting together—"the sharing of words and deeds"—is in fact the medium through which the self is defined—makes its appearance as something solid and worldly. A community, a shared world, a common space of appearance, is the fundamental condition for the achievement of selfhood. Further, it is by "acting together" that our sense of the world, and the sorts of things we deem fit to appear in it, are developed. That is to say, it is through political action that our sense of *justice*—of what we owe to our fellow citizens and to those who come after us—is both articulated and preserved. Without a "community sense," justice becomes mere legality.[21] For these and other reasons, the communitarians see Arendt as placing *community* at the very heart of politics, making it the cornerstone of selfhood, freedom, and justice. Arendt's theory of action is valuable because it recovers the dimension of shared purpose that Aristotle had claimed was central to the formation of a *political* association. By reasserting the Aristotelian notion of *koinonia*, Arendt's theory helps us escape the picture of the subject as sovereign that (to paraphrase Wittgenstein) held us captive. It frees us from the anomie of the "procedural republic" and gives us a taste of the "good in common" that only a robust political life can deliver.[22]

The three projects described above all draw heavily upon Arendt's theory of action in their attempts to come to grips with the ills of modern politics. Their criticisms and goals are diverse, but the readings of Arendt that they sketch or presume are remarkably similar. For the participatory democrat, it is Arendt's Aristotelian identification of action and politics, and her recovery of the conception of citizenship proposed in the *Politics*, that open new vistas to contemporary theory. For the Critical Theorist, it is her rediscovery of Aristotle's distinction between acting and making that is significant, since this makes possible a comprehensive theory of communicative action and consensual rationality. Finally, for the communitarian, Arendt restates the fundamental insight of the third book of the *Politics*; namely, that citizens must be bound together by more than a desire for mutual benefit if they are to experience the existential and moral enrichment that politics can provide.

These examples indicate just how tempting it is to locate Arendt's work comfortably within the Aristotelian horizon. Viewed as "the systematic renewal of *praxis*," Arendt's theory of action is astonishingly "ready-to-hand," available for various theoretical projects. It is hardly surprising that her appropriators have encouraged us to see her work as primarily an exercise in remembrance, as the recovery of traditional concepts and distinctions for critical employment in the present.

Admittedly, Arendt's text sometimes encourages us in such a reading. In the preface to *Between Past and Future* and in the essay "Tradition and the Modern Age," she vividly describes our age as one deprived of the transmissive mediation of tradition: "the past has ceased to throw its light upon the future," in Tocqueville's phrase.[23] *Our* dilemma seems to be precisely the opposite of the one Nietzsche diagnosed in *The Use and Abuse of History*: we suffer not from an excess of memory and its enervating effects, but rather from a peculiar forgetfulness. When the medium of remembrance—tradition—dissolves or is shattered, the only escape from the abyss of forgetfulness seems to reside in the theoretical project of aggressive, critical recovery. Excavating a tradition in ruins can, as Sheldon Wolin has observed, "remind us of what we have lost."[24] Such a reminder provides a standard against which the deficiencies of contemporary politics can be measured.

But while the trope of remembrance is inescapable in characterizing Arendt's project, it serves to suppress what is difficult, sometimes worrisome, and unquestionably original in her work. Ernst Vollrath has reminded us—and we *need* reminding—that Arendt's political theory is, in many respects, without precedent, literally incomparable.[25] To see her theory of action as essentially an exercise in renewal, recovery, or retrieval provides an immediate critical return, but it does so only at the cost of blinding us to the more radical nature of her project. This nature consists, as I indicated above, in the attempt to rethink action in an explicitly antitraditional manner. From Arendt's perspective, there is little choice: the "break in our tradition" accomplished by the fact of totalitarian domination in this century makes the recovery of traditional concepts both impossible and pointless. All attempts to "re-tie the broken thread of tradition," whether by a return to origins (Strauss) or through the vehicle of dialogue with the past (Wolin, Gadamer), are doomed.[26] The pressing problem is not to *recover* ancient concepts and categories, or to *restore* tradition in some form, but rather to deconstruct and overcome the reifications of a dead tradition. As Arendt reminds us, the fact that our tradition has come to an end does not liberate us from it; rather, "it sometimes seems that [the] power of well-worn notions and categories becomes more tyrannical as the tradition loses its living force and as the memory of its beginning recedes."[27]

Arendt's theory of action can be seen as part of a larger project of "remembrance," then, only if we are sensitive to the specific twist she gives this term. "Remembrance," as Arendt practices it, does not seek to revive concepts *qua* concepts, but to "distill from them anew their original spirit," to arrive at the "underlying phenomenal reality" concealed by such "empty shells."[28] The "irreparable break in tradition" requires, in Walter Benjamin's phrase, "a tiger's leap into the past."[29] The motive behind such interpretive violence is not simple preservation, but the destruction of the fossilized structures and contexts that deny access to the living kernel. The reward of such violence, of such tearing out of context, is never the renewal of a conceptual network, but "thought fragments" wrested from the past.[30] In her remarkable essay on Walter Benjamin, Arendt gives a description of Benjamin's "poetic" thinking, a description that applies equally well to her own thought:

> . . . this thinking, fed by the present, works with the "thought fragments" it can wrest from the past and gather about itself. Like a pearl diver who descends to the bottom of the sea, not to excavate the bottom and bring it to light but to pry loose the rich and the strange, the pearls and the coral in the depths and to carry them to the surface, this thinking delves into the depths of the past—but not in order to resuscitate it the way it was and to contribute to the renewal of extinct ages. What guides this thinking is the conviction that although the living is subject to the ruin of time, the process of decay is at the same time a process of crystallization, that in the depth of the sea, into which sinks and is dissolved what was once alive, some things "suffer a sea-change" and survive in new crystallized forms and shapes that remain immune to the elements, as though they waited only for the pearl diver who one day will come down to them and bring them up into the world of the living—as "thought fragments," as something "rich and strange," and perhaps as everlasting *phänomene*.[31]

In the same essay, Arendt notes the striking similarity between Benjamin's approach to the past, in which "the heir and preserver unexpectedly turns into a destroyer," and Heidegger's.[32] Heidegger's famous *Destruktion* of the history of ontology, announced in section 6 of *Being and Time*, was a response to the thoughtlessness induced by the rigor mortis of the tradition: "Tradition takes what has come down to us and delivers it over to self-evidence; it blocks our access to those primordial 'sources' from which the categories and concepts handed down to us have been in part quite genuinely drawn."[33] The task of destruction, as practiced by Arendt, Benjamin, and Heidegger, is never simply negative: it does not express the childish wish to "have done" with the past. It is undertaken precisely in order to gain access to primordial experiences whose very strangeness serves to shatter the complacency of the present.[34] This complacency does not result from our *forgetting* the tradition; rather, the point is that *the tradition is itself the primary form of forgetfulness*, essentially a reification.

In aligning Arendt's approach to the past and tradition with Benjamin's and Heidegger's, I am not accusing Arendt's appropriators of a misplaced antiquarianism. They, like Arendt, follow Nietzsche's dictum that "the past is understood in terms of what is strongest in the present, or not at all."[35] However, I want to insist upon the difference between a critical remembrance, which views the past as a resource of meaning, and a more radical form of remembrance, which aims to *intensify* our sense of "the gap between past and future."[36] The former is irreducibly dialectical in approach; like Hegel, it seeks to enter a dialogue with the past in order to create a critically powerful *bildungsroman* (story of education or development). The latter approach, in contrast, eschews the comfort to be gained by recasting the tradition in the form of dialogue; it takes the gap or break in tradition as its starting point, as the "non-place" that determines what Arendt calls the "contemporary conditions of thought."[37] In the first case, the appropriation of the past proceeds by a transvaluation of temporal distance: historical alienation becomes the productive ground of an understanding that occurs in the form of a "fusion of horizons" (Gadamer). Negativity appears as resource, continually reinscribed, in the manner of Hegel, in the *logos*.

The approach Arendt shares with Benjamin and Heidegger, on the other hand, steadfastly denies the totalization implicit in active—dialogical—appropriation. It insists instead upon the peculiar isolation of the present in a world from which authority, in the form of tradition, has vanished. It is one thing to acknowledge the primacy of our hermeneutical situation in every act of interpretation or understanding of the past, but quite another to insist that this situation is such that remembrance can only occur by a "leap"; that retrieval is concerned with fragments; and that all genuine recovery is in fact a brand of "poetic thinking."[38]

With these caveats in mind, we can begin to address the problem posed by Arendt's theory of political action. It is clear that some modesty is in order when it comes to assuming that *we* know what is strongest in the present; that is, the "context" for Arendtian remembrance. *She* did not start from a quarrel with liberal pragmatism or a fear of bureaucratic expansionism, although she is, of course, vehemently critical of both. Rather, for Arendt, what is strongest in the present, what feeds her "unhistorical" thought, is the fact of the rootlessness of modern humanity, our radical alienation from the world.[39] It was this rootlessness, this lack of place in the world, that in her view made totalitarianism possible.[40] Arendt's political thought seeks to trace the genealogy of this rootlessness (or "worldlessness") and to show how political action, and *only* political action, can combat it and the pathologies it creates. Taking "world alienation" as the central fact of the modern age, she did not attempt to enlist Aristotle in the fight against bureaucratic and technical rationality, but rather to use him to do something much greater. She wanted, in George Kateb's words, "to do what had never been done: to supply a philosophical account of the meaning of political action."[41]

Kateb's formulation has the merit of focusing our attention on the essential dimension of Arendt's theory of political action, that of *meaning*. In the context of a world characterized by the retreat of meaning, by a boundless instrumentalization that converts everything into a means for some subjectively posited end, the *meaning* of political action resides in its capacity to endow the world *with* meaning, to give it a significance and beauty it would otherwise lack. The meaning creative or revelatory capacity of political action gives it, in Arendt's eyes, an "existential supremacy" over all other human activities.[42] In so doing, political action redeems human existence and facilitates reconciliation with mortality. Only political action can refute the tragic wisdom of Silenus, that "Not to be born prevails over all meaning uttered in words; by far the second-best for life once it has appeared, is to go as swiftly as possible whence it came."[43]

This is an extraordinarily radical and profoundly original claim. In making it, Arendt "recovers" a sense of action found nowhere in the Western tradition of political philosophy. Indeed, it was that tradition, with its teleological model of action, that effaced the robust plurality of the public realm and robbed political action of any intrinsic worth. Arendt's theory of action proceeds by lifting *praxis*, in "crystallized" form, out of its philosophical context and resetting it in an existential one. It is for this reason that it takes the seemingly extravagant form it does. In theorizing action, Arendt provides us with nothing less than a phenomenology of meaning itself: its sources, conditions, modes of presencing, and possibilities for permanence.

Another way of putting this is to say that the motivation behind Arendt's theory of action is, partly, ontological. Her appropriation of *praxis*, poetic as it is, is guided by a desire to recover not concepts, but a certain way of being-in-the-world. Action creates a disclosive relation between plural individuals and their common world, a relation that is constantly threatened by the philosophical/human-all-too-human desire to escape its contingency and groundlessness and find a more stable alternative (politics as *technē*, as *epistēmē*, or as instrumentality). Arendt's thesis is that only the life of action in the public realm saves the world from being permanently "dimmed-down." The "worldlessness" of modern man, his pervasive subjectification of reality from Descartes to modern technology, incites a concern for dimensions of human existence—worldliness, the public realm, the spontaneous disclosive potential of action—that are in danger of vanishing forever. Any interpretation of her theory of action that ignores this concern does so at its peril, for it is here that Arendt's "renewal of *praxis*" comes together with her critique of modernity and her deconstruction of the Western tradition of political philosophy.

This set of concerns transcends the more immediately practical horizon drawn by Arendt's appropriators. In their rush to apply her insights, they dramatically underestimate the extent of her rethinking of political action and the political. They fail to see that Arendt views the teleocratic concept of *praxis* in Aristotle as internally linked to the modern instrumental view, in which action "is identified with effects guided by strategic reason."[44] Moreover, they fail to see that her emphasis upon the intersubjective nature of action is, as it were, only the first step in the displacement of the traditional concept of action. This leaves them consistently mystified by some of Arendt's more characteristic pronouncements concerning the nature of political action. For example, they cannot explain what motivates Arendt's argument that political action transcends the moral criteria that govern ordinary human behavior: in a theorist who adamantly opposes the use of force or violence in the public realm, this stipulation seems perverse. Further, they find Arendt's preference for describing political action in a vocabulary drawn largely from the performing arts is needlessly constricting and often misleading (she appears to be motivated by some inexplicable need to *aestheticize* action). Finally, and by far most commonly, her appropriators are exasperated by her unyielding and apparently dogmatic demand that the political realm be preserved untainted from the "vulgar" concerns for social and economic justice, not to mention the more prosaic array of social issues (housing, schools, health care, etc.) that we normally identify as the content of politics.[45]

I will return to these and other objections to Arendt's theory of action below (Section III of Chapter 1). Here, I simply want to note that her sympathetic readers typically explain away her apparently untenable desire for a "purely political" politics the same way they account for her critical power: they cite her debt to Aristotle. In *this* context, an asset (the "renewal of *praxis*") is reduced to a liability, the suggestion being that Arendt has taken the Aristotelian idea of political action as an end in itself far too literally, and for no good reason. Habermas speaks for many when he refers to the "clamps" of Arendt's overly Aristotelian theory of action, to conceptual distinctions dogmatically adhered to despite their irrelevance to modern politics.[46]

I mention this criticism in order to show the peculiar interpretive dialectic to which Arendt's political theory has been subjected. On the one hand she is praised for restoring a robust concept of political action, one derived from *praxis*; on the other hand she is accused of going too far in this endeavor, of falling prey to a kind of theoretical antiquarianism. The reader should note how Habermas's critique completes the circle: both what is living and what is (presumably) dead in the Arendtian conception of political action are traced back to the influence of Aristotle. We are left with a picture of Arendt's theory that, despite all protests to the contrary, renders it either unoriginal or arbitrary. Breaking out of this circle requires that we rethematize the political-ontological stakes of her theory of action, for much of what appears paradoxical in Arendt is in fact central to her project of radically reconceptualizing action. By focusing on the ontological dimension of her thought, the previously marginalized aspects are recuperated: they make sense, although in a way that is not harmonious with the characterization of "renewal." There are, of course, ample reasons for being critical of the resulting theory of action; my point, however, is that excessive respect for fossilized distinctions on Arendt's part is not one of them.

The most compelling reason for reading Arendt's theory of action against the tradition, and in light of her ontological concerns, is the desire to do justice to her enormous theoretical ambition. Responding to what Philippe Lacoue-Labarthe and Jean-Luc Nancy have called the "withdrawal of the political" (*le retrait du politique*) in the modern age,[47] Arendt sought to (1) expose the role philosophy has played in delimiting the Western conception of the political; and (2) affirm, against this delimitation, the importance of human plurality and the reality of the "space of appearances"—the public realm—that it makes possible. Paradoxically, Heidegger's thought provides the absolutely essential background for Arendt's rethinking of the political: without his "shift in paradigm," her project would be unimaginable.

Schematically, the Heideggerian project provides a basis for Arendt's in three broad areas. First, his book *Being and Time* provides a conception of human freedom that largely (but not totally) avoids the reductionist, antiworldly tendencies of the subject-centered conceptions of freedom that dominate the tradition. In this regard, Heidegger's articulation of man's disclosive relation to Being, and the way in which this relation gets covered over or forgotten, are of critical importance to Arendt's attempt to theorize political action in nonteleological, open, or "an-archic" terms.[48] Second, Heidegger exposes, in his subsequent work, the will to mastery and security that underlies the Western metaphysical tradition and that determines the tradition's conceptualization of action. Arendt appropriates Heidegger's deconstruction in order to show how the philosophical hostility to contingency and plurality, to *politics*, results in a self-conscious reinterpretation of action designed to exclude these dimensions. Third, and last, Heidegger's diagnosis of the alienation of the modern age, an alienation rooted in the attempt to cast the subject in a foundational epistemological and ontological role, provides Arendt with the frame for a critique of modernity that illuminates the *political* consequences of this pervasive subjectification—a critique Heidegger was himself ill-equipped to make.

In emphasizing Arendt's debt to Heidegger's thought, it is not my intention to reduce her political philosophy to the status of a footnote to someone else's, to replace Aristotle with Heidegger. I see Arendt as appropriating Heidegger in a highly agonistic manner; as twisting, displacing, and reinterpreting his thought in ways designed to illuminate a range of exceedingly *un*-Heideggerian issues; for example, the nature of political action, the *positive* ontological role of the public realm, the nature of political judgment, and the conditions for an antiauthoritarian, antifoundational democratic politics. Indeed, no small part of Arendt's originality resides in her ability to see the political implications of a body of work in a way that goes against the grain of authorial intent. Arendt is no epigone; it is important to stress that her appropriation of Heidegger is implicitly and explicitly opposed to "Heideggerian politics," whether by this phrase we are referring to what Bourdieu, Ferry, and other critics have called the "revolutionary conservatism" of the mid-thirties or to the antivoluntarism of *Gelassenheit* (releasement), which dominates the later work.[49] I am, of course, aware of the irony of enlisting Heidegger—the philosopher, Nazi rector, and critic of democracy—as a hermeneutical aid in reading Arendt—the political theorist, Jewish émigré, and champion of democracy. Nevertheless, the fact remains that her political theory, more than any other, "recovers" Heidegger's thought for the task of rethinking the political.[50] In the process she provides us with the tools for the most powerful and convincing critique of his philosophical politics.

One final note. Arendt does not attempt to "democratize" Heidegger—a clearly impossible project. My reading shows how she appropriates themes from his philosophy to aid her struggle against a tradition hostile to plurality, disagreement, and politics itself. While Heidegger's deconstruction of the Western philosophical tradition is an invaluable tool, it is no substitute for Arendt's own phenomenology of action and the public realm. In order to think action and politics without the appeal to extrapolitical ultimates, we must turn not to Heidegger the philosopher, but to Arendt the political thinker.

• PART I •

Arendt's Theory of Political Action

Arendt, Aristotle, and Action

... action and production are generically different.

—*Aristotle*, Nicomachean Ethics

I. ARISTOTLE AND ARENDT ON THE SELF-CONTAINEDNESS OF ACTION

Hannah Arendt begins *The Human Condition* by accusing the Western philosophical tradition of *effacement*. She contends that "the enormous weight of contemplation" in the Western philosophical tradition served, historically, to blur the inner articulations of the *vita activa*, the active life.[1] From Arendt's point of view, the Socratic tradition and Christianity share an obsession with an absolute Truth far greater than man and his deeds, a Truth available to man only through the cessation of all worldly activity. Contemplative stillness made a relationship to the eternal possible. From this ascetic-theoretical perspective, the classical hierarchy of human activities was leveled: the component parts of the active life—labor, work, and action—appeared equally base, equally constrained by necessity. Only contemplation, the *bios theoretikos*, seemed to offer a life of freedom, while the *bios politikos* seemed, if anything, to be more of an entanglement than either labor or work. While Arendt believes that Marx and Nietzsche, in their rebellion against the Socratic-Christian valuation, succeeded in reversing the traditional hierarchy of the contemplative and the active life, the very success of this reversal did nothing to remedy the original blurring of the inner articulations of the *vita activa*. Indeed, from Arendt's perspective, the violent anti-Platonism of Marx and Nietzsche served only to further efface these distinctions.[2] By setting life and labor over against the "eternal realm" of Being, they preserved the metaphysical tradition's conflation of labor, work, and action.

Arendt takes the failure of the Marxian/Nietzschean attempt to break out of the Western philosophical tradition's conceptual framework as the cue for her own project. She seeks to rearticulate the component parts of the *vita activa* in all their specificity and irreducibility. Her hope is that distinguishing clearly between these activities will pave the way to a revaluation of politics and political action, and to a new appreciation of human plurality and the world of appearances in which it finds expression.

This is no small task in an age that, according to Arendt, scorns the political and glorifies labor and its productivity: Marx and Adam Smith are equally contemptuous of the "unproductive" political sphere.[3] Nevertheless, the project must be undertaken, the revaluation attempted, for to forget the distinctiveness and value of action is tantamount, Arendt argues, to forgetting what makes us human.

Political action in its genuine form is disappearing from the world, both in fact and in theory. Should this process be allowed to complete itself, human beings will no longer be able to claim that they, alone amongst all animals, are free.[4]

One cannot fail to be struck by the supreme confidence with which Arendt makes her distinctions. Her descriptive conceptualizations of labor, work, and action in *The Human Condition* leave no room for confusion or conflation: each activity emerges in sharp contrast to the other two. It is precisely the sharpness of this contrast that disturbs critics, who see what starts as an admirable and overdue attempt to separate the political from the nonpolitical congeal into a rigid and dogmatic theory of political action.[5] They suggest that Arendt has indeed saved *praxis* from oblivion, but only at the cost of reviving quite dubious Aristotelian criteria for the articulation of a new hierarchy of human activities.

In this chapter, I want to take this charge seriously by examining the manner in which Arendt adopts Aristotle's conceptual apparatus for her own purposes. The question is the degree to which Arendt depends upon Aristotle's hierarchical criteria for the development of her own theory of action. I shall argue that, in this respect at least, Arendt's "Aristotelianism" exceeds the expectations of her critics. Her appropriation of crucial Aristotelian distinctions provides the very structure of her theory of action, the frame for her articulation of the *vita activa*. The Aristotelian influence is thus one key to understanding the Arendtian quest for a purely political politics. Yet her appropriation of Aristotle is, in an important sense, ironic, since she uses concepts from his political philosophy to deconstruct and overcome his own theory of action. In her eyes, this negative project is a prerequisite for a genuine "renewal of *praxis*." What this amounts to in a more positive sense I will discuss in later chapters.

We must begin, however, with Aristotle. In the *Politics*, Aristotle makes a strict distinction between the public and private realms, between the activities and relationships appropriate to each. The household realm (*oikia*) includes the economic or productive activities that aim at "the securing of life itself."[6] Its raison d'être is the provision of those necessities required for the preservation of individual life and the survival of the species.[7] Because it is organized to meet irreducible human needs and operates under constraints imposed by the necessity of guaranteeing continued physical existence, the household presumes relations of inequality. Relations of domination—of master over slaves, husband over wife, father over children—are unavoidable in this sphere and, according to Aristotle, are natural within its boundaries.[8] There must be a "head of the household" if this unit is to fulfill its basic economic functions.

The household realm, which makes material life possible, is contrasted with the political realm, the *polis*, which makes what Aristotle calls the "good life" possible.[9] The good life is one of noble and just actions, of ethical and intellectual virtue. The political association makes it possible by endowing its members with freedom and equality. Liberated from direct concern with the problems of life maintenance, citizens (the heads of households) are free to devote themselves to the pursuit and preservation of virtue in their community. It is only as a member of such a community, Aristotle argues, that a person develops his moral and intellectual capacities, and so becomes fully human.[10] An individual must have daily contact with fellow citizens concerning matters of a more than instrumental significance if he is to develop his potential for reasoned speech and his sense of justice. It is precisely in political interaction that the capacity for choice, judgment, and action is fully exercised, and that freedom is concretely realized. Without the *polis*, the individual cannot know *human* freedom: "He who by his nature and not simply ill-luck has no city, no state, is either too bad or too good, either sub-human or superhuman," a beast or a god.[11]

The ends of the household and the political association are, for Aristotle, distinct but nevertheless related. Aristotle poses a specific connection between the two spheres: the household is to be regarded as a means to, or condition for, the existence of the *polis*. Life has its primary value as a ground for the attainment of the good life. Aristotle puts this relationship in characteristically teleological terms when he states that all prepolitical forms of association (families, tribes, villages, etc.) have their natural end in the *polis*: "this association is the end of those others and its nature is itself an end; for whatever is the end-product of the perfecting process of any object, that we call its nature, that which man, house, household, or anything else aims at being."[12] The *polis*, or political realm, may be last in "the order of becoming," in the natural course of human development, but it is first in "the order of nature."[13] It is the end that all the other forms of association aim to attain.

The difference between the household and the political realm is, then, essentially one of rank or, as Aristotle likes to put it, relative priority: ". . . the city or state has priority over the household and over any individual among us. For the whole must be prior to the parts."[14] Only the "whole," the political association, is or can be self-sufficient; only the *polis* can meet the full range of human needs, from species preservation to moral development. All other forms of association, the component "parts" of the *polis*, fall short of this self-sufficiency (*autarkeia*), this perfection (*entelechia*). They fail to fulfill *all* of human nature. For this reason they cannot be said to possess full independent value; they must be viewed as inferior to the political association.

The Human Condition begins with an extended consideration of the household/*polis* distinction, which in Arendt's eyes is the basis for the all-important distinction between public and private.[15] Following Aristotle's discussion, she stresses the difference and hierarchy of these two spheres. The lesson to be learned from the Greeks is that the difference between public and private corresponds to the difference between freedom and necessity. Human beings are *driven* into the household realm by their wants and needs, by life itself. The community of the household "was therefore born of necessity, and necessity ruled over all activities performed in it."[16] In contrast, the *polis* "was the sphere of freedom, and if there was a relationship between the two spheres, it was a matter of course that the mastering of necessities in the household was the condition for freedom of the *polis*."[17] Household existence—what we would call private or social existence—serves to make politics possible: "As far as the members of the *polis* are concerned, household life exists for the sake of the 'good life.'"[18] The Greek conception forbids us from viewing the political order as an instrumentality of the social order, as *primarily* concerned with the protection of life (Hobbes), the preservation of property (Locke), or the promotion of the general welfare (Bentham, Mill).

Arendt makes this Greek distinction the axis of her political theory. Like Aristotle, she is convinced that politics is an end, not a means. To think otherwise not only robs politics of its dignity, but it strips human beings of their opportunity for freedom as well. For this reason, a sense of the separateness and hierarchy of the public and private realms must be preserved at all costs. Yet it is precisely this distinction that is threatened by what Arendt refers to as "the modern rise of the social," a phenomenon whose genealogical roots are to be found in the Christian/contemplative devaluation of the *vita activa*. The specificity of the political having been obscured by the contemplative tradition, the modern age witnesses the expansion without limit of a realm that is neither genuinely public or private, but a bastard hybrid.[19] Human community is increasingly framed in "social" terms, which is to say that the realm of the household, its "activities, problems, and organizational devices," gradually infiltrates the public sphere, usurping its importance and effacing the conditions and modes of action that made it *political*.[20]

The result of this "rise of the social" is that we moderns are unable to distinguish accurately between public and private realms, between the political and the prepolitical or nonpolitical. We view "the body of peoples and political communities in the image of a family whose everyday affairs have to be taken care of by a gigantic nation-wide administration of housekeeping."[21] The consequences are dire, in that our capacity for action withers as human plurality fails to find public expression.[22]

This is the broad phenomenological context within which Arendt provides a comprehensive theory of political action. The distinction between public and private has been hopelessly blurred, not only in the theory, but also in the experience of the modern age. Yet Arendt wishes to discover a set of criteria that will isolate genuinely political action from its various simulacra. Such criteria can be extracted from "an analysis of those general human capacities which grow out of the human condition and are permanent" (at least so long as that condition is not changed).[23] Only by identifying the irreducible differences between *types* of activity can our sense of the political be strengthened; only then can we recover some measure of the "clarity and articulateness" of the distinction between realms that was so self-evident to the Greeks. This is the first step to restoring dignity to politics, integrity to the public realm, and value to human plurality.

The stakes for Arendt are thus extraordinarily high. Redrawing distinctions within the *vita activa* is no mere exercise in the history of ideas. Most of her critics have granted the importance of this project, but have questioned whether her theory of action marks the distinctions between public and private, freedom and necessity, in a convincing, nonarbitrary way. Moreover, they ask whether the attempt to revive the Greek distinction is not doomed to failure, given the overdetermined character of contemporary political experience.[24] While these are important questions, I shall not pursue them here. At present I am less concerned with Arendt's success or failure in this project than I am with what might be called (for lack of a better word) her "method." *How* does she go about recovering the distinction between public and private? What set of criteria does she employ to differentiate and rank the various types of human activity? What, in short, is the standard by which she distinguishes freedom from necessity? Where does it come from, and what conception of politics does it imply?

•

Aristotle concludes the passage cited above on the "final" character of the political association by noting that the end of any process, its aim, ". . . can only be what is best, perfection; and self-sufficiency is both end and perfection."[25] The *polis*, in other words, is identified by its self-sufficient quality, by the fact that it alone is capable of providing the necessities of life *and* fulfilling the human desire for the good life. The kind of good it supplies is not partial, but final or inclusive: it encompasses the best, most complete life for man. The "self-sufficiency" of the *polis*, then, is not merely organizational; rather, it refers to the status of the political association as an end in itself. The *polis* is not a *means* to the good life, or one amongst several conditions necessary for its possibility, but the arena in which this life occurs. It is for this reason that Aristotle speaks of the "perfection" of the *polis*. As an end in itself, it is the actuality (*energeia*) contained only potentially in prepolitical forms of community.

We can elicit a "natural" principle of hierarchy from Aristotle's teleology, one rooted in the idea of development, and as applicable to the realm of human affairs as it is to the cosmos. This might be called the principle of self-sufficiency or, better, self-containedness.[26] It picks out those things or actions that exist or are undertaken for their own sake; that, possessing full actuality, contain their own *telos* and do not stand in an instrumental or developmental relation to anything else. For Aristotle, a self-contained activity is similar to a self-sufficient community or a self-sufficient life in that it is an end in itself. Such an activity is designated as higher in rank than activities that aim at some external good, just as the *polis* is higher in rank than forms of association whose raison d'être lies outside them.[27] In the *Nicomachean Ethics*, Aristotle states: "We call that which is pursued as an end in itself more final than an end which is pursued for the sake of something else; and what is never chosen as a means to something else we call more final than that which is chosen as an end in itself and as a means to something else."[28]

To call an activity "self-sufficient" or "self-contained," then, implies that it is undertaken for the sake of the activity itself, and not for some end beyond it. If, indeed, "it is for the sake of the end that all else is done" (*NE*, 1097a), then a genuinely self-sufficient activity must have its end in performance; otherwise, the activity must be viewed as incomplete and imperfect prior to its (logically and temporally distinct) end. As Aristotle says, ". . . in some cases the activity is the end, in others, the end is in some product beyond the activity. In cases where the end lies beyond the action the product is naturally superior to the activity."[29] Self-sufficient activities, with their connotation of full actuality or perfection, are atelic (*ateleis*): "we seek to derive nothing beyond the exercise of the activity" (*NE*, 1176b). Examples of such activities are virtuous action and contemplation.[30] Aristotle employs the term *energeia* (actuality) in a second sense to designate activities of this kind.

This line of thought leads to the well-known distinction between *poiēsis* or productive activity, on the one hand, and *praxis* or action, on the other. If a perfect or self-contained activity is *ateleis*, then it is clear that any form of making fails to fit the bill, as its guiding reality or perfection lies outside the activity itself, in the product. Production realizes itself as activity only in the achievement of some *result* (e.g., the shoe made by the cobbler, the building constructed by the architect): its "actuality" rests in this result. Hence, "production has an end other than itself," but *action* does not, for according to Aristotle, "good action (*eupraxia*) is itself an end."[31] The noble actions of the virtuous man *are* the good; they embody this perfection rather than merely indicate or reflect it.[32] Since the good of *praxis* is manifest in performance, Aristotle dubs it "unqualified" in contrast to the "qualified" good of the activity whose end appears only with the cessation or completion of the activity.[33]

Viewed in terms of relative self-containedness or perfection, *praxis* designates a clearly distinct order of activity in comparison to *poiēsis*. They are, as Aristotle says, "generically different."[34] It is precisely the self-contained quality of *praxis* and the "incomplete" nature of *poiēsis* that lead Aristotle to state categorically that "action is not production nor production action."[35] It is the clear corollary of this view that the "good life," the life toward which human beings naturally strive and which constitutes their end or "proper function" (*ergon*), must be a life "of action, not production."[36] The good or distinctively human life cannot be characterized by the instrumentality that is the essence of *poiēsis*, since this would rob it of value. Instead, it must be what Aristotle calls "an active life," a "life composed of the performance of virtuous and noble actions."[37] The gap between the virtuous and banausic ways of life is rooted in this ontological superiority of *praxis* over *poiēsis*. The actions of the citizen participate in, and contribute to, the good itself; the work of the artisan or laborer does not.[38] The life of action, available to the free citizen, manifests or is the good in the same way that flute playing is music: performance, not a product, is the end in each case. As Arendt puts it, summarizing Aristotle, good action cannot be a *means* in the usual sense, for in this case "the means to achieve the end would already be the end."[39] Thus, although Aristotle can say that "the actions of good and wise men have as their aim the production of a variety of excellent results" (*Politics*, VII.3), strictly speaking *praxis* lies outside the category of means and ends.

With Aristotle's distinction between the political and the household realms in mind, we can address the question of how Arendt approaches the parallel task of distinguishing the public from the private, the political from the nonpolitical, freedom from necessity. No reader of *The Human Condition* can doubt that the distinction between *praxis* and *poiēsis*, acting and making, is absolutely central. Indeed, it is no exaggeration to state that Arendt's theory of political action, her critique of the tradition, and her analysis of modernity would be impossible without it. Yet, precisely because of the immense importance of this distinction, we must be careful not to take her appropriation at face value.

Typically, Arendt's employment of the *praxis/poiēsis* distinction is seen as one way of reasserting the relative autonomy of the political order: the sphere of action is distinct from that of production. However, for Arendt far more is at stake. *Pace* Habermas, her appropriation attempts to do more than simply distinguish labor from interaction, or instrumental from practical reason. It seeks to illuminate a dimension of action and freedom that transcends altogether the Weberian problematic of rationalization and its discontents. Consider the following passage from her essay "The Crisis in Culture," in which she describes a kind of epistemological horizon that encloses humanity as producer, as *homo faber*:

> Fabrication . . . always involves means and ends; in fact, the category of means and ends derives its legitimacy from the sphere of making and fabricating where a clearly recognizable end, the final product, determines and organizes everything that plays a part in the process—the material, the tools, the activity itself and even the person participating in it; they all become means toward the end and are justified as such. Fabricators cannot help regarding all things as means to their end, or, as the case may be, judging all things by their specific utility.[40]

This passage and many others like it in her work indicate that Arendt has a profound suspicion of *poiēsis* as such, and not simply of its contemporary incarnation as technical rationality. *Homo faber*, she believes, has a natural tendency to generalize the fabrication experience. Motivated by a will to control or manipulate, he schematizes the world in terms of means and ends. The logic of production provides the ground of intelligibility: things make sense only as means or ends. With this "instrumentalization of the world," Arendt argues, usefulness and utility are established as "the ultimate standards for life and the world of men."[41] *All* things are ultimately degraded into means, thus losing whatever "intrinsic and independent value" they may once have had.[42] One primary result is that no *activity*, certainly not politics, can be comprehensibly regarded as "self-contained," as performed for its own sake. The universalization of the producer's "mode of comportment" toward the world creates the bizarre situation in which *utility*, the "in order to," is systematically confused with meaningfulness, the "for the sake of."[43]

Arendt does follow Weber insofar as she sees this paradoxical state of affairs as typical of modernity. Modern man is distinguished by his "trust in the all-comprehensive range of the means-end category."[44] According to Arendt, modernity is the age in which "the 'in order to' has become the content of the 'for the sake of'; in other words, utility established as meaning generates meaninglessness."[45] We can translate this back into Aristotelian terms by saying that the modern age has mistaken a *qualified* good for an *unqualified* one, and so destroyed the necessary conditions of intrinsic value: there is now "no way to end the chain of means and ends and prevent all ends from eventually being used again as means."[46] Such pervasive utilitarianism creates the "dilemma of meaninglessness" that haunts modernity (as we shall see, Arendt's description of the logic of this nihilistic dialectic owes much to Nietzsche). Arendt views *homo faber*'s confusion as resulting not only in the effacement of action's distinguishing characteristics, but also in a devaluation of its primary condition, human plurality.

With this effacement, *poiēsis* appears as the paradigmatic free activity: *action* and *making* are utterly conflated. *Homo faber*'s "matter-of-course identification of fabrication with action" extends the sovereignty of the means-end category to the political realm: ". . . the mentality of fabrication has invaded the public realm to such an extent that we take it for granted that action, even more than fabrication, is determined by the category of means and ends."[47] The gap between the political and the prepolitical is obliterated. It is as if the epistemological ground for distinguishing between the public and the private, freedom and necessity, plurality and univocity, had been dissolved.

It is the conflation of acting and making under the means-end category that permits "the admission of the household and housekeeping activities to the public realm."[48] For when the debate and deliberation of plural individuals appears devoid of "function" and (thus) meaning, the way is cleared for "the life process itself" to be "channeled into the public realm."[49] "The social" subsumes the political. Society, then, is "the form in which the fact of mutual dependence for the sake of life and nothing else assumes public significance and where the activities connected with sheer survival are permitted to appear in public."[50] Society's "conquest" of the public realm yields what Arendt calls "an unnatural growth of the natural," a public domain completely determined by the dictates of the life process itself.[51] Here, the realm of freedom has been completely submerged in that of necessity, all as the result of the "blurring" perpetuated by the instrumental mentality of *homo faber*.

Practically speaking, the "rise of the social" means that the "general interest" in economic self-reproduction is elevated to a position of unquestionable priority. This gives society its "monolithic," antipluralistic character. Where this interest reigns supreme, Arendt argues, the "head of the household" is dispensed with and "the most social form of government," bureaucracy, comes into being.[52] This "rule by nobody" is the form appropriate to an advanced, complex "national household." And, as Arendt is quick to add, "the rule of nobody is not necessarily no-rule; it may indeed, under certain circumstances, even turn out to be one of its cruelest and tyrannical versions."[53] The domination exercised by the economy (and by the bureaucracy in the name of the economy) creates an unprecedented demand for rationalized, disciplined behavior. Society "expects from each of its members a certain kind of behavior, imposing innumerable and various rules, all of which tend to 'normalize' its members, to make them behave, to exclude spontaneous action or achievement."[54]

The obvious resonance of this observation with the work of Weber, Adorno, or Foucault should not distract us from Arendt's main point, which is that society, "on all its levels, excludes the possibility of action."[55] It does so by absorbing the public realm and emasculating plurality. We are confronted, finally, not by a society of workers, of agents exercising a craft, but by a society of laborers, of masses who "consider whatever they do primarily as a way to sustain their own lives and those of their families."[56] The "factual transformation of the whole society into a laboring society" permeates human existence with a naturelike necessity and sameness. The survival of the species may be guaranteed on "a world-wide scale," yet *humanity*—human beings as public actors, as unique individuals—is threatened with extinction.[57]

Such are the vast and disturbing consequences Arendt sees flowing from *homo faber's* unlimited instrumentalism. The recovery of the distinction between *praxis* and *poiēsis* is clearly essential to delimiting a public realm distinct from the state and the economy, and to preserving a space for freedom and the expression of plurality. I should add that the *praxis/poiēsis* distinction is important not simply because it enables us to distinguish "communicative" from "purposive-rational" action, as Habermas suggests; rather, its real significance is that it reminds us that action and plurality have intrinsic value; that *freedom resides in the self-contained-ness of action*. It is only by deploying the distinction between *praxis* and *poiesis* in its original, rigorous, and hierarchical form that action's unique capacity to create meaning and to express plurality can be brought to light and the "gap" between public and private, the free and the unfree, can be revealed once again.

II. Applying the Criterion: Arendt's Descriptions of Labor, Work, and Action

Arendt's rearticulation of the component parts of the *vita activa* has drawn criticism from neo-Marxists, who have objected to the rigidity of her distinctions between labor, work, and action. What Arendt has missed, they say, is the dialectical relationship between these various activities, and between the realms of necessity and of freedom. The result is a political theory dedicated to the recovery of the public realm—to a "*polis* without slaves"—which ironically bars investigation of the ways the mode of production determines the form, content, and possibilities of political action. Arendt, it seems, is her own worst enemy: her Aristotelian hierarchy of activities effectively makes politics the province of the few, to the obvious detriment of her own democratic and participatory sympathies.

This line of criticism performs the valuable service of focusing our attention on *how* Arendt makes her distinctions, while highlighting the paradoxical consequences of her method. In his critique of Arendt, Bhikhu Parekh underlines the importance of "the degree of self-sufficiency of an activity" for her ranking of labor, work, and action.[58] I want to examine Arendt's distinctions in light of this criterion, in order to show just how integral it is to her theory of political action. Her application of it, however, is less myopic than her critics believe. Arendt does not attempt to escape the pradoxes of an autonomous politics; rather, she thinks them through to the end. From her perspective, the preservation of freedom and human plurality is at stake.

First, the distinctions themselves. *Labor*, according to Arendt, designates that part of human life devoted to subsistence and reproduction, to the fulfillment of the biological needs necessary for the preservation of the individual and the species. This dimension of existence fills the demands of the life process itself, and as such is under the sway of nature and necessity. Labor does not qualify as a specifically *human* activity, since our "metabolism with nature" (Marx) is something we share with all living things. Basing herself on the Greek view that "what men share with all other forms of animal life" ought not to be considered human, Arendt claims that "the use of the world 'animal' in the concept of *animal laborans* . . . is fully justified. The *animal laborans* is indeed only one, at best the highest, of the animal species that populate the earth."[59] (So much for the Marxian idea that labor is man's essence, that humanity creates itself through labor.[60] For Arendt, nothing could be further from the truth.)

The "pre-human" character of labor is displayed by the rhythm and "purpose" of the labor process itself. Marx's basic description of this process in *Capital* was, Arendt notes, entirely correct: labor is a ceaseless cycle of production for the sake of consumption and consumption for the sake of production, for the renewal of labor power.[61] In her view, Marx's description highlights the degree to which "labor and consumption are but two stages of the ever-recurring cycle of biological life."[62] Precisely for this reason, Arendt claims, it is a mistake to view labor as the source of value, as Marx does. For something to possess value, she argues, it must possess durability. The labor process, however, is concerned solely with the production of consumer goods, with "commodities" that meet man's biological need to consume, to reproduce himself. Hence, "it is indeed the mark of all laboring that it leaves nothing behind, that the result of the effort is almost as quickly consumed as the effort is spent."[63]

From Arendt's perspective, then, the labor process is a ceaseless cycle of production and consumption, essentially *un*productive insofar as what is produced has a most transitory existence. Consumer products appear only to be immediately resubmerged in the eternally recurring life process. As a result, there is no *telos* to labor. Labor assimilates human beings to nature, and nature, according to Arendt, is a realm without genuine beginnings or endings:

> . . . all human activities which arise out of necessity to cope with [the biological process of human existence and the fact of structural growth and decay] are bound to the recurring cycles of nature and have in themselves no beginning and no end, properly speaking; unlike *working*, whose end has come when the object is finished, ready to be added to the common world of things, *laboring* always moves in the same circle, which is prescribed by the biological process of the living organism and the end of its "toil and trouble" comes only with the death of this organism.[64]

The changeless, deathless repetition of nature is mirrored in the cyclical, repetitive, and ceaseless character of labor. It "never produces anything but life."[65] It is the most animal of human activities, the least self-contained, the least free.

Arendt admits that her distinction between labor and work is "unusual."[66] It is obviously foreign to the Hegelian/Marxian tradition. She believes, however, that the phenomenal evidence for such a distinction more than compensates for the lack of theoretical attention it has received. The main difference is rooted in the virtually prehuman character of labor. Work, in contrast to labor, is a distinctively *human* activity (although not *the* distinctively human activity). The distinguishing characteristic of work is its purposiveness; all work aims at the creation of a durable and lasting product, and so possesses a directionality, a teleological quality, that is utterly absent from labor.

Work *makes* things, from tools and chairs to art; it is essentially instrumental in character: "the process of making is itself entirely determined by the categories of means and end."[67] Moreover, "the fabricated thing is an end product in the twofold sense that the production process comes to an end in it . . . and that it is only a means to produce this end."[68] The achievement of a lasting result, an end, separates work from the circularity and necessity of the labor process: "To have a definite beginning and a definite, predictable end is the mark of fabrication, which through this characteristic also distinguishes itself from all other human activities."[69]

This way of distinguishing labor from work is by no means obvious: does not labor, after all, have an end (the reproduction of the individual and the species)? May we not also regard it as purposive? Arendt's position on this issue becomes clearer if we refer, once again, to Aristotle. "All art," Aristotle writes, "is concerned with the realm of coming to be"; thus, production "is concerned neither with things which exist or come into being by necessity, nor with things produced by nature: those have their source of motion within themselves."[70] What distinguishes work from labor is the *imposed* character of the end it achieves. This end—for example, the making of a table—is not dictated by nature, but is rather imposed on it. Work or fabrication, for this reason, is inherently violent: ". . . violence is present in all fabrication, and *homo faber*, the creator of the human artifice, has always been a destroyer of nature."[71]

Work, then, destroys nature through its creation of artifacts. The products of work, which Arendt calls "reifications," do not find their way back into the cycle of natural growth and decay, but endure outside it. It is *homo faber*, man as craftsman, who builds the world, not man as laborer.[72] In Arendt's view, work is the only genuine embodiment of a *human* negativity. *Homo faber* acts into nature and transforms it into something stable and solid, a "man-made home." It is on the basis of this stability that a specifically human life, a life removed from the ceaseless motion of nature, becomes possible.

Left at this, the difference between Arendt (and Aristotle), on the one hand, and Marx and Hegel, on the other, would appear largely semantic. Their descriptions of the character and significance of production seem quite similar, although they have chosen to designate this activity differently. The similarity, however, is superficial, since for Arendt the negativity of work, its violence, does not connote mediation in the Hegelian sense: work does not humanize nature. Rather, her view is that work creates a nonnatural space, the "world," which remains juxtaposed to the unarticulated positivity of nature. The realm of objectivity that human beings create is therefore *not* what Hegel referred to as a "second nature."[73] In Arendt's scheme, the world created by work does not *subsume* nature; it stands *between* nature and humanity. It provides distance *from* the natural, a distance that is necessary if we are to know or manipulate nature: "Only we who have created this objectivity of a world of our own from what nature gives us, who have built into the environment of nature so that we are protected from her, can look upon nature as 'objective.'"[74]

Keeping labor and work distinct and judging them in terms of their relative self-sufficiency are essential, then, to the establishment of a hiatus between the realms of freedom and necessity. The latter is limited by the nexus of instrumentality created by work. But the world created by artifice is not, in itself, a space of freedom; nor is the activity that creates it self-contained. Indeed, measured against this standard, the distance between labor and work, between necessity and instrumentality, diminishes. Labor's futility means that it is devoid of meaning, while the unquestionable hegemony of the end or product in work deprives the activity itself of any independent value: the production process "is only a means to produce this end."[75] Only *action*, Arendt states, following Aristotle, can lay claim to intrinsic meaningfulness, to self-containedness, and hence to freedom. But what specific activities *count* as action, from Arendt's point of view? Moreover, in what sense can these activities be said to "not pursue an end and leave no work behind," exhausting "their full meaning in the performance itself"?[76]

These are absolutely critical questions: they lead to the heart of Arendt's theory of political action and her paradoxical view of politics. I begin with the obvious. For Arendt, the political action and speech of citizens are, as Aristotle claimed, paradigmatic, self-contained activities. They are distinctively or fully human, whereas labor and work fall short. As Arendt puts it in one of her most fiercely Aristotelian (and anti-Hegelian) moments, in words intended to jar:

> Men can very well live without laboring. They can force others to labor for them, and they can very well decide merely to use and enjoy the world of things without adding a single useful object to it; the life of an exploiter or a slaveholder and the life of a parasite may be unjust, but they are certainly human. A life without speech and without action, on the other hand . . . is literally dead to the world; it has ceased to be a human life.[77]

Only the political life, the life of action and speech, is free; only the political life is human. To be human is to be a citizen, and citizenship, as Aristotle pointed out, is consonant with the exploitation or alienation of noncitizens.[78] Hegel to the contrary, where there are masters and slaves, only the master can enjoy genuinely *human* freedom, provided that the master is a citizen and acts with other citizens. Better that some should be free on the basis of the unfreedom of others than that all should be mired in the necessity of the household.

These judgments by Arendt seem harsh and foreign, "Greek" in the extreme. The difficulty of her position, and the discomfort it elicits, increase as she attempts to specify what exactly "self-contained" political action is. For if action is (as Aristotle says) politics, not all politics is action. The standard of self-containedness imposes severe limits on what deserves to be called *political*, on the kind of activity fit to appear in the light of the public realm. Distinguishing action from labor and work is only part of the job; equally important is making sure that politics lives up to the name of action. The question, then, is what conception of politics and political action results from the rigorous application of the Aristotelian standard? What does a "self-contained politics" look like?

I first want to note what is excluded by this standard. Any form of "politics" that replicates relations or functions appropriate to the household is unpolitical, since it would introduce the coercive force of necessity into the realm of freedom. The distinction between *praxis* and *poiēsis* also brackets all essentially instrumental or strategic action. Wherever action is *primarily* purposive, defined by its results, success, or failure, it ceases to be genuinely political. Concretely, these abstract prohibitions translate into a series of denials by Arendt that most of what *we* take to be political is in fact worthy of the name. Neither domination nor liberation counts as genuine political action; nor should the activities of administration or representation be viewed as properly political.

Although Arendt asserts that politics may be *based* on limited domination, she explicitly and vehemently denies the Weberian proposition that all politics is, finally, domination.[79] Domination is not political, because it imposes a monopoly on speech and action, a monopoly that destroys plurality. Where the prerogative of action is reserved by a ruler or a ruling clique, there are in effect no citizens, only subjects and their masters. The preservation of the lives and power of the rulers is the only real goal of such an association; the activity of subjects has value only as a means to this end. Politics as domination universalizes the master/slave relation, permeating all action with the necessity, inequality, and univocity characteristic of the household realm.[80]

One might be tempted to conclude that if domination is a specifically unpolitical form of activity, then action that overcomes it—*liberating* action—captures the essence of the political. Yet from Arendt's perspective, this assumption is flawed.[81] In her view, *revolutionary* action can be expressly political; indeed, in certain instances it has provided the modern age with a taste of the political life at its fullest and most intense. The American Revolution, the Paris Commune, the original *soviets* of 1905 and 1917, the *Räte* (workers' councils) of the German Revolution of 1918, the Hungarian revolt: all are cases in which the overthrow of tyranny led to the founding of a space for freedom and the (tragically brief) flowering of action and speech.[82] Yet, modern revolutionary action has also had an antipolitical impact, unleashing the tremendous "natural" forces bred by poverty, hunger, and exploitation. With the arrival of the poor on the political scene, Arendt asserts, the public realm and the freedom specific to it are overwhelmed by the torrent of unmet human needs released from their place of darkness. *Social* revolution, which elevates poverty to the rank of a "political force of the first order," creates a situation in which freedom has to be "surrendered to necessity, to the urgency of the life process itself."[83] The paradigm example that Arendt cites in this connection is the French Revolution, a revolution that justified itself not in terms of political freedom, but rather in terms of the needs of the people, their "rights" to "dress, food and the reproduction of their species."[84] Such needs are urgent, undeniable, *necessary*: the attempt to meet them through *politi-*

cal means inevitably produces terror; because while politics can "transcend" nature, it cannot overcome it. As Arendt notes, "It was necessity . . . that unleashed the terror and sent the Revolution to its doom."

Arendt's judgments on this issue seem exceptionally severe, bordering on the reactionary. Does she not realize that political freedom is meaningless where humanity remains enslaved to nature? The answer is, of course she does: a certain freedom from the burdens of life, from subsistence and reproduction, is a prerequisite for any real politics.[85] Her point is that so long as biological necessity forms an irreducible dimension of the human condition, freedom is possible only through the strict separation of activities relating to the life process and those relating to politics. The attempt to redress what she refers to as "the Social Question" through political means succeeds only in placing all of human existence under the aspect of necessity. Marxist revolutionairies, following the model of the French Revolution, had thought it possible to overcome necessity once and for all, to liberate humanity from biological necessity *tout court*.[86] But this goal makes natural need the sole content of revolutionary politics, and it leads not from necessity to freedom, but from necessity to violence. In Arendt's view, the attempt to liberate humanity from biological need and/or social inequality is responsible for returning men to the "state of nature."[87]

The standard of self-containedness also excludes what is, from our perspective, the stuff of everyday contemporary politics. Administration does not qualify as political action because its work, as Weber noted, is framed entirely in terms of means and ends.[88] The bureaucrat or manager is concerned solely with finding the most efficient means to achieve a pregiven end. Typically, these ends are derived in accordance with the imperatives of social reproduction. Conceived of as administration or management, then, government is concerned primarily with the life process of society, with its material conditions of existence and continued smooth functioning. Since their business is "dictated by the necessities which underlie all economic process," administration and management are, according to Arendt, "essentially non-political."[89] There can be no free or plural action where politics is reduced to the management of the "national household." As Arendt reminds us, "where life is at stake all action is by definition under the sway of necessity."[90]

The *praxis/poiēsis* distinction also leads Arendt to classify representation as unpolitical. Her polemical remarks about representative government are such that some have mistaken her for an elitist critic of democracy. This is not the place to deal with the details of her critique (elaborated in *On Revolution*) or the controversy it has stirred: we must limit ourselves to Arendt's main point.[91] In theory, she observes, the relation between those represented (the people) and their representative is entirely instrumental. The use of the representative is, in essence, a labor-saving device: to be a representative is to discharge the will of his constituents or to represent their interests in the public arena. His presence in government enables the electorate to get on with their "more urgent and more important" private business; he lifts from them the "burden" of attending to public business.[92] The representative system thus has its raison d'être in facilitating the pursuit of private economic interest. Indeed, *genuine* representation—representation that does not transcend its purpose as "glorified messenger boy or hired expert"—is possible only on the basis of a clear-cut, concrete *interest* such as the material welfare and prosperity of the represented group. (Where there is a wide range of individual *opinion*, as in more expressly political matters, the mechanism either breaks down or winds up usurping the power of the people.[93]) Where the representative system functions well, then, the public is once again an instrumentality of the private, and politics becomes a means to life or, more exactly, "commodious living." The end result, according to Arendt, is that "government has degenerated into mere administration" and "the public realm has vanished."[94] There is no space for freedom, for the articulation of plural popular opinion, or for the performance of "noble actions." Where the representative system does not function well, it devolves into oligarchy: "what we today call democracy is a form of government where the few rule, at least supposedly, in the interest of the many."[95]

Domination, liberation, administration, representation—determined by the force of necessity and destructive of plurality they are all prepolitical in character. Mistaken for the stuff of politics, they become antipolitical, denaturing the public realm by subjecting it to the life process. For Arendt, genuine political action is never a means to (mere) life, but the embodiment or expression of a *meaningful* life.[96] However, given the exclusions outlined above, what form can such action take? In what sense can political action be said to transcend necessity and instrumentality? Arendt has an answer to this seemingly unanswerable question, one that is, to all appearances, markedly Aristotelian.

The general mode of human activity that (potentially) breaks free of the life process is *speech*, speech with others. Genuine political action is nothing other than a certain kind of talk, a variety of conversation or argument about public matters. Aristotle had claimed that it is the capacity for reasoned speech (*logos*) that distinguishes men from such other "social" creatures as bees. Speech makes man a *political* animal in that it enables him to ascend from mere expression of appetite or aversion, or the perception of pleasure or pain, to the expression of *judgment*: only human beings can articulate and share a perception of what is good and what is bad, what is honorable and what is blameworthy, and this they do through speech.[97] It is this capacity of speech to raise human beings, so to speak, above life and its needs to the level of judgment that prompts Arendt to observe that "wherever the relevance of speech is at stake, matters become political by definition, for speech is what makes man a political animal."[98] The importance of *this* kind of talk, its fundamental significance for a *human* life, is underlined in her essay on Lessing: ". . . the world is not humane just because it is made by human beings, and it does not become human just because the human voice sounds in it, but only when it becomes the object of discourse. . . . We humanize what is going on in the world only by speaking of it, and in the course of speaking we learn to be human."[99] Although Arendt officially draws a distinction between action (deeds) and speech, it is clear that action without speech would not be action, since it fails to adequately express this capacity for judgment.

Speech is essentially political for the additional reason that it provides the basis for a noncoercive, nonviolent form of being and acting together. One point that Arendt consistently emphasizes about the *polis* is that, if it was ruled by anything, it was ruled by speech. Glossing Aristotle's differentiation between political and nonpolitical types of authority, Arendt notes that "to be political, to live in a *polis*, meant that everything was decided through words and persuasion, and not through force and violence. In Greek self-understanding, to force people by violence, to command rather than persuade, were prepolitical ways to deal with people characteristic of life outside the *polis*."[100] The political way of life, when contrasted to that lived in the household or the "barbaric" life outside a state, was characterized by the fact that here "speech and only speech made sense," for "the central concern of all citizens was to talk to each other."[101]

We can grant Arendt the point that speech serves to lift human beings above the level of mere need, and that it can create relations between individuals based on a kind of sharing—the "sharing of words and deeds"—rather than obedience, but in what way is political speech "self-contained"? What in the nature of such talk makes it one of those activities where "the means to achieve the end would already be the end," where *performance* is the goal?[102]

The answer to this question is that only a specific kind of speech is in fact political, deserving the title of action. Throughout her work, Arendt focuses on *deliberative* speech. Political speech has its end, typically, in the making of a decision, in the choice of a course of action. Political speech, then, is nothing other than the process of debate and deliberation, the "talk and argument," the "persuasion, negotiation and compromise" that precedes the deed.[103] It is "the speech-making and decision-taking, the oratory and the business, the thinking and the persuading" that counts as political speech, and (thus) as *politics*.[104] Deliberative speech, political debate, when engaged in by public-spirited citizens, is "an end in itself," because here the quarrel over "means," about the appropriate action to take, is always already a quarrel about ends. Deliberative speech in the *political* arena is never merely technical (as it is in the administrative sphere), since the "good" to be attained is articulated concretely only in the medium of debate about possible courses of action. Where all are agreed on the end, debate can take place, but it ceases to be political.[105] Political debate is end-constitutive: its goal does not stand apart from the process, dominating it at every point, but is rather formed in the course of the "performance" itself. Through such deliberation, individuals rise above merely strategic considerations and engage questions that have a direct bearing on the *kind* of political community they see themselves as part of. Genuine political deliberation does not move at the level of "in order to," but rather at the level of "for the sake of": it ultimately is concerned with the meaning of our life in common.

Arendt's attribution of inherent value to deliberative speech can be traced directly to Book VI of the *Nicomachean Ethics*, where Aristotle depicts practical/political deliberation as an activity valuable for its own sake. Practical wisdom (*phronēsis*), the primary intellectual virtue of deliberation concerned with action, is not merely concerned with the selection of means, as is *technē* or art. Rather, in deliberating, the man of practical wisdom, the *phronimos*, is more concerned with finding what is *good* for himself and his fellow citizens. This sets his deliberation off from the more limited, instrumental sort that is concerned with particular questions of policy. The latter type of deliberation, Aristotle calls "qualified": when done well it brings "success in the attainment of some particular end."[106] The former sort is "good deliberation in the unqualified sense": it does not concern itself with "what is good and advantageous in a partial sense, for example, what contributes to health or strength"; rather, it seeks "what sort of thing contributes to the good life in general."[107] The "correctness" of unqualified deliberation is measured not so much in terms of its success as in its ability to attain "what is good."[108] It does not have an end "other than itself," as does *poiēsis*, for "good action is itself an end."[109] To deliberate well, as the man of practical wisdom does, is to *do* well.

The distinction between *praxis* and *poiēsis* thus yields a focus on deliberative speech in the work of both Arendt and Aristotle. It is the unique character of deliberative speech that serves as the basis of Arendt's broad conception of politics. Debate "constitutes the very essence of political life,"[110] because it is only through the exchange, modification, and criticism of *opinion* that *political* deliberation proceeds. The public realm, the space of freedom and action, is then primarily an arena in which this unconstrained exchange of opinion can take place. It is "the common meeting ground of all," the place where everyone can "be seen and heard";[111] its paradigm is the assembly or *agora* of antiquity.[112]

But in order for such deliberation to occur and for such "sharing" to take place, certain preconditions are essential. First and foremost, politics as deliberative speech and common action presupposes a genuine *plurality*. Without plurality, without the diversity of perspectives implicit in "the fact that men, not Man, live on earth and inhabit the world,"[113] no action in Arendt's sense would be possible. Where this plurality has been neutered, as in the household, through force of common interest, or where it has been negated, as it has been under conditions of totalitarian domination, there political action is impossible. Under such circumstances, where a single perspective has been "prolonged" or "multiplied" to encompass all,[114] there can be no end-constitutive deliberation. This is because the ends are pregiven or imposed, and the space between individuals necessary for a variety of standpoints and the formation of opinion has been compressed or eliminated altogether. This is why Arendt calls plurality, with its connotation of spatial distribution and perceptual diversity, "specifically the *condition*—not only the *condition sine qua non*, but the *condition per quam*—of all political life."[115]

Secondly, deliberative or political speech presupposes *equality*. Deliberation can be unconstrained only when it takes place amongst peers; inequality introduces coercion and makes the exchange or sharing of speech false. However, in citing equality as an essential precondition of political action, Arendt is not subscribing to a doctrine of natural equality, such as that articulated by the Declaration of the Rights of Man or the Declaration of Independence. Equality is *not* a natural phenomenon. The Greeks knew this, and therefore created an artificial realm, the *polis*, in which individuals *qua* citizens could recognize one another on an equal footing. "The equality of the Greek *polis*, its isonomy, was an attribute of the *polis* and not of men who received their equality by virtue of citizenship, not by virtue of birth."[116] As *citizens*, each had equal opportunity to be seen and heard, and to participate in deciding public affairs. Political equality is therefore inseparable from political freedom, since the latter "means the right to be a participator in government; or it means nothing."[117]

A further precondition of political action understood as deliberative speech is *commonality*. Deliberative speech must be anchored in a shared world, since debate or disagreement concerning the direction of collective action presumes a certain minimum agreement in background judgments and practices. Where such agreement dissolves or is shattered, it is no longer possible to view the same thing from a variety of perspectives. The mediation necessary to the formation of opinions breaks down, with the result that politics (at least in the Arendtian sense) comes to a halt. Arendt attempts to convey the necessity of having such a "background consensus" by insisting upon the "worldly" character of political action. It is the world, that "relatively permanent home for man" created by *homo faber*, which makes politics possible by serving as "the common meeting ground of all."

Although she believes that "sharing a world" is a precondition of politics, we should not read Arendt as promoting an "organic" form of community. For her, the essential point about the public world is, as noted above, its objectivity, its "reified" quality. This objectivity "relates and separates men at the same time."[118] The world and the things in it bring individuals together by opening a (shared) space between them. It is the presence of such a palpable "in-between" that makes plurality—a genuine diversity of perspectives on the same phenomenon—possible. Where this shared sense of the world has become attenuated—whether as a result of the anomie and loneliness of mass society, or as the result of intensely intimate forms of community (for example, early Christianity) that collapse the "in-between," binding their members through force of love or shared belief—there politics is threatened in its very being.[119]

That politics is threatened by both too much and too little community leads Arendt to describe the appropriate relation between citizens as one of "friendship." Following Aristotle, she defines civic friendship in opposition to relations of intimacy or privacy. The substance of friendship is public talk: ". . . for the Greeks the essence of friendship consisted in discourse. They held that only the constant interchange of talk united citizens in a *polis*. In discourse the political importance of friendship, and the humanness peculiar to it, were made manifest."[120] Friendship in the political sense is a form of partnership, in argument and in conversation. It is based on mutual respect and mutual "commitment to a shared enterprise."[121]

A final precondition of properly political speech is *ability*. Arendt's espousal of citizenly equality as a condition of action does not make her an egalitarian. Far from it. Just as she believes that certain activities (labor and work) and subjects (administration and economics) are not fit to appear in the public realm, she feels that not all opinions are worth sharing and not all speakers are fit to be heard.

Political speech/action requires judgment (Aristotle's "excellence in delibera-tion"), integrity, impartiality, and a fierce commitment to the "public thing." As a result, the activity of politics has an irreducibly "elitist" dimension: only those of "authentically political talents" and public passion should be allowed to take up residence, so to speak, in the public realm. To demand that *all* participate, regardless of ability or degree of public-spiritedness, is to ensure the denaturing of political action and its corruption by extrapolitical concerns. Indeed, Arendt insists that we not delude ourselves about "the obvious inability and conspicuous lack of interest of large parts of the population in political matters as such"; the political way of life "has never been and will never be the way of life of the many."[122]

Arendt's insistence upon a public realm that is at once both open *and* exclu-sive, in which "those who belong are self-chosen, [and] those who do not belong are self-excluded,"[123] challenges "the democratic mentality of an egalitarian soci-ety." Yet she is unapologetic. Like Aristotle, she believes that the "good life" can be pursued only by "good" or the best individuals. Entry to the political realm should not be determined according to extrapolitical criteria, such as birth or wealth, but residence there should not be indiscriminately available to all. Arendt argues for a principle of distributive justice much like Aristotle's when it comes to the privilege of being seen and heard by one's peers. This opportunity is properly accorded to those with the abilities or virtues specific to politics, in-cluding trustworthiness, integrity, judgment, and courage.[124] Such individuals are deserving of public recognition and honor because they possess qualities that contribute directly to the vitality and freedom of the political community.[125]

Extracted from the *vita activa* by the criterion of self-containedness, political action emerges in Arendt's work as a certain kind of talk: the end-constitutive debate and deliberation of diverse equals on matters of common concern.[126] This talk occurs in the public realm, a sphere distinct from both the state and the economy, one structured by plurality, equality, commonality, and ability. The continuities with Aristotle on these aspects has already been noted; here, I simply want to underline how they contribute to what appears to be a broadly Aristote-lian conception of the political.

First, Arendt and Aristotle are one in their emphasis on the primacy of *partici-pation*. Politics *is* action for Arendt: her debt to Aristotle's conception of citizen-ship, which makes participation in "judgment and authority" the criterion that "effectively distinguishes citizens from all others," is manifest. Second, Arendt and Aristotle seem to focus on *community* as the foundation of action. For Aris-totle, the political association is bound not simply by interests, but by shared norms, purposes, and a harmony in basic judgments. Arendt's definition of action as "acting together" seems to imply a similar conception. Finally, both theorists have an essentially deliberative conception of politics, in which the debate and deliberation of diverse equals is granted an intrinsic value.

If the question about the *form* of genuine political action is answered by the appeal to such "unqualified" deliberation and debate, we are still left with the question of what such speech is actually *about*. The self-contained character of deliberative speech tells us nothing about the matters argued, debated, and decided upon in the public realm, as Arendt conceives it. "Household" or socioeconomic concerns are excluded; so what can the content of such talk be? This question takes us to the center of debates concerning Arendt's highly restrictive conception of politics and political action.

III. The Idea of a "Self-Contained" Politics

There is much in Arendt's appropriation of Aristotle that her critics applaud. Richard Bernstein, for instance, has drawn attention to the way in which deliberation, practical wisdom, and the nature of judgment stand at the center of the Arendtian view of political action.[127] This side of her thought provides a powerful weapon in the fight against the modern tendency to reduce political/practical questions to technical ones, and to grant experts an unquestioned hegemony over the collective judgment exercised by citizens. Ronald Biener and Hanna Pitkin have also highlighted this dimension of Arendt's work from slightly different perspectives.[128] But while the critics praise her conception of political action as coercion-free debate amongst equals, they balk at the transition from form to content. It is one thing to employ the criterion of self-containedness in order to isolate distinctively *political* modes of action; it is quite another to use this criterion to limit, and limit narrowly, what political speech can properly be *about*.

It is when one addresses the question of the content of political action that the "clamps" of Arendt's Aristotelian theory of action make themselves most sharply felt. The insistence upon self-containedness results in an apparently untenable and misguided attempt to sever the public from the private, the political from the social.[129] Even if one could separate these complexly intertwined strands, what would be left for citizens to talk about once such "extrapolitical" topics as wage justice, racial and gender inequality, social welfare issues, and the environment have been excluded? Hanna Pitkin expresses the frustration of many readers when she asks, "What keeps these citizens together as a body? . . . What is it that they talk about in the endless palaver of the *agora?*"[130]

The answer to this question is by no means obvious. How is it possible for the *content* of politics to be "self-contained"? How can political talk take place at a level abstracted from the "real interests" (Pitkin) of various social groups? What *does* political action deal with if not social problems and the demand for justice? Beyond the question of "What else is there"? one wonders whether the political and social can be distinguished at other than a merely conceptual level. One not need be a neo-Marxist in order to feel the force of Albrecht Wellmer's observation that virtually all our social problems are, at some level, also political problems.[131] Pitkin seems justified in decrying the "curious emptiness of content" that characterizes Arendt's image of politics and the public realm.

I shall return to these objections. For the moment, I want to concentrate on the paradoxical quality of Arendt's notion of a political action that, apparently, has no extrapolitical referent. Here it is crucial to see (1) that Arendt *does* want to limit the content of political talk to specifically *political* matters; and (2) that she does in fact have an answer to the charge of "emptiness of content." The answer, perhaps, is not totally satisfactory, and Arendt tends to obscure things by providing different versions. Nevertheless, she believes that it is both possible and necessary to limit the scope of properly political speech. The value of action, plurality, and the public sphere itself is at stake. For this reason Arendt, if anything, is even more rigorous than Aristotle in drawing out the implications of a "self-contained" *praxis*.[132]

If political action is to be valued for its own sake, then the content of political action must be politics "in the sense that political action is talk about politics."[133] The circularity of this formulation, given by George Kateb, is unavoidable. It helps if we make use of an analogy that Kateb proposes, the analogy between such a purely political politics and a game. "A game," writes Kateb, "is not 'about' anything outside itself, it is its own sufficient world . . . the content of any game is itself."[134] What matters in a game is the play itself, and the quality of this play is utterly dependent upon the willingness and ability of the players to enter the "world" of the game. The Arendtian conception of politics is one in which the spirit animating the "play" (the sharing of words and deeds) comes before all else—before personal concerns, group interests, and even moral claims. If allowed to dominate the "game," these elements detract from the play and from the performance of action. A good game happens only when the players submit themselves to its spirit and do not allow subjective or external motives to dictate the play. A good game, like genuine politics, is played for its own sake.

Illuminating as this analogy might be, it obviously fails to do justice to the *stakes* of politics, and to the seriousness that attends the "play" in this realm.[135] Political action entails great "responsibilities, sacrifices and dangers"; it is, in addition, far more of a response to events than any game.[136] Most important, the analogy is inadequate because it begs the question of what political action and speech is actually about. While it may give us a sense of the spirit appropriate to political action, we are still at a loss to describe how politics is or can be about itself.

The paradox is resolved, at least partially, if we look to the examples Arendt gives of exemplary political speech. These examples—the speeches of Athenian democracy, the debates attending the founding of the American republic, the deliberations of revolutionary councils, certain acts of civil disobedience—all revolve around the creation and preservation of the public sphere. Genuinely political speech concerns itself with "the creation of the conditions that make [politics] possible or with the preservation of those conditions."[137] This is the sense in which politics is or can be the content of politics. For the Greeks, such speech typically concerned the defense of the *polis* and its distinctive way of life against its neighbors, as in Pericles' Funeral Oration. For moderns, political speech has centered on the creation and maintenance of an institutional arrangement or framework of laws that serves to articulate and protect the public realm. It has centered, in other words, on the creation of a *constitution*, which Arendt understands to be less an instrument of limitation than a positive "system of power."[138]

According to Arendt, a constitution is an agreement by means of which a group of individuals constructs a space for action and for "tangible" freedom. Thus, the "foundation of a body politic," its constitution, is what "guarantees the space where freedom can appear."[139] The essential function of a constitution is not simply the safeguarding of rights and liberties, important as these are, but the creation and preservation of such a space. Understood as the creed of limited government and nothing more, "constitutionalism" ceases to be political in Arendt's sense. The act of founding a body politic and the debates and deliberations that precede the founding are evidences of exemplary political speech precisely because they concern the "creation of conditions"—for example, the guarantee of rights, the distinction between public and private, the institutionalization of popular participation—that transform political action into a relatively permanent way of being together. A space for action may "come into being whenever men are together in the manner of speech and action, and therefore predate and precede all formal constitution of the public realm,"[140] but it fails to become "a house where freedom can dwell" until this constitution takes place.[141] The speech of the revolutionary councils—of the French *sociétés populaires*, the soviets, the German workers' and soldiers' councils of 1918—is exemplary because this kind of speech *enacted* a new constitution of power, a people's constitution, so to speak. In the council system, the system of power not only created a space for action, but it *was* that space for action.[142] It becomes clear that for Arendt, as for the Greeks, "constitution" denotes less an institutional structure than a peculiarly political way of life.[143]

It would, of course, be self-defeating to hypostatize the moment of founding as *the* manifestation of genuinely political speech. The understanding outlined above demands that action be a continuing possibility. Thus, Arendt's understanding of what counts as political action expands to include all speech that serves to preserve a constitution from internal or external erosion.[144] In the case of the council system (where the system of power and the space for freedom coincide) or the *agora*, there is maximum opportunity for such speech. In representative democracy, on the other hand, the opportunity for deliberation and action tends to be limited. Civil disobedience, however, provides ordinary citizens with an additional outlet, a point Arendt makes forcefully in her essay on the subject. Unlike Thoreau, Arendt does not view civil disobedience as an expression of individual conscience. Its recent American manifestations (the civil rights movement, the antiwar movement) are viewed, instead, as exemplary forms of acting together—of *political* action.[145]

Genuinely political talk is concerned, then, with "preserving and promoting a way of acting and the values embodied in it."[146] This is the gist of its self-referential character. One must be careful, however, not to reify the constitution into an ideal entity separate from the system of power it creates and the modes of action it makes possible. It would be wrong, for example, to see the constitution as laying down a set of transcendent moral principles to guide the life of the political association. This way of construing the "foundational" character of the constitution merely succeeds in reducing all action to repetition; it separates the *content* of politics from the actual *performance* of political action. The implied or explicit constitutional concern of genuine political action hardly means that deliberation or debate is subject to a static, given set of intentions or ends that it must seek to uphold. The immanent ends of a *political* association, Arendt wants to argue, are not of this nature; their presence is rather a function of a continuing process of appropriation and transformation.

The structure of political action is one in which debate and disagreement reflect an overarching commitment to a particular public world and the mode of being together that it makes possible. It is therefore less a question of *what* is being debated, or *how* conservative or radical the outcome, so long as the participatory spirit remains and citizens "share a commitment to a mode of being together that recognizes and realizes the capacity for freedom in all individuals."[147] Genuine political talk must always, somehow, be concerned with the creation or preservation of this framework. But beyond this, the content of political action is neither given nor fixed, but generated in the course of performance. A constitution exists, as Kateb suggests, less for the realization of certain ends than for "indefinite future possibilities of political action . . . the frame is changed by what it contains—by the experience it shapes and accommodates."[148]

This rendering of the content of political action returns us to the charge of vacuity leveled by Arendt's critics. In his largely sympathetic reading of her work, Habermas praises Arendt for distinguishing between a genuinely political conception of power—power as the result of agreement and acting together—and the strategic model so often promoted by the tradition.[149] Yet Arendt's admirable attempt to separate communicative from instrumental or strategic relationships generates an unacceptably narrow view of politics, one "that is not applicable to modern relationships."[150] If her conception of politics is to be critically useful, it must be expanded to take into account socioeconomic relationships, an irreducible dimension of politics in the modern world.[151]

If Habermas's characterization of Arendt's "narrowing of the political" is correct, her political theory has a fatal weakness. Indeed, Richard Bernstein charges that the distinction between the social and the political engenders self-contradiction at the heart of her theory. For how are we to take seriously a political theorist who insists that "each person must be given the opportunity" to participate, but who turns a blind eye to the problem of how to create, through political means, the conditions that would help guarantee this opportunity?[152] Is not the narrowness of her conceptual structure the primary obstacle separating her view of political action from the realities of contemporary politics?

Arendt's conception of the content of politics is, as I have argued, deliberately exclusive. In fact, the desire to procure the "utmost possible autonomy" for politics is the driving force behind her thought on action.[153] Yet this need not render her conception irrelevant, or bar the possibility of revision. However, one must avoid exaggerating the degree to which Arendtian action is or can be "about" socioeconomic matters.[154]

Several issues need to be addressed in this regard. First, there is the obvious point against Habermas that Arendt's concept of action does not aim at descriptive generality: its critical power derives precisely from its foreignness and its oppositional quality. True, her notion of action and the distinction between action and violence are not much help in isolating the more sophisticated forms of coercion (for example, ideological distortion, manipulation by media) that often dominate our public realm. But insofar as the Habermasian project centers on identifying the criteria necessary for distinguishing *genuine* from *de facto* consensus, its aim is much different from Arendt's.[155] The "adequacy" of Arendt's concept of action ought to be judged according to its ability to distinguish the public realm from other spheres, and its capacity to preserve the fundamental phenomenon of plurality.

Second, the charge of self-contradiction that Bernstein levels against Arendt fails to hold water. Yes, to claim that "*every person* must be given the opportunity to participate in politics transforms the question of society," in that "it means we must honestly face the issue of how we can achieve or strive to realize a society where everybody has the opportunity to engage in politics."[156] But, strictly speaking, the issues raised by the goal of greater social justice are prepolitical. One needs to distinguish between the minimum conditions necessary for action and the achievement of genuinely equal access to the public realm (something no society has yet realized). Arendt sides with liberals against social democrats in viewing constitutionally guaranteed political rights as more fundamental than the abstract goal of social justice. Equality of citizenship, rather than greater equality of condition, is her primary concern. The relationship between the two, in her view, is a good deal looser than Bernstein suggests.

Third, Arendt's conception of *praxis*, while restrictive, is somewhat more flexible than Habermas, Bernstein, or Pitkin believe. When pressed by critics on the issue of her excessively narrow definition of "the political," Arendt indicated that (formal restrictions aside) her conception was "open" in two ways. First, she admitted that the *content* of political action—what citizens talk about—varies historically and culturally. Political talk is about the world. However, Arendt uses "world" in a very particular sense: the world is that "in-between" that "relates and separates men at the same time."[157] It is coextensive with "the public" in the broad sense of this term: "that which is common to us all of us."[158] The content of this world or this "in-between" necessarily "varies with each group of people."[159] As Arendt put it in response to a mystified query from Mary McCarthy:

> Life changes constantly, and things are constantly there to be talked about. At all times people living together will have affairs that belong in the realm of the public— "are worthy to be talked about in public." What these matters *are* at any historical *moment* is probably *utterly* different. For instance, the great cathedrals were the public space of the Middle Ages. The town halls came later. And *there* perhaps they had to talk about a matter which is not without interest either: the question of God. So what becomes public at every given period seems to be utterly different.[160]

This response relativizes the "proper content" of the public realm and political action without abdicating the various qualifications outlined above. Arendt's response may seem evasive, but it is in fact quite consistent with her "official" position. It is clear that any frame for action must possess certain formal qualities:

it must create a space of artificial equality from which violence and coercion have been largely excluded, and in which citizens have the opportunity to make their voices heard. It is also clear that politics must be about itself, in the sense that its primary concern must always be the health of this public sphere and the particular way of being together it makes possible. The self-contained quality of politics finds its chief expression in these dimensions of form and content. However, the *objects* of political speech—the worldly things that fill this public space—will vary and be subject to contestation. This is not to say that because *our* public space is filled by socioeconomic issues, these are or should be its proper content. Rather, it is to say that the question of content (understood now in the sense of the worldly referent of action) is secondary to the spirit and formal structure of political action. Certain kinds of concerns undermine the "care for the world," which, according to Arendt, animates all genuinely political life.

The "revisions" Arendt proposes thus do not seriously challenge her original notion of the properly political content of action. Arendt continues to apply the distinction between *praxis* and *poiēsis*, a distinction that bars coercive or essentially instrumental modes of action from the public sphere, as well as "household" or administrative matters. Her exclusionary strategy appears less strange if we recall the motive behind her theory of action. Arendt wanted, above all, to distinguish the life of action from the other activities that constitute the *vita activa*; moreover, she wanted to affirm the endless debate, deliberation, and plurality that characterize the *bios politikos*. By using Aristotle's distinction to focus on the atelic character of political action, she was able to free action from domination by the socioeconomic realm and thus restore, at least in principle, the inherent value of the plural realm of opinion.

Thinking Action against the Tradition

*Escape from the frailty of human affairs into the solidity of quiet and order
has in fact so much to recommend it that the greater part of political
philosophy since Plato could easily be interpreted as various
attempts to find theoretical foundations and practical ways
for an escape from politics altogether.*

—*Arendt*, The Human Condition[1]

I. TELEOLOGY VERSUS SELF-CONTAINEDNESS

The investigation of Arendt's political theory, thus far, has tended to confirm Habermas's judgment that its primary significance resides in "the systematic renewal of the Aristotelian concept of *praxis*."[2] Habermas's reading of Arendt presents her as a theorist of the communicative essence of political action, one who stresses the consensual nature of genuine politics, an emphasis grounded in the reinscription of Aristotle's distinction between *praxis* and *poiēsis*. It is an attractive reading in that it emphasizes the deliberative dimensions of Arendt's conception of politics while avoiding the drawbacks of its apparently classical structure. Arendt's theory of action need not succumb to "Hellenic nostalgia"; rather, it can be enlisted in the cause of articulating a fully dialogical conception of action and practical reason.[3]

The problem with this reading, as I argued in the Introduction, is that it keeps us from grasping just how radical Arendt's theory of action really is. Habermas is absolutely right when he states that "the teleological model of action" is Arendt's primary target.[4] However, his distinction between communicative and instrumental action (his "translation" of Arendt's distinction) prevents us from appreciating the inclusive character of Arendt's critique. Arendt's primary target is not merely the strategic conception of action propounded by Weber; rather, it is a teleological model that rules the tradition from beginning to end. Indeed, as I shall argue below, the Habermasian ideal of a purely communicative politics whose *telos* is rational consensus is, from the perspective Arendt provides, nearly as instrumental, and nearly as demeaning to plurality and politics, as Weber's strategic model. In order to preserve plurality and the phenomena it makes possible, we need an approach to action that truly treats it as an "end in itself."

To overcome the teleological model, Arendt needs to do far more than simply *revive* the classical concept of action. She needs to deconstruct that concept, since it obscures as well as preserves the phenomenon of genuine political action. Her appropriation of Aristotle is therefore neither mimetic nor slavish, as Habermas suggests. Instead, it is transformative and critical: she employs Aristotelian resources to radically reconceptualize the nature of action.[5] In this regard, a remark by Reiner Schürmann is instructive. "To deconstruct action," he writes, "is to uproot it from domination by the idea of finality, the teleocracy where it has been held since Aristotle. A deconstruction, then, is not the same as a destruction."[6] Arendt brings a certain amount of interpretive violence to the concept of *praxis*, not to destroy it but to "distill its original spirit," to reveal the "underlying phenomenal reality" that philosophical conceptualization has obscured.[7] Once the "empty shells" have been done away with, we are confronted with a notion of action that casts our entire network of inherited concepts—freedom, authority, autonomy, sovereignty, and power—in a radically new light.

I begin by tracing the way Arendt turns the criterion of action's self-containedness against Aristotle. Rather than "systematically renew" the notion of *praxis*, as Habermas suggests, Arendt pushes the inner tensions of Aristotle's original conception to the breaking point. This tactic is part of a comprehensive strategy designed to reveal the instrumentalism at the heart of Aristotle's account and to suggest why his concept of action is in many respects the source of the problem rather than its solution. For Arendt, the phenomenon of *praxis* can be revealed only if one reads Aristotle against the grain. Once we see this, the deeply antitraditional nature of Arendt's theory of action (and her political philosophy in general) begins to come into view. Her desire is to consider action as an autonomous phenomenon within the public sphere, rather than as a *means* to something else (whether power, truth, or even justice). Yet, as the case of Aristotle illustrates, the means/end category and the metaphorics of production from which it derives are so deeply rooted in our tradition that only a performance-oriented approach can reveal the peculiar freedom made possible by human plurality and the public sphere.

Arendt's single-minded focus on the "sharing of words and deeds" provokes intense anxiety on the part of her critics, who fear the implications of *politique pour la politique*. Surely, they argue, the phenomena of plurality and action can be preserved from reductionist absolutist or instrumental accounts without taking the radical step of isolating action from traditional moral or cognitive criteria. What value, after all, can an "autonomous" political action possibly have? This question leads many of Arendt's readers to ignore or even repudiate the strong formulation of her project and to opt, instead, for an antiteleological account grounded in a generalizable will or a procedural rationality. Such a Kantian/Rousseauian reformulation of Arendt finds support in On Revolution, her most extended consideration of *modern* political action. However, as I argue in Section IV, Arendt's objections to voluntarist and rationalist groundings of democratic politics run very deep. She is unwilling to accept an interpretation of action or freedom that, like Kant's or Rousseau's, denies that human plurality is both the "origin and goal" of political action. It is this staunch and indeed *ethical* commitment to human plurality and the "stage" where it can become manifest that leads Arendt to eschew the modern "philosophers of freedom" and their contemporary progeny. Paradoxically, the revolution in political thought that Arendt proposes can only be carried through with the aid of Nietzsche and categories appropriated from Heidegger's early philosophy. It is with Nietzsche and Heidegger that the depth of the problem of action is first revealed. It is with (and against) them that Arendt is able to articulate the open-ended freedom of action experienced by plural individuals on the public stage.

•

The picture of Arendt's theory of action as basically Aristotelian, as centered on the deployment of the *praxis/poiēsis* distinction, is complicated by three persistent themes in her work, which are particularly evident in her essay "What Is Freedom?" and the chapter on action in *The Human Condition*.[8] The first theme is the absolute priority she gives to *freedom*—the tangible, worldly freedom of the political realm—in all her discussions of action. Her most striking formulation appears in "What Is Freedom?":

> The field where freedom has always been known, not as a problem, to be sure, but as a fact of everyday life, is the political realm . . . for action and politics, among all the capabilities and potentialities of human life, are the only things we could not even conceive without at least assuming freedom exists. . . . Freedom, moreover, is not only one among the many problems and phenomena of the political realm properly speaking, such as justice, or power, or equality; freedom . . . is actually the reason that men live in political organization at all. Without it, political life as such would be meaningless. The *raison d'être* of politics is freedom, and its field of experience is action.[9]

The idea that freedom is "the *raison d'être* of politics" is, clearly, a *modern* one. In adopting Tocqueville's maxim for her own, Arendt distances her own conception of action and politics and Aristotle's. True, she uses the *praxis/poiēsis* distinction to distinguish between the realms of freedom and necessity, and she draws on Aristotle's distinction between the household and the *polis*. But there is a large gap between the Arendtian valorization of freedom as a phenomenon utterly divorced from the "natural" dimensions of human existence and Aristotle's more limited, and in some respects contradictory, claim that the *polis* is the arena in which man's distinctively human capacities are realized.[10] Arendt points to a radical discontinuity where Aristotle sees a structurally unified hierarchy. Moreover, Arendt's claim that freedom is the raison d'être of politics inverts the Aristotelian view of political association as a final end, a view that makes the liberation from necessity a step toward the self-sufficiency or perfection embodied in the state. Arendt views the political community as a "means" toward the end of freedom. This awards freedom an independence and a priority that it clearly lacks in the Aristotelian framework, where it is subsumed by the moral purposes of the state.[11]

The second theme that is difficult to reconcile with the Aristotelian paradigm is Arendt's identification of *action* with beginning or initiation. "To act," she writes in *The Human Condition*, "in the most general sense, means to take an initiative, to begin . . . to set something into motion."[12] The freedom of action is found in its capacity to "call something into being which did not exist before, which was not given, not even as an object of cognition or imagination, and which, therefore, strictly speaking, could not be known."[13] Arendt attaches the greatest importance to this human capacity, grounding it in what she refers to as man's essential "natality," his character as a *beginning* himself.[14] Action—understood as the human capacity for spontaneous beginning, for the creation of something utterly without precedent—verges, for Arendt, on the miraculous.[15] As Barker reminds us, the initiatory dimension of action was not unknown to the Greeks; however, Arendt attaches a significance to this dimension that they would have found incomprehensible.[16]

The final theme that problematizes the characterization of Arendt's theory as "Aristotelian" is her identification of *virtuosity* as the essence of action's freedom.[17] This description frames freedom of action in strictly *performative* terms. The freedom or self-containedness of action does not refer to some determining *telos* (e.g., virtue, the good for man); rather, it is expressed *solely* in terms of the virtuosity of performance.[18] While it is true that Aristotle emphasized the performative dimension of action in a number of contexts, and with particular vehemence in refuting the Socratic view that virtue is knowledge, the fact remains that the quality of performance alone could not be a satisfactory criterion of good action (*eupraxia*) for Aristotle.[19] Aristotle always emphasized the unity of performance and virtue, of good action and character (*hexis*).[20] He was especially concerned with distinguishing between genuinely virtuous actions and those with only the *appearance* of virtue. He therefore insisted that every performance of good action be grounded in a firm character; otherwise, virtue would not be actualized in action. In contrast, Arendt's description of freedom as virtuosity not only gives action a specific autonomy with respect to morality, but it locates the essence of freedom in precisely that realm of appearance from which Aristotle sought distance.

Arendt, then, describes freedom, rather than the good life, as the raison d'être of politics; she identifies the initiatory dimension of action as the chief locus of freedom; and she sees virtuosity of performance as its primary manifestation. When combined, these aspects suggest that Arendt's view of action is more than a little different from Aristotle's.[21] Aristotle sees the self-sufficiency of an activity as inextricably linked to its contribution toward the achievement of the good for man, the fulfillment of man's proper function (*ergon*). Virtuous or noble actions, *praxis*, appear as ends in themselves insofar as they help actualize this good (the life of intellectual and ethical virtue) in the course of their performance. This is why, as we have seen, that Aristotle characterizes the good life as an *active* life.[22] In making the distinction between *praxis* and *poiēsis*, he is claiming that action "attains" the good in a manner essentially different from the way in which instrumental activities attain their ends.[23] Virtuous action "is itself an end," because it constitutes "a certain kind of life";[24] because it is, in this special sense, "in conformity" with man's end.[25] The sort of immanent or internal relation articulated here—in which "the work of man" is "living well," a certain kind of activity—stands in sharp contrast to the means-end schema of production. Nevertheless, the self-containedness of *praxis* remains a function of the "highest good" itself. So, while the fulfillment of the *telos* of *praxis* may be immanent in the sense that "the means to achieve the end [are] already the end," the end retains a logical priority and distinctness.

According to Aristotle, the self-contained quality of *praxis* is significantly qualified. Generally speaking, we can say that the teleological model subsumes *all* activity, *praxis* included, as either the achievement of a good or the fulfillment of a function. While from one perspective *praxis* is intrinsically valuable, from another it is always subservient to a goal, with its value being a function of the peculiar nature of the "highest good," the work of man. The inclusiveness of the teleological framework is clear from the very first sentence of the *Ethics*: "Every art or applied science and every systematic investigation, and similarly *every action and choice*, seem to aim at some good; the good, therefore, has been well defined as that at which all things aim."[26] From *this* perspective, it is not really the case that "the specifically human achievement" of action "lies altogether outside the category of means and ends."[27] Rather, unless *praxis* is grounded by reference to its *telos* (*eudaimonia*), its status as *energeia* cannot be affirmed. The basis for the distinction between *praxis* and *poiēsis*, ultimately, is the difference between their respective ends; that is, the difference between the "highest good," happiness or the life of active virtue, and all other, less final, ends.[28] The highest good can be actualized only by a performance that is simultaneously a process of formation or creation. The realization of the *telos* demands that action produce a work, character, which fulfills "the work of man."

The formation of character, of course, is the theme that links Aristotle's ethics to his politics: ". . . the main concern of politics is to engender a certain character in the citizens and to make them good and disposed to perform noble actions."[29] Through law, political institutions, and education, citizens are guided toward an ideal of virtuous action—toward excellence. This collective formation of character is successful if citizens act in a virtuous manner toward one another. When virtue animates social relationships, the state can be said to realize justice concretely. For Aristotle, justice is less a function of rules than a quality of citizens themselves. He views "complete justice" as "the practice of complete virtue," or (in Ernest Barker's phrase) "virtue in action."[30] Justice, as the spirit animating social relations, is the sine qua non of a genuinely "happy" *polis*: through it the final good of the political association, its moral purpose, is realized. The *praxis* of the statesman and the citizen are therefore judged according to their contribution to the justice of the state; that is, the common good.[31] Power, office, and honors are distributed according to this standard.[32] Thus, while the political association, in Aristotle's understanding, is a field for action, such action has value to the degree to which it actualizes justice; for only just action enables the *polis* to realize its purpose, which is to make the good life accessible to its citizens. Here, as before, the value of action is seen to reside less in itself than in the creation of a work (the "production" of just citizens) or the fulfillment of a purpose (the final good of the state).[33]

For Aristotle, then, action is ultimately a *means*: to the development of character, to the actualization of virtue, to the realization of justice, and to the procurement of happiness. In this sense, the *praxis/poiēsis* distinction simply fails to square with the teleological character of Aristotle's ethics and political philosophy.[34] This is really no surprise, particularly since Aristotle's theory of causes universalizes the means-end category by its insistence upon the priority of the final cause. The result is a context in which the only thing that deserves to be called self-sufficient is the final product or goal (*eudaimonia*, the just *polis*). It is no exaggeration to state that, within the Aristotelian framework, *praxis* is ultimately subsumed by *poiēsis*.

Arendt's theory of political action should be read as the sustained attempt to think of praxis outside the teleological framework. Her argument is that teleological accounts of action are irreconcilable with the freedom born of human plurality and the public sphere. They deny the open-endedness of action, demanding a prior positing of goals in order for the activity—now viewed as *process*—to have either meaning or value. The contingency and "arbitrariness" that mark action are eliminated through the necessity injected into the "process of becoming" by the idea of a final cause. As Arendt remarks in *The Life of the Mind*, teleology not only compromises the autonomy of action by making its meaning conditional upon a goal but teleology also robs action of its essential initiatory power:

> The view that everything real must be preceded by a potentiality as one of its causes implicitly denies the future as an authentic tense: the future is nothing but a consequence of the past, and the difference between natural and man-made things is merely between those whose potentialities necessarily grow into actualities and those that may or may not be actualized.[35]

A teleological account of action therefore produces the two effects that Arendt's theory of action is most concerned to avoid: it instrumentalizes action while simultaneously effacing the gap between nature and the realm of human affairs. With respect to the former, Arendt argues that Aristotle's understanding of action is in fact derived from the fabrication experience, from *poiēsis*. She cites his description of the benefactor in the ninth book of the *Nicomachean Ethics*.[36] Aristotle describes the action of the benefactor as essentially creative, as artistic in nature: ". . . the recipient of their benefaction is the work of their own hands, and, accordingly, they love their handiwork more than it loves its maker" (1168a). The end of the benefactor's activity is "the work produced," and this work is not simply the enhanced life of the recipient but the life of the maker, the benefactor, as well. "In his activity the maker is, in a sense, the work produced": that is, the benefactor's existence, "produced" by his virtuous activity, is itself the chief *ergon*.[37] The determination of the meaning of the action in this way (and a quite peculiar determination it is, occurring as it does in the context of a chapter concerned with *friendship*) follows, according to Aristotle, from "the nature of things: what a thing is potentially is revealed in actuality by what it *produces*."[38]

Arendt's gloss of this passage emphasizes that the Aristotelian interpretation of action "actually spoils the action itself and its true result, the relationship it should have established."[39] Instead of creating friendship, a relationship *between* men, Aristotle's benefactor treats both the recipient and himself as raw material to be formed for a "higher" end. Arendt views this perversion as typical of all teleological accounts; she concludes that action "can result in an end product only on the condition that its own authentic, non-tangible meaning is destroyed."[40] If Aristotle thinks that even action between friends is a means toward the creation of a work, then, says Arendt, he clearly "thinks of acting in terms of making and its result, the relationship between men, in terms of an accomplished work (his emphatic attempts to distinguish between action and fabrication, *praxis* and *poiēsis*, notwithstanding)."[41]

The example of the benefactor is telling for Arendt, because it shows just how deeply teleology and the fabrication experience color Aristotle's thought. The account of deliberation given by Aristotle in Book III, Chapter 3, of the *Nicomachean Ethics* similarly displays the effects of the assimilation of *praxis* to *poiēsis*. Here, Aristotle stresses that "we deliberate not about ends but about the means to attain ends. . . . We take the end for granted, and then consider in what manner and by what means it can be realized" (1112b11–12). This characterization conflicts with the account of "unqualified" deliberation given in Book VI, Chapter 9, but it squares perfectly well with Aristotle's general teleological stance (more consistently adhered to in the *Eudemian Ethics*). For how could deliberation be end-constitutive in anything but the most partial sense if indeed "ends are inherent in human nature and the same for all"?[42] Arendt concludes that the freedom expressed in the act of deliberation is "very small" when the larger picture is taken into account. Aristotle's last word on the matter, according to Arendt, is "we deliberate only about means to an end that we take for granted, *that we cannot choose*."[43] Teleology, in other words, demands a basically instrumental (and highly restricted) account of deliberation.

Teleology further undermines the freedom of action by closing the gap between the political and the household spheres. While Aristotle certainly distinguishes the two spheres, his teleology reasserts a fundamental continuity between them. The natural order, culminating in the political association, is of a piece: there is no radical break between "life" and the "good life" because both are to be understood as "natural." The political realm, the realm of freedom, is naturalized, while the household is viewed as an important predecessor of the *politeia*. This raises the possibility of substantive similarity or parallel structure between the two realms. If "whatever is the end-product of the perfecting process of any object . . . [is] its nature," then it is man's nature "to live in a state."[44] But considered as *zōon politikon*, man's freedom presents itself as the result of natural (teleological) necessity. (How this continuity leads to what Arendt views as deformations in Aristotle's sense of the political will be shown in the next section.)

I should emphasize here that Arendt's objection to the teleological framing of action has both a narrow and an extended form. On the one hand, she clearly wants to assert, with Hobbes and the modern tradition generally, that the political realm is a supremely important *artifact*. Her constant use of architectural metaphors when discussing the public realm make this amply clear: the public realm is "a *house* where freedom can dwell."[45] The political realm is decidedly *un*natural, and this is what allows it to be a space of freedom. But Arendt is not simply objecting to the Aristotelian "naturalization" of human freedom; she is, moreover, objecting to the role performed by teleological explanation. So, for example, she takes just as strong exception to the Hegelian spiritualization of nature as she does to Aristotle's naturalizing of the *polis*. In both instances, teleology works to efface the difference between nature and human affairs. For Arendt, teleology is inherently dialectical. Whether in Hegelian or Aristotelian form, it attempts to "produce freedom" out of "the process of necessity."[46]

This is an important point for Arendt. It reveals the inner tendency of all forms of teleology, which is to restrict the autonomy of action by placing it in the context of a larger ("natural" or "speculative") necessity. Teleology, therefore, expresses *theoria*'s right to domination over action. Whether it takes as its object the necessity of the cosmic order or the historical dialectic, philosophical contemplation has, as Hegel said, "no other intention than to eliminate the accidental."[47] From such a perspective, the freedom or self-containedness of action can appear only as illusory or accidental; it is "unreal" compared to the necessity by which human freedom appears.[48]

II. THE ANTIPOLITICAL QUALITY OF ARISTOTELIAN *PRAXIS*

From Arendt's perspective, Aristotle's teleology is noteworthy for the way it universalizes the fabrication experience and encourages the view that the entire cosmos reflects the logic of production, of means and ends. This universalization is prompted by the superiority Aristotle attributes to the *vita contemplativa* and by his philosophical preference for necessity over contingency. For these reasons, Arendt's final judgment of Aristotle on action is quite severe. Rather than give him the benefit of the doubt, Arendt feels that the supremacy Aristotle claims for the contemplative life in Book X of the *Nicomachean Ethics* tells the whole story in a nutshell: his thought is colored throughout by a consistent and unquestionable devaluation of the realm of human affairs.[49] Genuine self-sufficiency, according to Aristotle, is never found in action or speech, for these "attempt to gain advantages beyond political action, advantages such as political power, prestige or at least happiness for the statesman himself and his fellow citizens, and that is something other than political activity."[50] Contemplation, however, is unquestionably an activity chosen for its own sake: "what is usually called 'self-sufficiency' will be found in the highest degree in the activity which is concerned with theoretical knowledge."[51]

In contrast, Arendt's adherence to the spirit of the *praxis/poiēsis* distinction results in a radically antiteleological stance, which aligns her *against* Aristotle and Hegel and (to a certain extent) *with* Kant. In the first and second *Critiques*, Kant maintained the autonomy of action (albeit in the guise of practical reason) in the face of theoretical and speculative reason. Arendt's hostility to the philosophic domination of action leads her to underwrite a limited Kantianism. Hence, in *The Life of the Mind*, she strongly endorses the Kantian distinction between *Vernunft* and *Verstand*, between Reason and what she translates as "intellect."[52]

It is difficult to overestimate the significance of this distinction for Arendt. In her eyes the primary accomplishment of Kant's "Copernican Revolution" in philosophy was the drawing of a rigorous distinction between matters of truth or cognition, on the one hand, and matters of meaning or practical import, on the other. Kant restricts theoretical reason to systematization of knowledge; it is not permitted to "transcend the limits of possible experience" and find speculative employment.[53] Those ultimate questions that human reason is "not able to ignore, but which, transcending all its powers, it is not able to answer," are placed forever beyond the province of *theoria*: the interest of theoretical reason is bound to the world of space and time.[54] As a result, practical reason emerges as autonomous and radically free, capable not just of determining the means but also the *goals* of human action. Practical reason in the Kantian sense signifies freedom as "a power of spontaneously beginning,"[55] and this marks a radical break with those who would define this faculty in terms of the power to *choose* between predetermined ends.

From Arendt's perspective, Kant's elevation of practical interest and his strict separation of modes of rationality mark a revolutionary moment in philosophy, as they signify philosophy's emancipation from the need to replace the "merely contingent" with the necessary. At least in principle, this emancipatory moment restored the integrity of the *praxis/poiēsis* distinction.[56] Thus, it is through a Kantian lens that Arendt's appropriation of Aristotle must be read.

How, then, does Arendt ultimately assess Aristotle's contribution to the conceptualization of action? The judgment Kant helps her make places Aristotle in a position structurally parallel to that which Plato occupies for Heidegger.[57] Each is seen as the origin of a particularly fateful interpretation—of action in Aristotle's case, of truth in Plato's—that strongly influences the course and development of the tradition generally.[58] Aristotle determines action instrumentally (thanks to his teleology), and the tenacity of this interpretation is revealed with the demise of the hierarchy of ends from which it emerged. For with the repudiation of the idea of a "final cause" at the beginning of the modern age, the means-end category is applied all the more rigorously, as the examples of Bacon and Hobbes amply demonstrate. Arendt, therefore, views the collapse of the *praxis/poiēsis* distinction and the rise of instrumentalism in the modern age as prefigured by Aristotle's teleological generalization of the fabrication experience.

The Kant-inspired perspective that Arendt brings to bear on Aristotle does not simply reveal a philosophical prejudice against action and politics, an elevation of theory over practice; of equal importance is the way it throws into sharp relief what Arendt refers to as "the inconsistency of his enterprise," the often self-contradictory nature of his depiction of the *bios politikos*.[59] Arendt's perspective reveals how Aristotle's ultimately instrumental view of action contaminates precisely those essential aspects of political life her positive appropriation of *praxis* highlighted.

Thus, the teleological assimilation of nature and the realm of human affairs (exemplified by Aristotle's statement that "the state belongs to that class of objects which exist in nature") does more than simply blur the line between freedom and necessity. There is, according to Arendt, a manifest transfer of concepts and categories from the household to the political realm. Aristotle's political philosophy is marked throughout by a tendency to "superimpose on the actions and life of the *polis* those standards which, as he explains elsewhere, are valid only for the behavior and life in the household community."[60] He is blind to his own insight. The most glaring contradiction concerns his original definition of the *polis* as "a community of equals for the sake of a life which is potentially the best."[61] This conception of the specific quality of the *political* association is contradicted by his subsequent determination that the good of the citizen consists in "knowing how to rule and be ruled."[62] Arendt reminds us that the idea of ruling and the distinction between rulers and ruled belongs "to a sphere which precedes the political realm . . . the *polis* is based upon the principle of equality and knows no differentiation between rulers and ruled."[63] Moreover, as she points out in *The Human Condition*, the very *idea* of ruling hinges upon a technical interpretation of action and the split between knowing and doing found in the fabrication process.[64] This split is transferred to the realm of human affairs in the form of the hierarchy of command and execution. By characterizing the good of the citizen in terms of the concept of rule, Aristotle undercuts equality and deliberation, thereby emasculating both *praxis* and plurality.

Aristotle, of course, does not ground his notion of rule by appeal to the Platonic idea of "the superiority of the expert over the layman." As Arendt notes, he is far too aware of the difference between acting and making to draw his metaphors *directly* from the sphere of production.[65] Nevertheless, his hierarchical, authoritarian rendering of the relation between "equal" citizens is not peripheral, but rather flows directly from a concept of action in which ends are pregiven, in which the *telos* rules from start to finish. The objective quality of these ends makes it hardly accidental that Aristotle's ideal *polis* has its raison d'être less as a field for action and debate than as a *school* for virtue. The primary political relationship is *not* between knowers and executors, masters and slaves; it is, however, between teachers and taught. Aristotle's substitution of *education* for *rule* intentionally suppresses the disanalogy between the two—the fact that the former occurs between people who "are potentially equals."[66] If one assumes that ends are found rather than made and that moral or practical knowledge, while not scientific, is nevertheless objective, then it follows that the primary task of the political community will not be to encourage end-constitutive debate, but rather to enforce the *nomos*—the laws and customs embodying the ends of the *polis*—upon the citizen body. It does this through a regime of moral education that lasts a lifetime, and that draws its effectiveness from its coercive power.[67]

For Aristotle, then, citizens participate, but they do so either by commanding or obeying; they are equal, but never all at once; they deliberate, but not about the most important things; they are, finally, not *one*, but neither can they be said to constitute a genuine plurality. The Aristotelian notion that the members of a community are identified by the ends they share imposes a substantive and severe restriction upon deliberative speech. It renders this speech technical in the last instance: only means to the community's ends, but never those ends themselves, are debated.[68] Aristotle cannot begin to define the political community without reference to its end; for Arendt, on the other hand, the question of "the end" of the political association is a non sequitur. The polity has no pregiven end other than to make the distinctive freedom of political action a permanent possibility for its citizens.[69] Because Aristotle unremittingly subjects *praxis* to the rule of *telos*, in Arendt's eyes he stands less as the antithesis to the Hobbesian "technification" of action and politics than as its genealogical origin.[70]

Aristotle's teleocratic model of action is thus mirrored in a basically authoritarian conception of the political association, one that suppresses equality and plurality and curtails deliberative speech in the name of a flawed educational analogy.[71] It is because Arendt places a premium upon plurality and doxastic speech that she ultimately rejects the Aristotelian conception of the political community and the severely restricted notions of action and deliberation at home in it. She substitutes the Kantian idea of a *sensus communis*, a "feeling for the world," for the more substantive *koinonia*.[72] Arendt's communitarian admirers are perplexed by this move; they fail to see that the "thick" community sense they find in Aristotle undermines the open-ended debate that Arendt identifies as the "very essence" of political life.[73] What needs strengthening, in her view, is not our sense of membership or a common moral vocabulary, but rather our commitment to the world. Where such commitment animates debate and disagreement, the talk that results is genuinely political; it rises above the mere clash of interests or the willful assertion of identity. Thus, the deliberative politics she champions is a contentious, agonistic, and often polemical exchange of opinion, one that stands in sharp contrast to the stately application of *phronēsis*. Against the Aristotelian norm of "correctness in deliberation" Arendt poses the example of Gotthold Lessing, whom she describes as a "completely political person" because he prized the friendship born of argument over the attainment of truth.[74] Such "friendship" harks back to *philia*, but differs from it by stressing plurality and open-endedness rather than harmony of judgments.

III. AUTONOMOUS ACTION: POLITICS AS PERFORMING ART

The force of Arendt's reading of Aristotle should now be clear. If the idea of *praxis* is to be effectively deployed in the fight against an undemocratic instrumentalization of action, then the first order of business is the thorough deconstruction of the teleological context from which this concept emerged. This makes it possible to think about the specific autonomy of action for the first time. Unless this reconceptualization is undertaken without reserve, any attempt to renew *praxis* will fall prey to the logic of instrumentalization that Aristotle sets in motion. Political phenomena—human plurality, the space of appearances, exchange of opinion—will continue to be degraded and devalued, with predictably undemocratic consequences.

The immediate question is whether anything "essential" remains of *praxis* after the "sea-change." Arendt certainly thinks so. For her, it is the performative character of action that provides the locus of action's intrinsic meaning or value, its freedom and "actuality." The peculiar self-sufficiency of action must be divorced from any obligation whatsoever to a pregiven *telos*. Arendt's appropriation of *praxis* proceeds, then, by detaching *energeia* from the metaphorics of production or growth that had made it the teleological concept par excellence. Once actuality is divorced from the notions of final causality or development, it can be seen to inhere fully in the activity itself. So transformed, *energeia* spawns an aesthetic or theatrical metaphorics, one in which the self-containedness of an activity no longer denotes "perfection" in the Aristotelian sense, but rather *virtuosity*. The virtuosity manifest in the performance of an action is action's true reason for being. Action embodies not "the good for man," but freedom.

This is the radical shift of ground that Arendt effects in order to "recover" *praxis*. The project is revolutionary, the formulations it yields paradoxical and often disturbing. By thinking of action in terms of what might be called a performance ontology, she preserves the autonomy of *praxis* while simultaneously de-emphasizing the categories traditionally employed in the analysis of action. Motives, goals, conditions, consequences: all become largely secondary to grasping action's peculiar significance and reality. "Motives and aims," Arendt writes, "no matter how pure or grandiose, are never unique; like psychological qualities they are typical."[75] The "specific meaning of each deed" is lost the moment we judge action according to such external criteria; this meaning can reside only "in the performance itself and neither in its motivation or achievement."[76] In order to grasp the atelic quality of action, we need a theory of presentation or appearance—a theorization of performance in the aesthetic as opposed to the technical sense.[77] Thus, in "What Is Freedom?" Arendt writes:

> Freedom as inherent in action is perhaps best illustrated by Machiavelli's concept of *virtu*, the excellence with which man answers the opportunities the world opens up before him in the guise of *fortuna*. Its meaning is best rendered by "virtuosity," that is, an excellence we attribute to the performing arts (as distinguished from the creative arts of making) where the accomplishment lies in the performance itself and not in an end product which outlasts the activity and becomes independent of it. The virtuoso-ship of Machiavelli's *virtu* somehow reminds us of the fact, although Machiavelli hardly knew it, that the Greeks always used such metaphors as flute-playing, dancing, healing and sea-faring to distinguish political from other activities, that is, that they drew their analogies from those acts in which virtuosity of performance is decisive.[78]

This passage, with its strong emphasis on virtuosity and performance, indicates just how far Arendt is willing to go in order to identify actuality and freedom with the activity itself. Arendt herself proposes the performing arts as the most apt analogy because their meaning, actuality, or "truth" is inseparable from the activity of presentation. Arendt claims that the performing arts "have a strong affinity with politics" because in neither case is the meaning "instrumental or objectifiable in character."[79] Indeed, in the case of action the appearance of freedom "coincides with the performing act" itself.[80] As Arendt puts it in "What Is Freedom?" "men *are* free—as distinguished from possessing the gift for freedom—as long as they act, neither before nor after; for *to be free and to act are the same*."[81] Freedom is therefore no more, but no less, than virtuosity, since this quality remains immanent to the activity.

The political realm is still the home of action and freedom, as Aristotle said it was. However, Arendt's transformation of *energeia* and *praxis* fundamentally alters our understanding of the nature of this "home." Once the teleological background is removed and the full "pathos of distance" is restored to the *praxis/poiēsis* distinction, the political realm emerges as essentially "a kind of theater."[82] To invoke Arendt's most characteristic description, it is that "space of appearances" in which action and freedom come to presence and can be remembered. The institutional form of the political association must be suited to serve as *stage*, for political actors like performing artists "need an audience to show their virtuosity"; they "depend upon others for the performance itself."[83] The *polis* was suited to this function: it was "precisely that 'form of government' that provided men with a space of appearances where they could act, with a kind of theater where freedom could appear."[84] In contrast, representative democracy limits the opportunity for performance/appearance—the "publicly organized space"—which, according to Arendt, marks a genuinely free people (a point she makes much of in *On Revolution*).[85] The political realm, viewed "autonomously" as a theater for action and freedom, is "the space where I appear to others as others appear to me" through the sharing of words and deeds; it is the space where "men exist not merely like other living things or inanimate things but make their appearance explicitly."[86]

If politics refers to itself, if action is essentially performance and freedom is essentially virtuosity, then the appropriate criterion for judging action is, as Arendt unhesitatingly affirms, *greatness*. Once again, this is something the Greeks knew but which we have forgotten:

> Unlike human behavior—which the Greeks, like all civilized people, judged according to moral standards—action can be judged only by the criterion of greatness because it is in its nature to break through the commonly accepted and reach into the extraordinary, where whatever is true in common and everyday life *no longer applies* because everything that exists is unique and *sui generis*.[87]

"Greatness" alone applies to the performance itself. To judge action according to its motivation or result inevitably degrades its autonomy, destroying "the specific meaning of each deed."[88]

Arendt's emphasis on "the shining glory of great deeds" seems far indeed from the deliberative model of politics. With its autonomy protected by the analogy of the performing arts, political action emerges now as *agon*, as heroic.[89] Action, performance, initiation, virtuosity, greatness: this configuration of concepts points to a politics driven by "a fiercely agonal spirit," to a public realm "reserved for individuality" in which "everybody had to constantly distinguish himself from all others, to show through unique deeds or achievements that he was the best of all."[90] In this context, the story of Achilles has a "paradigmatic significance," for this "doer of great deeds . . . and speaker of great words" gives expression to what Arendt describes as *the* political passion, the "urge toward self-disclosure at the expense of all other factors."[91]

Arendt's high modernist insistence on politics for the sake of politics, on preserving action from the reductive effects of external (moral or utilitarian) criteria, places her in an uneasy alliance with two other proponents of an agonistic, theatrical "politics of appearance," Machiavelli (whom I discuss here) and Nietzsche (see Chapter 3). She shares Machiavelli's strong distaste for the reduction of the political to the moral, to the point of insisting that consistent goodness leads, in the public realm, to disaster or at the very least to a lessening of our commitment to the world.[92] The priority of morality shifts the meaning of action away from the deed itself to either the intention behind it or its consequences. Machiavelli's concept of *virtu*, on the other hand, avoids any such displacement by focusing our attention on the *style* of action—action as a kind of play with the world:

> *Virtu* is the response, summoned up by man, to the world, or rather to the constellation of *fortuna* in which the world opens up, presents and offers itself to him, to his *virtu*. There is no *virtu* without *fortuna* and no *fortuna* without *virtu*; the interplay between them indicates a harmony between man and world—playing with each other and succeeding together—which is as remote from the wisdom of the statesman as from the excellence, moral or otherwise, of the individual, and the competence of experts.[93]

Virtu is the freedom of this play, the freedom of initiatory action. This freedom brackets the ethical criteria of everyday life and the instrumental dictates of politics as administration. From the point of view of initiatory, agonistic action, what matters most is not goodness or badness, nor the achievement of ends, but the ability to shine forth, to be glorious.[94]

The difficulties raised by Arendt's agonism are parallel to those encountered in Machiavelli, whose praise of great action attenuates, perhaps even severs, the relation between morality and politics. Arendt's critics are deeply troubled by what they see as a disdain for the standards of ordinary morality, and they fiercely denounce what appears to be a dangerous and uncalled-for aestheticization of action. Arendt's strategy for preserving the autonomy of action and the integrity of the public sphere threatens to degenerate into a politics of heroic display or, worse, an immoralist celebration of greatness as its own morality.[95]

I believe that such charges ultimately miss the point of Arendt's performative conception; nevertheless, they can hardly be dismissed out of hand. Arendt's critics point out that her theory of action encourages a celebration of virtuosity for the sake of virtuosity, of skill and ability for their own sake. Machiavelli's politics of *virtu* are illustrative in this regard, demonstrating that it is but one step from the "heroic" or glorious to the brazenly amoral: one need only recall his description of Cesare Borgia as the consummate political actor, as the possessor of great *virtu*.[96] Arendt, in contrast to Machiavelli, appears to have radically exaggerated the distance between a politics of appearance and virtuosity and a politics of deceit and manipulation. Her appeal to Machiavelli reminds us that there is a distinctively *political* conception of freedom; but it also reminds us how easily the politics-as-game analogy devolves into a Clauswitzian strategic encounter.[97]

As her distinctions between power and violence, action and coercion, make plain, Arendt hardly wants to go in *this* direction. All the more reason, then, to be surprised by her largely positive view of Machiavelli, the theorist most often credited with inventing the modern strategic conception of political action.[98] It is telling that Arendt focuses on the "theatrical" dimensions of *virtu*, particularly given her hypersensitivity to all traces of instrumentality in *praxis*. There appears to be a basic and inescapable self-contradiction at the heart of her theory of action, a contradiction between her Aristotle-inspired image of a deliberative politics based on equality, plurality, and the absence of coercion and her Machiavellian praise of the great, the agonistic, the virtuosic. How can she hope to combine the deliberative and the initiatory, the dialogical and the agonistic, in *one* theory of political action? Moreover, if I am correct in suggesting that the performative dimension has priority over the deliberative and dialogical, how is it possible to defend Arendt from charges that her agonistic conception of "politics for the sake of politics" promotes hero worship and immoralism?

George Kateb, I think, is the most compelling of Arendt's critics on this score: he emphasizes the marginalization of morality that a rigorous insistence upon the autonomy of action entails. Politics for the sake of politics apparently brackets moral judgment of all genuinely *political* action. According to Kateb, the "gist of Arendt's radicalism" is the view that "political action does not exist to do justice or fulfill other moral purposes. . . . The supreme achievement of political action is existential, and the stakes are seemingly higher than moral ones."[99]

Arendt's zeal to preserve the integrity of political action apparently leads her to deny the presence of binding moral limits to action, a denial that prompts Kateb to ask, "How can morally unlimited action be anything but gravely immoral?"[100] While Kateb disputes the idea that Arendt's position, in the final analysis, is immoralist, and while he makes a persuasive case for the presence of an "internal" morality in her theory of political action, he nevertheless stresses what he considers to be the highly dubious result of her violent anti-instrumentalism: a radical de-emphasis of the *consequences* of action. In Kateb's view, any theory of action that denies the priority of consequences is morally untenable. In Arendt's case, he maintains, a concern for consequences and a respect for moral limits must be on a par with "acting for the sake of action."[101]

Assuming Kateb is correct, we must ask whether Arendt's performative, agonistic conception is *too* successful in preserving the autonomy of action. Indeed, at times Arendt seems to surpass even Machiavelli in her insistence upon the antipolitical, unworldly quality of the moral life: "Goodness," she states, ". . . as a consistent way of life, is not only impossible within the confines of the public realm, it is even destructive of it."[102] It is the nature of purely moral activity, of genuine goodness, to "flee appearance," to be "as far removed from the public realm as possible."[103] The moment "good works" call attention to themselves, the moment moral motivation attempts to externalize itself in worldly form, the results are suspect. When the moral attitude suffuses the political realm rather than withdrawing from it (as Jesus did), the result is revolutionary terror and the destruction of the "world of appearances."[104] Hence Arendt's Nietzschean polemic against Rousseau's politics of compassion, a politics whose sensitivity to suffering leads it to eschew "the wearisome processes of persuasion, negotiation and compromise" and take direct, *violent* action.[105] Hence, also, her equally fierce opposition to the politics of authenticity, which demands that the actor's "innermost motives" be put on public display. Such a demand transforms all actors into hypocrites, a result that can be avoided only by a terroristic politics of virtue à la Robespierre.[106]

From a *political* point of view, then, "absolute goodness is hardly any less dangerous than absolute evil."[107] Arendt praises Machiavelli's insight in this regard, lauding his affirmation of glory over goodness:

> Nobody perhaps has been more sharply aware of this ruinous quality of doing good than Machiavelli, who, in a famous passage, dared to teach men "how not to be good." Needless to add, he did not say and did not mean that men must be taught how to be bad; the criminal act, though for different reasons, must also flee from being seen and heard by others. Machiavelli's criterion for political action was glory, the same as classical antiquity, and badness can no more shine in glory than goodness.[108]

It is, however, one thing to argue (with Machiavelli) that politics demands an ethic specific to it, one that necessarily departs from the strictures of ordinary morality, and another to argue (as Arendt apparently does) that glory is the appropriate criterion for action. Machiavelli does appeal to glory, both as an inducement to heroic action and as a reason for avoiding the baser roads to power.[109] Yet his primary purpose in *The Prince* is to point out the gap between public and private life and the respective ethics of each; to show how the virtues of the private citizen and ordinary morality may well lead to disaster when transferred without modification to the *public* realm. Thus, Machiavelli demonstrates how the virtues of generosity, mercy, and honesty, if strictly adhered to by the *political* actor, generate envy, faction, and violence, effects that are damaging to the state as well as to the prince.[110]

For Machiavelli, it is precisely the *consequences* of rigidly moral conduct that dictate a selective suspension of ordinary morality by the political actor. Like Weber, he sees violence as an unavoidable means in politics, as the instrumentality that distinguishes this "life sphere" from all others. The political actor must know "how not to be good" if the condition of violence is not to become pervasive; he must know when, and how, to use force or fraud in order to *reduce* the general level of violence.[111] Excessive care for one's soul leads just as assuredly to the ruin of the state—and the life of ordinary morality that the state makes possible—as does the unlimited violence of the tyrant.

The idea of a "specifically political ethic," therefore, does not imply a denial or inversion of ordinary morality; rather, it is predicated upon a kind of tragic knowledge.[112] As Weber puts it in "Politics as a Vocation," "he who lets himself in for politics . . . contracts with diabolical powers and for his action it is *not* true that good can only come from good and evil only from evil, but that often the opposite is the case."[113] There is present in Machiavelli not only the celebration of agonistic, glorious action that Arendt points to, but also something akin to Weber's "ethic of responsibility": the political actor must not, can not, elude personal responsibility for the "diabolical" means political necessity forces upon him. He must accept the fact of "dirty hands" if political evil is to be resisted effectively, all the while foregoing the appeal to *a priori* principles, absolute ends or his own glory as justifications that in any way lessen his responsibility for the violence he employs. Machiavelli and Weber reject absolutist morality for the Arendtian reason that it leads to an "unmanly" withdrawal from the world. More important, and in contrast to Arendt, they reject moral absolutism because it can so easily turn into an ethic of absolute ends, which is oblivious to the cost of achieving the goal: only the dogmatic absolutist truly believes that the end justifies the means.[114] The specifically political ethic that Machiavelli implies and Weber endorses begins with the premise that necessity sometimes forces the political actor to do that which is evil according to the standards of absolute or ordinary morality. The ethical conclusion that Machiavelli and Weber draw is that the peculiar responsibility of the political actor is not to choose only good means to good ends (a potentially disastrous policy), but to choose the lesser evil wherever necessity demands a departure from morality. The responsible political actor eschews means *and* ends whose cost is too high.

There is a striking difference between Arendt's view of the relation between politics and morality and Machiavelli's. While sensitive to the more spectacular and tragic excesses wrought by a politicized goodness or compassion, Arendt is generally unwilling to recognize the costs or consequences of action as the decisive criteria for judging ends and means. Indeed, unlike either Machiavelli or Weber, she wants to abolish the hegemony of the means-end category and overturn the teleological model of political action. This unwillingness to focus upon consequences can be explained and in part justified by the "internal" morality of her theory of political action—by her exclusion of violence, coercion, and essentially strategic action from the sphere of the political. From Arendt's perspective, the analysis of political action in terms of the means-end category cannot help but promote the view that political action *is* violence. As she notes in "On Violence," the "very substance of violent action is ruled by the means-end category."[115] Machiavelli and Weber both accept without question the hegemony of the means-end category; hence, their fundamental agreement that the calling of the political actor is to dispense violence in pursuit of goals, and their conviction that this peculiarly political means must be employed "responsibly," with the greatest possible precision. Arendt rejects the rationale underlying their position for the simple reason that, in the realm of human affairs, "the end is [always] in danger of being overwhelmed by the means which it justifies and which are needed to reach it."[116]

This praiseworthy rejection by Arendt of the ground of Machiavelli and Weber's "realism" notwithstanding, it is difficult to escape Kateb's conclusion that "a substantial revision would have to be made of Arendt's Greek conception if it is not to be charged with immoralism."[117] As is, the moral vacuity of "greatness" leaves Arendt's conception of political action all too vulnerable to charges of subjectivism or arbitrariness. It underlines the tension in her theory between "heroic," initiatory action and a more deliberative conception of politics. Unless Arendt can point to some ground or justification for action beyond display and virtuosity, or unless she can show how the criterion of greatness can be reconciled with an expressly deliberative conception of politics, her theory of political action will seem hopelessly at odds with itself.[118]

IV. Arendt's Critique of the Modern Turn to Will and History

Arendt's fierce insistence upon the autonomy of political action presents her readers with a paradox. On the one hand, her theory of action goes to great lengths to exclude all forms of violence and coercion from the political realm, giving it a strong normative dimension. On the other, the "purism" that generates these praiseworthy exclusions seems to lead her to the brink of immoralism. The paradox is intensified when we place the theory of action in the context of her political thought as a whole. How do we reconcile the tendency to bracket moral criteria with her monumental work on totalitarianism, her Eichmann-inspired analysis of the "banality of evil" in the twentieth-century bureaucracies of murder, and her preoccupation with the issues of conscience and judgment (our "faculty for telling right from wrong")? The link between politics and the possibility of evil was clearly a constant concern. Indeed, the arc of her thinking is in large part determined by the problem of political evil, beginning with totalitarianism and ending (in "Thinking and Moral Considerations" and the unfinished work on judgment) with a searching exploration of the mental faculties we must rely upon in coming to grips with such phenomena.

This fact, combined with Arendt's own experience as a refugee from the totalitarian terror of Nazi Germany, compels us to ask why she is so intent upon rescuing political action from the "tyranny" of moralizing categories? Why does she, of all people, give precedence to the claims of action rather than those of justice, morality, and rights?

The discomfort occasioned by Arendt's emphasis upon the autonomy of politics has prompted critics sympathetic to her work to propose a more Kantian reading of her political theory. The hope is that Kant—after Aristotle, the greatest "traditional" influence upon Arendt—provides an alternative way of affirming action and freedom, one that would put Arendt's "dramaturgical" theory in perspective. Seyla Benhabib and Jürgen Habermas, among others, have explored this vein, assimilating Arendt to a broadly modernist or universalist position by emphasizing the deliberative elements of her theories of action and judgment over the performative and agonistic ones.[119] They both argue that Arendt deploys an essentially intersubjective model of political judgment, one more indebted to

Kant than Aristotle insofar as it appeals to the criterion of universalizability in determining the justness or goodness of an action, norm, or policy.

A different, but equally Kantian, reading of Arendt is proposed by J. Glenn Gray,[120] who focuses not on the role of deliberation in Arendt's theory, but rather on her affirmation of freedom as a kind of spontaneous beginning. This idea, so central to her notion of action, has a clear pedigree in Kant's second *Critique*. In *The Life of the Mind*, as Gray points out, Arendt follows Kant in viewing the will as the faculty of such beginning, as our "organ for the future" rather than as a mere capacity for choice between pregiven alternatives. Nevertheless, she is dissatisfied by Kant's conflation of will and reason (in the form of "pure practical reason") and his domiciling of this faculty in an otherworldly ("noumenal") realm. Gray encourages us to read Arendt as a theorist intent on working out the aporias of Kant's philosophy of freedom, and on providing a basis for this philosophy that is "political, not metaphysical" (to use John Rawls's phrase).

This assimilation of Arendt's view of action and freedom to the most respectable of philosophical voluntarisms finds support in her celebration of spontaneous action and founding agreements in *On Revolution*. Indeed, this work—her most sustained encounter with the social contract tradition—shifts the focus of her theory of action away from "great" deeds to the questions of promising and democratic will formation. The voluntarist brand of participatory democracy that seems to emerge from *OR* leads James Miller to implicitly question the appropriateness of Arendt's hostility to Rousseau, whose formulation of moral freedom directly influenced Kant and whose conception of political community bears (at least *prima facie*) a striking resemblance to Arendt's.[121] Miller suggests that while Arendt is correct to criticize the "individualist" character of Rousseau's voluntarism, her conception of radical democracy rests upon normative foundations quite similar to his *moi commun* (common self). According to Miller, Arendt's voluntarism is of a collective order, predicated not upon the will of the individual but rather upon "the will to live together."[122] An ethos of democratic solidarity and participation permeates her "republicanism," with her critique of representative democracy echoing Rousseau's of Locke and representation.

These are only a few of the efforts that have been made to type Arendt as a "modernist" of sorts.[123] The advantages of such readings are perfectly clear: not only is one able to avoid the elitist baggage of her "Greek" theory of action, but one is also able to convincingly refute the charge of immoralism raised by Kateb and others. As portrayed by Benhabib, Habermas, Gray, and Miller, Arendt *grounds* her theory of action in (1) a kind of discourse ethic; (2) the autonomous will; or (3) the democratic community and the *moi commun*. It should be clear that whichever option is chosen, the problem of "moral foundations" has been solved.

In this section I want to probe Arendt's objections to the modern "philosophy of the will" and to elucidate the connections she sees between it and the historicism of Hegel and Marx. My purpose is twofold. First, I want to test the persuasiveness of the universalist and voluntarist readings of Arendt. Is she, in fact, an unknowing or "reluctant" modernist? Or do her criticisms of Kant and Rousseau, Hegel and Marx, reveal a set of theoretical objections to the modern formulation of autonomous freedom and action every bit as deep as her objections to Aristotle's teleology? If the latter is the case, we will be forced to revise our estimate of the scope and ambition of her rethinking of action. Moreover—and this is my second purpose—we will have to consider the possibility that Arendt's *limited* separation of the moral and the political has a strong justification. It may be that Kateb's sense of scandal is misplaced.

•

At first glance, a Kantian interpretation of Arendt looks both plausible and desirable. Combining Kant's "negative" definition of freedom as spontaneity (from the *Critique of Pure Reason*) with his positive account of freedom as autonomy or the capacity to act in accordance with self-given laws (from the *Groundwork* and second *Critique*) seems to provide just the sort of philosophical foundation that Arendt's theory of action demands. Kant preserves freedom as a form of radical initiation; he detaches the value of action from its success or failure in realizing goals; and he equates autonomy with universalizability. True, he locates the source of our freedom in an otherworldly ("noumenal") realm, and he assimilates the will (*qua* practical reason) to thought. Nevertheless, his practical philosophy appears to contain valuable resources for Arendt's project, a fact that she evidently appreciates in her later work. From her affirmation of the will as an "organ of free spontaneity" in *The Life of the Mind* to her focus upon the nature and specific validity of judgment in her earlier Kant lectures, Arendt appears to have come around to a Kantian reformulation of her earlier position, one that substitutes will and universalizability for the theatrical agonism of her "Greek" theory of action. Judith Shklar is not alone in holding that Arendt "quite deliberately ended her speculative journey into the past ... with Kant."[124] For Shklar and others, Arendt's "turn" to Kant is the guarantee of "the sanity of her enterprise."[125]

Yet, however attractive a Kantian reading of Arendt might be, it faces insurmountable obstacles. These come clearly into focus with a closer examination of her remarks on Kant, found in her posthumously published *Lectures on Kant's Political Philosophy* and in such earlier essays as "The Crisis in Culture" and "What Is Freedom?" Despite her great admiration for Kant, Arendt peremptorily dismisses the suggestion that his practical philosophy can add anything to the discussion of action, let alone clarify the nature of political freedom. Her view, simply stated in the *Lectures*, is that Kant's practical philosophy "nowhere takes action into account."[126] Whatever we take the subject of Kant's practical writings to be—the will, moral action, the nature of practical reason—it is not *action* in Arendt's sense. This radical disjunction flows, in part, from Arendt's firmly held conviction that the will is an antipolitical faculty.[127] It is not political because it excludes plurality, and plurality is the condition sine qua non of political action and freedom. Hence, "freedom as related to politics is not a phenomenon of the will."[128] The species of moral causality Kant proposes is prepolitical. For this reason, the autonomy of the moral agent cannot provide a basis for the autonomy of action. Indeed, Kantian moral autonomy denatures politics, as we shall see.

In "What Is Freedom?" Arendt questions the Western philosophical tradition's tendency to make freedom "an attribute of will and thought rather than action."[129] She rejects, in the strongest possible language, our almost automatic tendency to equate freedom with free will. This equation degrades the freedom of the public sphere and erects a nonpolitical standard (freedom as autonomy or sovereignty) over the realm of human affairs.[130] Kant, his affirmation of "spontaneous" freedom notwithstanding, clearly falls within the traditional paradigm: he displays the same bias against plurality, the same contempt for the realm of human affairs, as his philosophical brethren.[131] Kant's practical philosophy is centered on the reduction of freedom to will. This fact, combined with his conception of will as a rational faculty whose freedom is (in the last analysis) the spontaneity of reason, renders his practical philosophy irrelevant for thinking about action and politics.

Arendt provides the context for this judgment in her Kant lectures. There, discussing the questions with which Kant framed his philosophy, she draws out his essentially individualist and nonpolitical orientation:

> Kant repeatedly formulated what he held to be the three central questions that make men philosophize and to which his own philosophy tried to give an answer, and none of these questions concerns man as a *zōon politikon*, a political being. Of these questions—What can I know? What ought I to do? What may I hope?—two deal with the traditional topics of metaphysics, God and immortality. It would be a serious error to believe that the second question—What ought I to do?—and its correlate, the idea of freedom, could in any way be relied on to help us in our inquiry. . . . The second question does not deal with action at all, and Kant nowhere takes action into account. He spelled out man's basic "sociability" and enumerated as elements of it communicability, the need of men to communicate, and publicity, the *public* freedom not just to think but to publish . . . but he does not know either a faculty or a need for *action*. Thus in Kant the question what ought I to do? concerns the conduct of the self in its independence from others—the same self that wants to know what is knowable for human beings, . . . the same self that wants to know what it may reasonably hope for in matters of immortality.[132]

I quote this passage at length because it encapsulates Arendt's view of Kant as a thinker with a radically attenuated sense of the political. Arendt sees Kant's philosophy as circumscribed by concerns that are narrowly individualist; that center on a self detached from others and the realm of human affairs. The action and freedom of this self are different from, even opposed to, the action and freedom of the political actor who moves in the realm of plurality and appearance. It is significant, in this regard, that Arendt casually dismisses what usually pass as Kant's "political writings" ("Perpetual Peace," "What Is Enlightenment?" etc.) by noting that the concerns of these essays (including "freedom of the pen" and "the need to communicate") are, at best, prepolitical: they are conditions for action, not action itself. This distinction should make us wary of any premature reduction of Arendt's concept of *action* to *communication*. Arendt does stress the role of "communicability" and the "judicious exchange of opinion" in Kant's *aesthetic* theory; however, her concept of action is not reducible to these elements.[133]

It is because Kant's practical and "political" writings fail to address the question of action in the realm of plurality and appearance that Arendt attempts to tease out from the *Critique of Judgment* what she calls his "unwritten political philosophy."[134] The questions "What ought I to do?" and "What may I hope?" address man in his singularity, and appeal to his self-interest (in the broad sense of the health and preservation of his soul). It is only when the question "How do I judge?" is raised that Kant's philosophy engages the human condition of plurality, addressing human beings as "earthbound creatures, living in communities, endowed with common sense, *sensus communis*."[135] As judging individuals, we move in the realm of opinion; our interest is directed toward the world; and we actively seek to persuade our peers of the validity of our judgments. For these reasons, according to Arendt, Kant's philosophy is authentically political only in the first part of the third *Critique*, the critique of aesthetic judgment (or judgments of taste). Even here, however, the political implications of Kant's thought must be actively elucidated.

The suggestion that Kant's *real* political philosophy is to be found in his philosophy of art is, of course, a controversial one. Many commentators have balked at Arendt's exclusive focus upon the analysis of taste judgment in the third *Critique*. Contra Arendt, Patrick Riley argues that Kant "really did write a political philosophy," one that we cannot begin to understand unless we first acknowledge the fundamental place he reserved for *a priori* moral truth.[136] It is only in light of such truth, and *not* in the "judicious exchange of opinion," that we can make sense of Kant's universal republicanism and his hope that a constitutional legal order would promote the achievement of moral ends. Strictly speaking, Kant's practical philosophy may be "nonpolitical," but that does not prevent him from creating a political philosophy in which the first step, in the words of "Perpetual Peace," is to "pay homage to morals."

Riley's familiar portrait of Kant as a deontological theorist underscores the selectivity and idiosyncrasy of Arendt's interpretation. His point (*pace* Arendt) is that Kantian politics is not centrally about the exchange of opinion or intersubjective judgment: ". . . Kant himself would never have said that moral opinion, however 'general' or 'enlarged,' can replace moral truth."[137] Yet this criticism manages to miss Arendt's thrust. She does not deny that Kant begins with the moral law and justifies republican government in terms of it; rather, her point is that this very mode of proceeding brackets the realm of opinion, plurality, and appearance from the outset, and so denatures the political. Arendt seeks an "unwritten political philosophy" in the third *Critique not* because *Kant* sought "a new moral and political doctrine in aesthetic judgment," but because the world of aesthetic judgment is also the world of publicity, or politics.[138]

In order to appropriate Kant for politics, Arendt feels she must ignore the systematic intent that governs his political writings. As Riley correctly observes,

Kant's "official" political philosophy gives pride of place to his practical philosophy, to the ideas of moral truth and a pure (rational) will. There can be no doubt: Kant's "official" politics is a politics of truth, a politics derived, in deductive fashion, from an absolute. Yet it is for this very reason that Arendt dismisses it and looks elsewhere. The necessity of this search flows from her judgment that Kant's practical philosophy is "inhumane," intrinsically destructive of the realm of human affairs and its essential plurality:

> Kant argued that an absolute exists, the duty of the categorical imperative which stands above men, is decisive for all human affairs, and cannot be infringed even for humanity in every sense of that word. Critics of the Kantian ethic have frequently denounced this thesis as altogether inhumane and unmerciful. Whatever the merits of their arguments, the inhumanity of Kant's moral philosophy is undeniable. And this is so because the categorical imperative is postulated as absolute and in its absoluteness introduces into the interhuman realm—*which by nature consists of relationships*—something that runs counter to its fundamental relativity. The inhumanity which is bound up with the concept of one single truth emerges with particular clarity in Kant's work precisely because he attempted to found truth on practical reason; it is as though he who had so inexorably pointed out man's cognitive limits could not bear to think that in action, too, man cannot behave like a god.[139]

The Kantian appeal to such an absolute rips apart the "web of human relationships," degrading opinion and instrumentalizing human speech. Such effects, however, are not confined to Kant: they follow from *any* attempt to make an absolute the organizing principle of the realm of human affairs.[140] In order to grasp the specifically antipolitical character of Kant's grounding of human freedom in the pure (rational) will, it is necessary to examine how the machinery of the categorical imperative reconciles self-determination and the freedom of others through the rigorous effacement of plurality.

According to Kant, the will is genuinely free only when it acts in accordance with universalizable maxims, when it makes its ground of determination the sheer *form* of law itself. In Arendt's view, the legislating or lawgiving activity of such a pure will is nothing other than an extrapolation from the most fundamental rule of thought, the principle of noncontradiction. As she states it in "The Crisis in Culture," "the principle of lawgiving, as laid down in the 'categorical imperative'—'always act in a manner that the principle of your action can become a general law'—is based upon the necessity of rational thought to agree with itself."[141] This fundamental rule of thought is elevated to the status of a guiding practical principle, one that ensures "the correspondence of the self-will of one individual with that of another."[142]

This move hardly originates with Kant. As Arendt points out, it was Socrates who first proposed the standard of self-agreement as the determining criterion of ethical action.[143] In Kant, as in Socrates, the ethical ground is located in the thought process: ". . . it is the same general rule—Do not contradict yourself . . . that determines thinking and acting."[144] The specifically new wrinkle that Kant gives to this formula is to make the thinking ego—rather than the self per se—

the arbiter of consistency. The Socratic notion of self-agreement, of harmony with oneself, maintained a tenuous connection to plurality insofar as it internalized the dialogue form (hence the Socratic "two-in-one" of self and conscience). In Kant, however, this connection is severed with the interpretation of will (*Wille*) as practical reason.[145] So construed, the will in its legislative aspect eliminates all reference to plurality, whether internal or external. What matters is that the will will itself, that it will its own rational (universal) nature. Such a process is, as Hegel noted, utterly monological: it is "the pure unconditioned self-determination of the will."[146]

The universalizing power of Kant's absolute—the categorical imperative—flows entirely from the rational nature of the will. Autonomy is achieved when this will overrides all conditioning grounds and determines itself in accordance with the form of universal law.[147] Plurality and the possibility of agreement with others—the *political* topics broached in the third *Critique*—are extruded from Kant's practical philosophy as "heteronomy."

The conception of politics that follows from this will-based, antipluralist universalism, as Arendt ceaselessly points out, is fundamentally instrumental. Politics is a mere means: Kant favors a republican constitutional order because it supplies the apparatus necessary for the achievement of ends derived from analysis of the moral law.[148] If a "true system of politics cannot . . . take a single step without first paying tribute to morality," and if morality is conceived in *a priori* terms, then the importance of a space for deliberative politics—a politics of exchange of opinion and "incessant discourse"—is radically devalued.[149] To be sure, Kant famously insists upon the right to "public use of one's reason"; however, as Arendt points out, Kant sees such public use as indispensable to the freedom of *thought* and the scholar.[150] His prior reduction of action to will ensures that *this* freedom will be deprived of tangible reality. The Kantian conception of the public sphere, while suggestive, is thus critically undernourished from Arendt's perspective. Kant's real focus of interest is the instrument of what we would today call constitutional law.[151]

The Kantian reduction of action and freedom to will leads to a curious evacuation of meaning from the realm of human affairs. Viewed from a metaphysical perspective, freedom is a noumenal ground, the thing that gives the "good will" its intrinsic value.[152] However, when the will is considered as a "natural faculty" with effects in the world, its actions fall back within the "mechanism of nature" and it loses its claim to intrinsic value.[153] As a plural, *phenomenal* sphere, the realm of human affairs is governed not by reason, or even instinct, but by the clash of interest and inclination arising from empirical wills. As such, this realm necessarily elicits a "certain distaste" on the part of the philosopher: ". . . we find that, despite the apparent wisdom of individual actions here and there, everything as a whole is made up of folly and childish vanity, and often of childish malice and destructiveness."[154] If this realm (which Kant refers to as "the great world-drama") is to rise above the level of nihilistic farce, the philosopher is compelled to assume a providentially guided progress at work in this very discord. Thus Kant, in his "Idea for a Universal History with Cosmopolitan Intent," views discord as the *means* a purposive Nature employs in order to fully cultivate human capacities—a "civilizing" process that, although often violent, propels the species mankind toward greater peace and freedom. Without the assumption of such a "ruse of Nature" at work behind men's backs, the realm of human affairs is characterized by a "melancholy haphazardness" (*trostlose Ungefähr*) and appears, in Kant's view, senseless. As Kant's reply to Moses Mendelssohn makes clear, the particular actions of individuals, no matter how worthy, are incapable of redeeming a "spectacle" in which the human race does not constantly progress.[155]

From Arendt's perspective, the redemptive strategy adopted by Kant has important but largely negative implications for modern political thought. Kant escapes what he considers to be the self-evident meaninglessness of the particular by ascending to the level of the "whole."[156] Conflicting empirical wills and actions reveal an unsuspected meaning to the spectator who is able to frame human history as a process of species maturation. Obviously, such a strategy elevates the standpoint of the contemplative spectator to an epistemically privileged position: only the theorist is removed from the game enough to see its coherence and to judge its meaning.[157] Yet this supremacy of the spectator over the actor in Kant is ambiguous. On the one hand, it links up with themes from his aesthetic theory, and has important consequences for the activity of judgment (see Chapter 3). On the other, it sets the stage for a return to teleological explanation, and for the subsumption of politics by History. Kant's positing of a transsubjective actor (the species mankind) as the subject of history creates the pattern that the Hegelian and Marxian philosophies of history will emulate. Moreover, by positing peace and freedom as the *telos* that gives the whole of the historical process meaning, Kant opens the possibility of construing history as a kind of fabrication process, whose "product" is meaning itself.[158] In Hegel, the goal of this "production process" remains unknown to the human instruments who carry it out. It is only with the "end" of History that the "owl of Minerva" takes flight, and that human history reveals itself to the philosophical gaze as "the progressive unfolding and actualization of the idea of Freedom." In Marx, however, this teleological conflation of meaning with end takes a different, radicalized form: Kant's "ruse of Nature" and Hegel's "cunning of Reason" give way to the theoretically formulated demand that men, through conscious human action (*praxis*), *produce* the "end of History."[159]

Arendt views the Marxian attempt to derive politics from History as a distinctively modern version of "the age-old attempt to escape from the frustrations and fragility of human action by construing it in the image of making."[160] The point, in this context, is not so much the *violence* that accompanies any attempt to fabricate the end of History (although Arendt elsewhere decries the "you can't make an omelette without breaking eggs" reasoning born of this project); rather, what centrally concerns Arendt is the way the assumption of progress toward an end of History effaces the freedom of action itself. *Qua* "production process," history ceases to be characterized by a "melancholy haphazardness," revealing, instead, a dialectical necessity. Arendt's central theoretical objection to Hegel and Marx is that their assumption of a "movement of history" eliminates the possibility of a "radically new beginning." The notion of progress that underlies their theories is substantialist: it homogenizes historical time and ensures that (in Hegel's words) "nothing else will come out but what was already there."[161]

In Hegel, the realm of human affairs is ontologized as History. As Arendt notes, his "backward-directed glance," the glance of the philosophical spectator, reduces "everything that had been political—acts, and words, and events," to the historical.[162] It is this reduction that enables Hegel to get on with what he considers to be the central business of philosophy: distinguishing the contingent from the necessary in order to reveal the absolute in history.[163] In the Hegelian scheme, the contingent is equated, as in Kant, with meaninglessness; necessity with truth and significance. From the standpoint of the philosophical spectator, the progress toward freedom is a rationally necessary one. Arendt labels this a "fallacy," one born of the reification of the contemplative standpoint. It is from this fallacy that the paradox that "freedom is the fruit of necessity" emerges, a paradox that seduces not only Marx but the entire post–1789 revolutionary tradition.[164]

Arendt draws out the baneful consequences of the "magical spell of historical necessity" for political action and freedom in *On Revolution*. The phenomenal basis for the Hegelian-Marxian theoretical paradox was the *torrent revolutionnaire* of the French Revolution, the seemingly irresistible social and historical forces whose release "inevitably" destroyed the old regime. With the elevation of this "fact" to the status of unquestionable theoretical truth, the "men of revolution" themselves ceased to believe in action, preferring instead to worship the "pseudogod of History."[165] It was belief in this god that led the men of the October Revolution to acquiesce in their own elimination, to be the "fools of history." Their passive acceptance of this "fate" illuminates the degree to which Hegel's famous statement—*Die Weltgeschichte ist das Weltgericht* (world history is the world court of justice)—had been internalized as the *summa* of political morality. This principle of judgment stands in the sharpest possible opposition to Kant's. Yet while Arendt underscores this opposition (in the *Postscriptum* to the first volume of *LM*), her analysis in the Kant lectures reveals how the Kantian evacuation of meaning and freedom from the (phenomenal, plural) realm of human affairs prepares the way for Hegel's statement. For where freedom and meaning figure primarily as the *end* of History (as they do in Kant and Hegel's philosophies of history), the destruction of human lives is "redeemed" as a *means* (Kant's "discord," Hegel's "slaughterbench"). The victorious cause, whatever it may be, appears as the vehicle of progress.[166]

•

It may be objected that while Arendt's criticism of Kant's absolutism and philosophy of history is warranted, her root-and-branch repudiation of his practical philosophy is not. For Benhabib, this repudiation is premature, to say the least. It reflects Arendt's exaggerated concern for the autonomy of the political, a concern that puts her on the slippery slope of aestheticism. From Benhabib's point of view, this result is both dangerous and avoidable, since Arendt's own reading of

Kant points to a potential bridge between the second and third *Critiques*. The existence of such a bridge would allow us to break out of the monologism of the categorical imperative and recontextualize the Kantian concern with universalizability in the sphere of discourse and agreement. Such a discursive reformulation of the criterion of universalizability would overcome the denial of plurality built into the notion of will, while providing a firmer basis for action and judgment than can be offered by "mere" opinion. It is with this set of concerns in mind that Benhabib seizes upon Arendt's gloss on the Kantian notion of "enlarged thought."

In "The Crisis in Culture," Arendt contrasts the principle of lawgiving found in Kant's moral philosophy with the mode of thought he sees characteristic of judgment:

> In the *Critique of Judgment* . . . Kant insisted upon a different way of thinking, for which it would not be enough to be in agreement with one's own self, but which consisted of being able to "think in the place of everybody else" and which he therefore called an "enlarged mentality" (*eine erweiterte Denkungsart*). The power of judgment rests on a potential agreement with others, and the thinking process which is active in judging something is not, like the thought process of pure reasoning, a dialogue between me and myself, but finds itself always and primarily, even if I am quite alone in making up my mind, in an anticipated communication with others with whom I know I must finally come to some agreement. From this potential agreement judgment derives its specific validity. This means, on the one hand, that such judgment must liberate itself from the "subjective private conditions," that is, from the idiosyncrasies which naturally determine the outlook of each individual in his privacy . . . but which . . . lack all validity in the public realm. And this enlarged way of thinking, which as judgment knows how to transcend its individual limitations, cannot function in strict isolation or solitude; it needs the presence of others "in whose place" it must think, whose perspective it must take into consideration, and without whom it never has the opportunity to operate at all.[167]

In Benhabib's view, this passage contains Arendt's discovery of "a procedure for ascertaining intersubjective validity in the public realm."[168] The procedure outlined is one in which opinions are purified through a process of public dialogue and rational argumentation. Such dialogue strips opinions of their "subjective and personal conditions," filtering out what cannot be reconciled with either principled argument or the perspectives of our fellow citizens. Thus, an opinion framed in accordance with the strictures of "anticipated communication" and "potential agreement" will be far more likely to have a generalizable form, one that can win the universal assent of one's judging peers. In this way, what Benhabib calls "authentic processes of public dialogue" contribute to the formation of an "enlarged mentality," a faculty of judgment naturally oriented toward the universalizable.[169]

Benhabib is right to point out that Arendt's attraction to Kant's description of the "specific validity" of taste judgments rests on the discursive, public character he attributes to them (see Chapter 3). However Arendt, like Kant, thinks the model of reflective judgment clashes with the principles and machinery of pure practical reason: the former judges particulars without a concept, while the latter issues imperatives. For this reason, it is impossible to even harmonize the two, let alone combine them.[170]

Benhabib thinks that it is a mistake to erect a wall between practical reason and reflective judgment. As Arendt's gloss on Kant indicates, the specific validity of judgments of taste rests on the fact of their communicability. It is precisely this communicability that makes them fit candidates for universal assent. If we follow Benhabib's suggestion and read Kant's notion of "enlarged thought" as implying a discursive decision procedure, we see how the "monologue" of pure practical reason might be translated into the three-dimensionality of the public sphere. Arendt's gloss opens the possibility of reformulating the categorical imperative as "act in such a way that the maxim of your actions takes account of the perspectives of everyone else in such a way that you would be in a position to 'woo their consent.'"[171] In this formulation, the "universalist-egalitarian kernel" of Kantian morality becomes the basis for a deliberative democratic conception of practical reason, one liberated from the constraints of Kant's voluntarism and his two-world metaphysics.

This reading is ingenious insofar as it manages to combine Arendt's emphasis on plurality, deliberation, and exchange of opinion with the normative power of Kantian universalism. The advantages of such a combination are readily apparent. For example, it gives us a rational yet deliberative test for distinguishing between what Rousseau called the general will and the will of all (*volonté de tous*), the latter being a mere aggregate or coincidence of interests rather than a genuinely universalizable will. Why, then, does Arendt *not* make use of the "bridge" between Kant's moral philosophy and his theory of judgment, which the notion of "enlarged thought" supplies? The answer to this question is complex, and takes us to the heart of issues separating Arendt from her Habermasian appropriators.

Benhabib's object in promoting a deliberative, procedural interpretation of "enlarged thought" is twofold. First, such an account offers an avenue of escape from the monologism of the categorical imperative and the univocity of a will-based politics. Second, it enables Benhabib to overcome what she views as the dangerous separation of the moral and the political performed by Arendt. "Enlarged thought" is crucial in this respect, as it suggests that the "Aristotelian" brand of deliberative politics Arendt endorses need not be detached from a "principled moral standpoint" grounded in universalist-egalitarian commitments.[172] Benhabib agrees with Arendt that moral and political judgments concern particulars, and are (to use Kant's terminology) more reflective than determinant in character. Yet she thinks it is wrong to assume, as Arendt apparently does (along with neo-Aristotelians like Hans-Georg Gadamer and postmoderns like Jean-François Lyotard), that the reflective character of moral-political judgment makes us prisoner to the "practical arts" or to "local context and habit." If we as individual citizens enter public dialogues guided by the ethos implicit in the notion of "enlarged thought" (an ethos of generalization born of solicitation of other points of view), and if such public dialogues generate "public knowledge," then it is indeed possible to "weaken the opposition" between contextualist judgment and universalist morality.[173]

From an Arendtian perspective, however, the *Aufhebung*, or synthesis, Benhabib proposes is questionable. The problem is that Benhabib's redemption of the deliberative dimension of Arendt's political theory comes at the expense of the initiatory or performative dimension. The talk and judgment that occur in the public sphere have value, in Benhabib's view, primarily in terms of their contribution to "public knowledge," to the picking out of truly general interests from the welter of opinions, interests, and appearances.[174] The procedural interpretation of the public sphere abstracted from the ethos of "enlarged thought" *instrumentalizes* action and judgment by *reducing* them to dialogue or communication aimed at consensus. To be sure, in Arendt the notion of "enlarged mentality" performs a "universalizing" function of sorts: it strengthens an individual's opinion by eliminating the idiosyncratic and irreducibly particular. The result is a "disinterested" judgment, one more fit to appear in public. Yet what matters for Arendt is that such opinions or judgments *appear*, that the perspective of the political actor or judge achieve a *public* reality. Plurality is thus not merely an "input" in a larger process of achieving understanding and consensus; rather, for Arendt it is both origin *and* goal, the condition and achievement of action and judgment.[175]

The extent to which the dialogical/universalist reading deprives opinion, action, and judgment of intrinsic worth becomes clearer if we turn to Habermas. In his essay on Arendt, Habermas juxtaposes what he calls Arendt's "communicative model of action" with the instrumental or strategic conception of political action and power formulated by Weber: "The basic phenomenon [for Arendt] is not the instrumentalizing of another's will for one's own purposes, but the formation of a *common will* aimed at *agreement*."[176] Through a selective emphasis upon Arendt's Burke-derived definition of action as "acting in concert," Habermas manages to reduce the broad-range activities implied by "the sharing of words and deeds" to the phenomenon of communication and its putative *telos*, agreement. Thus, Arendt's theory of action is distinguished from the teleological model upheld by Weber insofar as "the consensus-building force of communication aimed at agreement is an end in itself."[177]

The contrast with Arendt here is both immediate and irreducible. For Arendt, it is not *agreement* that is "an end in itself for all parties," but *action* and *judgment*. The idea that either action or judgment reduces to communication and the process of "coming to an understanding" is foreign to Arendt. This is not to say that she devalues intersubjectivity; rather, it is to say that she views the approximation of "unimpaired intersubjectivity" and the cultivation of an "enlarged mentality" as preconditions for genuine political action and judgment. The rough approximation of these conditions gives voice to plurality—to debate, deliberation, and disagreement as well as consensus. The fallacy underlying Habermas's interpretation of her theory of action and Benhabib's modification of her theory of judgment is that the *removal* of systematic constraints or distortions to communication will result in the more or less natural emergence of a general interest, the "public knowledge" of which everyone can agree on. This fallacy has deep theoretical roots in the thought of Marx and Rousseau, both of whom desired an escape from politics—which they identified with faction, ideology, and class division—to the security and comfort of a harmonious general will. Habermas and Benhabib repudiate the Rousseauian ban on deliberative politics and the Marxian failure to take an institutionalized public sphere seriously.[178] Nevertheless, their mutual insistence, against Arendt, that "authentic processes of public dialogue" yield a cognitively based agreement with the force of truth marks them as inheritors of the rationalist attempt to reduce, if not eliminate, what Arendt calls the "incessant discourse" born of plurality.[179]

These considerations put Arendt's disjunction of judgment and practical reason in a new light. By holding these two faculties separate, Arendt hopes to preserve the political dimensions of performance *and* persuasion, deliberation *and* initiation, agonism *and* agreement. The attempt to recast the public sphere in accordance with a universalizing model of practical reason (whether deontological or discursive) is invariably an attempt to eliminate the performative dimension of politics. The isolation of the deliberative dimension effected by the Habermasian reduction of action to communication enables one to present the discursive rules governing theoretical or scientific discourse as an appropriate model for the political sphere.[180]

The idea of a discursive realm that operates through rational argumentation, the testing of propositions, and the gradual winning of universal assent is, of course, dear to all Enlightenment-inspired political philosophies, liberal as well as rationalist. Yet, as Lyotard emphasizes, the presumed homology between practical and theoretical discourse is dubious at best.[181] For one thing, it imposes a *teleology of consensus* upon the public sphere. Such a teleology may make sense in a community of researchers, but in the political realm it has the effect of emasculating plurality and diminishing the value of the public sphere as a "theater of freedom." Moreover, the idea of a strictly discursive public realm demands the hegemony of a given paradigm of argumentative rationality. Those rhetorics, discourses, and rationalities that depart from or are opposed to the hegemonic form will never have "the force of the better argument." Finally, and following from this, the institutionalization of a strictly discursive, argument-oriented public sphere reproduces the hazards of Kuhnian "normal science" in the political realm: spontaneity and what Richard Rorty describes as "revolutionary turns in the conversation" are discouraged insofar as these upset the regnant paradigm of discursive rationality.[182]

These criticisms apply as much to Socrates or Mill as they do to Habermas. It is important to keep them in mind, however, if we are to explain what Habermas calls Arendt's *abstention* from "conceiving the coming to agreement about political questions as a rational formation of consensus."[183] Contra Habermas, this abstention is rooted neither in an antiquated concept of truth nor in a "retreat into the tradition of natural right."[184] Rather, it is rooted in Arendt's profound suspicion of any attempt to rise above the realm of plural, conflicting opinion (*doxa*), to ground political action or judgment in truth.[185] Habermas and Benhabib reject this fear, underlining the discursive (as opposed to *a priori*) character of truth as unforced consensus. It is because the product of the "ideal speech situation" has the normative force of truth that this counterfactual provides (in Habermas's words) a "standard of criticism" capable of discriminating between "illusionary and nonillusionary convictions."[186] "Communication free from coercion" moves into the structural place vacated by Kant's "as if" interpretation of the social contract. So located, it provides, in Habermas's view, an indispensable test for separating out what is worthy of universal assent from the dross of ideologically tinged, systematically manipulated opinion.

Of course, Arendt's conception of the public sphere presupposes that force and fraud, coercion and manipulation, are kept to a minimum. However, her attempt to "read off the general structures of an unimpaired intersubjectivity" (Habermas) is hardly intended to provide anything more than a rough specification of the minimal conditions necessary for the emergence of *political* relations. Unlike Habermas, she has no desire to come up with a systematic set of criteria for distinguishing an authentic consensus from an inauthentic one. Yet for Habermas, as for Rousseau, this is the primary task of political theory. Hence, his attempt to elicit from Arendt a strong normative conception of the public sphere, one that does not merely emphasize the centrality of deliberation, but which isolates the specific form a deliberative politics must take if it is to provide *genuine* legitimation.[187] Arendt's refusal to treat "coming to agreement" as "the rational formation of consensus" is indicative of a very different approach, which more or less brackets the question of legitimacy in order to focus on the nature and meaning of political action itself. For the theorist of legitimation, the Rousseauian-Kantian question of when consent is genuine will always come first. For the theorist of political action, the "as if" deduction of legitimacy (or illegitimacy) is one of the more scholastic exercises inherited from the social contract tradition.

•

The ideal of a rational politics built on the unifying power of undistorted communication has deep roots in the Western tradition. Its appeal is obvious: it promises an escape from the more blatant forms of coercion and manipulation, as well as from the presumably destructive effects of faction and disagreement. Moreover, a politics guided by the ideal of pure communication or understanding manages to avoid the theatrical dimensions of political speech and action, which provide a medium for more sophisticated forms of manipulation. For Habermas, as for Socrates and Rousseau, the "force of the better argument" is necessarily obscured by a theatrical public space. Rhetorical speech—the "flattery" of the Athenian assembly or the modern political rally—is always under suspicion due to its performative, public character. This suspicion carries over to those forms of political speech and action that deliberately blur the line between performance and persuasion (for example, the theatrical politics of the American antiwar movement, of Act-Up, and of some groups within feminism).

Arendt's insistence upon participation, independent judgment, and the pivotal role of critical thinking makes it clear that the theatrical politics she champions is opposed to a politics of spectacle or image in which the "audience" figures as passive consumer.[188] She has no use for demagogues or the "political theater" of the prearranged media event. Nevertheless, she rejects as unpolitical any conception of a deliberative politics that desires to replace the "bright light" of the public realm with the more controllable illumination of the seminar room. For Arendt, to appear in public—to engage in political action—is necessarily to perform. She drives this point home by emphasizing how even Socrates' dialogues (which were conducted, pointedly, outside the assembly) were nevertheless performances. Whatever *political* quality Socratic dialogue has follows from the fact that Socrates "*performed* in the marketplace the way the flute-player performed at a banquet. It [Socratic dialogue] is sheer performance, sheer activity."[189] Considered as performance, Socrates' words are deeds—deeds undertaken in a public sphere (the agora) separate from, yet supplemental to, the assembly. Indeed, Arendt goes so far as to read Socrates' death as a deliberate and highly stylized performance, one intended to show his fellow citizens that he stood by his public speech and would not undermine his words by fleeing execution.[190]

For Arendt, even the "pure" argumentation of Socratic dialogue has an importantly theatrical dimension. In drawing our attention to it, she is not merely highlighting an unavoidable facet of discursive relations; rather, she is asserting this performative dimension as a *positive* value, as the thing most characteristic of action in the realm of appearances. "Public happiness"—what John Adams called "joy in action"—is impossible without a stage. Plurality cannot be manifest without an arena, institutional or otherwise, in which to appear. The desire to escape performance—to deliberate offstage, so to speak—is the desire to secure a realm in which one's words and agreements have a greater reality than "mere" opinion or promise. The only way to fulfill such a wish is to withdraw deliberation into the self; to make the self, rather than the public sphere, the scene of discursive purification. No modern theorist has understood this logical consequence of the demand for transparent communication and democratic will-formation better than Rousseau.

Arendt's comments on Rousseau in *On Revolution*, as James Miller notes, are relentlessly negative. Indeed, like many liberal critics, she discovers in his political philosophy seeds of totalitarianism. The liberal will find this shared judgment surprising, given the apparent similarities between Rousseau's political ideal and Arendt's. Both are proponents of direct democracy; both appeal to classical sources for images of a robust political life; both disparage the politics of interest and the mechanism of representation.[191] Moreover, Arendt and Rousseau insist upon the *conventional* basis of political power, emphasizing the abyss between a genuine "state of nature" and the world created by politics.[192] Their shared admiration for classical republicanism notwithstanding, they are uncompromisingly modern in their insistence that the reference back to nature (to natural law or right) is no longer possible. These affinities, however, do not prevent Arendt from seeing in Rousseau all that is wrong with the modern attempt to ground political freedom and power on will.

What precisely is wrong with this attempt, and what makes the Rousseauian version of it so anathematic to Arendt? Rousseau's voluntarism, after all, takes a straightforwardly political form, in sharp contrast to Kant's. The will in question is not a disembodied practical reason, but the will of a *moi commun*; that is, of a particular political *community*. Yet from Arendt's point of view, the move from a universalistic rational will to the "will of the people" or nation only underscores the plurality-hostile character of the faculty of will. Rousseau's political philosophy attempts to combine a classically inspired communitarianism with the modern individualist idiom of will and contract. The result, as Riley observes, is more than a little schizophrenic. What holds the two sides together, according to Arendt, is Rousseau's fierce desire to eliminate the divisive, "corrupting" effects of plurality. Viewed from this angle, the modern idiom of will is hardly an aberration; rather, it provides Rousseau with precisely the theoretical vocabulary necessary to overcome plurality and erect unity as the standard of the healthy political community.[193]

How does Rousseau accomplish this task? The answer, obviously, lies in his notion of the General Will (*volonté générale*), which Arendt describes as "the construction of a many-headed one."[194] Convinced by Hobbes of the necessity to have a single, indivisible sovereign power, but skeptical of his placement of this power in the hands of a sovereign "representative," Rousseau reconceived the constitutive pact of association—the "social contract"—so that the contracting individuals might be seen as delivering up their power to the community itself rather than to an individual or a group.[195] The "artificial and collective body" produced by this mutual alienation of rights and liberties enables its members to be both subjects of law and participants in sovereign authority. The will each member obeys as subject is in fact the will he has expressed in his public capacity as citizen. The social contract, this "reciprocal engagement between the public and its individual members," is the answer to the seemingly impossible task Rousseau sets himself: ". . . find a form of association which defends and protects the person and property of each member with the whole force of the community, and where each, while joining with all the rest, still obeys no one but himself and remains as free as before."[196]

The social contract genuinely solves this riddle, however, only if the moral and collective body it creates articulates a will that expresses the interest of the community as a whole. That is to say, the people, as members of the legislating sovereign authority, remain free only so long as the enactments of that authority express a truly general interest. Otherwise, a democratic procedure delivers one part of the community over to domination by another. The only way to avoid this unjust outcome, according to Rousseau, is to ensure, so far as possible, that citizens look into their hearts and vote what they sincerely believe to be in the public interest. When this is done—when "in their deliberations the citizens hold no communication with one another"—the General Will will be clearly manifest, and the results of voting on legislation will approach unanimity.[197] However, "when the social bond begins to loosen and the state to grow weak, when particular interests begin to make themselves felt and lesser associations to

influence the whole, then the common interest deteriorates and encounters opposition; unanimity no longer prevails in voting; the general will ceases to be the
will of all; contradictions and debates arise; and the best opinion does not by any
means go undisputed."[198]

For Rousseau, faction and debate are unmistakable signs of the corruption of
the body politic. The General Will—"constant, unalterable and pure"[199]—is always there, but citizens no longer correspond to it because the noise of particular
interests and debate have all but drowned it out. The recovery of the General
Will demands a constant *interrogation*—both in the assembly and in the self—
that is designed to arouse the clear yet obscured general interest. In this regard,
Arendt notes "the curious equation of will and interest on which the whole of
Rousseau's political theory rests."[200] According to Rousseau, the General Will is
the articulation of a general interest, the interest of the people or nation as a
whole. Yet it is clear, Arendt argues, that such an "objective," universal interest
has reality only insofar as it is opposed to "each interest or will in particular":

> In Rousseau's construction, the nation need not wait for an enemy to threaten its
> borders in order to rise "like one man" and to bring about the *union sacrée*; the
> oneness of the nation is guaranteed in so far as each citizen carries within himself the
> common enemy as well as the general interest which the common enemy brings into
> existence; for the common enemy is the particular interest or the particular will of
> each man. If only each particular man rises up against himself in his particularity, he
> will be able to arouse in himself his own antagonist, the general will, and thus he will
> become a true citizen of the national body politic. . . . To partake in the body politic
> of the nation, each national must rise and remain in constant rebellion against
> himself.[201]

This analysis of the dynamics of the General Will is revealing. For one thing,
the demand to produce a purified community will from which particularity has
been drained presupposes, in Arendt's view, an introspective turn of the Cartesian sort. "Deliberation" in Rousseau turns into the self-interrogation of an *âme
déchirée* (torn soul). It is only because our souls are torn in two, split between the
particularity of the individual and the generality of the citizen, that the general
interest has any chance of emerging with clarity. Just as Kant's rational will must
overcome the conditioning effects of all empirical grounds in order to realize
autonomy, so must the Rousseauian citizen strive to generate a general interest
through the opposition to who he is as an individual. The aim of this internal
struggle is something more than a harmony or concord of wills: it is the ascertaining of the *public will*, the uncovering of a perspective all would agree to if they
have rigorously bracketed their particularity. Rousseau effaces the "corrupting"
effects of plurality by assuming that every virtuous citizen will come to the same
conclusion, and by insulating the process of democratic will formation from the
muddying that occurs through the exchange of opinion.[202] Needless to say, it is
a short step from the self-interrogation Rousseau demands of virtuous citizens to
the "theory of terror" practiced by Robespierre, Lenin, and Stalin. What the

practitioners of terror share with Rousseau is the assumption that "the interest of the whole must automatically, and indeed permanently, be hostile to the particular interest of the citizen."[203]

Rousseau's theory of democratic will formation, while ostensibly more political than Kant's, is antipolitical through and through. Taking the idea of the single, sovereign will as his paradigm of genuine freedom, Rousseau attempts the systematic elimination of plurality and all its effects from the public sphere. The normative status he attributes to the ideal of unanimity, of *complete* consensus, guides the entire account of democratic decision procedure. Moreover, it reveals what Arendt calls the "pernicious and dangerous consequences" of modeling *political* freedom upon the idea of a genuinely free will.[204] In turning to the will as the ground of political freedom, both Rousseau and Kant perpetuate the tradition's error of identifying *freedom* with sovereignty or autonomy. This interpretation of freedom has deep roots in Greek and Christian thought, a fact Arendt emphasizes in "What Is Freedom?" However, she insists that the essential fact about freedom in the political sphere is that it is radically nonautonomous. To think otherwise, with Kant and Rousseau, is to radically devalue plurality and the public sphere. Ultimately, it is to question whether *worldly* freedom is possible at all.

Despite the harshness of her critique, there are those, like James Miller, who view Arendt's political theory as, essentially, a reformulation of Rousseau's social contract. Miller's reading of OR focuses on Arendt's fascination with the human ability to promise, a capacity that underlies the "collective effort to establish an abiding structure of shared public principles."[205] Through mutual promises, it is possible for a group of associated individuals to establish their own institutionally articulated reality, to constitute a new political order based on "the joint exercise of the will to live together."[206] For Miller, it is the constitutive power of promising that illuminates Arendt's emphasis upon the initiatory dimension of action: the "constitution of freedom" in the American Revolution is a radical beginning founded upon mutual pledges.[207] "Joint effort" takes the place of sovereignty; the "we can" substitutes for the "I will." Yet it is precisely in this emphasis upon the power of promising to establish new public realities, new "houses for freedom," that Arendt (according to Miller) reveals herself as "the unwitting heir of Rousseau's unrealized dreams."[208] Her "perfect image of public freedom" resonates most clearly with Rousseau's participatory, agreement-based ideal. Arendt's *real* enemy, Miller maintains, is not Rousseau, but the philosophical voluntarist (Nietzsche, Heidegger) who apotheosizes will and the heroic individual.[209]

Does this view of Arendt make sense? Bracketing, for the moment, Miller's characterization of Nietzsche and Heidegger, I should point out the parallel between Miller's textual strategy and Benhabib's. Like Benhabib on Kant, Miller acknowledges Rousseau's overly "individualistic" conceptualization of political freedom, but then he goes on to suggest that the kernel of Rousseau's ideal of self-rule can be given an intersubjective, plurality-friendly reformulation. Indeed, Miller argues that it is precisely such a reformulation that Arendt provides in OR, her refusal to acknowledge her fidelity to the Rousseauian ideal notwithstanding.

The problem with this reading is that it hypostatizes the moment of foundation as *the* paradigm of initiatory action. To some extent, Arendt shares the blame: her analysis in OR tends to focus on founding as the political act par excellence. Nevertheless, Miller's overemphasis upon the constitutive power of promising results in a skewed interpretation of her "perfect image of public freedom." What ultimately matters in OR is that the framework of mutual promises opens up an institutionalized space in which citizens can appear in word and deed. Thus the tragedy of the American Constitution, in Arendt's view, is that it establishes an extraordinary system of power without adequate provision for such public, theatrical spaces. The "lost treasure" of the revolutionary tradition is not the "will to live together" underlying founding conventions, but the desire to be seen and heard in public, to achieve "public happiness." Miller's reading of OR acknowledges this; however, his emphasis on the collective act of will underlying the formation of a new system of power leads him, like Rousseau, to exaggerate the role community plays in the preservation of a vibrant civic culture. Solidarity and communal veneration of "fundamental principles" take the place of agonistic debate and deliberation. The image of freedom moves from Athens to Sparta as plurality is confined within the exceedingly narrow limits set by civic republicanism.[210]

V. CONCLUSION: BEYOND ARISTOTLE AND KANT

Habermas is certainly right to juxtapose Arendt's "revival" of *praxis* to the strategic/instrumental concept of action propounded by Machiavelli and Weber. Political action, as conceived by Arendt, has an irreducibly intersubjective dimension, which puts it in sharp opposition to the goal of imposing one's will upon another. But while a kind of discursive ethos underlies what Arendt calls "the sharing of words and deeds," this sharing is finally not reducible to the communicative model of action Habermas proposes. "Action," in Arendt's sense, is no more reducible to dialogue aimed at understanding than it is to the fulfillment of the moral ends of the community. What is absent from both conceptions is an appreciation of the theatrical dimension of political action and the public sphere, of the intrinsic value of politics as an activity. We should not be surprised, then, that the "teleological model of action" encompasses Aristotle as well as Machiavelli, and Rousseau and Kant as well as Weber. From Arendt's perspective, the "instrumentalization of action" is a more perverse phenomenon than Habermas makes it out to be, and political theory carries much of the blame.

It is precisely in response to the deep-rooted devaluation of action and plurality in political theory that Arendt undertakes her radical reformulation. The radicalism of the project consists in her questioning *all* conceptions of action that submit it to the rule of a *telos*, whether strategic (success), moral (justice), or cognitive (truth). Thus, while Aristotle is useful for distinguishing acting from fabrication, he also contributes mightily to the philosophic institutionalization of the means-end schema. Similarly, while Kant affirms the spontaneity of human freedom, his practical-political philosophy rigorously deprives the realm of action and opinion of any intrinsic worth: only the quality of will or the contribution to progress redeems action in the realm of appearances. In Aristotle and Kant, the prejudices of the contemplative tradition are all too apparent. Whether in the name of a community ethos, the Moral Law, or the progress of the species, plurality and political action are denied an autonomous value.

What makes Arendt's criticism of Aristotle and Kant of more than passing interest is the remarkable ascendancy of neo-Aristotelian and neo-Kantian schools of political thought today. These schools (including communitarianism and Critical Theory) acknowledge a certain bias against plurality in the thought of the masters. Yet, we are told, this bias arises from the *metaphysics* of Aristotle and Kant, not from their political thought as such. Slough off the defects introduced by Aristotle's biologism or Kant's two-world metaphysics and what remains are resources of the greatest possible value in the ongoing struggle to reclaim a substantive role for the citizen in contemporary society.[211]

Arendt's readings of Kant and Aristotle should make us skeptical of such claims. The bias against a plurality-based politics is no excrescence of Kantian or Aristotelian political theory; on the contrary, it structures the basic categories (justice, community, will, universality) with which they think about politics and the public world. Unsurprisingly, this bias reappears in their contemporary appropriators. The communitarian regards action favorably so long as it does not split the community or undermine a fulfilling sense of membership; the Habermasian does so insofar as it contributes to a progressively rationalized and genuinely universal consensus. Plurality and disagreement are viewed by both schools as essentially problems in need of a solution. In this regard, it is difficult to escape the impression that liberalism, with its affirmation of pluralism and suspicion of group feeling, is more deeply rooted in the soil of politics than some of its contemporary competitors.

Arendt, of course, is no liberal: she demands too much of political action and the "stage" of the public sphere. Nevertheless, her affirmation of plurality and a publicly oriented individualism puts her in distinct opposition to the rationalist and civic republican virtues of solidarity, unanimity, and consensus. While appreciative of the role played by agreement and rational argumentation, she does not make the public sphere a function of these activities. As her remarkable essay on the Enlightenment critic Gotthold Lessing demonstrates, she values this sphere for the appearance and debate—ongoing, never-ending—that it makes possible.[212] She believes that our essential political obligation is not to ourselves, or the community, but to the *world*, that "shared home for mortal men."[213] It is care for the world, rather than care for the self or others, that Arendt sees as the moral impetus of politics. Where this care is lacking—where the desire for order, belonging, truth, or solidarity overtakes it—the energies of politics become destructive of this "in-between." Arendt's suspicion of moral absolutism is aroused by the lack of value such rigorism attributes to *this* life, *this* world. The otherworldly asceticism of Socrates in the *Phaedo*—or of a Kant who can endorse the sentiment "Let justice be done though the world may perish!"—repels her violently.

For Arendt, as for Lessing, the world is humanized through the agon of discourse—by argument, debate, and polemic flowing from a love of the world rather than a resentment of the conditions of human existence. *Inhumanity* flows from the resentful attempt to order the world of human relationships in accordance with some absolute (e.g., Justice, the Nation, Reason, or History). Humanity is found in the joyful acceptance of the "fundamental relativity" of this "interhuman realm"; that is, in acceptance of the fact that opinion is the stuff of politics and diversity of opinion the condition of a humane world.[214] The "internal morality of politics" makes itself felt only where the *ressentiment*-driven desire to re*make* the world (a necessarily *violent* undertaking) is suspended and a commitment to the world is allowed to flourish. But in order for this to happen, we must fundamentally change our attitude toward the world of appearances. In Arendt's view, a more aesthetic attachment to existence is the precondition of a more humane politics, a politics purged of the violence of the absolute.

Arendt, Nietzsche, and the "Aestheticization" of Political Action

O those Greeks! They knew how to live. What is required for that is to stop
courageously at the surface, the fold, the skin, to adore appearance, to believe
in forms, tones, words, in the whole Olympus of appearance. Those Greeks
were superficial—*out of profundity*. And is not this precisely what we are
again coming back to, we daredevils of the spirit who have climbed the
highest and most dangerous peak of present thought and looked around
from up there—we who have looked *down* from there? Are we not,
precisely in this respect, Greeks? Adorers of forms, of tones,
of words? And therefore—*artists*?

—*Nietzsche*, The Gay Science

An anti-metaphysical view of the world—yes, but an artistic one.

—*Nietzsche*, The Will to Power

The common element connecting art and politics is that they are
both phenomena of the public world.

—*Arendt, "The Crisis in Culture"*

I. INTRODUCTION

Arendt's rejection of the turn to will in modern political theory reflects her conviction that the interpretation of freedom as sovereignty or autonomy is incompatible with the nature and conditions of genuine political action. Far from
avoiding the plurality-hostile character of the teleological model of action, the
modern attempt to ground freedom in the autonomous will radicalizes its antipolitical tendencies. Moreover, Arendt believes that the reduction of action to
willing and the subsumption of politics by History destroys whatever remains of
the integrity of political action. The turn to will and to History continues and
deepens the degradation of politics, action, and plurality initiated by the contemplative tradition. The moderns provide no viable alternative to the "aesthetic"
approach to action that Arendt proposes as a way of preserving the dignity of the
public realm in the face of its philosophical and cultural devaluation.

In this chapter, I return to the question of Arendt's "aestheticization" of action, linking it to Nietzsche's struggle against Platonism. I suggest that Arendt's

performative approach to action decenters the political actor in a fashion parallel to Nietzsche's decentering of the moral subject. Both Nietzsche and Arendt are concerned with questioning a moral epistemology that rests upon a rigidified distinction between actor and act, agent and "effect." This distinction, they argue, deprives the realm of action and appearance of any intrinsic value. "Aestheticizing" action through the analogy of performance redeems its meaning, restores its innocence, places it "beyond good and evil" (to use Nietzsche's much misunderstood phrase). With respect to action, the performance model frees us from the nihilistic habit of justifying existence by the appeal to essence—that "true world" installed by Plato above the "shadow world" of mere appearance. Since, as Arendt repeatedly insists, the political world is the realm of appearance, a revaluation of the Nietzschean sort is absolutely imperative.

Viewing Arendt's "aestheticization" of action as continuous with the broad Nietzschean project of overcoming Platonism provides deeper insight into the strategic intent of her theory of political action. Yet it also has the effect of intensifying our unease with the agonistic conception of action. The second half of this chapter focuses on the difference between Nietzsche's and Arendt's respective "aesthetics of action." Arendt's emphasis on the agonistic dimension of action must be read, I maintain, in conjunction with her theory of political judgment. Based on an idiosyncratic appropriation of Kant's third *Critique*, this theory provides a forceful critique of the metaphysical and epistemological commitments of Nietzschean aestheticism (the will to power, perspectivism). Deploying Kant's notions of aesthetic "disinterestedness" and taste as a kind of *sensus communis*, Arendt avoids trading one reductionism (the Platonic/Aristotelian instrumentalization of action) for another (the Nietzschean reduction of action to an expression of the will to power). Her theory of political judgment invokes Kant in order to reassert the deliberative dimension as a necessary boundary—as a way of limiting the agon and keeping the play playful. She thus avoids the drawbacks of Nietzsche's aestheticism while reconciling the initiatory and intersubjective dimensions of her theory of political action. Most important, she preserves the disclosive nature of action from subsumption by subject-centered categories.

My interpretation of Arendt's theory of political judgment emphasizes its continuity with her theory of political action. In this regard I fully agree with Ronald Beiner's point that Arendt's "concern with the judging spectator is simply the extension of [her] definition of politics in terms of virtuosity or performance."[1] In addition to "completing" her theory of political action, Arendt's theory of political judgment serves to close the gap between the actor and the spectator, between the virtuosity of the performer and the apparent passivity of his audience. It therefore makes it possible to see judgment not simply as the fulfillment of action's disclosive potential, but as itself a kind of acting.[2] In this way, Kantian aesthetics serves as the unlikely mediator between Arendt's Machiavellian/Nietzschean emphasis upon initiation and virtuosity, and her Aristotelian emphasis upon deliberation, plurality, and equality amongst citizens.

II. Nonsovereignty and the Performance Model:
Arendt's Anti-Platonism

In the discussion of Arendt's theory of action thus far, I have drawn attention to Arendt's view that plurality—the fact that "men, not Man, live on earth and inhabit the world"—is "specifically the condition of all political life."[3] Plurality is the hallmark of action that, unlike labor or work, can only be carried on 22between individuals.[4] As the condition sine qua non of the "sharing of words and deeds," plurality makes possible the peculiar freedom of political action, a freedom that is *worldly, limited*, and *nonsovereign. Worldly* because this freedom is the freedom of a "plural We" engaged "in changing our common world."[5] As Arendt remarks, it is "the very opposite of 'inner freedom,' the inward space into which men escape from external coercion and *feel* free."[6] Such *philosophical* freedom—whether the tenuous freedom of the will or the unlimited freedom of thought—"remains without outer manifestations and hence is politically irrelevant."[7]

To be free and to act are the same, according to Arendt.[8] The freedom of action, however, is essentially a *limited* freedom. The fact that it occurs *in the world*, in the web of human relationships created by the fact of plurality, has a number of consequences.[9] First of all, it affects how we understand the initiatory dimension of this freedom—freedom as the capacity to spontaneously begin, "to call something into being which did not exist before, which was not given, not even as an object of cognition or imagination."[10] It is through this capacity for initiation that the actor "inserts himself into the human world."[11] This insertion—achieved through words and deeds—comes at a price, however. For while action is always a beginning, it is not a beginning over which the actor retains control. To act, to insert oneself into the human world, brings one face to face with the fact of plurality: the political actor "always moves among and in relation to other acting beings."[12] The political actor therefore is "never merely a doer, but also and at the same time a sufferer."[13] The freedom of political action is genuine, worldly, yet nonsovereign. Its authenticity is marked by its distance from the condition of mastery or autonomy. *Qua* political actors, we are anything *but* sovereign.[14]

Plurality, then, introduces an irreducible contingency to political action, a dimension that in many respects is the ground of action's peculiar freedom. Yet while contingency is presupposed by the idea of a virtuosic response to *fortuna*, and while it is manifest in the "startling unexpectedness" of every spontaneous beginning, it also invariably frustrates the achievement of the actor's purpose. Contingency of action—what Arendt calls action's "futility, boundlessness and uncertainty of outcome"[15]—gives rise to frustration with and, ultimately, hostility to action. This hostility, according to Arendt, lies at the root of *our* philosophical tradition.[16] Indeed, it gives this tradition its essential character:

> It is in accordance with the great tradition of Western thought to think along these lines: to accuse freedom of luring man into necessity, to condemn action, the sponta-

neous beginning of something new, because its results fall into a predetermined set of relationships, invariably dragging the agent with them, who seems to forfeit his freedom the very moment he makes use of it.[17]

Our tradition has been unable to accept the "absurdity" of the "simultaneous presence of freedom and non-sovereignty," or to understand "how freedom could have been given to men under the condition of non-sovereignty."[18] It has therefore repeatedly sought an escape from action, a substitute that would avoid the calamities of action and raise the realm of human affairs above "the haphazardness and moral irresponsibility inherent in a plurality of agents."[19] Plato, Arendt believes, saw the problem clearly: it was necessary to reinterpret action in a manner that gives the actor control over what he initiates. But if the political actor were "to remain complete master of what he had begun," then action would have to be recast in a way that would neutralize the effects of plurality and make the "ideal or uncompromising self-sufficiency and mastership" conceivable in political terms.[20] According to Arendt, Plato achieves this theoretical inversion, this neutering of plurality and politics, by reinterpreting action as a kind of making or fabrication. The political actor (the philosopher-king), like the craftsman, "sees" the product he wants to create before he acts: knowing and doing are separated. Action becomes simply the execution of operations necessary for the achievement of a given end.[21] The resulting split between theory and practice issues in a "natural" hierarchy of ruler and ruled, of knower and executer, a hierarchy seemingly demanded by the "nature" of action itself.[22]

While the doctrine of ideas, the metaphysical and epistemological ground of Plato's analogy, has not survived, his substitution of making for acting has proved foundational for a tradition desirous of suppressing plurality and contingency. The persistence and success of "the transformation of action into a mode of making" is measured, according to Arendt, "by the whole terminology of political theory and political thought, which indeed makes it impossible to discuss these matters without using the categories of ends and means, and thinking in terms of instrumentality."[23] It is important to note how the Platonic instrumentalization of action is structurally linked to the idea of freedom as sovereignty. Any theory of political action that genuinely desires to overcome the Platonic hostility to plurality and restore a sense of the intrinsic value of political action must, in Arendt's view, transcend not only the category of means and ends, but the interpretation of freedom as sovereignty that underlies the "transformation of acting into a mode of making." Overcoming the teleological model that governs the tradition demands an alternative model capable of preserving the very aspects of action covered over by Plato and Aristotle.

This gives us a new perspective on the performance model of action outlined in Chapter 2, Section III. In reading Arendt's description of the "frailty" of the realm of human affairs, one is struck by its substantial agreement with the view she ascribes to the tradition: both see this realm (and the action within it) as exceedingly fragile and contingent, as lacking solidity.[24] But what the tradition laments and seeks to escape, Arendt celebrates. First, she emphasizes how contingency is a structural feature of the freedom of action. Virtuosity manifests itself only in terms of the opportunities provided by *fortuna*: "There is no *virtu* without *fortuna* and no *fortuna* without virtu."[25] It is precisely the extraordinary contingency that pervades the realm of human affairs that gives freedom in the form of virtuosity the chance to appear. Second, she focuses attention on the *phenomenality* of political action, on the fact that words and deeds are heard and seen. She makes us appreciate the importance of the public realm as a "space of appearances," as a "kind of theater where freedom appears."[26] Finally, her emphasis on performance underlines the fact that *plurality* is the fundamental condition of political action. Without other actors, no opportunity for the expression of *virtu* arises; without an audience, action—words and deeds—fails to appear and generate meaning. The failure to achieve phenomenal expression, in Arendt's view, is equivalent to the failure to achieve reality: "For us, appearance—something that is being seen and heard by others as well as ourselves—constitutes reality."[27] Plurality is ontologically constitutive of the world.

The performance model, then, links freedom as virtuosity (Arendt's "agonistic" conception) with the condition of nonsovereignty. By highlighting this condition, Arendt effectively decenters the political actor: the freedom of political action cannot be captured by philosophies of action built around the notion of autonomous agency. The categories of "author" or "producer" are inapplicable to *political* agency.[28] Moreover, viewing action as nonsovereign performance allows us to move beyond the categories of means and ends, motives and aims. Not only do these categories fail to capture the phenomenon of political action, but they also obscure the variety of freedom experienced in it. In "What Is Freedom?" Arendt notes that "action, to be free, must be free from motive on one side, from its intended goal as predictable effect on the other."[29] Of course, motives and aims are important factors in any action, but "they are its determining factors and action is free to the extent it is able to transcend them."[30] Arendt's insistence on the nonsovereignty of political action frees it from it from its "determining factors," and, in so doing, helps us to see spontaneity, "the sheer capacity to begin," as the essence of action's freedom and the source of its "transcendent" quality.[31]

Arendt's focus on the nonsovereign freedom found in spontaneous political action raises the question of why this dimension is worth celebrating. Why take so much trouble to rescue it from obscurity, to preserve it through a radical reconceptualization of action as such? Her answer, implicit in her critique of *homo faber*'s disastrous identification of meaning with utility, is that the transcendent quality of great words or deeds is the source of a significance that is, in principle, unlimited. Great, initiatory, nonsovereign action is *boundless*: it creates myriad new relationships, unforeseen constellations, and—out of these—stories or lasting meaning.[32] No other human activity, according to Arendt, "produces" meaning as naturally as does action in the public realm. Again, this is something highlighted by the performance model, which emphasizes the embeddedness of action in the "already existing web of human relationships" while stressing its phenomenality, its need for an audience. Combined, these aspects of great or initiatory action work to transcend instrumentality and "produce" meaning. Indeed, in *The Human Condition*, Arendt directly links the meaning-creative capacity of initiatory action to its "futility, boundlessness, and uncertainty of outcome": "It is because of this already existing web of human relationships, with its innumerable wills and intentions, that action almost never achieves its purpose; but it is also because of this medium, in which action alone is real, that it 'produces' stories with or without intention as naturally as fabrication produces things."[33]

Political action thus possesses a unique *revelatory* capacity, the ability to illuminate the realm of human affairs in its specific phenomenal reality, and to endow this reality with meaning. The "revelatory character of action" and its "ability to produce stories and become historical" together "form the very source from which meaningfulness springs into and illuminates human existence."[34] This ability to *disclose* the world and the actors in it, to bring them to presence and endow them with meaning, is, in Kateb's words, the "existential achievement" of political action.[35] And it is precisely this disclosive or revelatory character of action that neither Aristotle, with his ultimately mimetic conception of *praxis*, nor Kant, with his reduction of action to motive and will, could comprehend or articulate. It is no wonder that Arendt attempts to distinguish her notion of the autonomy or specificity of action from theirs.

The performance model, then, reveals the nonsovereignty or "haphazardness" of action as the root of its specific freedom and meaning-creative power. It situates initiatory, agonistic action within a "space of appearances" (the public realm) in which the extraordinary or revelatory could become, in Arendt's words, "an ordinary occurrence of everyday life."[36] This was the reason for being of the *polis*, in Arendt's view. The *polis* also provided a "remedy for the futility of action," a way of preserving the "authentic, non-tangible, and utterly fragile meaning" created by action. Arendt goes so far as to suggest that political community originated as a form of "organized remembrance": "Not historically, of course, but speaking metaphorically and theoretically, it is as though the men who had returned from the Trojan War had wished to make permanent the space of action which had arisen from their deeds and sufferings, to prevent its perishing with their dispersal and return to their isolated homesteads."[37]

The creation of an institutionally defined public space ensured that "the most futile of human activities, action and speech, and the least tangible and most ephemeral of man-made 'products,' the deeds and stories that are their outcome, would become imperishable."[38] Great or initiatory action illuminates the world; such illumination presupposes a relatively permanent space where words and deeds can come to presence and be judged as appearances; that is, as a distinct and distinctly real realm of phenomena.[39]

We are now in position to appreciate Arendt's deepest motivation for insisting on the autonomy and dignity of political action. She combats the degradation of action by the philosophical tradition and modernity in order to save its disclosive essence from oblivion. Her deconstruction of the teleological model, her "aesthetic" reconceptualization, her violent anti-Platonism: all express her desire to preserve this all-important disclosive dimension. The disclosive nature of political action will be considered in greater detail in the next section. First, I want to investigate how the performance model overcomes the hostility to plurality, appearance, and politics that Arendt sees as shaping the Western tradition of philosophy and political theory.

•

In *The Genealogy of Morals*, Nietzsche questions the "slavish" tendency to take the actor out of the world by positing the "grammatical fiction" of a subject behind every deed.[40] By separating the actor from his acts in this way, the "slave" or reactive man is able to maintain the belief that *who we are* is, finally, independent of our style of action, our *virtu*. For the slave, the belief that identity precedes and stands apart from action is immensely comforting: it enables the reactive man to see his impotence, his inability to act and distinguish himself, as a *choice*, rather than as constitutive of who he is. According to Nietzsche, belief in the subject makes possible "for the majority of mortals, the weak and oppressed of every kind, the sublime self-deception that interprets weakness as freedom."[41]

Against the "slavish illusion" of a subject of agency that stands outside the world, Nietzsche argues simply that "there is no such substratum; there is no 'being' behind doing, effecting, becoming; 'the doer' is merely a fiction added to the deed—the deed is everything."[42] Arendt, in arguing for the interpretation of freedom as virtuosity and action as performance, is urging us, like Nietzsche, to reject the "slavish," moralizing tendency to posit a reality behind appearances, to take the actor out of the world and separate him from what he can do.[43] Freedom, according to Nietzsche and Arendt, is not found in the choice not to act, nor is identity something that precedes or is separable from action. Only the performing self knows freedom and only through performance can an otherwise dispersed or fragmented self be gathered together and display its uniqueness. Individuals become who they are, as Nietzsche would say, through action and the achievement of a distinct style of action.[44] Arendt makes a parallel point when she claims that individuals show who they are in virtuosic action.[45]

While Arendt's critique of the "traditional substitution of making for acting" reveals a great deal of the violence this interpretation does to the phenomenon of political action, it is only when we turn to Nietzsche's unmasking of the moral subject in the *Genealogy* that we come to appreciate just how violent our moral epistemology is. For while Arendt's account highlights those dimensions of action that get covered over by the teleocratic conception, Nietzsche provides a genealogy of the basic syntax that we impose upon action, a syntax appropriated, he argues, for the purpose of eliminating difference and constraining agonistic action. Nietzsche sees the reification of this syntax as originating in a slavish hostility to action even more primordial than the philosophical prejudice against the realm of human affairs cited by Arendt. By stressing just how hostile to plurality and difference the moral interpretation of action is, Nietzsche's analysis supports Arendt's view that we need a way of conceiving action that breaks decisively with the instrumental view. If, as Arendt argues, plurality is the origin and goal of agonistic political action, then it is essential to see how our grammar of action is always already at work in subverting the basic condition and primary achievement of action.

Nietzsche's suspicion regarding the subject not only uncovers the hostility to plurality and action built into our very language, but it also reveals how belief in this "fiction" underlies the basic Platonic/metaphysical distinction between appearance and reality.[46] Overcoming the reified actor/act distinction would, therefore, not merely enable a more affirmative account of agonistic action; it would also be a central moment in overcoming the Platonic/Christian/ascetic devaluation of *worldliness* and *appearance*. This larger overcoming is imperative if the nihilistic dialectic initiated by Plato's institution of the appearance/reality distinction is to be escaped (the Platonic valuation robs *this* world of meaning, yet is powerless to protect the transcendent grounds it posits from subsequent undermining by the same will to truth).

This, I think, is where Arendt's "aestheticism" draws closest to Nietzsche's. Both embrace the aesthetic as a strategic response to the exhaustion of meaning produced by the nihilistic logic the Platonic valuation sets in motion. If, as Nietzsche suggests, we read the last two thousand years as the story of "How the Real World at Last Became a Myth," of how *we* are left with only *this* world after belief in transcendent grounds withers, then the choice is between a positivistic/nihilistic embrace of "meaningless appearances," or an aestheticist revaluation of appearances as the privileged locus of meaning. Arendt and Nietzsche deploy the aesthetic against Plato, not out of mere skepticism regarding the existence of Truth or transcendent values (for both, the destruction of such ideals is an accomplished *fact* of recent Western history),[47] but rather as a way of rescuing the *possibility of meaning* in a nihilistic age.

Nietzsche's critique of a detached, autonomous ego and the moral interpretation of action that goes with it is thus of paramount importance to Arendt, and in many respects it sets the stage for her own reconceptualization of action. The moral/teleocratic interpretation of action must be overcome in order to avoid the reduction of plurality and difference, on the one hand, and that of meaning and appearance, on the other. But while framing freedom as sovereignty leads, in an obvious way, to the reduction of plurality, what is it about the distinction between actor and action that makes the moral interpretation so inimical to difference? What about the focus upon motives and goals, intentions and consequences, means and ends, is so hostile to action that we are *compelled* to "aestheticize" the phenomenon in order to save it? Nietzsche provides clues to these questions in the section from the *Genealogy* cited above, the most important clue being that the imposition of this distinction *alters the perspective* from which we view the phenomenon of action. We *now* view action, Nietzsche insists, from the standpoint of those for whom agonistic action was the greatest evil.

Nietzsche's argument takes the following form. From the point of view of the active man—the man who creates his own values as an exercise in self-affirmation, who is capable of great action, who can distinguish himself and lives to do so—the distinction between the "subject" and his effects makes no sense. The energies or forces of the noble man are, as Giles Deleuze reminds us, always acted:

such a man *is* his deeds and does not conceive himself otherwise.[48] The reactive man—the slave, in Nietzsche's terminology—needs to make this distinction in order to create the illusion of freedom in impotence. But he also needs this distinction in order to seduce the active man into believing that he is *responsible* for his actions because he could always have acted *differently*. The active man could, *qua* agent, *choose* not to act in an affirmative, agonistic manner; indeed, he could adopt a code of behavior based on the slavish denial of action. From the point of view of the slave, action is the original sin. It represents a form of life whose strength is manifest in its deeds, a form of life that is constantly individualizing and distinguishing itself through action.[49] The slave revolt in morality, in Nietzsche's eyes, is precisely a revolt against the life of action: the transvaluation of values it achieves is predicated upon the goodness of abstaining from action.

The trick is to get the agonistic actor to accept this radical change in perspective, to view his action as blameworthy rather than self-affirming. This, Nietzsche argues, is accomplished by means of the fiction of the subject, the fiction of a force separated from what it can do. Taken in by the tautological doubling of the deed present in language (for example, "the lightning flashed") that the slave presses upon him, the master succumbs to the idea that "the strong man is free to be weak and the bird of prey to be a lamb."[50] He accepts a moral epistemology that makes "the bird of prey accountable for being a bird of prey" and so becomes ashamed of his uniqueness and distinction. The active man willingly denies his agonistic spirit in order that he, too, might be "good," in the slavish sense of the word.[51] Thus, the strategic employment of a reified distinction between actor and act, subject and "effects," overcomes the "pathos of distance" between two radically different types. Through reflection, the vocabulary of justification, and shame, the forces of the active type are rendered reactive.[52] No longer evaluated in terms of style or virtuosity, action is brought down to size through constant monitoring of its motives and consequences.

The moral interpretation of action, then, reveals a hostility toward individualizing or great action *in its very structure*. It inserts a justificatory gap between actor and deed, ensuring that motives and consequences take precedence over the performance of action as such. At this stage, the stage of "bad conscience," the energies required for agonistic action are turned inward, channeled into the activity of self-surveillance and self-punishment.[53] The spontaneous, initiatory quality of action is increasingly smothered through the universalization of the standpoint of the one who does not act. The moralization of action (the story of which Nietzsche tells in the *Genealogy*) results in an antiagonistic attitude: the essential thing is to adjust one's behavior to the needs of the herd.[54] *Our* virtues, "namely, public spirit, benevolence, consideration, industriousness, moderation, modesty, indulgence and pity" are the virtues of a *tame* animal, an animal who does not act, an animal "easy to get along with and useful to the herd."[55]

Arendt's sympathy with Nietzsche's interpretation of the general tendency promoted by the moral interpretation of action (and its teleocratic counterpart) is clearly evident in her dramaturgical account, and in her sardonic admission that her "Greek" theory of virtuosic action is "no doubt . . . highly individualistic, as we would say today."[56] The trajectory of her analysis of modernity in *The Human Condition* attests, moreover, to her agreement with the Nietzschean thesis that action and difference are fatally undermined by a moralizing interpretation, one that elevates the perspective of utility and that culminates in the celebration of *behavior over action*.[57] From her emphasis on *homo faber*'s inability to grasp the meaning of action, to her conclusion that man as the *animal laborans* is increasingly incapable of performing it, Arendt's analysis presumes that Nietzsche's genealogy is essentially "correct," that the deep hostility to action manifest in the moral interpretation works itself out in modernity's reification of instrumentality, life, and material comfort.[58]

Of course, Arendt hardly endorses the principle of "rank ordering" that underlies Nietzsche's analysis and that guides the aristocratic radicalism of texts like *Beyond Good and Evil*. What she shares with Nietzsche is a deep suspicion of a moral epistemology that seems to breed docile subjects, and which systematically devalues agonistic action in the world of appearances. It is due to this "normalizing" tendency of the moral interpretation that she, like Nietzsche, opts for a performative conception of the self and a more action-friendly, theatrical conception of the public realm. Unlike Nietzsche, however, Arendt does not conflate democracy with a Christian or Socratic moral epistemology. In contrast to Nietzsche, *her* Greeks are democrats; hence, she can appropriate the greater part of his analysis in the name of a democratic agonism.

Is this move coherent? Can one be a "modern" with regard to formal political structures (democracy, constitutionalism, rights, etc.) while maintaining a Nietzschean skepticism toward the effects of universalist moral vocabularies? The contemporary debate on this issue has been fierce, resulting in a polarization of "universalists" (Habermasians and liberals), on the one hand, and "contextualists" (communitarians and postmodernists like Lyotard), on the other. As is often the case, Arendt's position straddles the dichotomy. Yet the question is an important one insofar as it underlines the political undecidability of the anti-Platonist project. As the example of Nietzsche illustrates, not all forms of this project are democratic. It should therefore come as no surprise that Arendt's "revaluation of appearance" substantively diverges from Nietzsche's. Before turning to this matter, however, I want to examine the *disclosive* character of Arendt's politics of appearance. What does political action disclose? How does this disclosure take place?

III. The Disclosive Nature of "Aestheticized" Action

According to Arendt, the primary phenomenon revealed by agonistic, virtuosic action in the public sphere is the unique identity of the agent.[59] Human plurality, she states, has "the twofold character of equality and distinction."[60] The distinctness of the human individual is not reducible to the quality of otherness or alterity, which he "shares with everything that is," nor to the quality of individuality, which "he shares with everything alive."[61] The form of being together implied by the notion of plurality enables the expression of a *unique* distinctness, a uniqueness that appears through words and deeds: "Speech and action reveal this unique distinctness. Through them, men distinguish themselves instead of being merely distinct; they are the modes in which human beings appear to each other, not indeed as physical objects, but *qua* men. This appearance, as distinguished from mere bodily existence, rests on initiative, but it is an initiative from which no human being can refrain and still be human."[62]

A life without action and speech is "dead to the world," because it is through action and speech that individuals disclose *who* they are. The "disclosure of who somebody is," according to Arendt, is "implicit in both his words and deeds." She hastens to add that "the affinity between speech and revelation is much closer than between action and revelation."[63] Without the accompaniment of speech, "action would not only lose its revelatory character but, and by the same token, it would lose its subject," the agent.[64] Action without speech ceases to be action because "there would no longer be an actor, and the actor, the doer of deeds, is possible only if he is at the same time the speaker of words."[65]

In speaking and acting, then, "men show who they are, reveal actively their unique personal identities and thus make their appearance in the human world."[66] If one reads this statement in conjunction with Arendt's remarks on the "fiercely agonal spirit" that pervaded the *polis* (where "everybody has constantly to distinguish himself from all others, to show through unique deeds or achievements that he was the best of all"), one is tempted to accuse her, as many of her critics do, of holding an overtly romantic, expressivist theory of the self.[67] They see the Arendtian political actor as a self that externalizes, uncovers, or "defines" itself through the tangible medium of words and deeds. However, it is important to see that Arendt's agonistic conception, like Nietzsche's, is based on the *rejection* of anything like an expressivist conception of self.[68]

What kind of self, then, *is* implied by the performance model of action? The expressivist conception assumes a core self, a basic or essential unity of innate capacities that are expressed, actualized, or concretized in the world of appearances. The "disclosure of the agent in speech and action" implies, from this perspective, an abiding subject, a reality, *behind* appearances. In contrast, the performance model deployed by Arendt and Nietzsche seeks to unmask this "fiction," to escape the slavish, moralizing prejudice against action, a prejudice manifest in the "necessary" positing of such a subject as the causal ground of all deeds/"effects."[69] Arendt interprets freedom as virtuosity precisely in order to keep the actor *in* the world, to frame his identity *qua* actor as coextensive with, rather than prior to, his actions. From Arendt's point of view, the self that *precedes* action, the biological or psychological self, is an essentially dispersed, fragmented, and plural self; it is a self whose lack of appearance deprives it of both unity and reality.[70] Like Nietzsche, Arendt challenges the assumption that a single, unified subject resides behind action; like him, she suggests that the unworldly self—the thinking as well as the biological and psychological self—is in fact a multiplicity of conflicting drives, needs, and faculties.[71]

The unity, coherence, or identity of the agent, then, is not a given; rather, it is an *achievement*, the product of action. But how does the performance of virtu-osic action give rise to an identifiable self, a self possessed of perceivable unity and, thus, of "unique distinctness"? Action, according to Arendt, provides us with an escape from the inner, determining, multiple self. Freedom as the sponta-neous beginning of something new is made possible by the transcendence of needs and psychology that entry into the public realm enables (since, to repeat, here neither the needs of life nor purity of motivation are at stake). Such an escape from the divided self is not found in man's other free activity, thinking, which is the freedom of a "two-in-one," of a self engaged in internal dialogue. The attempt of the philosopher to escape the realm of plurality through contem-plative withdrawal "always remains an illusion," for in his solitude he is, accord-ing to Arendt, "more radically delivered to this plurality inherent in every human being than anybody else."[72] Only entry into the public realm delivers us from such self-division: here the "companionship with others" calls "me out of the dialogue of thought" and "makes me one again—one single, unique, human being speaking with but one voice and recognizable as such by all others."[73]

Action, then, affords the self the chance to escape the "always changeable and somewhat equivocal" nature it has in private, and to assume a "definite and unique shape."[74] This definite, recognizable shape signals the achievement of a distinct style of action, which is to say that it reflects the actor's virtuosity.[75] It is also created by the principles that inspire an agent's action, and by the *persona*, the masks or roles, that the actor assumes in public appearance.[76] Arendt's essen-tial point is that if "the disclosure of 'who' in contradistinction to 'what' some-body is . . . is implicit in everything somebody says or does," then the achieve-ment of identity is reserved for those whose words or deeds reflect a consistency of style. The performance of action in public provides the opportunity for styliza-tion; and stylization, in turn, is the precondition for the kind of reification iden-tity demands and for the transformation of a public life into a memorable narra-tive or story.[77]

The idea that identity is not given, but is instead achieved through the cre-ation of a distinctive style, again recalls Nietzsche, who presented the problem of creating a self worthy of display and remembrance in a similar light. In *The Gay Science*, Nietzsche writes:

> *One thing is needful*—To "give style" to one's character—a great and rare art! It is practiced by those who survey all the strengths and weaknesses of their nature and then fit them all into an artistic plan until every one of them appears as art and reason and even weaknesses delight the eye. Here a large mass of second nature has been added; there a piece of original nature has been removed—both times through long practice and daily work at it. Here the ugly that could not be removed is con-cealed; there it has been reinterpreted and made sublime. Much that is vague and resisted shaping has been saved and exploited for distant views. . . . In the end, when the work is finished, it becomes evident how the constraint of a single taste governed and formed everything large and small. Whether this taste was good or bad is less important than one might suppose, if only it is a single taste![78]

Nietzsche's conception of the self as a work of art is importantly different from Arendt's idea of the revelation of self that occurs in political action. Nevertheless, Nietzsche sees selfhood, "becoming what one is," as an achievement wrested from diverse materials, and as consisting primarily in the attainment of style. As Alexander Nehamas notes, whether one has, in fact, attained this end is not something the *actor* can judge.[79] Nietzsche emphasizes that hardness toward oneself is necessary in order to bring coherence to welter, an emphasis Arendt echoes in stressing the discipline that playing a public role enforces.[80] But regardless of discipline, the final judgment about whether style or coherence is achieved—and what *kind* of character is displayed—resides with others—with the audience. Style and character, the marks of an achieved unity, are essentially *public* phenomena, utterly distinct from whatever feeling of unity the agent may experience himself.[81]

There is a third essential difference between the performance and expressivist models. The "disclosure of the agent in speech and deeds" implies, for Arendt, the absence of an underlying subject; identity as something achieved rather than given; and the *decentered* nature of such self-revelation. Arendt stresses that the disclosure of the agent—the "reward" of agonistic, individualizing action—is nothing like a project. Intentionality has the most tenuous connection to the "who" that action reveals.[82] Nor is the disclosure of the agent in words and deeds a process that necessarily increases self-knowledge or brings one closer to self-transparency. As Arendt states in *The Human Condition*, "disclosure can almost never be achieved by willful purpose, as though one possessed and could dispose of this 'who' in the same manner he has and can dispose of his qualities. On the contrary, it is more than likely that the 'who,' which appears so clearly and unmistakably to others, remains hidden from the person himself."[83] We cannot be the authors of ourselves, or of the stories that will be told about us.[84] The audience—our peers and those who come after—decides what the masks we wear in public signify and define, the "who" that they reveal.

As political actors, we disclose our unique identities, but we do *not* express ourselves. We do not do so for two basic reasons: first, there is no unified self to express; second, although action can be said to achieve or make identity possible, at the same time it conceals that identity. Nietzsche again is apposite. In the Preface to *The Genealogy of Morals*, he famously remarks that "we men of knowledge are unknown to ourselves . . . we are not 'men of knowledge' with respect to ourselves."[85] If we substitute "men of action" for "men of knowledge" in the first phrase, we approach Arendt's position. "Nobody," she states, "knows whom he reveals when he discloses himself in word or deed"; nevertheless, "he must be willing to risk this disclosure."[86]

The revelatory power of political action is not confined to the agent; action also discloses the *world*. For Arendt, "world" is virtually synonymous with the "public": it connotes that realm of phenomena that lies *between* men, and which, as such, is common to them.[87] Like every in-between, the world "relates and separates men at the same time."[88] Political action not only takes place *within* this "interspace"; it is, moreover, *about* it, in a double sense. First, political speech and action have a worldly content or referent that balances, to some degree, the agonistic urge to "self-revelation at any price." As Arendt puts it:

> Action and speech go on between men, as they are directed toward them, and they retain their agent revealing capacity even if their content is exclusively "objective," concerned with the matters of the world of things in which men move, which physically lies between them and out of which arises their specific, objective, worldly interests. These interests constitute, in the word's most literal sense, something which *inter-est*, which lies between people and therefore can relate and bind them together. Most action and speech is concerned with this in-between, which varies with each group of people, so that most words and deeds are *about* some worldly, objective reality in addition to being a disclosure of the acting and speaking agent.[89]

Arendt here emphasizes the world in its "objective" aspect, as a space articulated and defined by the durable things within it. Action is concerned with this world; however, it is important not to confuse the world-disclosive nature of action with the *creation* of this objective physical in-between. As noted in Chapter 1, Arendt identifies *work* as man's specifically world-building capacity.[90] In disclosing the world, action does not create it *qua* objectivity; rather, it constitutes it as a space of appearances, as a horizon for meaning. Action *transforms* the world by overlaying the "objective in-between" with a "subjective in-between," an in-between consisting solely of words and deeds. Such an in-between, Arendt remarks, is "altogether different" from the "physical worldly in-between with its interests."[91] The disclosive nature of action is found in the constitution of this subjective in-between: in "overlaying" the world, it transforms a space of durable things into a space of appearances, a space for meaning.

The world-disclosive nature of action refers, then, less to the realm of objectivity per se than to the illumination of the "world" as a public space (although Arendt strongly links the two aspects when she claims that "our feeling for reality depends utterly on appearance").[92] Stripped down to its thinghood, the world is the product of *homo faber*. While durable and lasting, it is a world in which appearance is not enough. In this world "everything must be of some use . . . must lend itself as an instrument to achieve something else."[93] It is a world, in short, where significance is a function of utility—and, as Arendt reminds us, "utility established as meaning generates meaninglessness."[94] The threat of meaninglessness posed by a potentially unrestricted instrumentality is escaped by the overlaying of the objective world with "the web of human relationships" created by action. The functional mentality of *homo faber* is limited by the care for the world, the commitment to the public realm and performance, that characterizes the agonistic political actor. The world can now appear as something more than an artificial space, a refuge from the repetition of nature: it now stands as a self-contained space of appearances, one where phenomena are judged in terms of their greatness or beauty rather than their utility.[95]

The world, considered as a space of appearances, is constituted "wherever men are together in the manner of speech and action."[96] Here appearance, and only appearance, has full reality ("In the realm of human affairs" Arendt writes, "being and appearance are indeed one and the same").[97] The publicity of this world, its shining brightness, clears an ontological space for appearance, a space "where freedom is tangible in words that can be heard, in deeds which can be seen, and events which can be talked about, remembered, and turned into stories."[98] The *phenomenality* of the public realm is seen by Arendt as the basic constitutive condition of its meaningfulness: virtuosic action is appearance that generates its own meaning. Indeed, according to Arendt, "if . . . we understand the political in the sense of the *polis*, its end or *raison d'être* would be to establish and keep in existence a space where freedom as virtuosity can appear."[99] As long as there is such a space for virtuosic action, the world is illuminated in its appearance, in its beauty; where such activities cease, the world darkens and the public space ultimately disappears.[100]

The world-disclosive nature of political action consists, then, in the way it illuminates the world as appearance; in the way virtuosic action glorifies appearance and makes it into a source of meaning. But for reality to present itself as appearance, for a space to be opened in which phenomena shine forth in their phenomenality, we need an undiluted plurality. The reality of the public realm relies "on the simultaneous presence of innumerable perspectives and aspects in which the common world presents itself and for which no common measurement or denominator can be devised."[101] Plurality, "the presence of others who see what we see and hear what we hear," confirms our feeling for the reality of ourselves and the world, and allows us to escape the "weird irreality" of a diffuse and isolated subjectivity.[102] However, the real ontological significance of plurality resides not in the simple confirmation provided by others, but in the fact that "everybody sees and hears from a different position."[103] Our "common world" can come to presence only through the play of perspectives that this difference in position creates: "only where things can be seen by many and in a variety of aspects without changing their identity . . . can worldly reality truly and reliably appear."[104] Plurality thus plays an ontologically constitutive role. For this reason, Arendt vehemently rejects the Platonic/philosophical privileging of truth, or *sophia*, and identifies opinion, *doxa*, as the stuff of political life.[105]

In Arendt's view, it is the nature of opinion to express perspective. Every opinion is relative to one's position in the world, and as such it formulates in speech what *dokei moi*, what appears to me.[106] Opinion in this sense is hardly the expression of subjective bias or arbitrariness; rather, it signifies the politically essential fact that "the world opens up differently to every man, according to his position in it."[107] It is precisely the variation implicit in the "it appears to me" that underlies the presencing of the common world. Moreover, through the expression of opinion one enters the public realm, revealing oneself in the process: "To assert one's own opinion belonged to being able to show oneself, to be seen and heard by others."[108]

Arendt's affirmation of the perspectival character of opinion returns us to one of her most prominent themes—the tension between truth and opinion, a tension that she sees rooted in the philosophic hostility to politics.[109] Through-out her work, Arendt persistently emphasizes the way truth denatures politics by marginalizing and degrading opinion. In "Truth and Politics," she flatly states that "every claim in the sphere of human affairs to an absolute truth whose va-lidity needs no support of opinion strikes at the very roots of all politics and government."[110] The claim to truth is destructive of politics in its denial of per-spective—the "it appears to me" that is essential to the presencing of the world as appearance. Seen from the viewpoint of politics, truth has a "despotic charac-ter"; it

> peremptorily claims to be acknowledged and precludes debate, and debate consti-tutes the very essence of political life. The modes of thought and communication that deal with truth, if seen from a political perspective, are necessarily domineering; they don't take into account other people's opinions, and taking these into account is the hallmark of all strictly political thinking.[111]

The Platonic instrumentalization of action, the separation and ranking of knowing and doing, hinges upon the appeal to a truth above opinion, a truth beyond perspective. Arendt repeatedly draws attention to the political context in which Plato formulated his concept of truth—the conflict between philosophy and the *polis* that led to the execution of Socrates.[112] Determined to make the *polis* safe for philosophy, Plato saw it as imperative that opinion be stripped of legitimacy. Hence, his "furious denunciation of *doxa* . . . ran not only like a red thread through his political works, but became one of the cornerstones of his concept of truth. Platonic truth . . . is always understood as the very opposite of opinion."[113] By framing truth in opposition to appearance and perspective, Plato creates one of the most effective weapons for reducing plurality and escaping the frailty of the realm of human affairs: "To the citizens exchanging opinions about human affairs which were themselves in a state of constant flux, the philosopher opposed the truth about those things which in their very nature were everlast-ing and from which, therefore, principles could be derived to stabilize human affairs."[114]

The Platonic demand that the philosopher replace the *phronimos*, that *sophia* replace opinion, results in a "tyranny of truth," a tyranny of absolute standards. That which is temporally good is always open to debate and persuasion; it is also irreducibly relative, as befits the "interhuman realm" that "by its nature consists of relationships." Here, according to Arendt, a "fundamental relativity" reigns.[115] Philosophical truth, in its concern with an absolute good, addresses man not in his plurality and relativity, but in his singularity; it abjures context and circum-stance; it compels rather than persuades. The will to truth—in its Platonic, abso-lutized form—undermines *doxa*, since it is no longer concerned, as Socrates was, with eliciting the truth of appearance and opinion. Its sole aim is to unmask these as illusion. The result is the creation of an abyss between truth and opinion and the destruction of "the specific political reality of the citizens," namely, the realm created or constituted by *doxa*, by the "it appears to me."[116] Because truth in the form of absolute standards destroys opinion and plurality, Arendt joins with those who, like Lessing, would willingly sacrifice the attainment of truth in order to preserve "the inexhaustible richness of human discourse."[117]

I should note that Arendt's hostility to a Platonic politics of truth does not encompass the domain of *factual* truth. While factual truths, like rational or religious truths, have a "coercive," persuasion-resistant character, Arendt considers their availability to be a fundamental presupposition for any genuine formation of opinion.[118] Where the line between fact and opinion has been systematically blurred, or where ideology and the rewriting of history succeed in producing a full-scale alternative reality, there a "politics of opinion" in Arendt's sense cannot take root.[119] While, from a doxastic perspective, it is possible to speak of the "despotism" of factual truth, this despotism is of a different order from that exercised by truths of reason or religion. The former provide nonpolitical boundaries to be realms of opinion and persuasion, while the latter invariably quash the plurality of perspectives that generates the "incessant discourse" Arendt cherishes.

While Arendt's preservation of the distinction between fact and opinion distinguishes her from some neo-Nietzschean interpretivists, she nevertheless agrees with Nietzsche that, in the public realm at least, there are no *moral* facts. In this discursive realm, even the most solid truths of reason, religion, and morality are transformed into the stuff of opinion. Thus, while it is always tempting for the statesman, no less than the philosopher, to endow certain propositions with the unquestionable force of truth, Arendt insists that this move is always made in bad faith. Her example is the set of "self-evident truths" that Jefferson appealed to in the Declaration of Independence. For Arendt, the "self-evident" characterization is a transparent rhetorical ploy by which Jefferson attempted to "put the basic consent among the men of Revolution beyond dispute and argument"; however,

> by saying "*we hold* these truths to be self-evident," he conceded, albeit without becoming aware of it, that the statement "All men are created equal" is not self-evident but stands in need of agreement and consent—that equality, if it is to be *politically relevant*, is a matter of opinion, and not "the truth." There exist, on the other hand, philosophical or religious statements that correspond to this opinion—such as that all men are equal before God, or before death, or insofar as they all belong to the same species of *animal rationale*—but none of them was ever of any political or practical consequence, because the equalizer, whether God, or death, or nature, transcended and remained outside the realm in which human intercourse takes place. Such "truths" are not between men but above them, and nothing of the sort lies behind the modern or the ancient . . . consent to equality. That all men are created equal is not self-evident nor can it be proved.[120]

Arendt's insistence that, politically speaking, the statement "all men are created equal" is in the realm of opinion is hardly intended to diminish its importance. On the contrary, she thinks this statement expresses a belief of the "greatest importance," namely, that "the joys and gratifications of free company are to be preferred to the doubtful pleasures of holding dominion."[121] What is at stake in her reading of Jefferson is the issue of whether, in the name of equality, the appeal to prediscursive grounds of validation should be allowed, regardless of the potentially stifling effect such appeals have on the realm of plurality. Arendt leaves little doubt as to her position: like Madison, she believes that "all governments rest on opinion," nothing more, nothing less.[122] To hold otherwise—to rely, with Jefferson, on the *crutch* of truth or to wield, with Plato, the *weapon* of truth—is to deny the fundamental transformation all propositions undergo when they enter the public realm. Moreover, it is to undermine the continuing commitment to the work of persuasion and dissuasion necessary to support such founding choices. In other words, it is not a question of instantiating a truth of God or nature in an inhospitable realm, but rather of persuading our peers that the pleasures of dominion, and of inequality, are indeed base.

Here, as elsewhere, Arendt explicitly repudiates the will to power or domination.[123] Nevertheless, her rejection of rational or religious truth as a meaningful or relevant guide to action in the public realm, combined with her deep suspicion of those who, like Plato, wish to transcend the arena of appearance and perspective, reflects the logic, if not the ideological substance, of Nietzsche's struggle against Platonism.

For Nietzsche, the claim to universality is a distinguishing characteristic of the moral interpretation of action. He suggests that one primary reason for the triumph of this perspective is that the reification of the subject occurs in language itself.[124] The grammatically instituted split between actor and action enables the moral interpretation to present itself, plausibly, not as one interpretive vocabulary, but rather as a representation or translation of the structure of the world and action in it.[125] Much of the power of the ascetic valuation derives precisely from its denial of perspective, partiality, and interests. And it is from this denial that the game of deducing actions from general principles is derived, a game that, as Lyotard reminds us, is as old as the West itself.[126] Indeed, its greatest monument is Plato's *Republic*.

Nietzsche, of course, denies the possibility of eliminating perspective, of coming up with a vocabulary that mirrors the structure of a reality beyond interpretation. As he says in GM III, 12: "There is *only* a perspective seeing, *only* a perspective 'knowing.'" This position frees us from the despotism of the ascetic will to power/will to truth (an ideal which "permits no other interpretation, no other goal"), affirming instead the essential pluralism of the world.[127] And this, moreover, makes possible a stronger, life-affirming kind of objectivity, quite distant from the contemplative ideal of a "pure, will-less, painless, timeless knowing subject": ". . . the *more* affects we allow to speak about one thing, the *more* eyes, different eyes, we can use to observe one thing, the more complete will our 'concept' of this thing, our 'objectivity,' be."[128]

Arendt's politics of opinion, her emphasis on the constitutive role of perspective and the coercive nature of truth, can be seen as a specifically political version of Nietzschean perspectivism, albeit one that retains a healthy respect for non-moral facts. Only by affirming the essentially perspectival character of opinion is the world saved from the reductive effects of the Platonic/moral interpretation of action, an interpretation predicated on the gap between reality and appearance, and on the untruth of appearance. The performance model adopted by Arendt from Nietzsche identifies reality with appearance, preserves plurality in the strong sense, and thereby maintains the value of action and the integrity of the public realm.

There is much, then, in Arendt's theory of agonistic political action that builds on Nietzsche's aestheticist struggle against Platonism. Yet, as I mentioned above, the parallels and continuities discussed so far do not touch upon Arendt and Nietzsche's deepest connection, their turn to the aesthetic as a way out of the nihilism that stretches from Plato to the present.[129] If, as Michel Haar notes, nihilism begins with the assertion that "this world is worth nothing and nothing in it is worth anything," and proceeds to invent a "true world" possessing all the attributes lacking in this one (unity, stability, identity, truth, goodness, etc.), *then* "the division of the two worlds, the feat undertaken by Plato, constitutes the nihilistic act *par excellence*."[130] It is so because this division denies meaning or value to the appearances themselves: only insofar as these are signs of some (non-apparent) reality are they granted significance.[131] Western man early gets into the habit of making meaning dependent upon some realm of essence beyond existence. An inevitable corollary of the will to truth or essence is the dialectic of enlightenment, the process by which all such "transcendent" grounds are dissolved in a corrosive skepticism: the true world becomes a fable. The central value of our culture, truth, drives us to ceaseless unmasking, to the destruction of life-affirming illusions and horizons, to the "truth that there is no truth"—God is dead.[132] The irony, as Tracy Strong observes, is that this discovery does not liberate us from the sense that we must have truth in order to have meaning, that meaning is somehow inextricably tied to truth or the universal.[133] We continue to search for what we know does not exist, confirming our growing sense of meaninglessness; worse, we come to be at home in this exhaustion of meaning.

Nietzsche's aestheticism—his championing of art against truth, his affirmation of illusion and appearance, his conviction that we need art to save us from truth—is obviously incomprehensible outside this context. Arendt's aesthetic approach to action is a parallel response to the same world-historical phenomenon, the self-devaluation of the highest values, the collapse of tradition and authority.[134] The realm of appearances—whether construed broadly as in the Nietzschean aestheticization of the world, or narrowly as in the Arendtian "aestheticization" of the political—holds the promise of meaning freed from the will to truth, from the nihilism implicit in all teleology, whether of Nature, God, or Man. The aesthetic attitude toward existence propounded by Nietzsche and the aesthetic approach toward political action proposed by Arendt have as their goal the redemption of a world rendered valueless by the collapse of absolutes and authority. Only by living "superficially"—as artists, as political actors, as glorifiers of appearance—do we escape the tragic wisdom of Silenus invoked by Nietzsche at the start of *The Birth of Tragedy* and by Arendt at the close of *On Revolution*.[135]

The glorification of appearance that takes place in art and action in the public realm endows the world with a meaning it otherwise lacks: both activities make the world beautiful; both escape the reduction of meaning that characterizes modernity.[136]

IV. LIMITING THE AGON: DIFFERENCE AND PLURALITY, PERSPECTIVISM AND JUDGMENT

It has been suggested that Arendt theatricalizes action as a way of overcoming its Platonic/Aristotelian instrumentalization; that the performance-oriented, agonistic dimension of the resulting theory of action is essential to the preservation of plurality; that this conception of action owes much to Nietzsche's anti-Platonic, "immoralist" aestheticization of action; and, finally, that she and Nietzsche are one in their celebration of a nonsovereign, decentered freedom of action "beyond good and evil." When viewed in such a light, Arendt's theory appears far indeed from what Habermas presents in his consensus reading. But this raises the question of whether Arendt's anti-Platonism leads her, like Nietzsche, into an uncritical endorsement of agonistic subjectivity. Can she be unaware of the dangers and distortions an unrestricted agonism invites—distortions that threaten to undermine the very *conditions* of political action (plurality, equality, commonality)?

Arendt, of course, is aware of the dangers of an excessive emphasis on the "fiercely agonal spirit" behind all genuine political action. In a previously unpublished manuscript, "Philosophy and Politics," she noted how this spirit constantly threatened to overwhelm the *polis*, to splinter it through centrifugal force.[137] She therefore broadens the Nietzschean focus on the agonistic quality of action by reasserting the deliberative element present in both action and judgment. This move on her part may seem a capitulation—an abandonment of an ill-advised aestheticization of action—and a return to the sound common sense embedded in the Aristotelian notions of *praxis* and *phronesis*. I would like to stress, however, that Arendt's modification of her "aestheticized" agonism does not employ external measures: the appeal she makes is not to reason or dialogue, but to *taste*.[138] Her theory of political judgment limits the agonal dimensions of politics not by abandoning the aestheticization of action, but by *completing* it. Hence, her highly idiosyncratic appropriation of Kant's third *Critique*, an appropriation that enables her to preserve plurality and politics from the subjectivism of Nietzsche's more purely agonistic model.

While Arendt's revised version of agonistic politics places her at a distance from consensus theorists like Habermas, it is also at variance with those who, following Nietzsche, tend to view discourse as war, as agon without limit (Deleuze, Lyotard, and Foucault, at various moments).[139] But here it might be objected that it is simply wrongheaded to accuse *Nietzsche* of promoting an overly agonistic, masculine model of subjectivity, one more intent upon self-display and self-composition than on being open to otherness. After all, the whole point of Nietzsche's archaeology of the moral, responsible subject in *The Genealogy of Morals* is to reveal the hidden coercions and violence that underlie the creation of any such centered subjectivity.[140] Contemporary appropriations of the *Genealogy* (e.g., Adorno and Horkheimer's in *Dialectic of Enlightenment*, Foucault's in *Discipline and Punish*) have stressed the violence, paranoia, and pathology that accompany the constitution of the self-identical subject.[141] Against such an essentially deformed subjectivity (a subject that would prefer any amount of self-inflicted pain, even death, to the relaxation of its all-too-dearly bought boundaries), Nietzsche, it is claimed, deploys a dissolvent notion of aesthetic experience, which halts the unending process of self-violation and self-mortification that *is* the ascetic ideal.

In this interpretation, increasingly dominant thanks to poststructuralism, Nietzsche stands as the great subverter of what Jochen Schulte-Sasse has called the "agonistic individuality of modern subjectivity."[142] It is important to take this reading seriously, if only because the critique of autonomy is such a central element in both Nietzsche and Arendt. Does the Nietzschean version of this critique result in the rejection of anything resembling an agonistic subjectivity? If we stick to the *Genealogy*, it is clear that Nietzsche's decentering of the subject, and his unmasking of the supposedly "free" agent, are not indictments of subjectivity *tout court*; nor can it be said that the positive image of subjectivity contained therein is antiagonistic. Contra Foucault, subjectification is not always or merely subjugation for Nietzsche.[143] If it were, then Nietzsche would be in the position of grounding the "joy in action" in the absence of a reflexive relation to self, in sheer instinctual behavior. However, occasional embarrassing remarks about the "blond beast" aside, the thrust of Nietzsche's analysis is that man only becomes an interesting animal as a result of this self-violence. "Breeding an animal with the right to make promises," the "tremendous labor" of the "morality of mores," does not bring forth *one* fruit.[144] There is the slavish will, to be sure, the will turned against itself, the will that is an instrument of self-surveillance, self-punishment, and adjustment to the herd. But there is also what Nietzsche calls "the sovereign individual," the "ripest fruit," the man in whom the process of discipline and interiorization has yielded a will strong enough to liberate itself from the morality of custom, and from morality as such.[145] *He* is responsible, this "master of a free will," but only to himself. He is freed from the constraints imposed by motives and goals and the moral criteria appropriate to them: *his* discipline is not in need of such props. Nietzsche's positive image of subjectivity is that of an individual who is "autonomous and supramoral," whose discipline is such that he "becomes what he is" by the imposition of a certain style upon the fragments that provide the raw material for his self. Such an individual masters himself, overcomes himself, in the activity of self-composition. This self-overcoming, which is also a self-creation, constitutes, in Nietzsche's view, genuine freedom:

> For what is freedom? That one has the will to self-responsibility. That one preserves the distance that divides us. That one has become more indifferent to hardship, toil, privation, even to life. That one is ready to sacrifice men to one's cause, oneself not

excepted. Freedom means that the manly instincts that delight in war and victory have gained mastery over the other instinct for "happiness." The man *who has become free*—and how much more the *mind* that has become free—spurns the contemptible sort of well-being dreamed of by shopkeepers, Christians, cows, women, Englishmen and other democrats. The free man is a *warrior*.[146]

Nietzsche's formulation of the virtuosic freedom of such a subject casts the "anti-agonistic" reading in doubt. It inevitably colors the way we view Arendt's parallel conception of virtuosic agency. If free action by definition transcends the categories of motives and goals, what possible meaning can it have apart from the aesthetic enjoyment, the feeling of power, which such self-conscious mastery, such display of one's own virtuosity, produces? Where "the deed is everything," it is abundantly clear that what matters is the *style* of action and not its origin or goal. Nietzsche's self-consciously aesthetic approach to action raises the question of how such "autonomous" action can ever amount to more than the form-giving "process of subduing" he refers to.[147] His celebration of the artist's will as a paradigmatic instance of such overcoming, of creative/appropriative interpretation, leads us to ask Arendt what prevents her conception of action from devolving into a similar subjectivism? How does one reconcile the imperative of *greatness* (the distinctive quality of "aesthetic" action) with the preservation of genuine plurality?

Nietzsche's aestheticization of action culminates, then, in an overstatement of the world- and self-creative potential of great, agonistic and/or artistic action. "Active" forces are "spontaneous, aggressive, expansive, form-giving"; they are constantly engaged in the process of imposing "new interpretations and directions" upon phenomena.[148] The "will to power" is the attempt by each interpreting force to assert its hegemony. The world, in this view, exists only as a "sign chain" awaiting investment. As Nietzsche puts it, "Whatever exists, having somehow come into being, is again and again reinterpreted to new ends, taken over, transformed, and redirected by some power superior to it; all events in the organic world are a subduing, a *becoming master*, and all subduing and becoming master involves a fresh interpretation."[149] Devoid of any intrinsic meaning, identity, or structure, the world and self offer unlimited opportunities for the Apollonian imposition of form, the affirmative creation of value. Through his virtuoso deployment of new tropes, the "artist" creates both new ways of seeing the world and new compositions of self.[150]

Another way of characterizing the deficiencies of Nietzsche's aestheticism is to say that it divides performer and audience, rendering the latter virtually superfluous. What does the creator of new values, and fresh illusions, care for the spectator? Like Nietzsche, he recognizes his own untimeliness. Insofar as the audience does have a place in the Nietzschean paradigm, it is in the contemporary form of interpretivism: the audience is seen as an aggregate of agonistic interpreters or critics, each seeking to impose his reading on any performance.[151] From this standpoint, the abolition of the "true world" really does do away with the apparent one as well: meaning and structure derive solely from the subjective positings of the actor or audience. In *Twilight of the Idols*, Nietzsche does not hesitate to link the unmasking of the "true world" to the unmasking of the apparent one.[152] As a result, there can be no meaningful talk of a *shared* world of appearances. The dissolution of any transcendent or transcendental ground of appearances implies that these have value or meaning strictly as a function of "perspective seeing." Nietzschean perspectivism ultimately denies appearance its own reality: belief in such a reality is only a metaphysical hangover.

How, then, does the appropriation of the third *Critique* enable Arendt to escape the excesses of an aestheticized, agonistic conception of politics? How does Kantian aesthetics help to reassert the intersubjective nature of the phenomena that Arendt wants to preserve? How, finally, can a theory of aesthetic judgment limit, without neutering, the agonistic conception of political action?

In her essay "The Crisis in Culture," Arendt compares works of art to the "products" of action, words, and deeds. What they share, she says, is "the quality that they are in need of some public space where they can appear and be seen; they can fulfill their own being, which is appearance, only in a world which is common to all."[153] Kant's aesthetic theory—which is particularly attuned to the *public* character of beauty, offering "an analytic of the beautiful from the viewpoint of the judging spectator"—gives us access to this reality in a way foreclosed by Nietzsche's (ultimately) reductionist view of appearance.[154] For Nietzsche, appearances are merely artifacts, errors, illusions created for the sake of life.[155] As a result, one ought not discuss the problem of the beautiful except in terms of the needs of the creator and the forces expressed in his creation. To approach the world of appearances or the beautiful from the *contemplative* standpoint, as Kantian aesthetics does, is one more sign of the decadence of the ascetic ideal. What Nietzsche specifically holds *against* Kant—namely, that he, "like all philosophers, instead of envisaging the aesthetic problem from the point of view of the artist (the creator) considered art and the beautiful purely from the point of view of the spectator" (GM III, 6)—is the primary reason that Arendt holds that his aesthetic theory has *political* relevance.[156]

In the third *Critique*, Kant goes out of his way to establish the specificity of aesthetic judgments and their objects. The broad distinction he draws between determinate and reflective judgments, between judgments for which "the universal (the rule, the principle, the law)" is given and judgments in which only the particular is given and "the universal has to be found," is intended to open a gap between the activities of judging an object as an instance of something, and judging it in its specificity, *qua* representation.[157] Aesthetic judgments are reflective precisely because they concern representations as representations, rather than as instances of a given concept. The extremely strong distinction Kant draws between aesthetic judgment—the judgment of whether something is pleasing or displeasing to us as representation—and cognitive judgment—the judgment of the objective qualities of a perception—is meant to underline the very different faces a phenomenon presents to us given the different attitudes with which we approach it. In the aesthetic attitude, we perform a kind of *epoche* by which the natural attitude, with its concern for and interest in things, is bracketed. As Kant says in section 2 of the third *Critique*: "When the question is whether something is beautiful, we do not want to know whether we, or anyone else are, or even could be, concerned with the real existence of the thing, but rather what estimate we form of it on contemplation."[158]

Kant's careful isolation of aesthetic experience and judgment enables us, contra Nietzsche, to conceive a way of judging appearances that does not reduce them to one more expression of an overflowing life.[159] His spectatorial approach, albeit exaggerated and rigidly formalistic, opens up a sphere removed from the pressing interests of life, a sphere where, in Arendt's version, "we are confronted with things which exist independently of all utilitarian and functional references, and whose quality remains always the same."[160] Kant's conception of the aesthetic has the merit, according to Arendt, of drawing our attention to the fact that "only works of art are made for the sole purpose of appearance."[161] Aesthetic objects are those "whose very essence is to appear and be beautiful. . . . The proper criteria by which to judge appearances is beauty,"[162] not because beauty is edifying, but because it lets the appearances shine forth as appearances.

"Saving the appearances," then, presumes something like the contemplative attitude Nietzsche scorned. From Kant's perspective, genuine aesthetic experience and judgment presuppose the achievement of a *disinterested* attitude.[163] Yet one is hard-pressed to see how such an attitude could be achieved in that other realm of appearances, the political realm. Arendt, however, claims that something like the aesthetic attitude is indeed necessary if we are to be open for *that* world. In "The Crisis in Culture," she glosses Kant's fundamental line of reasoning:

> The proper criterion by which to judge appearances is beauty. . . . But in order to become aware of appearances we first must be free to establish a certain distance between ourselves and the object, and the more important the sheer appearance of a thing is, the more distance it requires for its proper appreciation. This distance cannot arise unless we are in a position to forget ourselves, the cares and interests and urges of our lives, so that we will not seize what we admire but let it be in its appearance.[164]

Arendt's intention here is fairly clear. In order to do justice to political action, in order to redeem the meaning potentially disclosed by words and deeds in the public realm, the judging spectator must be able to assume an attitude similar to Kant's *uninteressiertes Wohlgefallen* (disinterested pleasure or satisfaction). Without it, nonsovereign political action would lose its revelatory capacity: action would be judged solely in terms of material or moral interests; worse, it might be seen as the mere manifestation of power. To appreciate the "play of the game" that characterizes a genuinely agonistic politics, the audience must be "released from life's necessity." Only then will they be "free for the world."[165] This is why Kant's formulation of aesthetic or taste judgments is an appropriate model for political judgment, for "taste judges the world in its appearance and in its worldliness . . . neither the life interests of the individual nor the moral interests of the self are involved here. For judgments of taste, the world is the primary thing, not man, neither man's life nor his self."[166]

While the question of the nature and degree of "abstraction from interest" appropriate to the political realm is a perplexing one, it is important to see the thrust of Arendt's reliance on Kant. Agonistic political action threatens to fragment the *polis*. One way of avoiding this is to cultivate an ethos whereby actors are more committed to playing the game than to winning.[167] Another equally important way of limiting the agon is to insist that political judgment—the meaning we draw from words and deeds—operates at a certain distance from the immediate interests of the audience. "Disinterestedness," in raising men above the pressing needs of life and the self, is essential to the appreciation of action and so to the intrinsic value of plurality, opinion, and politics itself.

But while some measure of disinterestedness is crucial to avoiding a politics of ideology, interests, or need, it seems ironic that Arendt would urge the adoption of a contemplative attitude toward political action. After all, *The Human Condition* identifies the contemplative (Platonic) impulse as specifically antipolitical.[168] Arendt, however, is careful to distinguish between the contemplative attitude that characterizes *theoria*, and the "objectivity" that characterizes the man of practical judgment. The latter arises not from achieving agreement with oneself (Socrates), but rather from being able, in Kant's words, to "think in the place of everybody else."[169] Having an "enlarged mentality," what Arendt calls "the ability to see things not only from one's own point of view but in the perspective of all those who happen to be present," presumes both distance and imagination.[170] Imagination—which Kant describes as the free play of the mind's power of representation—enables us to put ourselves "in the place of any other man," and thereby to abstract from "the limitations which contingently attach to our own judgment."[171] Aesthetic—and political—judgment achieves its disinterested character not through a complete withdrawal from the world, but by being representative, a point Arendt stresses in "Truth and Politics":

> Political thought is representative. I form an opinion by considering a given issue from different viewpoints, by making present to my mind the standpoints of those who are absent; that is, I represent them. This process of representation does not blindly adopt the actual views of those who stand somewhere else, and hence look upon the world from a different perspective; this is a question of neither empathy, as though I tried to be or to feel like somebody else, nor of counting noses and joining a majority but of being and thinking in my own identity where actually I am not. The more people's standpoints I have present in my mind while I am pondering a given issue, and the better I can imagine how I would feel and think were I in their place, the stronger will be my capacity for representative thinking and the more valid my final conclusion, my opinion.[172]

The representative thinking made possible by disinterested judgment is Arendt's Kantian version of Nietzsche's perspectival objectivity, the objectivity born of using "more" and "different" eyes to judge and to interpret a thing.[173] There is, however, an obvious and crucial difference between perspectives represented through the free play of imagination and the "perspective seeing" Nietzsche describes. For Nietzsche, having "more" and "different" eyes means the ability to relativize all accepted meanings, dissolving their apparent solidity in the free play of signifiers.[174] In Kant and Arendt, on the other hand, the free play of the imagination has the effect of focusing the judging agent's attention on the *publicly available* aspects of an issue.[175] The representative nature of judgment enables the transcendence of "individual limitations" and "subjective private conditions," thereby freeing us for the purely public aspect of the phenomenon.

The difference between genealogical "objectivity" and representative judgment, between the kind of aesthetic distance endorsed by Nietzsche and that endorsed by Kant and Arendt, is summed up by the contrast between Nietzsche's trope of "seeing things from another planet" and the Kantian/Arendtian appeal to "common sense," the *sensus communis*.[176] Nietzschean aestheticism, in the form of perspectivism, has the effect of either placing one *beyond* any community of interpretation (the genealogical standpoint), or denying that a viable "background consensus" exists, thereby robbing the public realm of its fundamental epistemological precondition. There can be no arena of common discourse, no genuinely public space, when the "death of God" leads to the advent of Weber's "warring gods."[177] Lyotard expresses a similar thought when he links the discovery of an irreducible plurality of incommensurable language games to the decline of the legitimizing metanarratives of modernity.[178] In such a situation, judgment and interpretation are inevitably aestheticized: we are left, in Nietzsche's phrase, with the "yay and nay of the palate."[179]

For Kant, the significance and implications of aesthetic distance are quite opposite. As noted previously, he is struck by the public character of the beautiful, despite the nonobjective quality of aesthetic experience.[180] The impartiality of detached aesthetic judgment, while not pretending to truth, guarantees that the object or ground of aesthetic satisfaction will be *communicable*. And this in turn reveals a quality of taste as judgment that is obscured by Nietzsche and our own subjectivist notion of taste. Taste judgments of the disinterested sort are characterized by a peculiar claim: the pure judgment of taste "requires the agreement of everyone, and he who describes anything as beautiful claims that everyone ought to give approval to the object in question and describe it as beautiful."[181] The communicability of taste judgments leads Kant to posit the existence of a common sense, a common "feeling for the world." Indeed, Kant describes taste itself as "a kind of *sensus communis*."[182]

The aesthetic distance achieved by representative thought thus points to the "grounding" of judging insight in common sense, a point Arendt emphasizes. "Common sense . . .", she writes, "discloses to us the nature of the world insofar as it is a common world; we owe to it the fact that our strictly private and 'subjective' five senses and their sensory data can adjust themselves to a nonsubjective and 'objective' world which we have in common and share with others."[183] The significance of Kant's theory of taste judgment for politics is that it shows how a nonfoundationalist theory of judgment can in fact serve to strengthen rather than undermine our sense of a shared world of appearances. Kant's analysis of taste judgment reveals how, in Arendt's words, "judging is one, if not the most, important activity in which this sharing-the-world-with-others comes to pass."[184] It does so by highlighting the public-directed claim implicit in all pure judgments of taste, by showing how the expression of approval or disapproval, satisfaction or dissatisfaction, appeals to the common sense of one's judging peers. In matters of taste, one "expects agreement from everybody else."[185] Oriented toward agreement, relying upon common sense, taste judgment emerges, contra Nietzsche, as the activity through which the public world presences itself as appearance; as the activity through which a community "decides how this world, independently of its utility and all our vital interests in it, is to look and sound, what we will see and what men will hear in it."[186]

Kant's theory of judgment thus opens a space between the false objectivism of Plato (political judgment as determinate, as a kind of *epistēmē*) and the subjectivism that accompanies Nietzsche's endorsement of perspectival valuation. Taste judgments are valid, but their "specific validity" is to be understood precisely in opposition to the "objective universal validity" that marks cognitive or practical judgments in the Kantian sense. As Arendt says, "Its claims to validity can never extend further than the others in whose place the judging person has put himself for his considerations."[187] Taste judgments are crucially dependent upon perspective, upon the "it appears to me," on "the simple fact that each person occupies a place of his own from which he looks upon and judges the world."[188] Nevertheless, they constantly refer us to a world of appearances "common to all its inhabitants." Kant's notion of taste judgment provides the perfect model for political judgment, in Arendt's opinion, because it preserves appearance and perspective without abolishing this world.

We can sum up the achievement of Kant's theory of judgment by saying that it removes the specter of subjectivism, yet without recourse to objective or cognitive grounds of validation.[189] Lacking an objective principle, taste judgments are necessarily difficult, and where their validity is questioned it can be redeemed only by persuasive means. As Arendt says in "The Crisis in Culture": "Taste Judgments [unlike demonstrable facts or truths demonstrated by argument] . . . share with political opinions that they are persuasive; the judging person—as Kant says quite beautifully—can only 'woo the consent of everyone else' in the hope of coming to an agreement with him eventually."[190]

Taste judgments are, in a word, redeemed deliberatively. Kant's conception of aesthetic judgment—departing from the exchange of viewpoints necessary for representative thinking and culminating in the persuasive exchange that accompanies the rendering of each judgment—is thus, for Arendt, political through and through.[191] It requires an ongoing process of exchange and deliberation, one "without criteria," as Lyotard would say.[192]

This is yet another reason why Kantian taste judgment is the appropriate model for Arendt's account of political judgment, the "receptive side" of virtuoso action. It reasserts the intersubjective nature of both appearances and judgment, while severing the links between the common or public and the universal. Our capacity for judgment rests on our feeling for the world, and this requires neither a transcendental ground for appearances nor universally valid criteria of argumentative rationality. Practical questions emphatically *do not* admit of truth.[193] Yet political judgment seen as a kind of taste judgment nevertheless helps to limit the agon by reintroducing the connection between plurality and deliberation, by showing how the activity of judgment can, potentially, reveal to an audience what they have in common in the process of articulating their differences. And what they have in common, contra Aristotle and contemporary communitarians, are not *purposes* per se, but the *world*. *Debate*, not consensus, constitutes the essence of political life, according to Arendt.[194] The Kantian conception of taste judgment reopens the deliberative space threatened by agonistic action, in a way that makes consensus not the assumed *telos* of political debate, but at best, a kind of regulative ideal.

The turn to Kant enables Arendt to avoid the antipolitical aspects of an actor-centered conception of agonistic action. The disclosive quality of political action comes to depend importantly upon the audience, conceived as a group of deliberating agents exercising their capacity for judgment. Thus, the meaning of action is seen by Arendt as predicated upon a twofold "death of the author": the actor does not create meaning as the artist does a work, nor can judging spectators redeem this meaning unless they are able, in some measure, to forget themselves. This is not to say Arendt's conception of political action and judgment extinguishes the self; rather, it is to say that self-coherence is achieved through a process of disclosure that is importantly decentered, for both actor *and* judge. As it turns out, the judging spectator is also engaged in the "sharing of words and deeds" in his capacity as a deliberating agent. And, as Arendt reminds us, "By his manner of judging, the person discloses to an extent also himself, what kind of person he is, and this disclosure, which is involuntary, gains in validity to the degree that it has liberated itself from merely individual idiosyncrasies."[195]

The agon is limited, then, not by retreating from the aestheticization of action, but by following its anti-Platonic impulse through to the end. The "completion" of the theory of action by a Kant-inspired theory of judgment retains the focus on action as something heroic or extraordinary. It does so, however, by shifting the emphasis from world- and self-creation to the world-illuminating power of "great" words and deeds, to the *beauty* of such action. As a public phenomenon, the beautiful can only be confirmed in its being by an audience animated by a care for the world. The difference between Arendt's "aesthetic" approach to politics and Nietzsche's aestheticization of life is nowhere clearer than in the connection Arendt draws between greatness and beauty in "The Crisis in Culture":

> Generally speaking, culture indicates that the public realm, which is rendered politically secure by men of action, offers its space of display to those things whose essence it is to appear and to be beautiful. In other words, culture indicates that art and politics, their conflicts and tensions notwithstanding, are interrelated and even mutually dependent. Seen against the background of political experiences and of activities which, if left to themselves, come and go without leaving any trace in the world, beauty is the manifestation of imperishability. The fleeting greatness of word and deed can endure to the extent that beauty is bestowed upon it. Without the beauty, that is, the radiant glory in which potential immortality is made manifest in the human world, all human life would be futile and no greatness could endure.[196]

Arendt's "aestheticism," an aestheticism predicated upon a love of the world, is critically different from Nietzsche's, which is the aestheticism of the *artist*. A persistent theme in Arendt's writing, one parallel to her emphasis on the tension between philosophy and politics, concerns the conflict between art and politics.[197] This conflict does not emerge out of the phenomenology of art versus that of political action; as we have seen, Arendt thinks these are importantly similar. Rather, the conflict centers on the mentality of the artist versus that of the political actor. The artist, according to Arendt, is a species of *homo faber*, who characteristically views the world in terms of means and ends. He is unable to conceive *praxis* independently of *poiēsis*: the work always retains priority over the activity itself. The result is that performance is denigrated, action misconceived.

Nietzsche, of course, has even less use for *homo faber* than Arendt, who takes pains to voice her criticism not against making as such, but against the universalization of a particular attitude. Nevertheless, if we take an Arendtian perspective, it is clear that Nietzsche, the artist-philosopher, must be counted amongst those who "fall into the common error of regarding the state or government as a work of art," as an expression of a form-giving will to power.[198] Plato's *Republic* stands as the initiator of the state as "collective masterpiece," as artwork, trope. The fact that Plato launched this metaphor in terms of what Lacoue-Labarthe calls a "mimetology," while Nietzsche repudiates again and again all metaphors of correspondence or adequation, does not alter their fundamental agreement: both regard action not as essentially performance, but as making.[199] *Poiēsis* has a radically different connotation for Nietzsche, to be sure, but the activity of self-fashioning and self-overcoming does not overturn the Platonic paradigm so much as bring it to closure. Nietzsche may explode the notion of *telos* in its classical sense, but the model of the work retains its significance. Thus, despite the importance of his anti-Platonism to the project of deconstructing the tradition's model of action, his contribution to the thinking of plurality and difference in a *political* way is subject to a crucial limitation. Thought essentially in terms of an "aesthetics of existence," in terms of a project of self-fashioning freed from any *telos*, the positively valorized notion of difference proposed by Nietzsche remains poetic. Like the activity of the artist, it "must be isolated from the public, must be sheltered and concealed from it," if it is to achieve adequate expression.[200] The poetic, ultimately antitheatrical framework assumed by Nietzsche prohibits the Arendtian thought that, under certain very specific conditions, it is precisely the public realm that is constituted by plurality, and which enables the fullest, most articulated expression of difference.

The critique of Nietzsche's aestheticism implicit in Arendt's theory of political judgment is thus of the utmost importance in coming to terms with what I have (somewhat misleadingly) called her "aesthetic" approach to politics. Arendt, unlike the tradition that runs from Plato through Schiller and Hegel to Nietzsche, studiously avoids the figure of the state as a work of art. Indeed, her "aestheticization" of politics stands in profound opposition to the conflation of art and politics performed by the German philosophical tradition after Kant.[201] The "poetic" character of Nietzsche's aestheticism suggests that he is not the "dynamite" he claimed to be; it suggests that he, like Kierkegaard and Marx, rebelled against the tradition without finally being able to extricate himself from its conceptual structures.[202] Nietzsche's failure is a predictable one, according to Arendt, because his transvaluation proceeds by turning the tradition upside down, by *inverting* its conceptual hierarchies. The inevitable result of all such "turning around" operations is entrapment within the structure one is trying to escape. Thus, Nietzsche's "inverted Platonism" stands, along with Marx's attempt to go beyond philosophy, not as a genuine break with the tradition, but as its point of closure.[203] Falling prey to the philosophical/Platonic identification of action as a kind of making, Nietzsche ultimately fails to provide the resources necessary for saving action and plurality from their philosophically induced oblivion. With Nietzsche, we are still unable to think the essence of action decisively enough.

PART II

Arendt and Heidegger

The Heideggerian Roots of Arendt's Political Theory

The essence of freedom is originally not connected with the will and even less with the causality of human willing.

—Heidegger, "The Question Concerning Technology"

Freedom as related to politics is not a phenomenon of will. . . . Man does not possess freedom so much as he, or better his coming into the world, is equated with the appearance of freedom in the universe. . . . Because he is a beginning, man can begin; to be human and to be free are the same.

—Arendt, "What Is Freedom?"

Dasein is its disclosedness.

—Heidegger, Being and Time

I. INTRODUCTION: THE ONTOLOGICAL-POLITICAL STAKES OF ARENDT'S THEORY OF ACTION

Arendt's turn to Kant throws the antipolitical aspects of Nietzsche's agonism into sharp relief; it also reveals the ontological commitments that inform her rethinking of freedom, action, and judgment. The appeal to Kant's aesthetics underscores not only the phenomenality of political action, but the being of the space of appearances—the *public* world—as well. It is precisely the reality of this flux-filled phenomenal realm that the metaphysical tradition (beginning with Plato and ending with Nietzsche) repeatedly denies. For Plato, the world of appearance—of democratic politics—is a mere shadow realm; for Nietzsche, the "apparent world" (understood as a shared realm of appearance) disappears with the unmasking of the "true" one.

We are now in a position to appreciate the gap that separates Arendt not only from Aristotle and Kant, but from Nietzsche as well. The dialectic of objectivism and subjectivism dramatized by Nietzsche's antimetaphysical thought appears, from her perspective, as antipolitical throughout. Both poles of this dialectic (which is to say, both ancients and moderns) obscure the world disclosed and illuminated by political action. Arendt's desire is to rescue at least the memory of the public world (and the action within it) from a philosophically induced oblivion. Escaping this dialectic, however, is no easy task; the stubborn persistence of the antipolitical metaphorics instituted by Plato and (to a lesser degree) Aristotle conspires with modern "world alienation" to make this world seem infinitely remote. In order to "recover" this world, and in order for action, freedom, judgment, and plurality to be thought *politically*, a peculiar strategy is required, one that makes possible a return to "the things themselves" prior to their distortion by the contemplative tradition.

Arendt facilitates this "return to the origin" by adopting the double Heideggerian strategy of deconstruction (*Abbau*) and repetition sketched in the Introduction to Heidegger's *Being and Time*. Her goal is to reveal the phenomenal core of the prephilosophic Greek experience of politics by dissolving the tradition's ontological prejudices (in favor of "true" Being) and by bracketing its translation of acting into the idiom of making.[1] The "negative" moment of this project closely parallels the "destruction of the history of ontology" announced, but deferred, in *Being and Time*. The "positive" moment, Arendt's construction of a phenomenology of action and the public realm on the basis of such originary experience, reflects fundamental ontology's attempt to delve behind a reified subject/object distinction in order to articulate the structure of our pretheoretical being-in-the-world.

The parallels between Arendt's project and Heidegger's thought go well beyond the question of "method," however. The thesis that serves as a point of departure for the present chapter is that Heidegger's ontological approach to the question of human freedom effects a radical shift in paradigm, a shift that turns out to be absolutely central to the thinking of freedom as a "worldly, tangible reality."[2] It is true that Heidegger himself failed to seize the opportunity presented by his framing of freedom as a mode of being rather than as a property of the subject. We can view Arendt, however, as appropriating his existential-ontological approach, eliminating its residual subjectivism in the attempt to do justice to the phenomena of political freedom, action, and judgment. Thus, her theorization of action as nonsovereign disclosure proceeds by the appropriation of some of the most important themes of *Being and Time* and the so-called "middle" works. Among these are Heidegger's emphasis upon finitude, contingency, and worldliness as structural components of human freedom; his conception of human existence as disclosedness (*Erschlossenheit*) or unconcealment (*Unverborgenheit*); the distinction between authentic (*eigentlich*) and inauthentic (*uneigentlich*) disclosedness; and his view of the "there" or "Da" of *Dasein* as a space of disclosedness or "clearing" (*Lichtung*).

These themes are discussed in Sections II and III of this chapter, where I show how they inform Arendt's hierarchy of human activities, her conceptions of political freedom and action, and her ontology of the public realm. The continuities are deep but never simple; Arendt is no mere "disciple" of Heidegger.[3] Moreover, these thematic links reveal only the first, most obvious level of Arendt's appropriation of Heidegger. A second, more profound level of influence is revealed when we turn to her transposition of the Heideggerian dynamics of transcendence and everydayness from an existential to a political context (Chapter 5). I contend that Arendt's controversial depiction of the relations between the public and the private, freedom and necessity, meaning and instrumentality, and the political and the social, need to be understood as reflections of the peculiar and complex relationship Heidegger constructs between authenticity and everydayness, unconcealment and concealment. Much of what Arendt has to say on these matters—from her contrast of the "shining brightness" of the public sphere with the "darkness" of the household, to her indictment of *homo faber*'s tendency to universalize the means/end category, a tendency that undermines the possibility of genuine politics—flows from her acceptance of the Heideggerian polarity of transcendence and fallenness. Like Heidegger, she views our capacity for transcendence as manifest in "authentically disclosive" pursuits; also, like him, she sees this distinctively human capacity as undermined by a tendency to prefer the "necessity" or "tranquillity" of everyday life to the contingency of freedom. Hence, her insistence that the public realm is a genuine space of disclosure only when animated by a "fiercely agonal" or "revolutionary" spirit, an insistence that resonates with Heidegger's problematic notion of "resoluteness" (*Entschlossenheit*). Hence, also, her pessimism regarding those few "islands of freedom" that men succeed in creating amidst a sea of "automatic" processes. Arendt is haunted by a profoundly Heideggerian sense of the evanescence of all such "open spaces."[4]

Few would contest the notion that Arendt was influenced by Heidegger: her debt has often been noted, although often in quite vague terms. Specific consideration tends to occur in the course of assessing the liabilities, even "dangers," of her political theory: those aspects that seem most questionable are, predictably, traced back to Heidegger. Thus, for example, we find Martin Jay, Luc Ferry and Alain Renaut, and Richard Wolin all emphasizing what they see as the "decisionistic" or irrationalist elements of Arendt's "dramaturgical" account of action— elements they relate back to Heidegger.[5] This line of criticism resonates with Leo Strauss's characterization of Heidegger's "existentialism." Strauss claims that existentialism "begins . . . with the realization that as the ground of all objective, rational knowledge we discover an abyss. All truth, all meaning, is seen in the last analysis to have no support except man's freedom."[6] Insofar as Arendt follows Heidegger in making freedom the "abyss-like ground" of action, she seems committed to a similar repudiation of standards provided by Reason, Nature, or even discursive rationality (the various "permanencies" Strauss opposes to modern "historicism").[7] This repudiation, Jay tells us, leads to the suspension of "all instrumental and normative constraints" upon "autonomous" action, a suspension that culminates in the untenable glorification of action for the sake of action, *politique pour la politique*. In this regard, Jay does not hesitate to place the "existentialist" Arendt in the company of Alfred Bäumler, Ernst Jünger, and Carl Schmitt.[8]

I think the appeal to Heidegger as a way of establishing guilt by association is both interpretively dubious and intellectually lazy. Arendt can appear as "decisionistic" only if one brackets her critique of will in politics, her strictures against violence, and her strong endorsement of a doxastically based rationality. Nevertheless, the rationalist/liberal anxiety elicited by Arendt's advocacy of an autonomous politics and her emphasis upon the initiatory character of action underlines a fundamental issue. What the critics are responding to—albeit through a glass, darkly—is one of the central drives of Arendt's political theory: the desire to think political action and judgment without grounds.

The groundlessness of action and judgment—the absence of any "bannisters" or transcendent yardsticks that might tell us how to act and how to judge—is a theme that runs throughout Arendt's work. Emerging for the first time in her skeptical treatment of the "rights of man" in *OT*, this theme becomes explicit in her reflections upon the collapse of the tradition and the loss of authority in the modern age, and it provides the backdrop for her unfinished work on the nature of judgment. One can without exaggeration describe her political theory as an extended meditation upon the problem of action and judgment *after* metaphysics. Seen from this angle, the Arendtian "uprooting" of action and judgment reflects less an existentialist privileging of the deed than a profound hostility to the "authoritarian" idea that reason or theory can secure an extrapolitical ground for these activities. Arendt sees the desire for such a ground as the wish to be relieved of the "burden" of our freedom and the need to think and judge for ourselves.

The idea of a ground beyond the realm of human affairs provides what Reiner Schürmann has called the "backbone" of metaphysics.[9] It makes possible the articulation of first and practical philosophy, the latter defined by its derivative relation to the principles or standards uncovered by the former ("ontology" in the strict or traditional sense). It also makes possible the separation of knowing from doing and the reconstitution of the political relation as one of hierarchy or authority—of ruler and ruled distributed according to a principle of superior virtue, reason, or knowledge. Arendt views the historical phenomenon of authority in the West as coextensive with the inception and decline of metaphysics.[10] As she emphasizes in her essay "What Is Authority?" the deployment of a nonviolent, generally accepted form of coercion (of reason, truth, ability, etc.) is the sine qua non of authoritarian rule, and this deployment hinges upon the appeal to transcendent standards. Yet this appeal is paradoxical, since the "transcendent" rarely makes its appearance in anything so ready-to-hand as rules for human conduct. The mediation between "true Being" (the realm available to contemplation) and the realm of human affairs was effected by the Platonic turn to the fabrication experience, which provided both a handy set of metaphors for "rephrasing" action and an image of the real (*qua* "idea") that was suited to practical requirements.[11] The resulting institutionalization of the split between theory and practice is authoritative for the entire tradition, as is the reduction of action to an instrumentality by which the truths revealed by philosophy are applied to the political sphere. This instrumental or teleocratic conception of action is never really questioned by the Western tradition, which views action as "the practical effectuation of the philosophical."[12]

For Arendt, the collapse of the tradition means, simply, that recourse to such standards-setting "firsts" is no longer possible. The demise of authority—the withering of ultimate grounds for action—confronts us with the demand to rethink our concepts of freedom, action, and judgment, concepts decisively shaped by their metaphysical origin. To refuse this challenge is to fall back into a theoreticist bad faith, wherein one props up the old bannisters or sets about discovering new ones. Today, the desire to prolong our self-incurred tutelage (a tutelage consisting in the submission of action and judgment to "ultimate" standards) is matched by the bland assurance that liberal democracy never really relied upon metaphysical justification, and can easily be made to "swing free" of the foundationalist impulses that animate the tradition. This view, associated with Richard Rorty and the more recent work of John Rawls, contains the effects of metaphysics by identifying it with a certain type of foundationalist argumentation, a species of justification that one can simply dispense with as one would any other quaint anachronism.[13] The trouble with this view is that it ignores the extent to which the language we use to talk about politics has been preformed by our antipolitical (contemplative) tradition. Thus, "postmodern bourgeois liberalism" dispenses with the quest for grounds only to leave the network of inherited concepts more or less intact. The shallowness of this kind of antifoundationalism becomes clear in its affirmation of the status quo: "philosophy leaves everything as it is"—in this instance, the vocabulary and unthought prejudices of political theory.

Foundationalists and antifoundationalists alike thus fail to grasp the opportunity presented by the implosion of tradition. For Arendt, this event offers the chance to theorize action and judgment as autonomous activities, which are freed not only from the domination of extrapolitical ultimates but also from the alien metaphorics imposed long ago on the realm of human affairs by a hostile philosophical tradition. Any objective assessment of Arendt's uprooting of action and judgment must begin with acknowledgment of *this* context: the peculiar space brought into being by the closure of metaphysical rationality, a space in which the demise of higher ends leaves untouched the view of action as means and judgment as the application of "preconceived categories" or "customary rules."[14] This habitual view does not merely deprive the political realm of its intrinsic dignity, but it also deprives us of the privilege of acting and judging for ourselves.

II. THE ABYSS OF FREEDOM AND *DASEIN'S* DISCLOSEDNESS: THINKING FREEDOM IN ITS WORLDLINESS AND CONTINGENCY

Throughout her work Arendt emphasizes the difficulty we have in thinking of freedom as a worldly phenomenon, one manifest in plural action. The problem (to oversimplify) is that our tradition extends and perpetuates the Greek philosophical and early Christian prejudices against such freedom. Greek philosophy dismissed the freedom found in the political sphere through its assertion of the superiority of the *bios theoretikos* (the contemplative life); early Christianity compensated for the loss of a secure public world by relocating freedom to an interior realm.[15] Historically, the Platonic ideal of self-mastery combines with the Pauline discovery of an internally divided will in a way that enables what Arendt views as a strictly derivative phenomenon—the freedom of the will, *inner* freedom—to usurp the place of freedom as it was originally experienced, as a "worldly, tangible reality."[16] The Christian/philosophical identification of freedom with will obscures the phenomenal reality of worldly freedom, a development that has "fatal consequences" for political theory.[17]

Our virtual inability to think about the nonsovereign freedom of the political sphere leads Arendt to strongly reassert the Montesquieuian distinction between *philosophical* freedom (the freedom of the will) and *political* freedom (the freedom of a "plural We").[18] It also motivates her search for models of action that effectively convey freedom's phenomenality, spontaneity, and contingency. This effort—to think of freedom in its nonsovereign worldly form, as a "mode of being" rather than as a capacity of the subject[19]—is complicated not only by our habitual reduction of freedom to will but also by our embarrassment with the idea of there being an "absolute" beginning. Kant, the only philosopher to truly affirm a faculty of "spontaneous beginning," noted the paradox of such a capacity, one that apparently shatters the temporal continuum itself.[20] Confronted with the seeming arbitrariness of such freedom (the human equivalent of *creatio ex nihilio*), is it surprising that our tradition has preferred to "trust in necessity" rather than to purchase freedom at the price of contingency?[21]

The groundless nature of the freedom of action—the fact that an "*abyss* of nothingness . . . opens up before any deed that cannot be accounted for by a reliable chain of cause and effect and is inexplicable in Aristotelian categories of potentiality and actuality"—goes a long way toward explaining the philosophers' preference for necessity and substantialist recuperations of novelty.[22] Moreover, as Arendt notes in the last chapter of *The Life of the Mind*, the philosophers are not alone in their fall into bad faith on this issue. Surprisingly, even "men of action," those "who ought to be committed to freedom because of the very nature of their activity," quail before what Arendt calls "the abyss of spontaneity."[23] This bad faith on the part of men of action is most apparent in the recourse the revolutionaries of the eighteenth century had to the "device" contained in the foundation legends of the Occidental tradition; namely, the trick of "understanding the *new* as an improved restatement of the old."[24] Just as the idea of an "absolute beginning" has proved to be too much for the "professional thinkers," so too has the "revolutionary pathos of the absolutely new" proved to be too much for the "men of action."

Where, then, do we turn in order to find an affirmation of the groundless freedom of political action? How do we go about overcoming the network of prejudices that frame this freedom as either illusory or unbearable? For reasons outlined above, Kant provides little aid in this project. In *The Life of the Mind* Arendt notes that only John Duns Scotus, the thirteenth-century theologian, was "ready to pay the price of contingency for the gift of freedom," and in *The Human Condition* and "What Is Freedom?" she more famously gestures toward Augustine's conception of freedom in the *City of God*: ". . . freedom is conceived there not as an inner human disposition but as a character of human existence in the world."[25] Yet, it seems clear that neither Scotus's affirmation of contingency nor Augustine's conception of human natality ("because he is a beginning, man can begin") by themselves effect the paradigm shift presupposed by Arendt's theory of political action. The ontological approach to human freedom presumed by this theory, together with its focus on nonsovereignty and disclosure, point unequivocally toward Heidegger, and specifically toward *Being and Time*.

In what follows I will sketch the way Heidegger's existential-ontological approach to the "problem" of human freedom effects the paradigm shift Arendt's theory of political action demands. By thinking of freedom existentially and ontologically, Heidegger breaks fundamentally with the ground of the will, opening the way to the elucidation of freedom as a mode of being-in-the-world. This is a necessary, albeit insufficient, step toward the elucidation of freedom as a mode of being-*of*-the-world, which Arendt's political theory undertakes.[26]

•

In his 1936 lecture course on "Schelling's Treatise: 'On the Essence of Human Freedom'" (1809), Heidegger observes:

> With [the] question of free will—which in the end is wrongly put and thus not even a proper question—Schelling's treatise has nothing whatever in common. For in this treatise freedom is not a property of man, but rather the reverse: man is at best a property of freedom. Freedom is the comprehensive and pervasive dimension of being in whose ambiance man becomes man in the first place. This means: the essence of man is grounded in freedom.[27]

In this passage, Heidegger gives less a paraphrase of Schelling than a concise characterization of his own approach to the question of human freedom. And while (as Frederick Dallmayr points out) the Schelling course represents a transitional moment in Heidegger's thinking of freedom, an anticipation of the coming "turning," or *Kehre*, it sums up themes present in the 1930 essay "On the Essence of Truth" and the lecture course *Vom Wesen der menschlichen Freiheit* ("Of the Essence of Human Freedom") from the same year.[28] These texts are sustained by Heidegger's desire to get beyond the traditional identification of freedom with free will or choice, and to clarify an ontological conception of freedom as the ground of human existence.

Heidegger's approach may be summarized as follows. Convinced that the traditional approach to the question of freedom presumed an answer to the question "What is man?" Heidegger sought to shift attention away from the will (conceived as a unique kind of causality) to the more primordial phenomenon of human openness or comportment toward Being. Thus, in "On the Essence of Truth," Heidegger writes:

> Freedom is not merely what common sense is content to let pass under this name: the caprice, turning up occasionally in our choosing, of inclining in this or that direction. Freedom is not mere absence of constraint with respect to what we can or cannot do. Nor is it on the other hand mere readiness for what is required and

necessary (and so somehow a being). Prior to all this ("negative" and "positive" freedom), freedom is the engagement in the disclosure of being as such. Disclosed-ness itself is conserved in ek-sistent engagement, through which the openness of the open region, i.e., the "there" ["Da"], is what it is.[29]

Unpacking this disclosive, ontological conception of freedom, and showing how it affirms the dimensions of worldliness and contingency, demands that we turn to *Being and Time* (1927). It is in this work that Heidegger begins his radical questioning of the identification of freedom with will and a certain kind of cau-sality. The break with this "subjectivist" view of freedom prepares the way for a questioning of the traditional teleocratic or teleological concept of action: action as guided by reason (which posits a goal) and sustained by will.[30] Thinking of freedom in ontological as opposed to causal terms allows us to appreciate the truth of Arendt's claims that "action insofar as it is free is neither under the guidance of the intellect nor under the dictate of will"; that "action, to be free, must be free from motive on one side, from its intended goal as predictable effect on the other."[31] In other words, it is only after we make the turn indicated by Heidegger in *Being and Time* that we are able to appreciate the nonsovereign freedom of action in the realm of plurality *as freedom*.

Being and Time would seem, at first blush, an odd place to turn to for aid in grasping the freedom peculiar to political action. The heavy emphasis upon au-thenticity, being-toward-death, and the "call of conscience"—to say nothing of the attack upon the "public interpretation of the world" perpetuated by the "idle talk" of the "they"—have led many to view *Being and Time* as a supremely unpo-litical text.[32] Indeed, Arendt blasts the book in the 1947 essay "What Is *Existenz* Philosophy?" in which she argues that the Heideggerian "Self" (*Selbst*) is the latest and most grossly inflated incarnation of romantic subjectivity.[33] Yet eight years later, in the lecture "Concern with Politics in Recent European Philoso-phy," she abandons the shrill tone for a more balanced appraisal. Significantly, Arendt downplays the importance of the "Self" in Heidegger, emphasizing in-stead his concepts of historicity (*Geschichtlichkeit*) and world (*Welt*). The latter concept she sees as standing "at the center of his philosophy."[34] And while she had previously praised her teacher Karl Jaspers's focus on communication at the expense of Heidegger's "existential solipsism," she now points out the fatal short-comings of Jaspers' dialogical model (the "I/Thou" relation, she says, can never be extended to the "plural We" of politics—a criticism she will repeat in *LM*).[35] Arendt hints that a potentially more fruitful starting point for the phenomeno-logical investigation of the political realm is to be found in Heidegger's concept of "world."[36]

Heidegger's ontological treatment of freedom grows out of his concept of "world," specifically out of his characterization of human being in *Being and Time* as "Being-in-the-world."[37] Heidegger deployed this somewhat awkward locution for a number of reasons. First, he wanted to avoid the tendency to treat human being as something present-at-hand, as basically an animal with reason added. Thus, "Being-in-the-world" serves to distinguish the kind of being peculiar to humans—*existence*—from other modes: only human being is "Being-in-the-

world." Second, this formulation is intended to combat the ontological prejudices built into Cartesian epistemology and the representational problematic
stretching from Kant to Edmund Husserl.[38] Heidegger's fundamental critical
point is that the epistemological approach *begins* by taking the agent out of the
world, reifying what is essentially relational into a substance/subject, and oppos-
ing this entity to the world considered as thing or object realm. The result is that
we lose sight of the essentially situated (and essentially *involved*) character of
human being, creating a largely artificial distance through the imposition of a
spectatorial metaphorics. Third, and following from this, Heidegger wants to
question the assumption that our primary or original encounter with entities is of
a cognitive or theoretical nature. The Cartesian splitting up of the world into
subjects, on the one hand, and objects, on the other, gives a false priority to
knowing as a kind of encounter, and this leads to a dubious characterization of the
"nature" of man. For Heidegger, "knowing the world" is a derivative relation:
existence (that is, Being-in-the-world), not cognition, constitutes man's essential
being. As Heidegger famously puts it, "'the essence' of *Dasein* lies in its existence."[39]

Originally, Heidegger argues, we do not stand over against or out of the world
(as the Cartesian picture would have it), but always already find ourselves within
a world, alongside other entities and beings like ourselves. Moreover, the "world"
in which we find ourselves is no mere container into which we, and the sum of
things, have been dumped, as if into a bag. Nor is the "world" something extra,
a kind of superentity. Nor, finally, does it denote the range of entities that we are
not. Rather, "world" is "a characteristic of *Dasein* itself."[40] It is one of the fundamental existential structures (*existentialia*) that Heidegger claims is constitutive of
human being, or *Dasein* (literally, "there-being"). The "world" is a totality of
relations, not things, an encompassing network of instrumental—or what Heidegger calls "equipmental"—relationships.[41] We first encounter entities not as
things present-at-hand (*vorhanden*), but rather as equipment, in terms of their
function, their place in a network of "in-order-to" relations. This network, this
totality of equipmental relationships, is given to us pretheoretically, by the
"sight" peculiar to practical involvement (what Heidegger calls "circumspection").[42] The "world" is not originally "beheld," but is dwelled in. And it is
through this dwelling that we become familiar with the various functional contexts within which entities are what they are. Thus, to take Heidegger's famous
example from *Being and Time*, a hammer is what it is not because, *qua* thing, it
possesses certain properties, but rather because it fulfills certain functions within
the nexus of our pragmatic concerns. The hammer is "ready-to-hand" (*zuhanden*)
in the workshop: it is situated within a set of "in order to" relationships; namely,
those constitutive of building.[43] And these relationships, in turn, are given direction by *Dasein*'s existential concerns, which structure what Heidegger calls the
"totality of involvements."

Our pretheoretical grasp of this totality provides the background understanding presupposed by all our activities and practices.[44] Thus, the "world" is a kind
of historicotranscendental condition for the possibility of meaning. It provides,
in Karsten Harries's phrase, a "space of intelligibility," the actuality of which we
consistently pass over in our everyday dealings.[45] It is only when the hammer

breaks that its inconspicuous being as equipment gives way to a confrontation with something present-at-hand as sheer object.[46] Moreover, it is only when equipment no longer functions that we become aware of the context of "in-order-to" relations. This context is pregiven by practical circumspection, yet "dimmed down": a "disturbance" is required for it to be "lit up," and, thereby, for the worldhood of the world to announce itself.[47] Otherwise, the horizon phenomenon of world, like the context of use itself, gets passed over in everyday "absorption" in our activities.

The "work world" (*Werke welt*) described by Heidegger, with its pervasive instrumentality and teleology (the "for the sake of"), clearly sets the pattern for Arendt's description of the "world" created and manipulated by *homo faber*. In contrast to Heidegger, Arendt emphasizes the durability of this world and the things in it, as opposed to its "transcendental" status as the set of background understandings and practices presupposed by our activities. Nevertheless, the similarity is striking; and, as we shall see, both Heidegger and Arendt juxtapose a certain kind of "authentic" activity and its "sight" or understanding to the everyday way of viewing the world manifest to *homo faber* or "absorbed" *Dasein*.

I have given a preliminary characterization of the "world" of Being-in-the-world. Following Heidegger, I turn now to the second component of this "structural totality," the entity that has being-in-the-world. Phenomenologically, the being of this entity—*Dasein*—is in fact "in each case mine." *Dasein* is not something present-at-hand: it is not a "what," but a "who."[48] And the answer to the question of the "who" of *Dasein* is always, as Heidegger says, "in terms of the 'I' itself, the 'subject,' the 'self.' The 'who' is what maintains itself as something identical throughout changes in its experiences and ways of behavior."[49] Yet this way of answering the question of "who is *Dasein*?"—while avoiding the temptation of treating *Dasein* "like any other entity" (namely, as a "what" or something present-at-hand)—nevertheless misleads us. It points us toward the "indubitable I" of Descartes, toward a subject which is who it is by virtue of its isolation. However, as Heidegger reminds us, "in clarifying Being-in-the-world we have shown that a bare subject without a world never 'is' proximally, nor is it ever given. And so in the end an isolated "I" without others is just as far from being proximally given."[50] The "others"—the knowability of which had been such a problem from Descartes to Husserl—"already are there with us": we are always already *with* others, just as we are always alongside entities. Considered from the perspective of the "who" of *Dasein*, the world of Being-in-the-world is a "with world" (*Mitwelt*); "Being-in," according to Heidegger, is a "Being-with-others."[51] As beings-in-the-world, we are originally amongst others like ourselves (hence the Husserlian "problem" of intersubjectivity dissolves).

Arendt similarly eschews the tendency to substantialize human being into a "what," or to see "human nature" as an appropriate response to the attempt to characterize human existence.[52] If "the 'essence' of *Dasein* lies in its existence," then something called "human nature" cannot be isolated without regard to the historical-existential conditions of human being. Rather, what is called for is the phenomenological description of the "worldly" conditions under which existence is given to human beings, and the delineation of the existential structures and capacities of the "who" so enabled. The point, crucial for Arendt and for Heidegger, is that the *conditions* of human existence might change so radically (whether as a result of technology or totalitarianism) that capacities which were previously viewed as intrinsic, as "part of human nature," disappear.[53] In addition to subscribing to what is pejoratively described as Heidegger's "historicism" on this score, Arendt presses his suggestion that the world of *Dasein* is a "with world" further than he did himself. Transformed into the notion of "plurality," *the* condition of political action, Arendt takes the Heideggerian notion of "co-being" in a radically un-Heideggerian direction.[54]

The third structural component of Being-in-the-world is the relation of "Being-in" itself, a relation that, in Heidegger's lingo, is "equiprimordial" with "world" and *Dasein*. Actually, it is in terms of this relation that the polarities "world" and *Dasein* appear as such. As Heidegger puts it, "Being-in is not a characteristic that is effected, or even just elicited, in a present-at-hand subject by the 'world's' Being-present-at-hand; Being-in is rather an essential kind of Being of this entity itself."[55] Heidegger moves quickly to avoid the misunderstanding that "Being-in" simply refers to the "*commercium* that is present-at-hand *between* a subject present-at-hand and an Object present-at-hand."[56] Closer to the truth would be to say that "*Dasein* is the Being of this 'between'"—a nothingness, gap, or in-between that resides in the space opened by its world.[57]

The "Being-in" of Being-in-the-world thus gives to *Dasein*'s existence the character of a "there": "The entity which is essentially constituted by Being-in-the-world *is* itself in every case its 'there.'"[58] By Being-in the world in a concerned way, by the fact of its existential care for its own Being, *Dasein* "clears" or opens a world, a space of significance, a "there." Moreover, it is precisely as this "there"—as a particular, historical way of Being-in-the-world—that *Dasein* has its fundamental character, its "there-being" (*Da-sein*). As "there," *Dasein* is not closed off, an enspirited substance that must somehow establish links to the "external world." The "there-being" of *Dasein* is an *open* structure, a mode of being at odds with the bundle of prejudices we have inherited from substantialist metaphysics.[59] *Dasein* as Being-in is not simply open; it *is* this openness:

> When we talk in an ontically figurative way of the *lumen naturale* in man, we have in mind nothing other than the existential-ontological structure of this entity, that it *is* in such a way as to be its "there." To say that it is "illuminated" means that *as* Being-in-the-world it is cleared in itself, not through any other entity, but in such a way that it *is* itself the clearing. Only for an entity which is existentially cleared in this way does that which is present-at-hand become accessible in the light or hidden in the dark. By its very nature, *Dasein* brings its "there" along with it. If it lacks its "there," it is not factically the entity which is essentially *Dasein*; indeed, it is not this entity at all. *Dasein is its disclosedness.*[60]

At this point Heidegger's basic description of human existence as Being-in-the-world takes on a more specific character. Anticipating a bit, we can say that the notion that *Dasein* is its "there," or disclosedness, captures, for Heidegger, the general nature of man's relation to Being. As "there-being," *Dasein* possesses, through its practices and involvements, a pretheoretical understanding of the world; and this understanding—presupposed by all subject/object relations—in turn presupposes an unthematized (preontological) comprehension of Being. The practices and beliefs of every culture—whether ancient Greek, Aztec, or modern European—are built upon such precomprehensions, understandings of Being that find expression in the various "worlds" these cultures create and inhabit. That the understandings or disclosures of Being which animate these cultures are different—that Greek *existenz* expressed a comprehension of Being different from that of the Aztecs or ourselves—is hardly a controversial thesis. Moreover, it helps to explain what, in *Being and Time*'s existential analytic, remains somewhat unclear. Heidegger is maintaining that human existence, at its most fundamental level, is nothing other than the "disclosure of Being," the opening of a particular economy of presence, accomplished by specific historical ways of Being-in-the-world.

This view of human existence has a number of consequences. First, as the "Da" of *Dasein* implies, every clearing or disclosure of Being is, by its very nature, partial, finite. There can be no such thing as a full or final disclosure of Being, since Being itself is nothing other than the series of "theres"—particular historical economies of presence and absence—opened or "cleared" by *Dasein*. Hence Heidegger's well-known (and often misunderstood) statement in *Being and Time* that "only as long as *Dasein is* (that is, only as long as an understanding of Being is ontically possible) 'is there' Being."[61] "Being" is neither a "super thing" nor a self-subsistent ground of presence; least of all is it (as some commentators have claimed) a kind of metasubject.[62] When Heidegger speaks of Being, he is (as he constantly reminds us) speaking of something *different* from entities: he is speaking of the presencing process manifest in this series of "theres," or clearings (which, for our purposes, may be identified with the complex network of beliefs and practices we call "cultures").[63]

Second, the description of *Dasein* as its disclosedness means that human existence has the basic character of "uncovering" or discovering, in the double sense of "creating a clearing for Being" (a "there") *and* bringing new "entities" (things, discourses, cultural achievements from art to political forms) to stand within it. As Heidegger puts it in Section 44 of *Being and Time*, "uncovering is a way of Being for Being-in-the-world . . . disclosedness is that basic character of *Dasein* according to which it *is* its 'there.'"[64] As the rest of this section (and much of Heidegger's subsequent work) clarifies, disclosedness is to be understood in contrast to the trope of correspondence upon which traditional theories of truth and definitions of man (as *animal rationale*) are based. As disclosedness, *Dasein* does not bring itself into accord with truth; rather, thanks to its preontological comprehension of Being, *Dasein* is always already "in the truth."[65] Moreover, it is this "primordial" phenomenon of "truth" at the level of clearing that makes the truth of assertion—and particular knowledge discourses—possible.[66]

The third and final consequence of the notion that *Dasein* is its disclosedness (the "clearing" of the "there") is that all attempts to achieve a full, final, complete disclosure of Being—to get behind the obscuring web of appearances, to get in touch with something "larger and stronger" than ourselves (Rorty)—are doomed to failure. None of man's cognitive, moral, or aesthetic vocabularies can claim to be "right" or "correct" by virtue of their correspondence to a Nature, a human essence, or a beauty beyond the ontologically constitutive presuppositions of human practice. The effort to achieve such a full or final disclosure is (to stick with Heidegger's preferred metaphor) tantamount to dragging the forest into the clearing. Since every "open region" or clearing presupposes a surrounding darkness—a more primordial realm of unconcealment or hiddenness—all disclosure is necessarily partial.[67] There can no more be a "correct" science or "correct" political theory than there can be a "correct" art, since the notion of "correctness" (*orthotes*) hinges upon the availability of an unsituated perspective, a realm of full or enduring presence available to human reason (hence the traditional definition of truth as *adequatio intellectus et rei*).[68] Of course, the fact that one cannot speak of "correctness" at a level of vocabularies (what would it mean, for example, to call the vocabulary of representative democracy "correct" or "true"?) does not mean that one cannot make judgments about it; it is just that these judgments are shaped by our hermeneutic situation, rather than delivered *sub specie aeternitatis*.[69]

Heidegger's characterization of *Dasein* as its disclosedness, and the consequences this characterization has for how we view human freedom, are further clarified if we turn to his discussion of *Dasein* as an open structure of possibility or "thrown projection" (Sections 31 and 44 of *BT*). The description of *Dasein* as Being-in or the Being of the "there" provides the basis for Heidegger's polemic against a substantialist interpretation of selfhood, a polemic that crescendos in the declaration that *Dasein* is the Being of the "between" (Section 28). What precisely Heidegger means by this formulation is elucidated in Section 31 of *Being and Time*, where we learn that *Dasein*'s originary disclosedness—its having a "world"—is accomplished by a projective understanding that "clears" the world, and orients itself within the horizon of significance, in terms of *Dasein*'s existential possibilities or "potentiality for Being."

> The kind of Being which *Dasein* has, as potentiality-for-Being, lies existentially in understanding. *Dasein* is not something present-at-hand which possesses its competence for something by way of an extra; it is primarily Being-possible. *Dasein* is in every case what it can be, and in the way in which it is its possibility. This Being-possible . . . is essential for *Dasein*. . . . Possibility as an *existentiale* is the most primordial and ultimate positive way in which *Dasein* is characterized ontologically.[70]

As its disclosedness, then, *Dasein* is a projective structure of understanding, an open structure of possibility.[71] And as possibility or structure of projection "ahead of itself," *Dasein* is not a something, but a *nothing*: the *place* where beings disclose themselves in light of *Dasein*'s care or concern for its own Being. In "What Is Metaphysics?"—his inaugural lecture at Freiburg University (1929)—Heidegger draws attention to how this projective structure forms the basis of *Dasein*'s *onto-logical* freedom: "Holding itself out into the nothing, *Dasein* is in each case already beyond beings as a whole. This being beyond beings we call 'transcendence.' If in the ground of its essence *Dasein* were not transcending . . . then it could never be related to beings nor even to itself."[72] Which is to say (to return to Section 31) that *possibility*, considered as a fundamental existential structure, or *existentiale*, "does not signify a free-floating potentiality-for-Being in the sense of the 'liberty of indifference' (*libertas indifferentiae*)."[73] Rather, it signifies the mode of Being-free (*Freisein*) that comes from being "thrown" into a definite range of possibilities, which *Dasein* can recognize as constitutive of its "ownmost" Being or which it can externalize as ontic alternatives awaiting its choice.[74] For Heidegger, the important point is that freedom as a mode of Being—as thrown projection—makes the *liberum arbitrium* (the will as faculty of choice or decision) possible.[75]

So, what kind of freedom is Heidegger talking about when he moves from the "nothingness" or transcendence of *Dasein*'s "Being-possible" to what he calls *Dasein*'s "ownmost potentiality-for-Being"? If this freedom is not a "liberty of indifference," is it, perhaps, a form of *positive* freedom—a freedom *for* the mode of Being that would be *authentic* ("ownmost") for *Dasein*?

Heidegger's language, especially in *Being and Time*, tends to promote such a misinterpretation. However, we must bear in mind the assertion he makes in "On the Essence of Truth," cited above. The kind of freedom Heidegger is pointing to is neither "mere absence of constraint" nor "readiness for what is required and necessary" (an "ought" or duty); it is, rather, a freedom *prior to* negative and positive freedom, a freedom that is the condition of possibility for both. *This* freedom—the ontological freedom of the being whose Being is thrown projection—is the freedom of the "open region," the freedom found in the "engagement in the disclosure of beings as such."[76] It is the freedom of disclosedness; the freedom of an "open comportment" toward the world that both animals and things lack, and that the will (our organ of choice or purposiveness) covers over; it is the freedom of the "there," a freedom *for* the world.

As the thrown projection of possibilities, *Dasein*'s disclosedness, its Being-in-the-world, is essentially care (Section 41 of *BT*). According to Heidegger, this "primordial structural totality" has three moments: thrownness (*Geworfenheit*), projection (*Entwerfen*), and fallenness (*Verfallenheit*). I have discussed *Dasein*'s projection with regard to its Being as possibility; before turning to Heidegger's central distinction between authentic and inauthentic disclosedness, I should like to discuss thrownness and fallenness.

The notion of "thrownness" is deployed by Heidegger to emphasize the "already-being-in-the-world," which is constitutive of *Dasein*'s projection and disclosedness. *Dasein* "finds itself" (*sich befindet*) within a world; it is "already in a definite world and alongside a definite range of definite entities within-the-world."[77] Disclosedness always occurs within a world whose conditions of constitution *Dasein* does not control. The range of possibilities open to it is finite in the sense that the outermost horizon of possibility is historically and culturally pregiven. Thus, when Heidegger says that "disclosedness is essentially factical," he is underlining the *conditioned* nature of *Dasein's* Being as possibility, as projection.[78] Facticity—that which confronts us as thrown beings-in-the-world—is not something separate that can be overcome or eradicated via a Fichtean assertion of will; nor is it something that *inhibits Dasein's* projection of possibilities. Rather, it is that in terms of which such projection becomes possible.

This emphasis on thrownness as a structural characteristic of *Dasein* is frequently overlooked in the attempt to portray Heidegger as the inheritor of the German idealist "philosophy of freedom."[79] A genealogical line is drawn from the radical conception of freedom in the second *Critique*, through Johann Fichte and Friedrich Schelling, down to Nietzsche and, finally, Heidegger. What prompts this "voluntaristic" reading of *Being and Time* is the mistaken view that the repudiation of the idea of "human nature" somehow implies the removal of any and all constraints: Heidegger's dictum "higher than actuality stands *possibility*" takes on Faustian overtones.[80] In fact, Heidegger's questioning of the assumption that "man has a nature or essence in the same sense as other things" (Arendt) promotes a renewed appreciation of human finitude.[81] The initial modern response to the demise of Nature as a teleological order of Being may have been to cross what Arendt calls the "rainbow bridge of concepts" to a radically unsituated concept of human freedom and the myth of total human self-creation; however, if *Being and Time* stands for nothing else in the history of modern philosophy, it definitively repudiates this Cartesian-Kantian-idealist heritage.[82] Fundamental ontology highlights our worldly or conditioned character in a philosophically unprecedented way, a point not lost upon Arendt, who begins *The Human Condition* by questioning the concept of human nature and stressing the conditioned character of human existence:

> Whatever touches or enters into a sustained relationship with human life immediately assumes the character of a condition of human existence. This is why men, no matter what they do, are always conditioned beings. Whatever enters the human world of its own accord or is drawn into it by human effort becomes part of the human condition. The impact of the world's reality is felt and received as a conditioning force. . . . because human existence is a conditioned existence, it would be impossible without things, and things would be a heap of unrelated articles, a *nonworld*, if they were not the conditioners of human existence.[83]

Heidegger's description of the disclosedness of *Dasein* as thrown projection thus implies a continuing taking up or creative appropriation of possibilities that are "given" to us, but unrealized as possibilities. As disclosedness, *Dasein* is constantly at work bringing new "entities"—vocabularies, practices, beliefs—to light within the clearing. However—and here we encounter one of the most important themes of *Being and Time*—*Dasein* has a built-in tendency to "forget" its disclosive or projective character. In its "everydayness," *Dasein* is "absorbed" or "fascinated" by the world; that is, by the things, people, and concerns it encounters daily. This tendency is especially manifest in what Heidegger calls "the public interpretation of the world," an interpretation embodied in "idle talk, curiosity, and ambiguity" (Sections 35–37). These modes express the understanding or disclosedness peculiar to the "they," to the self that has been thrown into "publicness."[84]

The problem with "publicness"—the reason why Heidegger devotes so much energy decrying it—is that it conveys an "average intelligibility" which is ready-to-hand and available to all. This intelligibility—a kind of degenerate form of what Arendt has in mind with the Kantian notion of a *sensus communis*—creates the impression that the disclosure or openness embodied by our everyday practices constitutes a full, adequate, and complete grasp of existence. It creates the impression that things could not be otherwise than they are, that there is nothing else to disclose. Practices and understandings that are in fact contingent take on the appearance of naturalness; the given and, as it were, accomplished way of Being-in-the-world is reified. It is this reification of a current set of practices that Heidegger has in mind when he speaks of our "fallenness" or our being "lost in the world." Through this reification, the truth of *Dasein* becomes untruth: a *partial* illumination is mistaken for a full one, with the result that our disclosive character falls into oblivion. *This* forgetting, Heidegger points out, is tremendously reassuring: it provides an escape from a finitude and contingency that are otherwise overwhelming; it subjects the unknown and uncontrollable possible to the domination of the actual:

> . . . the way in which things have been publicly interpreted . . . holds *Dasein* fast in its fallenness. Idle talk and ambiguity, having seen everything, having understood everything, develop the supposition that *Dasein*'s disclosedness, which is so available and so prevalent, can guarantee to *Dasein* that all the possibilities of its Being will be secure, genuine, and full. Through the self-certainty and decidedness of the "they," it gets spread abroad increasingly that there is no need of authentic understanding or the state of mind that goes with it. The supposition of the "they," that one is leading and sustaining a full and genuine "life," brings *Dasein* a *tranquillity*, for which everything is "in the best of order" and all doors are open. Falling Being-in-the-world, which tempts itself, is at the same time *tranquillizing*.[85]

In reading Heidegger's descriptions of fallenness, it is of the utmost importance to remember two points. First, "falling" is *not* a "bad and deplorable ontical property of which . . . more advanced stages of human culture might be able to rid themselves"; it is, rather, "a definite existential characteristic of *Dasein* itself."[86] "Falling" is "the basic kind of Being which belongs to everydayness" and, as such, is not something that can gradually be eliminated or left behind.[87] This is crucial for the understanding of Heidegger's idea of "authentic" *existenz*: we are dealing here not with a binary opposition, but a kind of dialectic, a dialectic of transcendence and everydayness. As Heidegger himself warns us, "*authentic* existence is not something which floats above falling everydayness; existentially, it is only a modified way in which such everydayness is seized upon."[88] In many respects, this qualification is what makes Arendt's positive appropriation of Heidegger possible.

Secondly, we must not lose sight of the fact that fallen Being-in-the-world is itself a kind of disclosedness. In Heidegger, there can be no opposition between a Being-in-the-world that discloses and one that does not: after all, *Dasein* is its disclosedness. The opposition or tension that Heidegger develops with his distinction between authentic (*eigentlich*) and inauthentic (*uneigentlich*) existence is between a disclosedness that grasps itself as such and a disclosedness that forgets itself, which views itself as something *vorhanden*. Thus, when Heidegger says in "On the Essence of Truth" that "every mode of human comportment is in its own way open," he is stating the obvious (a point he later drives home in "The Question Concerning Technology," where even technological "enframing" is presented as a "mode of revealing").[89] This does not, however, prevent some modes of comportment (and some preontological comprehensions of Being) from being more open than others. The hallmarks of an "inauthentic" understanding of Being—the kind of understanding possessed by "fallen" *Dasein*—are its passing over of the "world" as horizon phenomenon, its forgetting of the projective character of the self, and its hypostatization of the "open" or clearing as (in Wittgenstein's phrase) "everything which is the case."

This thought is perhaps made clearer if, borrowing from Thomas Kuhn, we identify inauthentic understanding with a specific vocabulary or practice. The Kuhnian equivalent of inauthenticity is an established "normal science" that has utterly forgotten its "revolutionary" origins, to the point of forgetting its own historicity and losing the ability to conceive a shift in paradigm.[90] When any vocabulary, practice, or space of disclosure becomes this rigidified, it begins to conceal more than it reveals. The "truth" of its mode of comportment becomes "untruth":

> That which has been uncovered and disclosed stands in a mode in which it has been disguised and closed off by idle talk, curiosity, and ambiguity. Being towards entities has not been extinguished, but it has been uprooted. Entities have not been completely hidden; they are precisely the sort of thing that has been uncovered, but at the same time they have been disguised. They show themselves, but in the mode of semblance. Likewise what has formerly been uncovered sinks back again, hidden and disguised. *Because Dasein is essentially falling, its state of Being is such that it is in "untruth."*[91]

How, if at all, is it possible to prevent this seemingly inevitable movement by which "truth" passes over into "untruth," by which disclosure becomes concealment? To some extent, this movement *is* inevitable, an inescapable process of reification by which the revolutionary becomes everyday, poetry becomes prose. Yet within this "proximally and for the most part fallen" existence, Heidegger holds out the possibility of a different *kind* of comportment, a different *mode* of disclosedness. And this mode—authentic existence—sets the pattern for Arendt's idea of political action as nonsovereign disclosure.

III. HEIDEGGER'S DISTINCTION BETWEEN AUTHENTIC AND
INAUTHENTIC DISCLOSEDNESS AND
ARENDT'S APPROPRIATION

I now want to examine Heidegger's articulation of *Dasein*'s disclosedness in terms of the *Eigentlichkeit/Uneigentlichkeit* distinction. This distinction frames the relationship between the kinds of activity and understanding that are genuinely disclosive, and those that are not. It expresses the peculiar dynamic Heidegger sees between our transcendence and our everydayness, a dynamic in which an authentic striving to disclose or uncover is juxtaposed to our tendency to seek out the security of the "ground" of the everyday. Heidegger's identification of the everyday with publicness (*Öffentlichkeit*) leads him to see the achievement of authentic disclosedness as contingent upon an inward turn: only the individual's confrontation with his own groundlessness or mortality is enough to shatter the tranquillity of the everyday. Arendt is obviously hostile to this turn to the self; yet this does not prevent her from appropriating Heidegger's general description of human existence and the distinction between authentic and inauthentic disclosedness. Arendt takes up this distinction, spatializing or externalizing it in such a way that the public realm—now the arena of agonistic politics—is seen as the proper venue for authentic disclosedness, the realm in which the "Da" of *Dasein* is illuminated. "Groundless freedom" is made manifest in political action, in a way that transforms the world into "a home for mortal man" (something it could never be for Heidegger, the philosopher of *Unheimlichkeit*, [uncanniness, or the sense of not being at home]).

According to Heidegger, the world in which fallen everyday *Dasein* finds itself is the world of work or daily preoccupation. "Proximally and for the most part," *Dasein* is absorbed in its environment (*Umvelt*), encountering things and others through the "sight" or understanding provided by practical circumspection and concern. Such a world is "dimmed down": the preoccupied self, engaged in productive comportment toward entities, sees only things that are "handy" for one purpose or another.[92] Absorbed in its daily routine, everyday *Dasein* passes over not only the world, but its "self." Indeed, *Dasein* is so deeply enmeshed in the objects of its concern that it universalizes the type of seeing, the mode of understanding, that guides it in the workplace: equipment "announces itself" as present-at-hand, while *Dasein* interprets itself and its mode of existence as something *vorhanden*. As we shall see, Heidegger views the metaphysical delimitation of the meaning of Being as "presence" as the result of Greek philosophy's naive universalization of the understanding of Being appropriate to the fabrication experience.[93] Against this naïveté, *Being and Time* insists upon the existential temporality of *Dasein* as the more primordial horizon within which every understanding of Being originates. The important point in the present context is that the universalization of productive comportment toward entities (a universalization characteristic of everyday *Dasein*) obscures our Being as disclosedness, as thrown projection. The result is that *Dasein*'s "ownmost potentiality for Being"—its capacity for making possibilities its own, for individuation—is dispersed in the "they" self.

For Heidegger, this fallen or inauthentic way of grasping ourselves and the world is a decline from a higher mode, one that (as Jacques Taminiaux puts it) is "adequately adjusted to the ownmost Being of *Dasein*."[94] In other words, there is a different kind of "sight," geared to a different mode of comportment or activity, one more genuinely expressive of our capacity for transcendence *qua* Being-in-the-world. Such understanding and activity is *authentically* disclosive; it is not undertaken for a variety of posited (limited) ends, but rather arises from *Dasein's* care for its own Being. As such, it is undertaken for its own sake. As Heidegger says, "*Das Dasein existiert umwillen seiner*" (*Dasein* exists for the sake of itself).[95] This mode of existence stands in tension with average everydayness, yet the two are related.

How, then, are we to understand "authentic disclosedness"? Assuming the "built-in" quality of *Dasein's* fallenness, what makes this kind of existence, this mode of activity and understanding, possible?

It is all too easy to lose the thread of Heidegger's argument, particularly if we fall back upon existentialist clichés (what Theodor Adorno called the "jargon of authenticity"). Heidegger's foremost desire is to indicate a way of Being-in-the-world that does not settle into the security and familiarity of the everyday world, the world in which "everything is 'in the best of order' and all doors are open." Authentic disclosedness, unlike its inauthentic counterpart, objectifies neither its self nor its world: it maintains a sense of the fluidity of the possibilities available to it, while grasping its own situated character. An authentic understanding is one that resists the reification of the status quo into a "full disclosure" by actively pursuing its vocation as possibility, as the disclosing or uncovering of "entities." Authentic existence, in this sense, is nothing other than disclosedness that knows itself to be such; which eschews notions of correspondence or the idea that the world is "everything that is the case"; which recognizes its historicity and the futility of erecting "permanencies" or grounds for an existence that has none. Against such attempts, authentic *Dasein* strives to keep its horizon open, to prevent its "truth" from slipping into "untruth." Authentic disclosedness in this sense signifies a wresting or contentious relation to Being, a relation best conveyed by the notion of "creative appropriation." The "ethos" of authentic disclosedness is expressed by Heidegger in Section 44 of *Being and Time*, where, after describing the way "fallen" *Dasein* "disguises" what it has revealed (as given, or ready-to-hand), he states:

> It is therefore essential that *Dasein* should explicitly appropriate what has already been uncovered to defend it *against* semblance and disguise, and ensure itself of its uncoveredness again and again. . . . Truth (uncoveredness) is something that must always first be wrested from entities. Entities get snatched out of their hiddenness. The factical uncoveredness of anything is always, as it were, a kind of *robbery*.[96]

Only through such striving to disclose, a process Heidegger refers to as "making one's own," does *Dasein* fully realize its transcendence, its capacity for uncovering or disclosure, its Being as "discoveredness." Seen in this light, the distinction between authentic and inauthentic disclosedness provides us, first and foremost, with a hierarchical relation between reified (everyday) disclosedness and an unreified form that (potentially) prevents the "clearing" from "dimming down"; one that illuminates through its ability to uncover the new, through its creative or originary spontaneity. This configuration of genuine disclosedness and inauthentic understanding reformulates the relation between transcendence and everydayness. Authenticity "tears itself away" from the everyday; however, the "uncovering of anything new," according to Heidegger, "is never done on the basis of having something completely hidden, but takes its departure from uncoveredness in the mode of semblance."[97] Authentic disclosedness, in other words, neither removes itself from its "there" nor creates a world of its own; rather, it is a mode of activity and understanding that breathes new life into the familiar.

This point is frequently overlooked, usually in favor of the more familiar "existential" themes of Division II of Being and Time. Yet it is, perhaps, the central strand of Heidegger's thought, insofar as it represents his continuing attempt to think the relationship of man and Being.[98] Thus, in the 1936 essay on "The Origin of the Work of Art," Heidegger returns to the question of how the "clearing" is to be kept "open," of how the inevitable process of reification and "dimming down" is to be forestalled. In this essay, Heidegger turns away from authentic disclosedness as a kind of praxis to the ability of poiēsis and the artwork to "clear" a world and maintain a "strife" between the "world" and its primordial hiddenness (what he calls the "earth").[99] While the focus of the "striving" or "wresting" has shifted importantly—the agon of disclosure has ceased to be something intraworldly and has become more profoundly ontological—the central concern remains the same. The somewhat threatening talk of "creators" and "preservers" obscures this continuity, which is an expression of the desire to prevent culture from freezing over. In this desire—in his preference for the metaphorics of disclosing, uncovering, and revealing over those of correspondence or correctness—Heidegger overlaps not only with Nietzsche, but also with J. S. Mill (and, more recently, Richard Rorty).[100]

In turning to consider what makes authentic disclosedness possible, we confront those aspects of Heidegger's account most antipodal to Arendt. Yet even these more familiar "existential" facets of Heidegger are (as I shall argue below) taken up and transposed by Arendt in her appropriation of the Eigentlichkeit/ Uneigentlichkeit distinction. Thus, while Heidegger's "authentic self" signals a Kierkegaardian turn that Arendt deplores, his emphasis in Division II upon Dasein's groundlessness sets the stage for Arendt's conception of the nonsovereign freedom of the public realm. Moreover, while the Heideggerian category of "resoluteness" (Entschlossenheit) has overtones of willfulness (as his critics have been quick to point out), it also stands for the acceptance of nonsovereignty as the basic precondition for the exercise of human freedom.[101] Again, this is a lesson not lost upon Arendt.

For Heidegger, the possibility of authentic disclosedness hinges upon our capacity not simply to tear ourselves away from everydayness, but to affirm our thrownness or contingency. If authenticity means anything, it means a willingness to put oneself at risk in the opening of new possibilities, the willingness to abandon the security and tranquillity of the ground provided by everydayness. "Proximally and for the most part," we cover up the contingency of human existence, of "thrown projection," with the preoccupations of everyday life. However, intimations of this contingency (the groundlessness of the "there") are found, as Heidegger famously argues, in the phenomenon of anxiety (Section 40 of BT). With the onset of anxiety, the familiar and secure world of things slips away, and the nothingness that underlies it is revealed. Anxiety "takes away from Dasein the possibility of understanding itself, as it falls, in terms of its 'world' and the way things are publicly interpreted"; it "throws Dasein back upon that which it is anxious about—its authentic potentiality-for-Being-in-the-world."[102] In this manner, anxiety individualizes Dasein by bringing it "face to face with itself as Being-in-the-world"; which is to say that it reveals Dasein to itself as Being-possible, as (in Heidegger's phrase) a "Being-free-for."[103] Unable to get a hold on things, thrown back upon itself, anxious Dasein is unheimlich, not-at-home.

Insofar as anxiety confronts us with the nothingness of our Being-possible, it can either lead us "back to ourselves" or precipitate a flight away from our "ownmost Being." Thus, as Karsten Harries notes, "authenticity and inauthenticity have their ground in anxiety."[104] The experience of Unheimlichkeit (uncanniness) makes the familiarity and security of the "they" self all the more tempting. While anxiety can be said to shatter the tranquillity of fallen Dasein, it nevertheless heightens the desire to retreat to this inauthentic self and to a public interpretation of things that present possibilities as "secure, genuine, and full." Only the "silent call of conscience," according to Heidegger, calls us away from this self-forgetting world to care for our "ownmost" Being.[105]

What, then, does conscience demand? It demands, above all else, the acknowledgment of what Heidegger calls Dasein's "guilt."[106] With this theme, we arrive at the essential precondition of authentic disclosedness. "Guilt," in Heidegger's lexicon, does not denote moral imperfection or original sin. It signifies, rather, Dasein's facticity or thrownness, considered from the angle of our existential "ground." The basis of Dasein's existence (the horizon in terms of which it projects itself, the world in which it finds itself) is not in Dasein's power. Insofar as Dasein's existence can be said to have a ground, this ground does not have the character of a foundation.[107] There is no overcoming either the contingency of this ground or the fact that Dasein must nevertheless bear responsibility for it. Heidegger sums up the existential consequences of Dasein's thrownness or contingency thus: "In Being a basis—that is, in existing as thrown—Dasein constantly lags behind its possibilities. It is never existent before its basis, but only from it and as this basis. Thus, "Being-a-basis" means never to have power over one's ownmost Being from the ground up. This "not" belongs to the existential meaning of thrownness."[108] In other words, because "Dasein is not itself the basis of its Being" but, as thrown projection, the "Being of its Basis," Dasein "as such is guilty," without foundation.[109]

The intent of such formulations is to drive home the uncertainty and lack of security implicit in our finitude and our character as projecting beings. The acknowledgment of "guilt" equals *Dasein*'s recognition of its incapacity to ground itself; it is *Dasein*'s self-recognition as "groundless ground," or *Abgrund*. Negatively, such recognition reveals the futility of attempting to fix man a place in an "order of Being" or to identify a proper *telos*. Positively, it serves as an affirmation (on the existential level) of the ontological freedom of the "there." This freedom, it will be recalled, is prior to the will and essentially nonsovereign. The theme of *Dasein*'s "guilt" gives this ontological freedom—the freedom of *Dasein*'s original openness—an existential concreteness. Authentic *existenz* demands an abandonment of everyday preoccupation *and* foundational schemes, along with the affirmation of the finitude manifest in *Dasein*'s thrownness. It demands, in other words, an affirmation of the nonsovereign freedom made possible by the fact of human finitude.

This brings us to the role of resolve as "resoluteness" (*Entschlossenheit*) in Heidegger's thought. In Section 60 of *Being and Time*, resoluteness is presented as the authentic response to the call of conscience. *Dasein* can choose to submerge itself in the "lostness" of the "they," or it can resolutely take up its thrownness, be "ready" for anxiety, and accept the burden of its contingent, projective character. As "a distinctive mode of *Dasein*'s disclosedness," resoluteness implies a steadfast acknowledgment of "guilt"; it stands for "an openness to the uncertainty of human existence," a surrender "of all claims to something like a ground."[110] As the mode in which authentic disclosedness becomes actual, resoluteness entails concrete choices, commitments, and actions—in the world and with others—lest it fall back into an inauthentic solipsism:

> Resoluteness, as authentic *Being-one's-Self*, does not detach *Dasein* from its world, nor does it isolate it so that it becomes a free-floating 'I.' And how should it, when resoluteness as authentic disclosedness, is *authentically* nothing else than *Being-in-the-world*? Resoluteness brings the Self right into its current concernful Being-alongside what is ready-to-hand, and pushes it into a solicitous Being with Others.[111]

We see here how far Heidegger's idea of "authentic *Dasein*" is from Kierkegaard's "knight of faith."

Resoluteness, then, "is always the resoluteness of some factical *Dasein* at a particular time."[112] But, Heidegger asks, "on what basis does *Dasein* disclose itself in resoluteness? On what is it to resolve? *Only* the resolution itself can give the answer."[113] Heidegger's critics have seized upon this formulation and others like it in order to accuse him of holding a position indistinguishable from decisionism. Thus Leo Strauss, for example, see historicism as the "truth" of existentialism, and decisionism as the "truth" of historicism: "Existentialism appears in a great variety of guises but one will not be far wide of the mark if one defines it . . . as the view according to which all principles of understanding and action are *historical*, i.e., have no other ground than groundless human decision."[114] Richard Wolin, in his recent critique of Heidegger, claims that Strauss has identified "a crucial intellectual historical dynamic"; for "once the arbitrariness and contingency of human belief-structures has been demonstrated—and once traditional moral claims have been dissolved amid the eternal flux of historical emergence and passing away—"values" themselves become an arbitrary posit, and the only power that is capable of establishing them proves to be a *sovereign act of human will*."[115] With the unmasking of moral objectivism and the "naturalness" of traditional norms, the sole remaining basis for moral-political orientation appears to be "*decision ex nihilo*, a radical assertion of will."[116]

Since I argue that Arendt appropriates Heidegger's notion of authentic disclosedness, it is necessary to pause and consider the validity of this charge. As indicated above, I think the reading of *Being and Time* as voluntarist is dubious, largely because Heidegger is addressing an openness of comportment prior to will.[117] Nevertheless, in transposing this ontological point into existential terms, Heidegger certainly seems to stress sheer decision or the *will* to authenticity or resoluteness. Two points, however, serve to reveal the one-sidedness of Strauss's and Wolin's interpretation. First, insofar as BT emphasizes *Dasein's* historicity, it does in fact reveal our "values" as contingent. But what does this mean? Only that our moral horizons are *horizons*, informed by a complex intersection of traditions and beliefs, and by certain large-scale historical processes (secularization; the gradual growth of a "universalist" moral consciousness). *Dasein's* thrownness does not imply a *void*. The thesis that our moral horizons are historical in this broad sense implies a radical subjectivism *only* to those who have internalized the metaphysical/psychological need to *ground* moral vocabularies on some originary source of value. In Strauss's and Wolin's view, there *must* be some such grounding source; and if it is not Nature, God, or an unsituated Reason, then it must be (so the argument goes) human *will*: the willing subject provides the lost ground in a disenchanted world. Heidegger, however, does not frame resoluteness as the *source* of value; rather, he offers it as a response to the *weight* of judgment and action in a disenchanted world. The absence of pregiven measures (or "yardsticks," as Arendt calls them) focuses our attention on the *difficulty* of moral and political judgment, and upon our responsibility for our commitments.[118]

The second reason the "decisionism" charge will not hold true follows from the first. On Strauss's and Wolin's reading, authenticity, *qua* resoluteness, implies the radical devaluation of all socially encountered norms and values as "inauthentic": the authentic individual, in tearing himself away from everydayness, must, like Nietzsche's *Übermensch*, create his own set of values out of nothing. Yet this reading totally distorts what Heidegger means by "authentic disclosedness." *Dasein's* disclosedness, in its "authentic" mode, has the character of a "making one's own," not a *creatio ex nihilo*. To repeat what Heidegger says in Section 44, "The uncovering of anything new is never done on the basis of having something completely hidden, but takes its departure rather from uncoveredness in the mode of semblance."[119] In other words, authenticity in Heidegger's sense is a certain way of taking up what is given yet "dimmed down," the creative appropriation of contents and possibilities that are encountered *within* our lifeworld yet which have, in their codified, reified, or clichéd forms, ceased to signify. Hence, Heidegger's insistence that *Dasein* needs to "explicitly appropriate what has already been uncovered . . . assure itself of its uncoveredness again and again" lest vocabularies and practices sink to the level of thoughtless habit. Therefore, it is not a question of *dispensing* with what is given, but of trying to breathe life into it by taking it seriously, as something that one desires to make one's own.[120] After all, authentic existence is "not something that floats above falling everydayness; existentially, it is only a modified way in which such everydayness is seized upon."[121]

•

In turning to Arendt's appropriation of Heidegger's distinction between authentic and inauthentic disclosedness, I should underline the broad lines of continuity. First, Heidegger's ontological approach to human freedom (what I have called his "paradigm shift") clearly sets the stage for Arendt's own phenomenological account, in the double sense that it questions the priority of will and insists upon finitude, contingency, and worldliness as *structural* aspects of human freedom. Second, Heidegger's conception of existence as disclosedness provides Arendt with a postmetaphysical framework for considering the *vita activa*, one that abandons the teleological approach based on human nature and its ends in order to focus upon conditions, capacities, and the ability to create or disclose meaning.[122] Third and last, Heidegger's description of the nonsovereign freedom of the "there" prefigures Arendt's account of the transcendence peculiar to political action and the kind of freedom we encounter in the plural, public realm (itself a "space of disclosure").

These continuities serve to create something like a common problematic for Arendt and Heidegger, despite radical differences in emphasis and ultimate concern (the "meaning of Being," on the one hand, politics and the public realm, on the other). It is, however, Heidegger's articulation of the relation between authentic, open, or resolved activity and the preoccupied comportment of everydayness that really drives home the importance of fundamental ontology for Arendt's project. I wish to make two claims. First, I think that a full understanding of the distinction Arendt draws between the world of work and the activity of *homo faber* (on the one hand) and political action in the public realm (on the other) is possible only in light of Heidegger's distinction. The relation Arendt sets up reproduces—albeit in a very different context—the dynamic Heidegger poses between transcendence and everydayness in the existential analytic. The second claim follows from the first: the hierarchy implicit in the *Eigentlichkeit/Uneigentlichkeit* distinction sets the pattern for Arendt's hierarchy of human activities—not, to be sure, in terms of an order of ends (Aristotle), but rather in terms of relative disclosive or meaning-creative capacity.

Taken together, these two claims suggest that we view Arendt's theory of political action and her hierarchy of human activities as attempts to "spatialize" or externalize the very distinction that "regulates" Heidegger's entire project.[123] Yet this suggestion runs up against immediate objections. Is it plausible to suggest that Heidegger's distinction can be transposed from an existential to a political context, without doing great violence to the phenomena of politics? (Heidegger's own formulations during the thirties would seem to confirm this.) How coherent is it to "spatialize" the distinction between authentic and inauthentic disclosed-ness? After all, if "authentic disclosedness" is "only a modified way in which everydayness is seized upon"—if, in other words, it is not separated by an abyss from the "fallen" world of everydayness—then how is it possible to maintain that Heidegger's distinction informs Arendt's articulation of the relation between the world of work and the public realm?

We need to recall, first, that the world created by *homo faber* (what Arendt calls the "human artifice") is *not* a different world from that inhabited by human be-ings *qua* political actors. The world created by work and the world "illuminated" by action are the *same* world, notwithstanding Arendt's insistence that these activities occupy quite different places *within* the world.[124] For Arendt, the world-liness of human existence first becomes manifest in the activity of work—man as *animal laborans* being a specifically worldless creature.[125] To be sure, labor also takes place "in the world"; however, the harder the forces of nature, necessity, and life press upon us, the more the world "de-worlds" itself. In Arendt's view, labor is a mode of activity so driven by the needs of life that it sinks below the horizon of instrumentality. As laboring beings we are, so to speak, prior to preoc-cupation; we are absorbed not by the world, but by ourselves, by our sheer bodily existence.[126] Thus, while labor clearly presupposes a particular kind of "sight," Arendt's analysis implies that this sight is not really disclosive: what it reveals is not so much a world as an *environment*. For this reason, labor does not distinguish us from animals so much as link us to them. As Arendt writes, "The *animal laborans* is indeed only one, at best the highest, of the animal species which populate the earth."[127]

If labor, in this sense, is predisclosive, the same cannot be said of work. Ac-cording to Arendt, it is precisely the activity of work that gives us a world, an artificial, durable "home" that removes us somewhat from the immediacy of the natural and destructive cycle of production and consumption.[128] This world, the world of *homo faber*, is a more or less stable structure whose being consists in its reified quality and whose meaning is circumscribed in terms of instrumentality.[129] The world of *homo faber* is in essence a reification, because work creates a realm of objects that outlasts consumer goods and individual life span. This realm of objects *is* a world, and not just a heap of unrelated articles, insofar as it is entirely framed in terms of the category of means and end.[130] Utility, in other words, provides the horizon of vision or understanding for *homo faber*, who negotiates his world as a totality of "in order to" relations posited in accordance with the stan-dard of usefulness.

Arendt's analysis is quite close to Heidegger here: they both view the "work world" as our everyday form of worldliness. And, despite her emphasis upon the objective or reified quality of this world, Arendt more or less accepts the Hei-deggerian description of it as a totality of equipmental relations. This is made plain by her adoption of his vocabulary of the "in order to" (*das Um-zu*) and the "for the sake of" (*das Worumwillen*) to convey the understanding characteristic of *homo faber*'s productive comportment. Following Heidegger, Arendt argues that *homo faber*'s productive approach to the world necessarily discloses the world as a series of "in order to" relations structured according to the criterion of utility. Moreover, she argues that this particular "ontological precomprehension" is so pervasive—so absorbing or totalizing—that meaning itself is grasped in terms of utility.[131] Because *homo faber* "judges and does everything in terms of 'in order to,'" the place of the "for the sake of which" is occupied by utility. Thus, as Arendt puts it, "the 'in order to' has become the content of the 'for the sake of.'"[132]

The result of this universalization of the productive comportment characteristic of *homo faber* is that the world is simultaneously disclosed and "dimmed down." Heidegger's claim that *Dasein's* everyday comportment toward entities disguises or covers over phenomena is echoed by Arendt's assertion that *homo faber* has "an innate incapacity to understand the distinction between utility and meaningfulness"; that "insofar as he is nothing but a fabricator and thinks in no terms but those of means and ends which arise directly out of his work activity, [*homo faber*] is just as incapable of understanding meaning as the *animal laborans* is incapable of understanding instrumentality."[133] This incapacity lies at the root of the conflation of meaning and utility referred to above, the practical effect of which is to rob the public world of inherent value, to reduce the realm of appearances to a collection of use objects for the sake of an "ultimate" end—namely, man.[134] Such a reduction, Arendt argues, is typical of *homo faber* and is exacerbated by the submersion of "the limited instrumentality of fabrication" in the life process itself. The result is a reification not in the sense of an objectification, but in the Heideggerian sense of an ontological one-dimensionalization: the "limitless instrumentalization of everything that is" levels the world down to a set of familiar contexts of use, one we encounter in our everydayness, yet one deprived of all revelatory capacity.[135]

This brings us to the possibility of transcending the world as *Zeug*, as equipment or use objects. For Heidegger, an "immanent" transcendence of this "dimmed down" world hinges upon the breaking away from concernful absorption and the recovery of a higher mode of sight and activity, one undertaken for its own sake. In Arendt, the possibility of transcendence is concertized through the entry into the public realm that, as "space of appearances," provides the site for authentically disclosive action and speech. The meaningfulness of such action and speech has nothing to do with utility or success; indeed, the illuminative or revelatory capacity of action springs from its ability to transcend these criteria. Thus, just as "authentic disclosedness" illuminates the world through a certain "wresting" or taking up of the everyday, so political action in the Arendtian sense places the world under a new and unexpected aspect. The result, if not exactly a "transfiguration of the commonplace," is something similar, for what political action does, according to Arendt, is to reveal or disclose an unsuspected meaningfulness at the heart of the familiar, public, and everyday world. It endows this world with a significance it otherwise lacks. As Arendt puts it, "the meaningfulness of everyday relationships is disclosed not in everyday life, but in rare deeds, just as the significance of a historical period shows itself in the few events that illuminate it."[136] What matters, in short, is the *event* of authentic disclosedness, an event that, in both Arendt and Heidegger, signifies a wrenching free of every-dayness and its illumination through the unpredictable uncovering of the new. Through such disclosive spontaneity, the world is revealed in its worldliness, the actor or *Dasein* (anonymous in his everydayness, *qua* laborer or producer) re-vealed in his individuality.[137]

This juxtaposition of Arendt and Heidegger in terms of the relation between everydayness and disclosedness, the world of work and political action, serves to highlight just how important the *Eigentlichkeit/Uneigentlichkeit* distinction is for Arendt. Moreover, it provides a new perspective on the agonistic public realm as theorized by Arendt. This "space of appearances," the site of the authentically disclosive activities of speech and action, is, potentially, the one place in the world where both the functionalism of life and the utility of work are tran-scended; where, in Heidegger's words, "the semblance and disguise that covers over phenomena in their everydayness is at last penetrated."[138] Arendt is ada-mant about the ability of political action to achieve this "penetrating" effect. As laborers we are preoccupied by the needs of life and subject to its rhythms; as producers we are absorbed by the imperative of usefulness, by the question of means and ends. It is only in tearing ourselves away from *these* preoccupations and entering the public realm—a true "space of disclosure"—that we manifest our disclosive capacity and become free for the world.

Heidegger's distinction clarifies Arendt's theory of political action in another respect. I mentioned how Arendt's rhetoric concerning the realms of freedom and necessity encourages us to view the "worlds" of action and work as absolutely separate, even though, strictly speaking, only the activity of labor is determined by necessity per se. This impression is reinforced by Arendt's insistence upon the self-containedness of action and the need for an autonomous public sphere. Hei-degger's distinction will appear discontinuous with Arendt's theory so long as we view her call for an "autonomous" politics as an attempt to seal off a zone of transcendence from the rest of the world. However, as the preceding reading indicates, the relation Arendt describes between the world of work (the "human artifice") and the public realm is more complex, complementary, and "Hei-deggerian." The central question for Arendt is whether the world built by *homo faber* provides a stage for authentically disclosive (revelatory) action, or remains simply the site of productive comportment. Thus, action concerns the world originally disclosed through work, the "subjective in-between" of words and deeds not taking leave of the world, but "overlaying" it.[139] This confirms the suggestion made in Chapter 1, that the relation between action and work, or what we would call the political and the social, is somewhat more permeable than it first appears. What seems an arbitrary and *a priori* demarcation of the political in terms of a hyper-idealized content pales beside the more important criteria of the kind of understanding, interaction, and spirit that permeates the public sphere. As theorized by Arendt, the public realm is first and foremost a space of disclosure, one not intended to detach action from the surrounding world, but rather to provide a space where (in Arendt's words) "the extraordinary becomes an ordinary occurrence of everyday life."[140]

These, then, are a few of the ways Heidegger's *Eigentlichkeit/Uneigentlichkeit* distinction informs Arendt's political theory, particularly her reappropriation of the Aristotelian distinction between *praxis* and *poiēsis*. Heidegger's distinction mediates Aristotle's, bracketing the latter's teleological apparatus in favor of the criterion of relative disclosedness. Thus, when Arendt takes up Aristotle's distinction between acting and making, she is in fact reformulating *praxis* as authentic *existenz*. This brings me to my second claim, namely, that Arendt's hierarchy of human activities reproduces the order Heidegger inscribes in the contrast between a preoccupied, everyday disclosedness and an open or "resolved" mode, one predicated upon the affirmation of contingency. According to Arendt, as laboring beings we can hardly be said to disclose at all, our world having the character of a "non-world" or environment.[141] As fabricators or producers, our disclosive capacity takes the form of the reification of things, an activity that, with the exception of works of art, is circumscribed by the dim light of the in-order-to.[142] It is only as actors in the public sphere that we are *genuinely* disclosive, of ourselves and of our world in its tangibility and durability—as a place of dwelling, a "home for mortal men."

While Heidegger's distinction importantly structures Arendt's political theory, we must not lose sight of the transformative nature of her appropriation. The characterization of *action* as our disclosive capacity par excellence, combined with the depiction of the public realm as a space of disclosure, serves to wrench Heidegger's "regulating" distinction away from the individualist, quasi-Kierkegaardian context of *Being and Time*. Eschewing Heidegger's residual subjectivism and his philosopher's distaste for the realm of human affairs, Arendt transforms his distinction by spatializing or externalizing it. Authentic disclosedness is identified with a particular worldly activity—political action—and this activity is seen as having a "proper location in the world," namely, the public sphere.[143] Arendt's conviction that each human activity has its "proper place" means that her hierarchy of human activities takes the form of a phenomenological topography of the *vita activa*. The ironic and supremely *un*-Heideggerian result is that authentic disclosedness is "localized" or domiciled in a realm of opinion and talk. As we have seen, Heidegger views this realm as irredeemably "fallen," and this precipitates his turn to the self (*Selbst*). Arendt, free of the philosophical prejudice against the realm of human affairs that motivates this retreat, sees Heidegger's strategy as futile and self-deluding. She opposes it with the same vehemence with which she opposes all romanticism, particularly the "politics of authenticity" invented by Rousseau.[144] Arendt combats the modern "flight from the world to the self" by asserting that individuation occurs in the context of plurality, through the performance of action in a "theatrical" public space. Nothing could be further from the Heideggerian identification of individuation with being-toward-death. Thus, in politicizing Heidegger's *Eigentlichkeit/Uneigentlichkeit* distinction, Arendt can be said to turn it inside out: the "proper" and the "improper," which Heidegger aligns with interiority and publicness, respectively, are transposed.[145]

An abyss, then, separates Arendt's celebration of disclosive political action in the public sphere from Heidegger's repudiation of the "public interpretation of the world." However, the vast difference between them concerning the "place" of authentic disclosedness should not lead us to assume—as some have—that Heidegger's "publicness" and Arendt's "public realm" have precisely the same referent.[146] In fact, as we shall see, there is much in Heidegger's critique of *Öffentlichkeit* (publicness)that Arendt endorses. Moreover, we should not assume that Arendt's appropriation of the *Eigentlichkeit/Uneigentlichkeit* distinction dispenses with all of the more well known themes of Division II. Generally speaking, Arendt avoids Heidegger's identification of authenticity with an affirmation of our mortality. Yet, as noted above, she retains his emphasis upon the "groundless" or "guilty" character of authentic disclosedness. Where Heidegger presents our "guilt" as an essentially *individual* phenomenon—as the lack of foundation confronted by thrown, mortal *Dasein*—Arendt once again "externalizes" this *existentiale*, emphasizing the intersubjective dimensions of *Dasein*'s thrownness. Our finitude or nonsovereignty is phenomenologically most apparent in the "futility, boundlessness, and unpredictability" of action in the public world. Our thrownness or contingency is highlighted when we initiate actions that change constellations in unforeseeable ways. Groundlessness, then, is concretely encountered in the realm of plurality, not the self. This is why Arendt identifies natality (the ontological condition of the actor *qua* beginner) and not mortality as "the central category of political, as opposed to metaphysical, thought."[147]

Arendt's reemphasis on plurality as constitutive of our thrownness and her relocation of "groundless" freedom to the public realm transform the role and nature of *Entschlossenheit* (resolve). It is true that Arendt nowhere employs the category of "resolve"; indeed, in her Heidegger critique in *Life of the Mind*, she eyes it suspiciously as a substitute for the will. Nevertheless, it is clear that the non-sovereign freedom of the public sphere requires something like *Entschlossenheit*, if only because the temptation to forgo this freedom—to retreat to the darkness of the private realm or to escape contingency through instrumental/strategic action—is so strong. The freedom of political action demands, first, the affirmation of plurality and contingency; second, it demands a commitment to a public way of Being-in-the-world. Not for nothing does Arendt insist that the entry into the public realm requires courage.[148] It is in the "fiercely agonal spirit" of the Greeks and the "revolutionary spirit" of the bourgeois revolutions, the original soviets, the Hungarian revolt, that we find the mixture of affirmation and commitment required of every new beginning. Without insisting upon too neat a parallel, it is possible to view the heroism of the nonsovereign political actor as a concrete, worldly form of *Entschlossenheit*, so long as we are careful not to identify "resolve" with "blind decision" or commitment for the sake of commitment (Sartrean *engagement*, of which Arendt was decidedly critical).[149]

Reading Arendt's theory of political action in this way raises two obvious objections. The first is that it is simply not coherent to "spatialize" Heidegger's distinction between authentic and inauthentic disclosedness: the attempt to "localize" either in terms of activity or place makes a hash of the distinction. The second objection is more categorical. It is that the structure of Heidegger's distinction, so completely framed in terms of individual *Dasein*, defies anything like a political appropriation. The only way to give Heidegger's distinction a political twist is to plug in the *Dasein* of a people for the resolved self, a substitution that politicizes "authenticity" in a patently totalitarian direction.[150]

In response to the first objection, it should be noted that Heidegger's early and middle work prepares us for just such a spatialization, prefiguring Arendt's identification of freedom with an open space of disclosure through a historicizing of the "there," or clearing. Thus, we find the "Da" of *Dasein* reformulated as a particular historical open space in Heidegger's *Introduction to Metaphysics* (1935) and "The Origin of the Work of Art" (1936). These works go so far as to identify the *polis* with the original or most primordial space of disclosure, the place where the world "worlds" itself.[151] The agon is also present, albeit in a highly speculative, undemocratic form, namely as the "striving" or "struggle" initiated by the "world-opening work" of the "creator." The result is the lamentable and peculiarly Heideggerian mix of an ontological conception of freedom with a metaphysical conception of the state. Following Plato and Hegel, Heidegger casts the state as fulfilling an essentially speculative function, as the place where Being is brought to presence.[152]

The issues raised by the second objection are more complex, centering on the alleged subjectivism of *Being and Time*. The more we view the *Eigentlichkeit/ Uneigentlichkeit* polarity as circumscribed by *Dasein*'s individual ("in each case mine") existence, the more odd the suggestion of a *political* appropriation appears, particularly one devoted to preserving the essential dimension of plurality. My claim that Arendt's distinction between action and work constitutes such an appropriation will appear less outlandish if, following Taminiaux's suggestion, we see Heidegger's distinction as itself a reappropriation (and transformation) of the Aristotelian distinction between *praxis* and *poiēsis*.[153] This perspective on the "regulating" distinction of *Being and Time* clarifies the hierarchy Heidegger draws between the sight and comportment peculiar to "preoccupied" *Dasein* and the higher mode (undertaken for its own sake) characteristic of authentic *existenz*.[154] Thus, despite the apparent "oblivion of *praxis*" in Heidegger's work, the case can be made that "authentic disclosedness" represents the early Heidegger's attempt to recuperate *praxis* as transcendence. This suggestion gains credence from a passage in *The Metaphysical Foundations of Logic*, the book derived from a lecture course Heidegger gave in Marburg in 1928. After noting the Greek philosophic propensity to identify transcendence with *theoria*, Heidegger observed, "Nevertheless, *Dasein* was known to antiquity also as authentic [*eigentliche*] action, as *praxis*."[155]

As Taminiaux notes, "The use of *eigentlich* to characterize Greek *praxis* is in itself extremely significant."[156] In the context of the present discussion, it provides a vital clue, one that not only illuminates Heidegger's project, but also enables us to see how, structurally speaking, Arendt could appropriate Heidegger's distinction for her own purposes—namely, an antiteleological reading of Aristotle's distinction between acting and making. Arendt positively appropriates Heidegger's emphasis upon a genuinely disclosive, wresting, and individuating "mode of comportment," upon a transcendence inherent in being-in-the-world. While going along with the gist of Heidegger's transformation of Aristotle, she strongly reasserts the plural, public, and doxastic dimensions of the original *against* him. Unlike Taminiaux, I do not think we can view this as a "return" to Aristotle on the part of Arendt. In addition to the reasons cited above, it is clear that Arendt follows Heidegger's lead in insisting upon the groundless and "end"-less quality of the freedom of action. She may quarrel, violently, with Heidegger's location of freedom as a "mode of being," wanting nothing to do with his turn to the self. Nevertheless, she sees in his articulation of transcendence and everydayness a path beyond teleology and will, a path of the greatest significance to post-metaphysical political theory.

Groundless Action, Groundless Judgment: Politics after Metaphysics

> Do we not smell anything yet of God's decomposition? Gods
> too decompose. God is dead. God remains dead. And we
> have killed him. How shall we, the murderers of
> all murderers, comfort ourselves?
>
> —*Nietzsche,* The Gay Science *#125*

> The pronouncement "God is dead" means: The supersensory world is with-
> out effective power. It bestows no life. Metaphysics, i.e., for Nietzsche
> Western philosophy understood as Platonism, is at an end.
>
> —*Heidegger, "The Word of Nietzsche"*[1]

> What has come to an end is the basic distinction between the sensory and
> the supersensory, together with the notion, at least as old as Parmenides, that
> whatever is not given to the senses—God or Being or the First Principles and
> Causes (*archai*) or the Ideas—is more real, more truthful, more meaningful
> than what appears, that it is not just *beyond* sense perception but *above*
> the world of the senses. What is "dead" is not only the localization
> of such "eternal truths" but also the distinction itself.
>
> —*Arendt, Introduction,* The Life of the Mind[2]

I. The Second Level of Appropriation: The Dialectic of Transcendence/Everydayness and Arendt's Ontology of the Public World

Many critics, including Hanna Pitkin and Sheldon Wolin, have charged Arendt with elitism. Adverse to what they view as the exclusionary dimension of Arendt's "Greek" theory of action, they stress its tension with the more popular impulses of (modern) participatory democracy.[3] Support for this critique may be found in the way Arendt's agonistic conception echoes Nietzsche's distinction between active and reactive agents (the "masterly" and "slavish," respectively).[4] Like Nietzsche, Arendt appears to draw a thick black line between the affirmative, robust creators of heroic values (on the one hand) and the unworldly, reactive naysayers (on the other). This creates the impression of a certain aristocratism. In championing agonistic action, Arendt appears to make authentic disclosure the prerogative of a *type*.

For some, the Heideggerian perspective I propose will simply confirm their suspicion that there is an antidemocratic bias at the heart of Arendt's apparently democratic political theory. It is quite easy to twist the *Eigentlichkeit/Uneigentlichkeit* distinction so that it reproduces Nietzsche's hierarchy: the authentically disclosive or creative individual appears as a higher "rank order" than the herdlike "they."[5] Indeed, Heidegger himself was not above recasting his distinction along vulgar Nietzschean lines.[6] Yet such an interpretation misleads us, and not only with respect to the nature of Heidegger's distinction. In confounding Arendt's hierarchy of activities with a hierarchy of types, this interpretation creates a fundamentally false picture of her political theory.

The hierarchy inscribed in the *Eigentlichkeit/Uneigentlichkeit* distinction refers to "modes of comportment" and understanding, *not* groups of agents. The distinction frames a dialectical relation between transcendence and everydayness, one that belies the Nietzschean idea of a "rank order." Most significantly, it presumes fallenness as a built-in tendency of *Dasein*. Viewed as a structural characteristic of existence, fallenness is not something that can be left behind or "overcome" (Heidegger's attempted *Überwindung* of Platonism/nihilism in the thirties notwithstanding).[7] The notion of fallenness highlights two of Heidegger's basic convictions: every mode of comportment is both open and closed; every revealing or disclosure is also a concealment. Bearing this in mind, fallenness denotes our tendency to give in to the "tranquilizing" understanding of everyday concern, a tendency that intensifies reification and causes us to lose sight of our original open or disclosive character (what Heidegger calls "the truth of Being").

The idea of fallenness, then, ties transcendence to everydayness while setting the distinction between authentic and inauthentic disclosedness into motion. "Fallenness" presents us with an everydayness that is not simply a static background, but rather an expansive, colonizing force, one that is presupposed by authenticity/transcendence but also threatens it. Thus, the idea of authentic disclosedness implies, on the one hand, an original (primordial) concealedness and a "world" or clearing that is relatively "dimmed down."[8] But it also implies a dialectic of transcendence and everydayness in which the reifying forces of security and daily preoccupation constantly threaten to transmute the openness of the "there" into mere semblance or disguise.

We can view Arendt's primary distinctions—between public and private, work and action, freedom and necessity, the social and the political—as reflecting both the formal structure of concealment/unconcealment (*aletheia*) and the threatening dynamic suggested by the idea of fallenness. Like Heidegger, Arendt insists that the space of disclosure (the public realm) presupposes a surrounding area of hiddenness or darkness (the private). Also like him, she fears the reifying power of "average everydayness," of the sight characteristic of work and labor, which is capable of plunging the entire public sphere into the realm of semblance (the "social"). For Arendt, the fallenness of *homo faber* poses a constant threat to the very arena built by him. The universalization of *homo faber*'s instrumentalizing mode of comportment—the drawing of everything within the horizon of ends and means (a phenomenon that, in Arendt's view, is constitutive of modernity)—

creates the conditions under which the pressing needs of life are channeled into the public sphere. The effect of this colonization of the public realm by social concerns is the radical "dimming down" of the space of disclosure. The *telos* of this process, equivalent to the triumph of fallenness over "wresting" or initiatory disclosure, is the substitution of normalized behavior for agonistic action, and the replacement of individualizing politics by "household administration."

Here we arrive at what I referred to in Chapter 4 as the second level of Arendt's appropriation of Heidegger. This stratum reveals itself when we interrogate the structure of Arendt's distinctions and her narrative about the fate of the public realm in our time. What we find is a working out of Heidegger's dialectic of transcendence and everydayness in a political register. This project is propelled by Arendt's Heideggerian sense that the "dimming down" of our space of appearance has passed beyond the crisis point. The freedom of the public sphere, and with it the ontological dimensions of the public world and self, have been crowded out by the needs of life and the "socialized" pursuit of happiness (consumer society). This development takes on an additional pathos when viewed from the perspective of the fate of modern revolutions: our "treasure"—the *public* freedom created by revolutionary founding—has been lost.[9]

•

In "On the Essence of Truth," Heidegger extends the ontological approach to truth initiated in Section 44 of *Being and Time*. Setting aside the correspondence theory of truth, he famously redescribes truth in the Greek manner, as *aletheia*. When thought of as *aletheia*, truth is no "accordance" of matter and knowledge, object and intellect; rather, it is an *event* of disclosure, a happening that issues from a dialectic of concealment and revealment.[10] The strong anti-Platonic, anti-Kantian thrust of Heidegger's conception is apparent. But what does Heidegger mean by "concealment," and how is it central to the phenomenon of truth?

"Concealment" for Heidegger indicates that more primordial realm of hiddenness or darkness out of which every "clearing," every historico-ontological happening of truth, occurs. Thought of ontologically, truth is possible only on the basis of the "concealment of beings" or *untruth*.[11] There can be no disclosure without concealment, no truth without an "older," more original untruth. Yet this concealedness (what Heidegger dubs "the mystery") is forgotten by man, who is absorbed by what is "readily available and controllable."[12] According to Heidegger, this constitutes our normal (fallen) state of affairs: we are in untruth. This untruth is not a preserving concealment, but rather an everyday form that Heidegger calls "erring." Thus, as Heidegger puts it, "man's flight from the mystery toward what is readily available, onward from one current thing to the next, passing the mystery by—this is erring."[13]

Heidegger identifies all active comportment towards beings as, simultaneously, openness and erring. This identification extends and simplifies the analysis in *BT*. We can already detect the abandonment of the notion that authentic disclosure resembles *praxis*, an abandonment that leads Heidegger to turn to thinking as the only possible avenue for overcoming forgetfulness and penetrating *l'écume des choses* (the froth of things).[14] As we might expect, Arendt is profoundly critical of this withdrawal and of Heidegger's prejudice in favor of that which does not appear (Being—which remains, strictly speaking, "forgotten" or partially disclosed in a "disguised," concealing way). Nevertheless, she is deeply influenced by Heidegger's framing of disclosure in terms of concealment/unconcealment. Arendt appropriates this polarity for her "disclosive" theory of action. Giving it an intraworldly twist, she identifies the realms of concealment and revealment with the private and the public, respectively. The articulation of her political theory's central distinction is thus rooted in Heidegger's ontological treatment of truth.

Arendt has taken a pounding for the rigidity of her distinction between public and private. Feminists, critical theorists, and deconstructionists have all underlined the hazards of reifying this distinction. Insofar as Arendt presents this distinction as "natural" or self-evident, the pounding is deserved: nothing is easier to demonstrate than the historicity of what we deem "fit to appear" in the "bright light" of the public realm. The critics are wrong to assume, however, that Arendt is motivated to draw this distinction by a reactionary desire to keep certain "household" matters (or agents—e.g., women, workers) out of bounds. What is of fundamental importance to Arendt is not so much the content of the "public" or the "private" as the availability and integrity of each of these distinct realms. A political theory that identifies political action as our most authentically disclosive activity demands *both* a public space of disclosure and a surrounding darkness, a place of retreat from the bright light of the public sphere. As Arendt puts it, "a life spent entirely in public, in the presence of others, becomes, as we would say, shallow. While it retains its visibility, it loses the quality of rising into sight from some darker ground which must remain hidden if it is not to lose its depth in a very real, non-subjective sense."[15]

Contrary to some misreadings, then, Arendt's disclosive theory of political action does not denigrate the private realm; rather, it sees it as fundamentally important. Indeed, like the Greeks and Romans she so admires, Arendt views this realm of concealedness as "sacred":

> The sacredness of this privacy was like the sacredness of the hidden, namely, of birth and death, the beginning and end of mortals who, like all living creatures, grow out of and return to the darkness of a underworld. The non-privative trait of the household realm originally lay in its being the realm of birth and death which must be hidden from human eyes and impenetrable to human knowledge. It is hidden because man does not know where he comes from when he is born or goes when he dies.[16]

Without privacy, the "dark and hidden side of the public realm," neither action nor freedom are possible. Like *aletheia*, disclosive action ("the highest possibility of human existence") presupposes hiddenness and the concealing preservation of the "mystery"—the place from which we arise and disappear.[17]

When Arendt laments the "rise of the social," then, she is not simply mourning the public sphere's loss of integrity. She is mourning, equally, the loss of an authentically private sphere. The "contradiction" between public and private that had so worried Marx is resolved, in our time, by "the utter extinction of the very difference between private and public realms," an extinction wrought by the rise of the social and the "submersion" of public and private in a hybrid realm of concealment and "disguise." The "social" creates a reality in which nothing is authentically public or private; in which the space of disclosure is "dimmed down" by the needs of life; in which action is submerged in a tide of conformist behavior and interiority takes the place of individuality.

This last point underlines the progressive or cumulative nature of the "dimming down" of the public sphere. This process is accelerated by the rise and triumph of "the social," but it has its roots in *homo faber*'s "fallen" tendency to view everything in terms of means and ends. Arendt has no desire to place instrumentality as such on trial.[18] The problem, as she sees it, is the built-in tendency to generalize this mode of comportment, a tendency that leads to the instrumentalization of politics as household administration and to the absorption of the public sphere by the needs of life.[19] Thus, the "admission of household and housekeeping activities to the public realm" carries with it an "irresistible tendency to grow, to devour the older realms of the political and the private."[20] This progressive tendency—the "unnatural growth of the natural"—amplifies the forces of automatism at the expense of action and spontaneity. The result is a "mass man" characterized by "mass behavior" and a situation in which Heidegger's "perverse sounding statement" that "the light of the public obscures everything" goes "to the very heart of the matter."[21] As in Heidegger, the gravitational pull of fallenness exerts greater and greater force, with the polarity of everydayness and transcendence becoming more and more lopsided. For Arendt, the advent of mass society means that "rare deeds" are not simply juxtaposed to behavior; increasingly, they are subsumed by it. Thus, as Arendt writes,

> The unfortunate truth about behaviorism and the validity of its "laws" is that the more people there are, the more likely they are to behave and the less likely they are to tolerate non-behavior. Statistically, this will be shown in a leveling out of fluctuation. In reality, deeds will have less and less chance to stem the tide of behavior, and events will more and more lose their significance, that is, their capacity to illuminate historical time.[22]

One possible outcome of this negative dialectic of fallenness and transcendence, automatism and spontaneity, is a pervasive conformism wherein the "oneness of mankind" overrules the plurality of the human condition. Arendt's fear is that the hegemony of the "they-self" wrought by the rise of the social will deprive our disclosive capacity of both place and occasion. The possible eclipse of this disclosive capacity—an eclipse foreshadowed by the totalitarian obliteration of the last spaces of freedom within mass society—confronts us with a paradox. On the one hand, the rise of the social and the creation of mass society apparently guarantees the survival of the animal species mankind "on a world-wide scale."

On the other hand, this very development threatens humanity—human beings considered as disclosive agents—with extinction.[23]

The same Heideggerian dynamic of transcendence overwhelmed by fallenness provides the narrative thread of Arendt's *On Revolution*. Despite the impression sometimes given in *The Human Condition*, Arendt's interpretation of revolution (a distinctively *modern* phenomenon) leaves no doubt that freedom is indeed a defining aspect of modernity. Revolutions are "the only political events which confront us directly and inevitably with the problem of beginning."[24] In other words, it is only with the modern revolutions that the full pathos of freedom— the consciousness of a radical new beginning, a *novus ordo saeclorum*—becomes manifest. Yet the story Arendt tells in *OR* is, in fact, a tragedy, the story of a "lost treasure." The radical new beginnings of the French and American revolutions come to a bad end. In the French case, the clearing of a new space for freedom begun by the revolution is almost immediately overwhelmed by the "social question." The desperate poverty of millions, combined with the heritage of a sovereign model of power and the violent compassion of the Jacobins, ensured that the emergence of a new democratic public sphere would vanish in the violence of a prolonged, and ultimately futile, struggle for liberation.[25] In contrast, the American Revolution, unburdened by the crushing poverty of the Old World, succeeded in founding a new space for freedom.[26] Yet the promise of the ingenious "new system of power" created by the American Constitution goes unfulfilled, due largely to an ambiguity or ambivalence regarding the kind of freedom it was to house and protect. The original focus on the "pursuit of public happiness"—on the right of all to enter the public sphere and become, in Jefferson's words, "participators in government"—gives way to the pursuit of private happiness and material welfare. For Arendt, the equivocal American attitude toward public freedom is manifest in what she calls Jefferson's slip of the pen in the Declaration of Independence: the "pursuit of *public* happiness" is elided to the "pursuit of happiness."[27] This elision foreshadows the historical shift away from the "contents of the Constitution" (*qua* system of power) to the Bill of Rights. This is a shift away from public freedom to civil liberty: the "share in public affairs" promised by the Constitution is traded for a "guarantee that the pursuit of private happiness would be protected and furthered by public power."[28]

In the case of the French Revolution, the founding of a space for freedom is fatally sabotaged by the overwhelming forces of necessity; in the American case, a successful founding is undone by the failure to remember "public happiness" and to provide the requisite institutions for its maintenance.[29] What we find in both instances is the "resoluteness" of the revolutionary spirit giving way to the self-objectification implicit in submitting to the *torrent revolutionnaire*, or the desire for commodious living.[30] This bad faith makes the "need for action" appear transitory: the creation and preservation of a space for freedom fades as a motivating force for revolution, with its place being usurped by the question of public welfare and the administration and management of economic processes.[31] The more such processes rule our lives and our political sphere, the greater the loss of our revolutionary "treasure" (public freedom, public happiness). For Arendt, the fate of the political in the modern age is to be read in the history of its revolutions, a history in which "islands" of freedom emerge amidst a sea of automatic processes, only to be overwhelmed and disappear:

> The history of revolutions—from the summer of 1776 in Philadelphia and the summer of 1956 in Budapest—which politically spells out the innermost story of the modern age, could be told in parable form as the tale of an age-old treasure which, under the most varied circumstances, appears abruptly, unexpectedly, and disappears again, under mysterious conditions, as though it were a fata morgana. There exist, indeed, many good reasons to believe that the treasure was never a reality but a mirage. . . . Unicorns and fairy queens seem to possess more reality than the lost treasure of the revolutions.[32]

In modernity, the dialectic of transcendence and fallenness is played out in terms of the colonization of the political by the social. The proliferation of "automatic processes" denatures the public sphere and diminishes the space for freedom.[33] In the context of *this* reality, the political is essentially *evanescent*, the champion of freedom a champion of lost causes. To be sure, public freedom has not disappeared from the world; yet the primacy of life processes—of the social and economic—has starkly and dramatically curtailed a phenomenon whose being always was, at best, episodic.[34]

II. Being as Appearing: Post-Nietzschean Ontology and the Evanescence of the Political

The evanescence of the few "islands of freedom" that Arendt picks out in modernity confirms, apparently, the contemplative tradition's low estimate of the realm of human affairs. The political realm is one of flux or becoming, lacking the permanence that is the benchmark of value for the metaphysical tradition. Political philosophy overcomes the disdain felt by the *vita contemplativa* toward this sphere; yet, owing to its origins within this tradition, it is informed by the same ontological prejudices. Thus, while Plato's attempt to model the realm of human affairs upon the structure of true Being may have lost plausibility long ago, his two-world theory has continued to provide the basic architecture of political thought. Natural or divine law, right reason, the greatest good for the greatest number, distortion-free communication: these are a few of the principles called on to provide a ground to the flux, an extrapolitical normative ground from which stability and permanence might flow. Of the great Western political theorists, only Machiavelli refused this temptation, creating his own "political metaphysic" of flux and appearance to combat the inherited prejudices of Platonism and Christianity.[35]

As we have seen, Arendt is extremely critical of the "Platonic" tendencies of our tradition of political thought.[36] This perspective, however, does not lead her (as it does some postmoderns) to celebrate flux for the sake of flux.[37] Arendt's conviction that "in the political realm, Being and appearance coincide" does not prevent her from insisting upon a certain structural or institutional permanence for the public realm. In her view, the public realm can nurture our worldliness, provide a "home" for mortals, and preserve the meaning and memory of action *only* insofar as it outlasts the life span of the individual.[38] This insistence upon the need for a stable, relatively permanent structure marks another respect in which Arendt's anti-Platonism diverges from Nietzsche's.[39] Insofar as Nietzsche responds to the tradition's reification of Being as self-subsistent ground by affirming flux and becoming, he merely inverts the metaphysical hierarchy.[40] The drive for immortality that Arendt opposes to the contemplative yearning for eternity implies a different sort of ontology, one in which Being is not simply opposed to appearance, nor dismissed as mere error or illusion.

How, then, can Arendt assert the reality of appearance without falling into the Nietzschean trap? How can she reconcile the desire for a (limited) permanence with her tragic historical sense of the evanescence of the political (its "lingering awhile in presence")?[41] One way of answering the first question is to insist upon the ontological dimensions of publicity (a tack Arendt takes in her Kantian, aestheticizing mode). Another is to delve behind the ontological prejudices that inform our tradition and that promote the degradation of the political. This is the tack taken by Arendt in her "repetition" of the Greek prephilosophic experience of politics, a repetition undertaken not merely to escape the distortions perpetuated by a hostile tradition but—more profoundly—in order to "retrieve" an experience of Being as appearance lost long ago. As noted above, this anti-Platonic, post-Nietzschean turn echoes the methodological strategy of *Being and Time*. However, Arendt's "repetition" resonates more strongly—and more troublingly—with another of Heidegger's texts, the 1935 lectures *An Introduction to Metaphysics*. These lectures represent Heidegger's own attempt at surmounting Platonism and nihilism, at escaping the dialectic of objectivism/subjectivism. Prefiguring Arendt, he draws on the Greeks to rethink Being as appearing. Yet it is also in this text that Heidegger notoriously refers to the "inner truth and greatness" of the National Socialist movement.[42]

The fact that Arendt's attempt at overcoming Platonism intersects sharply with *this* text leads us to ask what are the *politics* of rethinking Being (or "the real") as appearance; that is, against substantialist metaphysics and its "invertors"?

Like Arendt, *An Introduction to Metaphysics* frames the recovery of the Greek experience of Being as appearance as a profoundly *political* project. Heidegger begins by thematizing the *Seinsvergessenheit* lodged in the heart of metaphysics—a forgetfulness of Being that he views as the source of the technonihilism threatening Europe, and especially Germany, from both sides (Russia and America, "metaphysically speaking" the "same").[43] The *spiritual* crisis of the West—a crisis manifest in "the darkening of the world, the flight of the gods, the destruction of the earth, the transformation of man into a mass, the hatred of everything free and creative"—flows from the *Seinsvergessenheit* of an exhausted subjectivism (expressed by the Nietzschean characterization of Being as a "mere vapor and a fallacy").[44] The only hope for escaping this crisis, according to Heidegger, resides in the possibility of repeating "the beginning of our historical-spiritual existence, in order to transform it into a new beginning."[45] In the question of Being—the

Seinsfrage—nothing less than the "spiritual destiny of the West" is at stake; hence, "the beginning must be begun again, more radically, with all the strangeness, darkness and insecurity that attend a true beginning."[46]

For Heidegger, the core of this all-important repetition is a recovery of the originary experience of Being *qua* presence before its reification into constant presence by the tradition. Heidegger's attempt to retrieve this Greek experience of presence proceeds by the dissection of the four most basic distinctions upon which metaphysics is based: the distinctions between Being and Becoming, Being and Appearance, Being and Thinking, Being and the Ought.[47] These distinctions play an essential role in the delimitation of Being as constant presence and, thus, as ground.[48] Yet they all retain the trace of another, more primordial, experience of Being, one that Heidegger believes has the power to save the West from the "flimsily covered abyss" opening up before it.

Heidegger's discussion of the distinction between being and appearance in Chapter 4 of *An Introduction to Metaphysics* is notable in two respects. First, it undertakes a thorough revaluation of the ontological significance of appearance. Second, Heidegger insists that the differential relation between being and appearance presupposes a primordial bond or unity. Both are highlighted when Heidegger declares: "Only the tired latecomers with their supercilious wit imagine that they can dispose of the historical power of appearance by declaring it to be 'subjective,' hence very dubious. The Greeks experienced it differently. They were perpetually compelled to wrest being from appearance and preserve it against appearance."[49]

Deploying one of his famous etymological arguments, Heidegger maintains that the primordial or hidden "unity of Being and appearance" echoes faintly in the senses of appearance (*Schein*) found in everyday German. He specifies three primary modes: *Schein* as "radiance or glow"; as appearing or coming to light; and as mere appearance or semblance.[50] It is the second mode of *Scheinen* (appearing, in the sense of showing itself) that, according to Heidegger, underlies the other two. Thus, "the essence of appearance (*Schein*) lies in the appearing (*Erscheinen*)."[51] Appearing is "self-manifestation, self-representation, standing-here, presence"; and "to be present," to appear or to shine (as, for example, stars do), "means exactly the same thing as being."[52]

The "inner connection" between being and appearance attested to by everyday usage refers us to the Greek experience of this unity in the presencing they called *physis*. According to Heidegger, *physis* denotes "self-blossoming emergence (e.g., the blossoming of a rose), opening up, unfolding, that which manifests itself in such unfolding and perseveres and endures in it; in short, the realm of things that emerge and linger on."[53] *Physis*, as "emergence," can be "observed everywhere"; yet the Greeks did not learn what *physis* was through natural phenomenon, but vice versa. Their ontological precomprehension of the world was entirely colored in terms of this "power that emerges and the enduring realm under its sway."[54] Thus, the "standing-in-itself" we associate with the being-present of a thing was, for the Greeks, "nothing other than standing-there, standing-in-the-light," a "shining appearance."[55] The experience of *physis* as emergence, as coming into the light, meant that to the Greek mind "appearing is not something subsequent that sometimes happens to being"; rather, "appearing is the essence of being," "being means appearing."[56]

Heidegger's interpretation is very close to the ontological primacy of appearance posited by Arendt in *The Human Condition* and *On Revolution*, a primacy she generalizes beyond the political sphere in *The Life of the Mind*: "In this world which we enter, appearing from a nowhere, and from which we disappear into a nowhere, *Being and Appearing coincide*."[57] What is implied here is not the turning upside down of the metaphysical hierarchy, in which appearance or "illusions" are opposed to the "error" of Being; rather, Arendt is suggesting that we view appearances or "surfaces" as the highest mode of being.[58] This, of course, is a lesson gleaned from the Greek experience of politics, in which "appearing to all" coincided with the fullest reality. Heidegger's starting point is different; nevertheless, he emphasizes the continuity between the experience of *physis* as self-emergent appearance and the Greek understanding of the political realm as a space of appearance. That the essence or "truth" of being lies at least partly in appearance is shown by the Greeks understanding of "the supreme possibility of human being": the glory or glorification achievable through political action. As Heidegger notes, "Glory is in Greek *doxa. Dokeo* means 'I show myself, appear, enter into the light.'"[59] As we have seen, it is precisely this understanding of "the shining glory of great deeds," of the illuminative capacity of action in the space of appearances, that guides Arendt's anti-Platonist theorization of the public realm. Prefiguring Arendt yet again, Heidegger underlines the perspectival constitution of the arena in which "glorious action" stands as the highest mode of being. The regard in which an individual stands, the magnificence of a city: these realities, Heidegger points out, are constituted by *doxa*, by opinion. The "aspect of a thing" first offers itself and changes through the "diversity of viewpoints" found in the public realm.[60]

The Greek understanding of being as appearance thus reveals the ontologically constitutive power of *doxa*. Arendt's and Heidegger's "repetitions" are in remarkable accord here. For Arendt, the superior reality of the public realm is found precisely in its doxastic dimensions, which Plato had dismissed as akin to shadows on the wall of a cave cut off from the light of the Real and the True. Heidegger stresses the historicity of the Platonic devaluation of appearance, a devaluation he sees as marking a turning point in the "spiritual" life of the Greeks and the "destiny" of the West:

> It was in the Sophists and Plato that appearance was declared to be mere appearance and thus degraded. At the same time being, as *idea*, was exalted to a supersensory realm. A chasm, *chorismos*, was created between the merely apparent being here below and real being somewhere on high. In that chasm Christianity settled down, at the same time reinterpreting the lower as created and the higher as creator. These refashioned weapons it turned against antiquity (as paganism) and so disfigured it. Nietzsche was right in saying that Christianity is Platonism for the people.[61]

This passage clarifies the political stakes of the "destruction of the history of ontology." It also reveals the way in which the Arendtian revaluation of worldliness and appearance is continuous with, and indebted to, Heidegger's "surmounting" of Platonism in the nineteen thirties. There is, however, a clear and important difference between their respective "overcomings," a difference that creates an abyss between these two attempts at post-Nietzschean ontology. The difference reveals itself, symptomatically enough, in the course of Heidegger's discussion of *doxa* in *An Introduction to Metaphysics*. Heidegger turns from discussing the importance of *doxa* for the reality of appearance to Sophocles' *Oedipus Rex*. Significantly, the lesson he wishes to extract from the tragedy is that appearance, by its very nature, is self-distorting: appearance reveals, but this revelation is always and at the same time a concealment, or a deception.[62] Sophocles demonstrates the Greek recognition that "this deception lies in the appearance itself": "Only because appearance itself deceives can it deceive man and lead him into illusion."[63] The structurally deceiving nature of appearance means that the all-important Greek passion was not, as Arendt believes, the agonistic urge to action and self-display; rather, the Oedipus story attests to "the passion for disclosure of being." The Oedipus story presents us with, in the poet Friedrich Hölderlin's words, a "tragedy of appearance"; one that enacts, according to Heidegger, "the enduring struggle between being and appearance," a struggle in which the drive to unconcealment is constantly at war with the concealing powers of appearance.[64]

Here we see the gap that separates Heidegger's dialectic of concealment and revealment from Arendt's appropriation. Heidegger's equation of disclosure or unconcealment with truth (*aletheia*) leads him to identify the illuminative activity of the Greeks not with doxastic political action, but rather with the poetic or creative activity that "wrests" the truth of Being concealed by the "dimmed down" appearances of the public realm. Harkening back to the polarity of authentic disclosedness and everydayness in *Being and Time*, Heidegger underlines the structural ambiguity of appearance, and the resultant imperative to wrest being from it: "If he [man] is to take over [his] being-there in the radiance of being, he must bring to stand, he must endure it in appearance and against appearance, and he must wrest both appearance and being from the abyss of non-being."[65]

In framing the dialectic of concealment/revealment—*aletheia*—as an "enduring struggle between being and appearance," Heidegger reveals the depth of his philosophical prejudice against the realm of human affairs. While this framing hardly resurrects Plato's metaphysical hierarchy, it *does* create a clear ranking of authentic, wresting, "bringing-into-the-light," on the one hand, and the inauthentic, obscuring character of everyday opinion and discourse, on the other. The ambiguous appearances of the latter have value only insofar as the authentic creator—the poet, thinker, or statesman—can mold them into something utterly novel, bringing forth a new clearing for Being through the world-disclosive capacity of his work.[66] Heidegger's "repetition" of the Greek experience of Being as appearing thus presents us with a privileging of the poetic, world-disclosive activity of the creator over the *praxis* of the many. His ontology of appearance is irreducibly political insofar as it shifts the disclosive agon from an intersubjective context (the public realm) to that of the enduring struggle between being and appearance. *This* struggle—the struggle for the truth of Being—is one that remains the province of "leaders" or "creators" *alone*.[67]

Heidegger's thinking of being as appearance is determined throughout by a philosophical bias in favor of "the hidden ground" of presence. This bias leads Heidegger to emphasize the structurally ambiguous character of appearance and to aim his "repetition" at the forgotten sources of Western ontology. Arendt's "repetition" goes one step farther—or deeper—than Heidegger's. Her "destruction" of the Western tradition of political philosophy returns us not to the originary (speculative) sources of a presence subsequently reified as constant presence by metaphysics, but rather to an experience of the being of appearance drawn entirely from the plural, doxastic, and public dimensions of *praxis*. Heidegger, as the discussion in *IM* indicates, was quite aware of this alternative phenomenal origin; yet his privileging of Greek ontology prevents him from seeing the experience of appearance born of plurality and politics as anything other than a derivative mode.[68] What is lacking in Heidegger (as Arendt points out in a note to her essay "What Is Authority?") is an appreciation of the *political* context in which Plato initiates the degradation of appearance and the reification of truth as correspondence.[69] The result is a political ontology of appearance whose center of gravity remains the struggle for truth (now *aletheia*); a struggle inscribed, as in Plato, in the gap between the few and the many. We should not be surprised, then, that the disclosure of the being of appearance takes two radically opposed forms: the poetic agon by which the truth of Being is wrested from appearance versus the agonistic "sharing of words and deeds" characteristic of a radically democratic politics.

III. THE PROBLEM OF GROUNDLESS ACTION AND JUDGMENT

Arendt's "debt" to Heidegger has occasioned stern and often quite hostile criticism. Rationalists of the left and right take strong exception to her characterization of the freedom of political action as spontaneous or groundless, a characterization they view as a theoretical Pandora's box. In an essay on Arendt, Martin Jay identifies her emphasis upon the "sheer capacity to begin" with an existentialist glorification of the deed, a linkage that puts her theory of political action on the slippery slope to *violence*.[70] Richard Wolin raises a related but somewhat different objection, focusing on the affinity between Arendt's "dramaturgical" model of action and Heidegger's notion of the "clearing" as a locus of unconcealment. Wolin suggests that Arendt's disclosive conception of politics, like Heidegger's disclosive conception of existence, fails to provide criteria for distinguishing between "legitimate and illegitimate modes of self-unveiling."[71] Arendt's political philosophy, he thinks, is plagued by the same "criterionlessness" that haunts Heidegger's *Being and Time*.[72] The lack of "normative grounding" is viewed as placing Arendt in a theoretical position indistinguishable from *decisionism* (a conclusion Jay arrives at also). It comes as no surprise when these critics turn Strauss's critique of Heidegger upon Arendt, charging that her commitment to freedom as the "abyss-like ground" of action leads her into relativism and irrationalism.

Arendt's political theory will appear "irrationalist" to those who believe that the task of a "rational" political theory is the establishment of normative foundations that are, strictly speaking, beyond argument and that can be called upon to provide extrapolitical criteria of legitimacy for any given consensus.[73] From this perspective, the Just remains immanently connected to the True, and the specification of the conditions necessary for the circulation of true statements provides an analogical model for what constitutes legitimate agreement in the political realm.[74] As noted above, Arendt thinks this analogy is a false one: theoretical discourse provides a misleading model for practical discourse. Its advantages (for example, a more subtle set of criteria for distinguishing authentic from inauthentic consensus, or right from might) are outweighed by its disadvantages (the fetish made of a particular model of procedural rationality; the overvaluation of agreement as the *telos* of action and discourse). In fact, nothing in Arendt's position signals a hostility to rationality as such, despite Jay's suggestion that the appeal to prephilosophic experience manifests a "Heideggerian denigration of *Logos*."[75] That Arendt values rational discourse highly is clear from her antipathy to a romantic politics of will or feeling à la Rousseau or Robespierre.[76] It is precisely *against* such a politics that she insists upon *opinion* and *judgment* as rational and political faculties of the first order.[77] From Arendt's point of view, the scandal of the Western tradition of political thought is the way it consistently ignores the specific rationality of these faculties, reserving the honorific "rational" for discourses whose object is truth.

Martin Jay's main charge—that Arendt's celebration of initiatory action veers unavoidably toward violence—is even more questionable. Jay argues that Arendt's forcefully made (and often repeated) distinction between action and violence will not stand due to the inner "affinity between beginnings and violence."[78] In making this claim (which he sees as born out by the *aporias* of Arendt's text), Jay repeats one of the West's oldest and most pernicious prejudices, namely, that "in the beginning was a crime"; that "no beginning could be made without using violence, without violating."[79] This prejudice, given mythic form in the legends of Cain and Abel, and of Romulus and Remus, owes its plausibility to the metaphorics of fabrication. When viewed through the prism of making, political beginnings appear essentially violent; the truth of the statement "you can't make an omelette without breaking eggs" seems incontrovertible. Yet the whole point of Arendt's radical reappropriation of the distinction between *praxis* and *poiēsis* is to force us to question the ease with which we impose *this* metaphorics upon the realm of human affairs. Thus Arendt, like Locke, views violence as a legitimate means to resist tyranny, as almost by definition part of the struggle for liberation. However, this struggle is prepolitical, and it lacks the existential glamour (and ontological significance) attributed to it by Georges Sorel, Jean-Paul Sartre, and Frantz Fanon.[80] Like the social contract theorists of the Enlightenment, Arendt insists upon an irreducible gap between this prepolitical sphere (the "state of nature") and the realm of political action constituted by the act of founding. The deliberative nature of the latter act, manifest in the American case, must not be overlooked.[81] The "unique lesson" of the American Revolution is lost at the moment the act of founding is absorbed by metaphors drawn from the plastic arts or natural processes.

With regard to Richard Wolin's charge that Arendt's political theory is beset by the same "criterionlessness" found in Heidegger, I need only note the obvious. Arendt clearly provides a set of stringent criteria for distinguishing genuinely political actions and relations from nonpolitical ones. These criteria—derived, for the most part, from the idea of a "self-contained" politics—rule out violence, coercion, and deception, along with the more blatant forms of technocratic high-handedness. Arendt is adamant that a public sphere is truly possible only where plural equals interact through persuasive speech.[82] It may be objected that her criteria are too rough and ready to provide an adequate defense against the subtler forms of ideological manipulation. What is lacking, we are told, are standards tight enough to rule over the redemption of validity claims.[83] Arendt's response to this criticism is to insist that such concerns fall *within* the arena of political judgment and cannot shape it from without. There are, in other words, no theoretical shortcuts that might substitute for the faculty of political judgment or compensate for its deficiencies. Such a response is in line with one of her most basic and firmly held convictions, anathema to the inheritors of classical rationalism and *ideologiekritik* alike, namely, that citizens must be treated, for better or worse, as adults, capable of acting and judging for themselves.

The charges, then, are wide of the mark. Their vehemence, however, bespeaks an anxiety whose source is hardly Arendt's failure to provide sufficient criteria for determining a "genuine" consensus. The accusations of irrationalism, "criterionlessness," and violence convey a (distorted) recognition of the magnitude of Arendt's project. Her political theory attempts nothing less than the rethinking of action and judgment in light of the collapse of the tradition and the closure of metaphysics (the "death of God"). The negative, "destructive" side of this project consists in demonstrating how our instrumental or "technical" interpretations of action, thought, and judgment fall under the shadow of a "dead God." Arendt's positive tasks are the uprooting of action and judgment from the patterns imposed by metaphysical rationality and the rethinking of these activities in their autonomy and freedom; that is, without grounds (in the metaphysical sense). Such an unprecedented rethinking is the only "authentic" response to the collapse of the tradition and the crises of authority and judgment that follow in its wake.

•

One of the more familiar canards about Arendt is that she is somehow nostalgic for authority.[84] This misreading is occasioned by her discussion of the modern "crisis in authority" in the essay "What Is Authority?" Here, she identifies the "loss of authority," its "vanishing from the world," with the "loss of worldly permanence and reliability."[85] This identification resonates all too well with the communitarian yearning for a more rooted, grounded political association. At the same time, it provides liberals with the ammunition they need to accuse Arendt of nostalgia for a premodern social order in which tradition, religion, and authority worked together to supply a stable basis for politics.[86]

As we shall see in Chapter 6, Arendt can with some justification be accused of harboring a desire for rootedness or "at-homeness," a desire in conflict with the energies of modernity. Nevertheless, it is wildly inaccurate to accuse her of (or praise her for) a nostalgia for authority. According to Arendt, one salient characteristic of the current "crisis" is that we "are no longer in a position to know what authority really is," experiences of it having vanished from our life-world.[87] The result is that we are prone to confuse authority with power or violence. Yet, as Arendt points out, "authority precludes the use of external means of coercion; where force is used, authority itself has failed."[88] Similarly, authority is "incompatible with persuasion, which presupposes equality and works through a process of argumentation."[89] Persuasion denotes an "egalitarian order," while the exercise of authority presupposes hierarchy. The "essence" of authority is the hierarchical relation between "the one who commands and the one who obeys," a relation that rests "neither on common reason nor on the power of the one who commands."[90] What makes authority possible is the mutual acceptance, by rulers and ruled, of "the hierarchy itself, whose rightness and legitimacy both recognize."[91]

As a political principle, then, authority conflicts with Arendt's basic convictions as to what authentic politics is (namely, something that occurs only in "the egalitarian order of persuasion").[92] How to explain the impression that she mourns its passing? This impression is created, in part, by her citing the decline in authority as one element in the constellation that made the totalitarian seizure of power possible.[93] But—and this is a point overlooked by her communitarian admirers as well as her liberal critics—while the demise of authority creates clear dangers (it is, she says, "tantamount to the loss of the groundwork of the world"), it also creates unprecedented opportunities.[94] The loss of authority, according to Arendt, "does not entail, at least not necessarily, the loss of the human capacity for building, preserving, and caring for a world that can survive us and remain a fit place to live for those who come after us."[95] Indeed, it may be that this loss makes a new, stronger form of "care for the world" possible.

The principle of authority created stability by providing the political order in the West with a certain kind of foundation. Arendt's project in "What Is Authority?" is to specify the nature of this foundation and to show why it is no longer possible. Hence, the real question of the essay is "what *was* authority?"[96] Placed in the context of Arendt's political thought as a whole, the essay makes a strong case for relief at the passing of authority. The overarching argument is that while authority may have provided a ground for theory and practice from the Romans up to the Enlightenment, it is only with its demise that the "elementary problems of human living-together" once more come into view.[97] The central role played by the concept of authority in Western political thought contributes mightily to the perversion of our concepts of political action, power, judgment, and freedom. By tracing the opening and closure of what could be called the "epoch of authority," Arendt points us toward a postauthoritarian concept of the political.

What, then, was authority? In answering this question, Arendt insists (in proper Heideggerian, historicist mode) that we avoid any appeal to ahistorical generalization. What is in question is not "authority in general" but "a very specific concept of authority that has been dominant in our history."[98] What is the nature of this "specific concept," and where did it come from?

According to Arendt, the concept of authority operative in our tradition is one that legitimates the political order by reference to some transcendent, extrapolitical force. This specification is clarified by the contrast between authoritarian and tyrannical forms of government, a contrast liberalism tends to obscure:

> The difference between tyranny and authoritarian government has always been that the tyrant rules in accordance with his own will and interest, whereas even the most draconic authoritarian government is bound by laws. Its acts are tested by a code which was made either not by man at all, as in the case of the law of nature of God's Commandments or the Platonic ideas, or at least not by those actually in power. The source of authority in authoritarian government is always a force external and superior to its own power; it is always this source, this external force which transcends the political realm, from which the authorities derive their "authority," that is, their legitimacy, and against which their power can be checked.[99]

The principle of authority demands, in short, that human affairs "be subjected to the domination of something outside their realm."[100] It is only upon the supposition of some such transcendent, dominating force that authoritarian regimes (in the strict sense) are possible. Which is to say, simply, that our concept of authority is, at its heart, metaphysical. Authority presupposes metaphysics' two-world theory; its demise, moreover, is inseparable from the closure of metaphysical rationality as traced by Nietzsche and Heidegger. To the question What was authority? then, the short answer is *metaphysics*.

That the "epoch of authority" and what Heidegger called the "epoch of metaphysics" are roughly coextensive is borne out by the genealogical dimension of Arendt's inquiry. The kind of "public-political world" brought into being by the notion of authority did not always exist: as Arendt notes, the word and concept are Roman in origin.[101] Even more important is the fact that "neither the Greek language nor the varied political experiences of Greek history show any knowledge of authority and the kind of rule it implies."[102] The Greeks did not recognize the relation of rulership as a political relation, since it inevitably implied force and violence (prepolitical modes of interaction). The idea that there could be a hierarchy not based on force or violence, and which would be accepted by both rulers and ruled as just and binding, was an idea that had to be introduced into Greek political discourse, precisely *against* the experience of the *polis*. According to Arendt, this introduction (subsequently built on by the Romans and Christianity) was performed by Plato and Aristotle.[103]

Arendt views the Platonic-Aristotelian attempt to "introduce something akin to authority into the public life of the Greek *polis*" as fraught with paradox. Authority "implies an obedience in which men retain their freedom."[104] Yet the various examples of rulership available to Plato and Aristotle in the public and private spheres all framed relations predicated upon the denial of freedom. The tyrant, the general, the household head, the master of slaves: taken individually, each provided a model of unquestionable authority, yet none could be said to preserve either the public sphere or the freedom of citizens.[105] Thus, the concept of rule had to be introduced by some other means, which preserved at least the appearance of freely given obedience. The "other means," of course, was the rule of reason, an innovation through which the "Socratic school" transferred the compelling force of truth from the sphere of theoretical insight or logical demonstration to the realm of human affairs. Reason provided a nonviolent (and hence "legitimate") principle of coercion, which enabled Greek thought to rise above persuasion (a clearly inadequate means, as illustrated by the trial of Socrates) without resorting to despotism. But in order for reason to rule, it had to be demonstrated that the genuine standards for human conduct transcended the realm of human affairs, and were available only to those capable of contemplative "seeing"; that is, philosophers. Such a demonstration is undertaken by Plato in the *Republic*; "nowhere else," Arendt writes, "has Greek thinking so closely approached the concept of authority."[106]

The Platonic-Aristotelian turn to reason as a way of introducing the idea of rule into the political sphere is laden with implications for our tradition. As Arendt states it, "The consequences of expecting reason to develop into an instrument of coercion perhaps have been no less decisive for the tradition of Western philosophy than the tradition of Western politics."[107] Politically, this appeal entails splitting thought off from action and creating a hierarchical relation between the two. Rationality ceases to be a doxastic capacity exercised by the actor in the context of plurality. It becomes, instead, the monopoly of the "thinking class" (in Plato, those by nature suited to the contemplative life). One reason the *Republic* is paradigmatic for the Western concept of authority is that in Plato's utopia this class is not, strictly speaking, a ruling class. The ruler in the *Republic* is neither a group nor an individual, but a set of transcendent standards. Such standards—the sine qua non of genuine authoritarian rule—are available only to the mind's eye, a kind of sight not possessed by the hoì polloi. The "philosopher-kings" are, in fact, selfless instruments to whom true Being is revealed, and who translate this moment of vision into standards for the realm of human affairs.[108] The question of whether reason reveals that which is "just by nature" to an intellectual elite or (as the Enlightenment would have it) to all is less fundamental than the peculiar relation this appeal institutes between first and practical philosophy. The Platonic politicization of reason creates a relation of derivation between "general" and "special" metaphysics, ontology and practical (ethical or political) philosophy.[109]

The "authoritarian" appeal to metaphysical rationality made by Plato thus has two key effects. First, it disentangles thought from action, firmly coupling reason to the unseen realm of the universal; second, through the idea of transcendent standards, it attributes a prescriptive power to thought such that it "rules over" action.[110] The splitting off of thought from action accomplished by the Platonic move is, if not the origin, clearly the institutionalization of the theory/practice distinction. This distinction is irreducibly metaphysical insofar as it rests upon what Heidegger terms a "technical" interpretation of thought and action.[111] From Plato forward, action is viewed primarily as a means to an end, as the production of an effect. Thought, on the other hand, is stripped of its purely contemplative (useless) status and is functionalized: its primary role, *qua* theory, is to guide action by the rational securing of first principles and the positing of ends in accordance with these principles. For metaphysical rationality (as Schürmann notes), action is essentially teleocratic and thought is essentially foundational.[112] The latter's job is to secure the truth with which the former may be brought into accord. The Platonic appeal to transcendent standards—to the "authority" of reason as a "legitimate principle of coercion"—establishes the familiar pattern wherein action proceeds from and is legitimated by a grounding, extrapolitical "first" revealed by reason.[113]

Within the field of metaphysical rationality, then, action is delineated as "the practico-political effectuation of the philosophical."[114] Yet despite Plato's success in articulating a new configuration of thought and action, his attempt to introduce "something akin to authority" into the political sphere suffered from a significant weakness. Arendt describes Plato's predicament:

> The trouble with coercion through reason, however, is that only the few are subject to it, so that the problem arises of how to assure that the many, the people who in their very multitude compose the body politic, can be submitted to the same truth. Here, to be sure, some other means of coercion must be found, and here again coercion through violence must be avoided if political life as the Greeks understood it is not to be destroyed. This is the central predicament of Plato's political philosophy and has remained a predicament of all attempts to establish a tyranny of reason.[115]

Plato solved this predicament by introducing (at the end of the *Republic*) a myth about rewards and punishments to be meted out in the hereafter.[116] Christianity is notable for the way it appropriates both Plato's "invisible spiritual yardsticks" and the myth of otherworldly sanctions, a combination which proved so powerful that even the thoroughly enlightened and secular revolutionaries of the eighteenth century felt compelled to cite the fear of hell as an indispensable grounding for the maintenance of social order.[117] It was, after all, through religion and belief in the hereafter that the authoritarian positing of transcendent yardsticks for human affairs became a political fact of the first order, successfully establishing what had previously been viewed as the negation of the political relation (authority or hierarchy) as its essence.

In Arendt's view, authority and religion, in combination with tradition, formed a tremendously powerful and resiliant "groundwork" for premodern European civilization.[118] She sees the relative stability of the West as a function of the mutually reinforcing elements of this constellation, an "amalgamation" that first attained its political perfection with the Romans (for whom Greek philosophy provided an unquestioned authority).[119] The problem is that none of these elements can fill its foundational role if any one of the others is in decline. Thus, the process of secularization has the ultimate effect of making a "grounded" social order impossible. And this, in turn, produces a generalized crisis—not only in authority, but also (as we shall see) in judgment. The crucial point in Arendt's analysis is that the closure of metaphysical rationality—the withering of ultimate grounds for action, the "death of God"—would have remained an event of strictly local (philosophical/theological) significance were it not for the fact that Christianity had indeed (as Nietzsche said) brought Platonism to the people. The result is that the various "modern deaths" which haunt contemporary intellectual life (the deaths of "God, metaphysics, philosophy, and, by implication, positivism") have "been events of considerable historical consequence": since "the beginning of our century, they have ceased to be the exclusive concern of an intellectual elite and instead are not so much the concern as the *common unexamined assumption of nearly everybody*."[120] Without the belief in otherworldly sanctions, transcendent standards become empty husks—still repeated and respected, but deprived of their effective power. The only thing that survives the "modern deaths" unscathed is the *habit* of legitimating action via the appeal to such standards. This is the situation Arendt has in mind when she speaks of a generalized "crisis in authority," a situation Nietzsche and Heidegger described as *nihilism*.[121]

Arendt is under no illusions concerning the political ramifications of this situation. On the one hand, she freely acknowledges the disastrous possibilities opened by this crisis. At Toronto, in response to the philosopher Hans Jonas's call for a revived inquiry into ultimate grounds, Arendt replies: "I am perfectly sure that this whole totalitarian catastrophe would not have happened if people still had believed in God, or in hell rather—that is, if there were still ultimates."[122] On the other hand is the simple and devastating fact that "there were no ultimates to appeal to," no extrapolitical principles that retained an unshakable validity and effectivity for the average person, or that would make him or her prefer death to complicity with a criminal regime.[123] Nor does our discomfort end there; Arendt continues:

> And if you go through such a situation [as totalitarianism] the first thing you know is the following: you *never* know how somebody will act. You have the surprise of your life! This goes throughout all layers of society and it goes throughout various distinctions between men. And if you want to make a generalization then you could say that those who were still firmly convinced of the so-called old values were the first to be ready to change their old values for a new set of values, provided they were given one. And I am afraid of this, because I think that the moment you give anybody a new set of values—or this famous "bannister"—you can immediately exchange it. And the only thing the guy gets used to is having a "bannister" and a set of values, no matter. I do not believe we can stabilize the situation in which we have been since the seventeenth century in any final way. . . .
>
> We wouldn't have to bother about this whole business if metaphysics and this whole value business hadn't fallen down. We begin to question because of these events.[124]

The import of these remarks is clear. Arendt does *not* believe that nihilism at the "practical level" is combated by a return to tradition, a reassertion of "values," or—worse yet—the movement for "traditional values" (as she puts it elsewhere, the Fascist is "a good family man").[125] It is precisely the reliance upon such "banisters" in our tradition that has led to the separating out of thought and action and to the positing of an overly simple (deductive) relation between "yardsticks" and action. Corresponding to these (historical) developments is a precipitous decline in our capacity for moral and political judgment. Plato's postulation of extrapolitical, transcendent yardsticks had the effect of equating judgment with the "capacity for subsuming," a simplification much in evidence in the monological character of Kant's moral philosophy.[126] Our powers of reflective and intersubjective judgment have atrophied under the weight of such objectivist regimes. The result is that the crumbling of these "yardsticks" leaves us dangerously susceptible to those who offer the narcotic of a revivified set of values, the "moral" means by which to prolong our mechanical habits of judgment and escape the complexity—and effort—of thinking and judging for ourselves.[127]

For Arendt, then, the imperative issuing from the generalized "crisis in authority" is not (as Karl Jaspers wrongly assumes) to preserve whatever fragments of authority remain; rather, it is to join Nietzsche's and Heidegger's "destructive" enterprise, in order that we might face the "elementary problems of human living-together" more honestly, without dogma or prejudice.[128] The description she gives of her efforts in *The Life of the Mind* applies equally to her attempt to extricate action, freedom, judgment, and an opinion-based rationality from the tyranny of what Schürmann calls metaphysics' "attributive-participative" schema:[129]

> I have clearly joined the ranks of those who for some time now have been attempting to dismantle metaphysics and philosophy with all its categories, as we have known them from their beginning in Greece until today. Such dismantling is possible only on the assumption that the thread of tradition is broken and that we shall not be able to renew it.[130]

The "dismantling" of the remains of the substantialist machinery of legitimation and judgment according to first principles is rendered unavoidable by the "horrible originality" of totalitarianism, whose actions "constitute a break with all our traditions; they have clearly exploded our categories of political thought and our standards for moral judgment."[131] Totalitarianism shatters what is left of conventional wisdom, leaving us with a "topsy-turvy" world in which inherited notions no longer have any purchase.[132] However, the caesura introduced by totalitarianism had long been in preparation, its "shattering" effect being the result of a deeper, subterranean crisis at work in the Western tradition itself, the movement by which our highest values devalue themselves.[133] From Arendt's perspective, the self-undermining character of the appeal to transcendent values (what Nietzsche saw as the irony of the will to truth) leads to the destruction of a crucial component of the "groundwork" of the West. This creates a situation in which political structures are held together (as Montesquieu presciently noted) solely by customs and traditions.[134] The increasingly hollow foundations of political society correspond to a "moral and spiritual breakdown of occidental culture," the extent of which is revealed by the relative ease with which totalitarian societies succeeded in inverting our most "sacred" moral precepts. As Arendt notes in her 1953 essay "Understanding and Politics," the frightening thing about totalitarianism is not so much its radical novelty as the fact that "it has brought to light the ruin of our categories of thought and standards of judgment."[135] The bankruptcy of our "foundations" is revealed once and for all; the political consequences of an authoritarian/nihilistic investment in transcendent standards and ultimate grounds comes home to roost.

The crisis in authority, then, is inseparable from a crisis in judgment. But just as the closure of metaphysical rationality opens the possibility of thinking action in its freedom and autonomy as something other than a means, so too does the loss of "customary rules" open the way toward a renewed appreciation of our capacity for judgment. We may live "in the shadow of a great catastrophe," but the break in our tradition is also liberating:

> Even though we have lost yardsticks by which to measure, and rules under which to subsume the particular, a being whose essence is beginning may have enough of origin within himself to understand without preconceived categories and to judge without the set of customary rules which is morality. If the essence of all, and in particular of political, action is to make a new beginning, then understanding [judgment] becomes the other side of action.[136]

Our cause for hope comes from the fact that, just as our capacity for action does not hinge upon the availability of ultimate grounds, our capacity for judgment outstrips the availability of general rules or "yardsticks." The independence and spontaneity that characterize our capacity to "think without rules" make it possible to begin the assessment of the unprecedented (and generally horrific) political phenomenon of the twentieth century. The policy of systematized murder implemented by totalitarian regimes, for example, reveals the inadequacy of our "preconceived" categories. Totalitarian violence, manifest in "the blotting out of whole peoples" and the "clearance" of whole regions of their native populations, is no simple extension of tyranny, and the nature of its criminality is obscured by the traditional rubrics of "war crimes" or "pogrom."[137] Such categories conceal the unprecedented nature of this (bureaucratic-technological) crime of the state, the horrible novelty of which is glimpsed in the industrialized (factory-like) production of corpses in the Nazi death camps. The inadequacy of traditional juridical concepts to deal with this new criminal reality was implicitly recognized at Nuremburg by the introduction of a new category of crime—"crimes against humanity" or, as the French prosecutor François de Menthon put it, "crimes against the human status"—a category that has become irreplaceable in the historical as well as legal judgments of state crimes of the twentieth century.[138]

In the case of totalitarianism, the work of judgment is impeded not only by our propensity for "preconceived" categories, but also by a juridical discourse which insists that evil motives constitute the core of the guilt of the accused. Murder as a state policy reveals the theological assumptions concerning the nature of evil built into legal discourse, a point driven home to Arendt in the course of the trial of Adolf Eichmann. For Arendt, the Eichmann case presented the paradoxical juxtaposition of evil deeds on a gigantic scale with a patently unmonstrous, non-demonic doer—an actor whose most striking characteristics were "an extraordinary shallowness" and a "curious, quite authentic inability to think."[139] It was precisely the gap between the monstrousness of the deeds and the "ludicrousness of the man" that put Arendt "willy-nilly" in the possession of a concept: the "banality of evil."[140] This concept—born of the specific phenomenon of Eichmann's personality, and scarcely intended as a global characterization of the perpetrators of the Holocaust—is a prime example of the capacity of reflective judgment to begin with particulars and "ascend" to a universal. *Qua* concept, the "banality of evil" focuses our attention on a crucial dimension of twentieth-century state-sponsored violence: the *thoughtless* individual who, lacking wickedness, pathology, or even ideological conviction, willingly becomes a cog in the new bureaucracies of murder.

If, in response to these contemporary crises, Arendt emphasizes the *autonomy* of action and judgment, she does so in order to underline their freedom and spontaneity, their continued viability in a disenchanted age. Considered as our capacity for initiation, action does not stand in need of the guidance of grounding (transcendent) principles: it is, in fact, denatured by the Platonic-Aristotelian imposition of the substance/attribute, ground/action schema. Similarly, our capacity for judgment does not hinge upon the availability of "customary rules," and it is indeed undermined by the simplistic subsumptive model of judgment such rules promote. The antinostalgia of Arendt's perspective on the eclipse of authority and the break in tradition is evident in her conviction that the "faculties" of action and judgment come truly into their own precisely when there are no "bannisters" to lean on.[141]

Here we come to one of the more important ironies of Arendt's political thought, one completely overlooked by her rationalist critics.[142] In Arendt's hands, the closure of the deductive relation between first and practical philosophy does not lead to decisionism or relativism, but to a recovery of the phenomena of action and judgment in their autonomy and complexity. This recovery, in turn, sets the stage for the restoration of the ethicopolitical dimension, so gravely foreshortened by the instrumentalizing dialectic Plato sets in motion. The "irony" of Arendt's aesthetic approach to political action is that it rescues the phenomenon of reflective judgment (judgment "without criteria") from the oblivion into which it had been thrust by a dogmatically rationalist (and ultimately nihilistic) tradition. Thus, while Arendt's Kantian appeal to taste judgment as the appropriate model for moral-political judgment flows, first and foremost, from a desire to "save the phenomena" of the public-political world, it also provides the reorientation we need to begin the "reconstruction of moral horizons" (Beiner) in terms of shared judgments.[143] And this is the first step toward a postmetaphysical recuperation of the question of *justice*—which, as Arendt notes toward the end of her Eichmann book, is not fundamentally a question of knowledge or truth, but of *judgment*.[144]

IV. The Tradition as Reification: Productionist Metaphysics
and the Withdrawal of the Political

For Arendt the Western tradition of political thought represents a sustained and deeply rooted effort to escape the "frailty" of human affairs, the hazards of political action, and the relativity of the realm of plurality. The haphazardness and contingency that permeate this realm call forth a succession of theoretical attempts to overcome politics, to introduce a firm (extrapolitical) ground for action or to point to a social order in which the need for action is transcended. As we had seen, what unites these efforts is the tendency to substitute making for acting, to submit *praxis* to the dominance of *poiēsis*. Such a substitution makes the idea of sovereign political freedom plausible; moreover, it leads us to look at the realm of human affairs through a very different lens, one that promotes the idea of mastery or control. Whether the grounds for this "technical" interpretation of action *qua* making are metaphysical (the Ideas, Nature, the rational will, History) or pragmatic (Nietzsche's "life," Richard Rorty's "desires") in the end makes little difference. What matters is that both action and politics are denatured, their essential characteristics buried under an epoch-old forgetting.

Arendt's depiction of our tradition as animated by a will to escape politics (or, at the very least, to bring it under control by instrumentalizing political action) adds the dimension of historical depth to the "inauthenticity" of *homo faber*'s productive mentality. This mentality, which gains ascendence in the modern age, resonates with the tradition's repression of action. The result is that the "withdrawal of the political" is one of the outstanding characteristics of our time.[145] In singling out the tradition as being in no small way responsible for our "forgetting" of the political, Arendt is clearly following Heidegger's own historical reworking of the theme of inauthenticity. This reworking, beginning with works published in 1930, led Heidegger to view the metaphysical tradition as a "science of grounds" that systematically covered over the "mystery" of presencing and the primordial phenomenon of the unconcealment of Being in favor of a hypostatized, leveled-off account of the "Being of beings." Such an account, Heidegger argues, allows Western man to circumscribe Being as something representable and thus (in principle) controllable. By thinking of Being on the model of beings—by effacing what Heidegger refers to as the "ontological difference" between Being *qua* presencing and entities—metaphysics thrusts the primordial phenomenon of the "clearing" or disclosure of Being into oblivion. This forgetting lays the groundwork for the eventual "regulating and securing" of all that is, for planetary domination.[146] From the start, then, metaphysics's will to ground is seen, simultaneously, as a will to security and a will to power.

The narrative Heidegger develops after 1930—in which the history of metaphysics conceals a closet "history of Being," the tale of Being's self-withdrawal and subsequent oblivion[147]—clearly diverges from the "fundamental ontology" of his *Being in Time*. This divergence becomes more pronounced with the *Kehre*, the "turning," that occurs in the course of the Nietzsche lectures (1936–40), a turning that spurs his critique of technology and the development of the notion of *Gelassenheit* as an alternative to metaphysical/technological "enframing."[148] Nevertheless, it is important to grasp the basic thematic continuities between early, middle, and late Heidegger; otherwise we risk misinterpreting not only his turn to *Seinsgeschichte*, but also the way his history of metaphysics decisively influences Arendt's view of the "contemplative tradition's" escape from politics.

•

In *Being and Time* Heidegger argued that our disclosive relation to Being is covered over by our propensity to understand ourselves and the world around us as *vorhanden* (present-at-hand), in terms of the categories of subject and substance. This propensity is rooted in our everydayness but also, more deeply, in our Greek and Cartesian heritage. As such it is symptomatic of a fundamental lack of resolve, an unwillingness to acknowledge either the pervasiveness of finitude or the fact of our groundlessness. The desire for security and tranquility prompts us, on the one hand, to lose ourselves in everydayness and, on the other hand, to presuppose the availability (and validity) of preestablished standards. These tendencies of inauthentic *Dasein* conceal the anxiety-producing freedom of disclosure by reifying our contingent vocabularies into quasi-natural entities and by stripping the world of its horizonal (historical) status.

In turning his attention to the origins of the Western metaphysical tradition, Heidegger sought to provide a genealogy of the ontological prejudices that predispose us toward such forgetfulness. Early on, Heidegger claims, metaphysics installs at the root of our culture a particular and fateful interpretation of the Being of beings, one that freezes the ontological horizon of the West so that Being loses all connotation of temporality and is understood, instead, as something permanent and selfsame, something we can take up a position toward and (ultimately) dispose of. By reifying the presence of the present and taking it as the model for Being, metaphysics disentangles man from Being and plunges the human vocation of disclosure into oblivion.[149] The forgetfulness it promotes is similar to the "numbing" effect of everydayness, but it occurs at a much more profound and historically diffuse level. Insofar as metaphysics's reifying approach to Being and the "is-ness" of entities successfully seals off the temporality of presencing from thought, it constitutes a "destiny" (*Geschick*) for the West, one that culminates in the hegemony of the "standing-reserve."[150]

The rudiments of this story can be grasped by returning to Heidegger's gloss (in *IM*) on the pre-Socratic comprehension of Being as *physis*, as self-emergence or coming-into-the-light.[151] Heidegger's return to the "first beginning" of the West is undertaken to reveal what he considers to be a more authentic understanding of the disclosive character of human being. This understanding, he argues, is inseparable from an experience of Being as an overpowering event or activity (the process through which what is comes to presence). With the pre-Socratics (specifically with Parmenides), the fateful identification of Being with presence is made, yet presence is understood temporally, as an occurence. With Plato, however, the eventlike character of Being as appearing is lost as the *consequence* of this process—appearance or visibility—is hypostatized as pure or timeless form. As *ontos on*, the realm of essence or idea provides a *paradeigma*, or model, from which the particular and temporal derives its being. A *chorismos* (chasm) is inserted between the real and permanent prototype and the merely apparent (transient) copy:

> From the standpoint of the idea, appearing now takes on a new meaning. What appears—the phenomenon—is no longer *physis*, the emerging power, nor is it self-manifestation of appearance; no, appearing is now the emergence of the copy. Since the copy never equals its prototype, what appears is mere appearance, actually an illusion, a deficiency.... Because the actual repository of being is the idea and this is the prototype, all disclosure of being must aim at assimilation to the model, accommodation to idea. The truth of *physis*, *aletheia* as the unconcealment that is the essence of the emerging power, now becomes *homoisis* and *mimesis* . . . a correctness of vision, of apprehension as representation.[152]

The "transformation of Being from *physis* to idea" thus gives rise to "one of the essential movements in the history of the West," insofar as it covers over both disclosure and concealment (the mystery) with a relation of correspondence.[153] The installation of a relation of representation between intellect and "the matter" (or of mimesis between essence and thing) rests upon the reinterpretation of Being as enduring, constant presence. Thought of as *eidos* (form or idea) or *ousia* (substance), Being is delimited by its permanence, self-identity, and pregivenness.[154] This reification facilitates the recuperation of the ontological difference between Being and beings (between presencing and what is present) as the distinction between "whatness" and "thatness," essence and existence.[155] Heidegger calls this recuperation "an event in the history of Being," because with it, Being takes up its metaphysical position as the ground of beings. As Otto Pöggeler puts it, in metaphysics "the difference between Being and beings is thought from going beyond what is present (a being) toward constant presencing (Being). Being thereby becomes a ground in which a being is grounded."[156] This gives a decidedly ominous spin to Heidegger's statement in "What Is Metaphysics?," where he calls metaphysics "inquiry beyond or over beings, which aims to recover them as such and as a whole for our grasp."[157] The interpretation of Being as constant presence or ground guarantees, so to speak, the possibility of an inclusive grasp of all that is. With this promise the metaphysical project of a total representation and securing of Being announces itself.[158]

For Heidegger, then, the root of metaphysics's inauthenticity—its will to security and power, its "spirit of revenge" (Nietzsche)—is found in its approach to the *Seinsfrage*, the question "What is Being?" For the pre-Socratics, this question remained suspended, open-ended, the most uncanny of questions. Yet for metaphysics (the science of grounds founded by Plato and Aristotle) the question is easily answered: Being is the *ontos on*, the ground from which "beings as such are what they are in their becoming, perishing, and persisting as something that can be known, handled, and worked upon."[159] The abyss out of which economies of presence and absence happen is covered over and the role of human beings in this unmasterable event forgotten.

The manner in which metaphysics converts Being into a ground deserves somewhat closer attention. Developing a line of thought from *Being and Time*, Heidegger emphasizes how the understanding of the Being of beings as constant presence or present-at-hand derives from the fabrication experience—from the comportment of *Dasein* as producer.[160] Greek ontology is seen as performing a hypostatization similar to that by which *Vorhandenheit* (present-at-handness) obscures *Zuhandenheit* (ready-to-handness). In both the historical and phenomenological cases, certain aspects of entities as they are encountered in the production process (e.g., their outward appearance, independence, their standing-in-itself [*Ansichsein*]) are radically decontextualized.[161] This decontextualization makes it possible for these aspects to be projected as the essential characteristics of the Being of beings. As early as *The Basic Problems of Phenomenology* (written directly after *Being and Time*), Heidegger saw the historical genealogy of *Vorhandenheit* as leading back to the "productionist" prejudices of the Greeks. In his subsequent work on the history of metaphysics, the productionist character of Western ontology becomes a persistent theme.[162]

From Heidegger's perspective, the Greek reliance upon the fabrication experience for a more "solid" understanding of Being initates a metaphysical tradition in which the metaphorics of production exercise an unquestioned dominance.[163] The Greek universalization of a regional ontology leaves its trace in Plato's thinking of constant presence along the lines of an idea or a prototype, and in Aristotle's understanding of actuality (*energeia*) in terms of "embodied form" or work (*ergon*). Indeed, according to Heidegger, Aristotle was "more Greek than Plato" in the transparency of his productionist prejudices.[164] The Christian understanding of the Being of beings as "created being" (*ens creatum*) deepens and extends the Greek productionist view of the world by casting God in the role of supreme artificer.[165] With Descartes, the creative representing power of the divine intellect is transferred to the human subject, who, as "thing that thinks," is the most real being and whose prerogative it is to delimit reality in terms of the clarity and distinctness of its representations.[166] The predominance of *poiēsis* in the metaphysical tradition reaches its culmination in Nietzsche's "artist's metaphysics," in which the Being of beings and truth in all its forms are seen simply as *products* of a creative will to power bent on increasing and enhancing its power.[167] Nietzsche's "inversion" of Platonism/metaphysics brings the will to grasp and control beings (sublimated by the representational paradigm) front and center, revealing the will to planetary domination driving metaphysics from the beginning.[168] This will, shorn of its "bad conscience," reaches its fulfillment in technological "enframing" (*Gestell*).[169]

Heidegger's path after *Being and Time* was, of course, by no means straight. Yet while he was to disown the transcendental impulses of fundamental ontology (its residual subjectivism and "humanism"), the concern with recovering our disclosive relation to Being remains constant. The truly big change after 1930 is that he comes to see the tradition, rather than everydayness, as the primary locus of inauthenticity. Fallenness comes to be seen as (so to speak) a derivative phenomenon. The real lack of resolve first surfaces in the Greek "securing" of Being as constant presence or ground, a securing accomplished through the tacit decontextualization and universalization of the productive comportment toward entities.

The point of contact between Heidegger's critical "history of productionist metaphysics" and Arendt's view of our tradition as a series of attempted "escapes" from politics is clear. If, as Heidegger maintains, the originary thrust of the metaphysical tradition is to deny human "guilt" and finitude; to relieve the anxiety of disclosure with the security of correspondence (to some "order of Being"); and to reassure that the possession of the ground enables us to dispose of the real as we see fit; then, we should not be surprised by what happens when *this* tradition turns to confront the phenomenological realm of politics and political action. If, as Arendt suggests, political action is our most groundless and disclosive activity, we can expect a peculiarly tenacious attempt to "disguise" it or cover it over. This, on Arendt's reading at least, is precisely what happens, as the arc of the tradition—from Plato and Aristotle to Marx and Nietzsche—traces the recuperation of acting as making, politics as art or *technē*, freedom as sovereignty or control. The antipolitical implications of this "productionist" approach to politics have been described; what I wish to stress here is the way Heidegger's deconstruction of metaphysics affords us a glimpse into the rootedness of this tendency. Because the predominance of *poiēsis* is built into our most basic ontological categories, the subsumption of *praxis* by *poiēsis* is almost a foregone conclusion. Arendt's single-minded attempt to rescue action from the distorting metaphors of politics as making or plastic art flows, I would suggest, from her appreciation of the political implications of what Heidegger discovered when he went back to the "ground" of metaphysics. Unsurprisingly, Heidegger was to remain blind to his own insight.[170]

The Critique of Modernity

The fundamental event of the modern age is the conquest
of the world as picture.

—Heidegger, *"The Age of the World-Picture"*

World alienation, and not self-alienation as Marx thought,
has been the hallmark of the modern age.

—Arendt, The Human Condition[1]

Nothing in our time, it seems to me, is more dubious than
our attitude towards the world.

—Arendt, *"On Humanity in Dark Times"*

I. INTRODUCTION: ARENDT AND HEIDEGGER AS CRITICS OF MODERNITY

The Human Condition presents Arendt's phenomenology of human activity. This analysis, however, is interwoven with a narrative about the decline of action and the public realm throughout the modern age. "The purpose of the historical analysis," she tells us, ". . . is to trace back modern world alienation, its twofold flight from the earth into the universe and from the world into the self."[2] The story she unfolds is not an optimistic one. The modern "rise of the social" promotes the absorption of the public realm by household concerns, while *homo faber*'s consistent utilitarianism results in the "limitless instrumentalization of everything that exists."[3] Add to these developments the tendency, born of modern science, to view the earth (which Arendt calls "the very quintessence of the human condition") as merely one more object, and the transformation of work into a form of labor via technological automatism, and the result is a pervasive and radical *worldlessness*. Politically, worldlessness manifests itself in the "atrophy" of the space of appearances and the "withering" of common sense, a loss of feeling for the world.[4] Existentially, worldlessness is experienced as a kind of homelessness, a lack of place that results from the modern destruction of the durability of the "human artifice."

Insofar as worldlessness—"always a form of barbarism"—is homelessness,

Arendt agrees with Heidegger's sentiment in the "Letter on Humanism": homelessness is coming to be the destiny of the age.[5] The forces unleashed by modernity—the forces of capitalist expropriation and accumulation of wealth, of modern science (with its presupposition of an "Archimedean point"), and of technology—are, according to Arendt, directly responsible for this state of affairs. Each has contributed mightily to the undermining of the "human artifice," to the transformation of relatively stable structures into fluid processes. The result is an alienation from the world even more extreme than that of the early Christians. Like them, we have no faith in, or feeling for, the durability of our world; unlike them, we have no bond strong enough to replace the world.[6]

For Arendt, the modern project of technological mastery has an essentially ironic outcome. Freedom is not enhanced by the extension of control and the overcoming of necessity; rather, it is gradually eliminated as it loses its place in the world. In taking this stance, Arendt seems very much on the terrain of the Frankfurt School. Her critical thrust, however, is decidedly different from that of Theodor Adorno and Max Horkheimer. Where they emphasize the domination of nature and the ways it inevitably boomerangs on a subject who is also nature, Arendt stresses the extent to which technology assimilates human existence to the "natural."[7] The problem is not, or not merely, the modern will to expunge otherness and subjugate nature (a project that leads to increased domination). What is at stake for Arendt is not the natural basis of the self but the integrity and durability of the world that stands between humanity and nature.

This crucial difference is linked to another. From Arendt's perspective, it is not *fear* of otherness that underlies the project of technological mastery; rather, she believes this peculiarly modern project is driven by a deeply rooted existential *resentment*, a resentment of finitude and limitation as such.[8] Modernity rebels "against human existence as it has been given"; it is driven by the desire to exchange the givenness of the human condition for "something he [man] has made himself."[9] From the perspective of late modernity, the world appears to be a prison. Technology presents itself as the means by which the boundaries of this prison may be removed. Yet technology reveals itself to be something much more than a means: it is a specifically world-destroying power, one that renders the very category of means and ends irrelevant through its focus on process. In the "pseudo-world" of technology, even the "equipmental totality" is "dimmed down."

Arendt's focus on existential resentment (the very opposite of all "thankfulness for Being") refers us directly to Heidegger's critique of the modern "will to will," just as her description of the process whereby the instrumentalism of *homo faber* gives way to the worldlessness of the *animal laborans* evokes his critique of technology. Like Arendt, Heidegger understands the modern age as one of "insurrection" against what is (in Arendt's phrase) a "free gift from nowhere."[10] The "will to will" is a will to overcome finitude and contingency, to remake the world and establish man in the position of "lord and master." Such a project, however, requires a radically transformed understanding of the real, an ontology in which man, *qua* subject, becomes "the relational center of that which is as such."[11] Heidegger's writings—from *Nietzsche* (1936–40) and "The Age of the World Picture" (1938) to "The Question Concerning Technology" (1954)—trace the modern subjectification of the real, the process through which the real is reduced to dimensions set out by a representing, willing subject. For Heidegger, this process coincides with what *An Introduction to Metaphysics* calls the "darkening of the world." It culminates in the "ordering revealing" of technological "enframing" (*Gestell*), a mode of presencing that brings humanity to "the very brink of a precipitous fall."[12]

Heidegger's concern, shared by Arendt, is that man, in making himself "lord of the earth," destroys the very conditions necessary for the exercise of his disclosive capacity. Thus, what Heidegger fears from technology as a "mode of revealing" is the way it "drives out every other possibility of revealing"; that is, its peculiarly closed or leveling character.[13] Arendt's *The Human Condition* provides a less abstract account of the modern subjectification of the real, one that focuses upon the "destruction of the common world" promoted by the Faustian energies of modernity.[14] The animating worry, nevertheless, is parallel to Heidegger's: we seem to be creating a "world" in which there is no viable stage for action, and in which "normalized" behavior subsumes disclosive spontaneity. The decline of a genuinely public reality in the modern age raises the possibility that the "survival of the species mankind" will be secured at the cost of extinguishing the disclosive capacity—the capacity for action—that makes us human.[15] The paradoxical logic of modern existential resentment is that an age that "began with such an unprecedented and promising outburst of human activity" may in fact end "in the deadliest, most sterile passivity history has ever known."[16]

This chapter examines the antimodernism of Arendt and Heidegger in light of this fear. At the most general level, I want to show how Arendt's concern for the world and action leads her to appropriate leading themes from Heidegger's critique of modernity, including the subjectification of the real, the "de-worldling of the world," and the technological dis-essencing of our disclosive capacity. As in Chapters 4 and 5, my desire is not to place Arendt in Heidegger's shadow; rather, it is to reveal the way she extracts novel and unexpected *political* implications from a critique mired in cultural conservatism. This is not to say that Arendt's antimodernism is entirely free of such conservatism; however, it is to draw attention to the "sea-change" these themes undergo as they migrate from Heidegger to Arendt. As always with Arendt, what is taken up is transformed, often to the point where it is no longer recognizable. This is especially true in the case of modernity and its pathologies. As a result, Arendt's understanding of politics, her democratically motivated "care for the world," places Heidegger's ontological concerns in a context he would not have recognized.

This is an important point, one frequently overlooked by those who would dismiss the Arendtian critique of modernity as "rejectionist" or "totalizing." It is true that Arendt fails to play the game of immanent critique: her purpose is not to sing to liberal bourgeois society its own tune. In this respect, she barely qualifies as even a "reluctant" modernist.[17] Closer to the mark, I think, is George Kateb's characterization of her as a "great antimodernist."[18] Yet even this description is offered with polemical intent. Kateb would have us view Arendt as the kind of cultural critic who wishes to see modernity undone. This way of framing the issue strikes me as a liberal version of what Foucault calls "the blackmail of Enlightenment"—the insistence that one take a stand "for" or "against" bourgeois democracy, enlightenment rationality, and so forth, before delivering the specifics of one's critique. While Arendt is unquestionably antimodern in a broad sense, she hardly shares the cultural conservative's wish to return to the premodern. Arendt refuses to deal in this type of nostalgia, a fact evident throughout her theoretical work. If nothing else, this work is a prolonged and multifaceted account of why the structures of meaning, morality, and politics defining the premodern world are no longer possible.

What is it, then, that makes Arendt's critique of modernity *seem* like a paradigmatic instance of rejectionist critique? Partly (as Kateb notes) it is her unyielding focus on the downside of modernity: she describes its horrors and pathologies at length, but none of its greatness.[19] Another explanation, less obvious but no less important, is that this critique moves on explicitly ontological terrain. Just as her rethinking of action and freedom centered on the mode of being and type of reality implied by an authentically political existence, so her critique of modernity focuses on the destruction of the "space of appearances" and the decline of a genuinely *public* reality. Hence the distance that separates her critique from one that takes the Weberian concept of rationalization as its central category of analysis.[20]

The impression that *The Human Condition* is an exercise in "Hellenic nostalgia" is created when we hypostatize Arendt's ontological concerns into a static phenomenology of human activity. The old hierarchy of the *vita activa* then appears as the means to condemn the new—a "stick to beat modernity with." Yet this phenomenology is not as conceptually static as it first appears, and in fact it relies upon an implicit historical ontology. Unlike many of her critics, Arendt refused to reify the capacities and conditions of human existence into a transhistorical human "nature."[21] As her rejoinder to Eric Voegelin makes clear, she was intensely aware of the internal connection between individual capacities and the conditions necessary for their exercise.[22] Thus, she could easily imagine situations in which the effacement of certain conditions necessary for action (e.g., plurality or worldliness) had progressed to the point where this capacity itself began to wither. It is not, in other words, simply a question of the relative status an activity has in the hierarchy of the *vita activa*; it is also a matter of the peculiar historical reality the activity inhabits. Hence the possibility not only of a change in rank (the "reversal" within the *vita activa* that helps define the entry into modernity), but of a dis-essencing or transformation of the capacities themselves. It is the resulting inseparability of the ontological and the political that makes Arendt's critique of modernity at once so powerful and so frustratingly *final*.

II. Heidegger: The Metaphysics of the Moderns and the Subjectification of the Real

> Collapse and desolation find their adequate occurrence in the fact that meta-physical man, the *animal rationale*, gets fixed as the laboring animal.
>
> —Heidegger, *"Overcoming Metaphysics"*[23]

Self-Assertion as Self-Grounding: The "Inauthenticity" of Modernity

Heidegger views the modern age as the age of the autonomous subject, of the "will to will" and boundless human self-assertion (*Selbstbehauptung*). Yet he also sees it as an advanced expression of the inauthenticity that characterizes the tradition of Western metaphysics. The apparent paradox—the idea that self-assertion might somehow be "irresolute"—dissolves when we realize that for Heidegger, the will to will (the will to increased power) is essentially a will to security.[24] The dynamism of modernity, its ceaseless application to the project of remaking or (to use Kant's figure) *completing* the world, is essentially reactive. It is driven by the characteristically metaphysical desire to grasp and secure Being as a whole, to render Being as something permanently present. Human self-assertion takes the form of a perpetual "making secure," an ordering of all that is that reaches its culmination in the technological presencing of the real as "standing-reserve" (*Bestand*).

The modern goal of planetary domination, and the overcoming of finitude this implies, proceeds via a radicalization of the productionist prejudices of the tradition. According to Heidegger, both Greek philosophy and Christianity equated "to be" with "to be produced." In the modern age, this understanding is given an explicitly anthropocentric twist. "Being" is no longer an attribute dispensed by the Creator God of Christianity; rather, it is identified with the realm of objectivity set out by the active, self-conscious subject. That which is finds its measure and ground in the "planning and calculating" of this subject, who represents and "sets before."[25] The world, in Heidegger's famous phrase, "becomes picture" as man becomes, at the threshold of modernity, "the primary and only real *subiectum*."[26]

The "dominance of the subject in the modern age" is announced by the work of Descartes, whose work Heidegger singles out as the beginning of modern metaphysics.[27] Descartes's subjective turn (by way of the *cogito*) illustrates, for Heidegger, the inextricability of self-assertion and the will to security within modernity. On the one hand, the *cogito* signifies the liberation from a medieval *ordo* and the traditional concept of truth as revelation. It is a symbol of a newfound autonomy, which Heidegger describes as "the emancipation of man in which he frees himself from obligation to Christian revelational truth and Church doctrine to a legislating for himself that takes its stand upon itself."[28] This autonomy, however, is possible only on the basis of a new ground, a new certainty. The eclipse of the *lumen naturale*, the suspension of the divinely guaranteed correspondence (*adequatio*) between "the matter" and truth, precipitated a crisis in ground, which could be resolved only by the substitution of a new ground for the old. Thus, as Heidegger puts it, "liberation *from* the revelational certainty of salvation had to be intrinsically a freeing to a certainty in which man secures for himself the true as the known of his own knowing."[29] The other side of the liberation preformed by Cartesian doubt is Descartes's claim to have found the *fundamentum absolutum inconcussum veritas* within man himself.[30]

The significance of the *cogito* hardly ends here. The epistemological move, while revolutionary, points to a deeper ontological transformation, one that results from Descartes's appeal to self-consciousness as the paradigmatic instance of presence.[31] By offering the self-consciousness of the subject as his one indubitable point, as that which is "firmly fixed," Descartes implicitly makes this ground of truth the ground of being. Heidegger points to this in a gloss of the *cogito* offered in the *Nietzsche* lectures:

> *Cogito* then does not merely say that I think, nor merely that I am, nor that my existence follows from the fact of my thinking. The principle speaks of a connection between *cogito* and *sum*. It says that I am as one representing, but that my representation, as definitive *repraesentatio*, decides about the being present of everything that is represented; that is to say, about the presence of what is meant in it; that is, about its being as a being. The principle says that representation, which is essentially represented to itself, posits Being as representedness, and truth as certitude. That to which everything is referred back as to the unshakeable ground is *the full essence of representation itself*.[32]

The "thing that thinks" finds its clearest and most distinct idea, its most real idea, in consciousness of self. This provides the basis for its drawing an ontological horizon around itself in terms of representation: "The Being of the one who represents and secures himself in representing is the measure of the Being of what is represented as such."[33] The subject's capacity for foundational (self) representation is that upon which the objectivity of the object can first appear. Thus, the epistemological turn performed by Descartes at the beginning of the modern period serves as a kind of Trojan horse for metaphysics, in that the *cogito* establishes and secures the truth of Being within the space opened up by representation.[34] The *cogito* is the vehicle through which man implicitly assumes his specifically modern role as "that being upon which all that is, is grounded as regards the manner of it Being and its truth."[35] It symbolizes the moment in which "man becomes the relational center of that which is as such"; in which ontology becomes anthropology; in which the real is subjectified through the reduction of Being to representation.[36]

According to Heidegger, it remained for Kant and German Idealism to strip Descartes's argument of its scholastic anachronisms and tease out its full ontological implications. By focusing upon the *a priori* contribution of transcendental logic (the categories) and imagination (the schematism of concepts), Kant's "Copernican revolution" in epistemology explicitly grounded the objectivity of the object in the subjectivity of the subject. The tacit reduction of the real to an objectivity (*Gegenstandigkeit*) constructed or "posited" (Fichte) by a transcendental subject resolved the old metaphysical question concerning the Being of beings into an *anthropological* one.[37] Radicalizing the basic Cartesian strategy, the first *Critique* grounds Being (thought metaphysically, as the totality of beings) as that which "stands-against" the subject.[38] Thus, Heidegger's reading reveals transcendental philosophy as indeed the "modern form of ontology."[39] The critique of pure reason presents an anthropocentric narrowing and reification of our ontological horizon, a "demarcation, on the basis of our reason, of the determinations of the Being of beings, of the thingness of things; it means an admeasuring and projecting of those fundamental principles of pure reason on whose basis a thing is determined in its thingness."[40]

Heidegger famously sees Nietzsche as the culmination of this modern, anthropocentric and reductionist, ontologizing. He interprets Nietzsche's doctrine of the will to power as a metaphysics, in which "that which is in being" is whatever a will driven to increase its own power sets before itself.[41] Nietzsche consummates the "modern metaphysics of subjectness" in that he takes the Cartesian demarcation of the real (as that which the *ego cogito* sets before itself) to its logical extreme. Cartesian certainty assures the self of its fixedness, its availability as ground. Nietzsche "activates" this certainty in the form of a will to power whose securing of itself demands that it surround itself "with an encircling sphere of that which it can reliably grasp at."[42] Such an encircling sphere "bounds off the constant reserve of what presences," and transforms reality into something "fixedly constant," something that can be "immediately at the disposal of the will."[43] The "inauthenticity" of the moderns, first expressed in the Cartesian turn to the subject as ground and measure of the real, reaches a new level in Nietzsche's reduction of Being to that which can be "made secure," which can provide the raw material necessary for the will to power's preservation and increase. With Nietzsche, the Cartesian quest for certainty reveals itself to be driven by a deep-seated existential resentment.

Heidegger's interpretation is quite controversial: he manages to see Nietzsche as animated by the "spirit of revenge."[44] I want to leave this controversy to one side in order to focus on the role Nietzsche plays in Heidegger's narrative about modernity; for it is with the framing of Nietzsche as Descartes's heir, as the most extreme expression of modern subjectivism and self-assertion, that the practical implications of Heidegger's analysis reveal themselves. If (and it is a big "if") one accepts Heidegger's contention that "metaphysics grounds an age, in that through a specific interpretation of what is and through a specific comprehension of truth it gives to that age the basis upon which it is essentially formed," then it becomes possible to view the progressive subjectification of the real in modern philosophy as signaling a fundamental alteration in man's "precomprehension of Being," and (thus) an equally fundamental change in his modes of comportment toward Being.[45] Where "the whole of that which is as such . . . has been drunk up by man," where man "rises up into the subjectivity of his essence," into "the I-ness of the *ego cogito*," there

> Man enters into insurrection. The world changes into object. In this revolutionary objectifying of all that is, the earth, that which first of all must be put at the disposal of representing and setting forth, moves into the midst of human positing and analyzing. The earth itself can show itself only as the object of assault, an object that, in human willing, establishes itself as unconditional objectification. Nature appears everywhere . . . as the object of technology.[46]

The subjectivism of Descartes, Kant, and Nietzsche—their reduction of that which is to representation and will—prefigures the destiny of the modern age. From Heidegger's perspective, it is the destiny of this age to remake the world, to *actualize* the productionist ontology of the tradition. For Heidegger, it is a straight line from Plato's presentation of the fabrication experience as a lasting image of the real (*eidos* as blueprint) to the subject of modern philosophy who produces by representing and setting before.[47] It is a similarly straight line from this "merely" theoretical objectification to the "unconditional objectification" of modern science and technology. The end result is not simply an exchange of grounding images (the world viewed as clock or mechanism rather than text), but rather the creation of an instrumentalized, and utterly anthropocentric, reality, in which that which is appears as raw material.[48] As we shall see, for Heidegger the horror of the technological age is that humanity also "comes to presence" as raw material.

The Will to Will and the Conquest of the World as Picture

Heidegger's 1938 essay "The Age of the World-Picture" (*Die Zeit des Weltbildes*) approaches the modern subjectification of the real from a different angle. In contrast to the contemporaneous Nietzsche lectures, it does not offer commentary on philosophical texts, but rather a transcendental argument in the broadly Kantian sense. Beginning with phenomena he considers essential to the modern age—science, machine technology, the subjectification of art in aesthetics, the framing of human activity as "culture," and "the loss of the gods"—Heidegger attempts to uncover the particular historical understanding of what it is that makes them possible.[49] By elucidating the "modern interpretations of that which is," Heidegger believes he can help the "essential character of the modern age" to reveal itself.[50]

The importance of this essay, for my purposes, is twofold. On the one hand, it provides a more concrete version of the subjectification thesis, one that concentrates on the exemplary character of modern science in a manner which anticipates Arendt's own analysis in *The Human Condition*. On the other hand, the essay provides a striking formulation of this subjectification (the "reduction of the world to picture") that clarifies the link between modern anthropocentrism and productionism.

Heidegger begins his quest for the understanding of what *is* that underlies the modern age by limiting his investigation to the phenomenon of modern science. By isolating the "essence" of modern science, Heidegger hopes to uncover the metaphysical ground that provides its foundation. And, he thinks, once this is accomplished "the entire essence of the modern age will have to let itself be apprehended from out of that ground."[51]

The first in Heidegger's series of descending questions is, then, "In what does the essence of modern science lie?"[52] The answer, in a word, is *research*.[53] In marked contrast to the *epistēmē* of the Greeks or the *doctrina* and *scientia* of the Middle Ages, *modern* science takes the form of research. As a form of knowing, research is characterized by the projection of a "fixed ground plan" or object realm, rigorous procedure (methodology), and ongoing, institutionalized activity. With this approximation of the "essence" of modern science, Heidegger now asks, "What understanding of what is and what concept of truth provide the basis for the fact that science is being transformed into research?"[54]

Research, whether scientific or historical, aims at calculating the future or verifying the past. Such calculation and verification presume that "nature and history [can] become the objects of a representing that explains. Such representing counts on nature and takes account of history."[55] The transformation of science into research presumes that "the Being of whatever is, is sought in objectiveness."[56] It presumes, moreover, that "truth has been transformed into the certainty of representation."[57] The "objectifying of whatever is," accomplished in "a setting before, a representing, that aims at bringing each particular being before it in such a way that man who calculates can be sure of that being," constitutes the metaphysical ground of science as research.[58]

This objectifying of whatever is through representation does not merely make science as research possible; according to Heidegger, it determines "first and long beforehand" the essence of the modern age generally. How so?

In answering this question, Heidegger returns to the theme of self-assertion as self-grounding. The objectifying of whatever *is* signifies that man "frees himself to himself," extricating himself from the web of obligations built into a teleological *ordo*.[59] Yet this "freeing"—the self-assertion of the modern age—while "correct" as a characterization of modernity, is not "decisive." In fact, Heidegger states, it "leads to those errors that prevent us from comprehending the essential foundations of the modern age."[60] What is "decisive" is not that such objectification dissolves the encompassing teleological hierarchy of the Middle Ages, but that with this objectification "the very essence of man itself changes, in that man becomes subject."[61] This means that man becomes *subiectum* (the translation of *hypokeimenon*), the "that-which-lies-before," which, "as ground, gathers everything onto itself."[62] Man becomes the "relational center of that which is as such"; but this event, according to Heidegger, is possible "only when the comprehension of what is as a whole changes."[63]

Heidegger's transcendental argument seems, at this point, to become dangerously circular. *Qua* research, science presumes the objectification of whatever is and the transformation of truth into certainty of representation. This transformation, in turn, points to the fact that man (and not God or *physis*) has become *subiectum*, the being upon which all that is "is grounded as regards the manner of its Being." However, we are now told that this shift in ground rests on a prior change in "the comprehension of what is as a whole."

In fact, there is a circle here, but of the hermeneutic sort. The change in "the comprehension of what is as a whole" that makes man as *subiectum* possible is that the world becomes "picture."[64] In claiming this, Heidegger is not saying that the "world" (a name for "what is in its entirety") becomes an object susceptible to representation; rather, he is saying that the horizon of world is itself transformed. By "becoming picture," this horizon phenomenon frames the Being of that which is as representedness, a transformation that makes possible the emergence of man as subject and the objectification of whatever is.[65]

The "becoming picture of the world" thus signifies the most fundamental transformation of the modern age, a transformation in the way the world provides a space of disclosure or unconcealment. In modernity, the world "worlds" as picture. Within such a space, that which is can appear only as something represented and set before:

> . . . world picture, when understood essentially, does not mean a picture of the world but the world conceived and grasped as picture. What is, in its entirety, is now taken in such a way that it is in being and only in being to the extent that it is set up by man, who represents and sets forth. Wherever we have the world picture, an essential decision takes place regarding what is, in its entirety. The being of whatever is, is sought and found in the representedness of the latter.[66]

In modernity, things come to presence otherwise, as picture. This is what distinguishes the essence of the modern age; namely, "the fact that the world becomes picture at all."[67] Modernity is distinguished from other ages not by the character of its world picture, but by the fact that it *has* a world picture. For the Middle Ages, that which is appears as *ens creatum* (God-created entity); for the Greeks, that which is "is that which arises and opens itself"—*physis*. In neither age is the being of what is understood as, first and foremost, something that can be represented by man.

Representation thus constitutes the uniquely modern mode of comprehending the real. For modern man, to represent means "to bring what is present at hand before oneself as something standing over against, to relate it to oneself, to the one representing it, and to force it back into this relationship to oneself as the normative realm."[68] It is through this type of representation that modern man "gets into the picture," and in a peculiarly hegemonic way: "man sets himself up as the setting in which whatever is must henceforth present itself, i.e., be picture."[69] Such universal setting-before makes the world appear as picture *for us*, as a coherent and systemic whole framed in accordance with human needs, as something that is at our disposal.[70] As the setting in which the world, as picture, presences as objective, man takes on a distinctive status: he becomes, in Heidegger's words, "the representative [*der Repräsentant*] of that which is."[71]

It is tempting to read Heidegger's characterization of the modern understanding of what is as implying no more than a change in the relative position of humanity vis-à-vis the real. Thus, assuming Heidegger's broad descriptions of the medieval and Greek understandings of Being to be correct, one might say that what distinguishes modernity is a more detached or alienated perspective: we are no longer "looked upon" by Being (as were the Greeks), nor implicated in its hierarchical structure (as was medieval Christendom). Instead we comprehend the real in terms of a relation of representation, as object for a subject. The problem with this simplified way of putting things is that it implies that here is a "position" of man in relation to the real in all epochs; moreover, it implies that the comprehension of what is has always been, at base, a matter of representation. Heidegger vigorously disputes this reading, challenging the idea that what is at stake is distinguishing the modern world picture from the world pictures of the Middle Ages or antiquity.[72] Only modernity has a world picture, and only in modernity can there be such a thing as a "position" of man:

> The newness of this event by no means consists in the fact that now the position of man in the midst of what is, is an entirely different one in contrast to that of ancient and medieval man. What is decisive is that mankind himself expressly takes up this position as one constituted by himself, that he intentionally maintains it as that taken up by himself, and that he makes it secure as the solid footing for the development of humanity. Now for the first time is there any such thing as a "position" of man.[73]

For Heidegger, the radical novelty of modernity consists in the fact that this epoch, in contrast to all others, defines itself through an explicit and self-conscious redrawing of its ontological horizon. All ages have a comprehension of what is; only in modernity is this comprehension thematized and placed in service of a *project*; namely, "gaining mastery over that which is as a whole."[74] Hence, Heidegger's emphasis, in the passage cited above, on the "decisive" fact that man "expressly takes up this position as one constituted by himself," that he "intentionally maintains it" and "makes it secure." The self-conscious and purposive reduction of Being to that which can be represented—a reduction accomplished through the projection of methodologically rigorous "ground plans"—ensures that humanity will encounter only that for which it is "prepared."[75] What metaphysics had previously attempted only "in theory," modernity accomplishes in fact: the imposition of an ontological horizon that, at every point, refers back to the "solid footing" as its maker. "What is, in its entirety, is now taken in such a way that it first is in being and only is in being to the extent that it is set up by man, who represents and sets forth."[76]

The transformation of the world into picture is thus equivalent to its anthropologization. The life of man, *qua subiectum*, becomes the assumed reference point for everything. The ultimate effect is to extend Kant's "Copernican Revolution" to all spheres. It is just such an extension that Heidegger depicts at the outset of his essay: art moves in the purview of aesthetics, and is considered as the object of subjective experience or as an "expression" of human life; similarly, the relation to the divine is transformed into "religious experience."[77] Thus, according to Heidegger's interpretation, the loss of metaphysical comfort arising from the demise of a teleological, anthropocentric world order is more than compensated for by modernity's relentless anthropologism—its reduction of the world to "experience."

The transformation of the world into picture is also inseparable from the *conquest* of the world. The imperialism of the subject leads Heidegger to declare that "the fundamental event of the modern age is the conquest of the world as picture."[78] The world picture is "the creature of man's producing which represents and sets before"; which calculates, plans, and molds all things; and which "secures, organizes, and articulates itself" as world view.[79] The productionist interpretation of Being installed by the Platonic *eidos* comes full circle as the *eidos*, *qua* world view, is made a creature of the productivity of life. "To be" still means "to be produced," but to be produced by the animal species mankind in accordance with the ranking of needs and appetites systematized in world views. Thereby, reality is fully instrumentalized; metaphysics comes to culmination in the technological remaking of the world.

Technology as a Mode of Revealing: The "Brink of a Precipitous Fall"

The essay "The Age of the Word Picture" traces the process by which Kantian schematization is taken off the drawing board, so to speak, and put to work. The result is an instrumentalized reality approximating the "totality of equipmental relations" described in Heidegger's *Being and Time*.[80] Yet this instrumentalist mode of revealing, in which human positing and "setting before" create the illusion of mastery, is rapidly subsumed by a different, more comprehensive ordering, the "enframing" (*Gestell*) of technology. For Heidegger, the advent of the technological world signals the culmination of the metaphysical project of grasping and securing all that is; but it also signals the "death of the subject" insofar as it marks the transformation of anthropocentric instrumentalism into a "framing" that attacks or "challenges" humanity itself. With the advent of the technological world-ordering, "self-assertive man," the initiator of the modern project, becomes "the functionary of technology," the creature of an "ordering revealing."[81]

It is the irony of the modern project—the fact that self-assertion drives humanity to "regulate and secure" itself—that forms the underlying theme of "The Question Concerning Technology" (1954).[82] Heidegger's explicit purpose in this essay is twofold. First, he wants to disabuse us of the current "correct" (instrumental and anthropocentic) conception of technology. Technology, he argues in the first half of the essay, is something quite different from a means, or an instrument. Second, Heidegger wants to show how an unbounded instrumentalism outstrips itself, creating a world in which the means/end category is no longer meaningful. The new reality is more accurately characterized by the "inclusive rubric" of "standing reserve."[83] In the technological framing of the world, Heidegger argues, everything that is comes to presence as essentially raw material. Humanity is not exempt from this framing; indeed, "The Question Concerning Technology" seeks to illuminate how technological revealing threatens humanity with a loss or dis-essencing of its disclosive capacity. According to Heidegger, the attempt to ground and solidify the place of humanity amidst that which is (the metaphysical project) leads, in its technological form, to the "brink of a precipitous fall"[84]—to the "fixing" of man as laboring animal.

For Heidegger, it is the possibility of such "fixing" that makes technological revealing a "threat" to humanity's disclosive nature.[85] The question concerning technology is, ultimately, a question about human dignity. What is at stake is the preservation of a sense of humanity's disclosive (nonteleological) relation to Being, a relation that has been concealed by the metaphysical tropes of correspondence and self-grounding. This relation, Heidegger maintains, is all but destroyed by technological enframing, an economy of presence that provides a truly definitive (that is, final) answer to the metaphysical question of *why* man exists.[86]

"Human dignity" may seem an odd category for Heidegger, the critic of humanism, to invoke. The confusion here, however, arises from a superficial reading. When, in the "Letter on Humanism," Heidegger famously (some would say, notoriously) suggests abandoning humanism to its fate, he does so precisely because this humanism, in its metaphysical determination, "does not set the humanity of man high enough."[87] Metaphysical humanism reifies the "open possibility" of human existence into a "what," the better to provide an answer to the question "Why is it necessary for man to exist at all?" This question—a *degrading* question, as Kateb notes[88]—lies at the root of all metaphysical attempts to "jump over our own shadows" and delimit humanity from a God's-eye perspective. Metaphysical humanism presumes that existence must be redeemed by essence; that the world has value only in relation to this essence; and that human inessentiality is equal to nihilism.[89] In these ways, such humanism promotes what Heidegger calls "forgetfulness of Being" (*Seinsvergessenheit*). Heidegger's point in "The Age of the World Picture" is that the modern anthropologizing version of metaphysical humanism sets the stage for an even more radical forgetting: the "fixing" of humanity not as subject, but as "the most important raw material."[90] It is this more radical forgetting that Heidegger addresses in "The Question Concerning Technology" and elsewhere, under the somewhat misleading rubric of the "threat" to man's "free essence."[91]

Heidegger's stated aim in QCT is to prepare a "free relationship" to the "essence" of technology (QCT, 4). To inquire into the essence of something means, traditionally, to ask *what* that thing is. The answer given to the question What is technology? is, typically, one of two statements: technology is a means to an end; it is a human activity (QCT, 4). These broad characterizations belong together, according to Heidegger, since "to posit ends and procure and utilize the means is a human activity" (QCT, 4). And this is how we normally think of technology, namely, as a "complex of contrivances" for the achievement of human ends. Technology is "the manufacture and utilization of equipment, tools, and machines, the manufactured and used things themselves, and the needs and the ends they serve" (QCT, 4). This description of the "what" of technology Heidegger calls "the instrumental and anthropological definition of technology," a definition that possesses an "uncanny" correctness insofar as it applies to modern as well as older handwork technology (QCT, 5). Who, after all, would question that to "power plant with its turbines and generators is a man-made means to an end established by man" or that the "jet aircraft and the high frequency apparatus are means to ends"? (QCT, 5). Technology, whether primitive or advanced, is a tool, an *instrumentum*.

It is in terms of the "correct" definition of technology (as a means to an end) that the "problem" of modern technology has been framed as an issue of control. Since the industrial revolution, man's tools have appeared to take on a life of their own: means have transformed themselves into ends, and humanity has become the servant of its instruments. This is the phenomenon that Marx addressed as reification, and that Weber analyzed under the rubric of rationalization.[92] Where means become ends, it is a question of reasserting human control—of regaining our alienated subjectivity, as Marx would say. In this way, the instrumental conception of technology conditions "every attempt to bring man into the right relation to technology": everything seems to depend upon our manipulating technology in the proper manner as *means* (QCT, 5). Thus, the task we set for ourselves: "we will, as we say, 'get' technology 'spiritually in hand.'" We will master it" (QCT, 5). The more technology threatens to slip from control, the more urgent becomes the will to mastery.

Heidegger, however, poses an unsettling question: "Suppose that technology were no mere means, how would it stand with the will to master it?" (QCT, 5). This question implies that the "correct" definition conceals at least as much as it reveals. And indeed, according to Heidegger, "the correct instrumental definition of technology still does not show us technology's essence" (QCT, 6). But this essence—the "true"—can be pursued only by way of the "correct." Accordingly, the question concerning technology must proceed by first inquiring into the nature of the *instrumental* as such: "Within what do such things as means and ends belong?" (QCT, 6). The answer to this question is that a means "effects" or "attains" something; it is a *cause*. Likewise, the end that determines the choice of means in also considered a cause. Thus, "wherever ends are pursued and means are employed, wherever instrumentality reigns, there reigns causality." (QCT, 6).

Heidegger, at this stage in his argument, departs on what seems an inexplicable tangent. He inquires into the Greek understanding of causality, an understanding that, he argues, has been obscured by the tradition's reification of Aristotle's doctrine of fourfold causality. Underlying the instrumental or teleological understanding of causality as effect or goal is an older, "poetic" notion of causality: "The four causes are the ways, all belonging at once to each other, of *being responsible* for something else" (QCT, 7). Thus, for the Greeks, a silver sacrificial chalice is not produced by an artisan who imposes form on material, in order to create an object that fulfills a particular purpose. Rather, the "material," silver, and the "form," the "aspect of chaliceness," are contained in advance within the realm of "consecration and bestowal" (QCT, 8). This "bounding" determines what the thing will be: it is the space out of which the sacrificial chalice is what it is. This bounding, together with the silver itself and the "aspect" of chaliceness, are "coresponsible" for the presencing of the chalice. The silversmith "gathers" these three modes of responsibility together, indebting himself to them as he participates in the "bringing-forth" of the vessel (QCT, 9).

Heidegger's description of the "fourfold coresponsible bringing-forth" at work in the presencing of the sacrificial vessel appears, at first glance, to be a classic example of Heideggerian kitsch. Causality is transformed into something mysterious through the invocation of the primordial powers of the pastoral and the sacred. The description, however, has a point; namely, to show that causality experienced as "bringing-forth" is a form of *poiēsis* or presencing (QCT, 10). *Poiēsis*, thought of primordially, is a bringing into appearance, just as *physis* is. Both involve the "bringing-forth" out of concealment into unconcealment; both are forms of *revealing*, or *aletheia* (QCT, 12).

What does *this* have to do with causality as effecting and instrumentality? What has the essence of technology to do with revealing? (QCT, 12). The answer, of course, is everything. For not only is every bringing-forth a revealing, but all causality, all instrumentality, and all technology arise from this "domain" of bringing-forth. Technology, thought of "correctly" as means, refers us to causality, and the essence of causality lies in bringing-forth, in revealing: "If we inquire, step by step, into what technology represented as means, actually is, then we shall arrive at revealing" (QCT, 12). Thus, technology is no mere means; technology is a way of revealing (QCT, 12).

The essence of technology may lie in revealing, in bringing to presence, but it is clear that the mode of unconcealment that rules in technology is radically different from a "bringing-forth in the sense of *poiēsis*" (QCT, 14). The latter was harmonious with *physis*; indeed, Heidegger describes *physis* as "*poiēsis* in the highest sense" (QCT, 12). In contrast, "the revealing that rules in modern technology is a challenging, which puts to nature the unreasonable demand that it supply energy that can be extracted and stored as such" (QCT, 14). Heidegger deploys a set of contrasts designed to underline this challenging. The windmill, for example, did not "unlock energy from the air currents in order to store it," whereas "a tract of land is challenged into the putting out of coal and ore" (QCT, 14). Similarly, the work of the peasant did not "challenge the soil of the field," whereas the "mechanized food industry" sets upon nature to set it in order, to make it deliver up the resources necessary to keep the endless cycle of production and consumption going (QCT, 15).

If Heidegger were simply bemoaning the loss of pastoral wholeness, it would be easy to dismiss his analysis with Adorno-esque contempt. But the German romantic examples—culminating in Heidegger's horror that the Rhine of Hölderlin's hymns has become a "water power supplier"—serve a larger purpose. They help to elucidate the kind of revealing that holds sway in our world:

> The revealing that rules throughout modern technology has the character of a setting-upon, in the sense of a challenging-forth. That challenging happens in that the energy in nature is unlocked, what is unlocked is transformed, what is transformed is stored up, what is stored up is, in turn, distributed, and what is distributed is switched about ever anew. Unlocking, transforming, storing, distributing, and switching about are ways of revealing. But the revealing never simply comes to an end. Neither does it run off into the indeterminate. The revealing reveals to itself its own manifoldly interlocking paths, through regulating their course. This regulating itself is, for its part, everywhere secured. Regulating and securing even become the chief characteristics of the challenging revealing (QCT, 16).

The world created by technological revealing imposes an inclusive instrumental grid, in which the activities of unlocking, transforming, storing, distributing, and switching about occur. What distinguishes *this* world from the more familiar equipmental totality of *Being and Time* is that the *ends* of the nexus of instrumental relations have been transferred to the level of the system as a whole. The result is that a continual (and, strictly speaking, endless) "regulating and securing" subsumes purposive activity per se. The instrumental totality is automatized in the perpetual self-activity that constitutes the different modes of regulating and securing. This has a peculiar—and, from Heidegger's point of view, decisive—consequence. When the only "goal" is that "everywhere everything is ordered to stand by, to be immediately at hand, indeed to stand there just so that it may be on call for a further ordering," then everything presences—is revealed—as "standing-reserve" (QCT, 17). With this "inclusive rubric," Heidegger designates "nothing less than the way in which everything presences that is wrought upon by the challenging revealing" (QCT, 17).

Heidegger's thesis, then, is that the revealing of technology projects an ontological horizon limited to the standing-reserve. As an inclusive ontological rubric, standing-reserve designates a fundamental transformation. Things no longer stand over against us, as objects; rather, they stand by us (QCT, 17). Tools and instruments lose whatever residual autonomy they might have had as their "standing" is framed by the "ordering of the orderable." Of course, machines can still be represented as objects; for example, the airliner on a runway. But such a representation acts to conceal what and how the machine now is: the airliner stands ready to provide transportation. It is not a tool, but part of the "stock" of the transportation industry.

The claim that things no longer presence essentially as objects or tools implies that the subject or producer has, somehow, disappeared. This raises the question of "who accomplishes the challenging setting-upon through which what we call the real is revealed as standing-reserve?" (QCT, 18). The answer, obviously enough, is man. Through his "conceiving, fashioning and carrying through," man "accomplishes" this revealing. However—and the point is key for Heidegger—man "does not have control over unconcealment itself, in which at any given time the real shows itself or withdraws" (QCT, 18). But what does it mean to *accomplish* a revealing without *controlling* it? Heidegger gestures here to one of the fundamental tenets of his historical ontology, a thought explicitly at odds with all forms of metaphysical humanism. Particular epochal economies of presence are never consciously deployed by man; rather, they form that outermost horizon within which humanity orients itself, structuring its practices and projects. Against the Cartesian assumptions of the moderns, the network of background assumptions and practices that form a "world" cannot be rendered transparent or reduced to an object of manipulation. In other words, the "light" in which Being reveals itself is not reducible to the projection of the subject. Heidegger expresses this thought metaphorically when he states that such precomprehensions of what is are "sent" us, and "send" us on a way of revealing (QCT, 24).

As a mode of revealing, then, modern technology is "no merely human doing" (QCT, 19). Through it, man is "challenged" to reveal the real in a particular way, as standing-reserve. Just as the "bringing-forth" of *poiēsis* called or "gathered" man to reveal the real as *physis*, so the "challenging claim" of technology "gathers" man into an ordering, and concentrates him "upon ordering the real as standing-reserve" (QCT, 19). The name Heidegger gives to this challenging claim is *Gestell*, Enframing: "Enframing means the way of revealing which holds sway in the essence of modern technology and which is itself nothing technological" (QCT, 20). As the "challenging ordering" that "sets upon" man to reveal the real as standing-reserve, Enframing stands in the starkest possible contrast to the bringing forth of *poiēsis*. Yet, Heidegger reminds us, they "remain related in their essence," as modes of revealing (QCT, 21).

Enframing designates "nothing technological, nothing on the order of a machine" (QCT, 23). It is a mode of revealing that "sets upon" man and thereby "puts him in position to reveal the real, in the mode of ordering, as standing-reserve" (QCT, 24). The self-understanding of the moderns, in which science enables man to assume a position, a kind of Archimedean point, from which the world can be reduced to the representable and "disposed" of, is revealed as an illusion. We are "in the picture," to be sure, but not in the hegemonic way presumed by the modern subjectification of the real. Man "stands within the essential realm of Enframing. He can never take up a relationship to it only subsequently" (QCT, 24). In other words, he is always already "framed, claimed, and challenged" by a destining that sends him into this way of revealing: "Always the destining of revealing holds complete sway over man" (QCT, 25). But, as Heidegger gnomically adds, "that destining is never a fate that compels" (QCT, 25).

The paradoxical nature of this statement is lessened when Heidegger reminds us of the nature of freedom understood from his ontological perspective. *This* freedom, the freedom of revealing, is the freedom that governs the open space of any "clearing" (QCT, 25). It consists "neither in unfettered arbitrariness nor in the constraint of mere laws," but in "the destining that at any given time starts a revealing upon its way" (QCT, 25). Only within a space so destined does a set of possibilities emerge, and do practices and projects appear. In this sense, every revealing, every clearing, is a "destining" in that it situates man in a particular world and furnishes a field for his disclosive activity. Yet in addition to being the site of primordial (ontological) freedom, the "destining of revealing" is also a *danger* (QCT, 26): it raises the possibility that man may reify a given set of practices/possibilities and thereby lose sight of—"forget"—his disclosive character. Beyond this essential (one could say, structural) danger lies what Heidegger calls the "supreme danger":

> . . . when destining reigns in the mode of Enframing, it is the supreme danger. This danger attests itself to us in two ways. As soon as what is unconcealed no longer concerns man even as object, but does so, rather, exclusively as standing-reserve, and man in the midst of objectlessness is nothing but the orderer of the standing-reserve, *then he comes to the very brink of a precipitous fall*: that is, he comes to the point where he himself will have to be taken as standing-reserve. Meanwhile man, precisely as the one so threatened, exalts himself to the posture of lord of the earth. In this way the impression comes to prevail that everything man encounters exists only insofar

as it is his construct. This illusion gives rise in turn to one final delusion: It seems as though man everywhere and always only encounters himself. *In truth, however, precisely nowhere does man today any longer encounter himself, i.e., his essence.* (QCT, 27; the first emphasis is mine)

Enframing is the "supreme danger" because, more than any other mode of revealing, it thrusts the phenomenon of revealing into oblivion. It radicalizes *Verfallenheit* (fallenness) by enabling the regulating and securing of both man and world as standing-reserve. With this securing, the dream of metaphysical humanism is realized: the "open possibility" of *Dasein* (there-being) is replaced by a grounded actuality, a humanity that encounters only itself when it looks upon nature or the world. Technology is thus the vehicle of *Geist*'s (spirit's) return to itself. But what appears, from a Marxian or Hegelian standpoint, as the moment of reconciliation is, in fact, the extreme degree of alienation or "homelessness," or of disconnection from the essential contingency of disclosure. As "lord of the earth," the subject extends its instrumental horizon through "uncreative positing" and the reduction of the real to the representable. The "brink of a precipitous fall" is reached when this disclosure no longer even takes the form of a relentless objectification. The step beyond modern self-assertion is Western humanity's late modern submission to the regime of ordering as such. The contingency of this regime is lost sight of as the "orderer of the standing-reserve" accepts its "fate" as "the subject of all consumption," as the "most important raw material."

The irony of the subjectification of the real reveals itself. The framing of the world as picture turns out to be merely the prologue to the universalizing of *Gestell* (Enframing), of the technologizing attitude that "drives out every other possibility of revealing" (QCT, 27). "Banished" into an ordering revealing, man *seems* to encounter only himself; in fact, Western humanity's acceptance of the "fate" of technology and its role in the ordering revealing ensures that it will never encounter itself, its disclosive essence, within the frame of technology. Western humanity gets what metaphysics has always desired: a release from "guilt" (finitude), a secure basis, and the constant presence of all that is (as standing-reserve). Metaphysics's will to ground, power, and security culminates in the technological framing/dis-essencing of man as standing-reserve. The "completely humanized world" is, in fact, a technonihilistic world—a world driven by the demand for increased power and orderability, a world in which global cycles of production and consumption "fix" man as the laboring animal.

III. Arendt on Modernity: World Alienation and the Withdrawal of the Political

Modern World Alienation and the Subjectification of the Real

At first glance, Arendt's critique of modernity seems to have little in common with Heidegger's. Arendt's analysis is determined, largely, by her desire to preserve the autonomy of action from the instrumentalizing attitude of *homo faber*.

This, needless to say, is not *Heidegger*'s worry. Indeed, viewed from the perspective of *Gestell*, all forms of human activity—acting as well as making—appear as expressions of the "will to will." For Heidegger, the only "cure" for modernity's will-to-will is *Gelassenheit*, letting beings be (a kind of "will-to-not-will," as Arendt puts it). *Praxis* provides no response to the pathologies of modernity; rather, it is part of the problem. Hence Heidegger's statement in "Overcoming Metaphysics" that "no mere action will change the world," a sentiment he echoes in the *Spiegel* interview.[93]

The gap between Arendt and Heidegger seems to widen when we note that Heidegger's entire story about the modern subjectification of the real is presented in terms of *Seinsgeschichte*; that is, in terms of a metanarrative about Being's self-withdrawal. The *idealism* of this metanarrative (in which the history of metaphysics provides the trace of a secret, "all-determining" history of Being) stands in stark contrast to Arendt's focus on specific phenomena and events.[94] Moreover, Arendt's hostility to narrative structures of the Hegelian sort rules out any easy assimilation of her story to Heidegger's.

The differences, however, ought not to hide the continuities. Arendt's *The Human Condition* can be read a number of ways; for example, as a phenomenology of action, or as a contribution to public realm theory. Yet such readings become misreadings if they try to detach what Arendt has to say about action or the public realm from her narrative about the "loss," "destruction," and "disappearance" of the public world in modernity.[95] *Everything* Arendt has to say about action and the public realm is framed in terms of an analysis of the de-worldling of the public world in the modern age. The fact from which she begins is the loss of this specific reality, what she calls "the eclipse of the common public world."[96] This is not to say that Arendt denies that we late moderns *have* a public realm; rather, her point is that this realm has "lost its power" to gather us together, to "relate and separate" us as a world properly should.[97] In *our* public realm, being and appearance hardly coincide: the plurality of perspectives necessary for such a space of disclosure has both fragmented and flattened into the uniform gaze of mass society.[98] The reasons for this state of affairs are complex and constitute the heart of *HC*; the result is more straightforward. According to Arendt, the human condition of late modernity is characterized by the *deprivation* of an authentically public reality: the "shining brightness" has become an obscuring glare.[99]

The "innermost story of the modern age," then, concerns the destruction of this common world, the public reality, and the correspondingly fugitive nature of the political.[100] The ontological thrust of Arendt's analysis in *HC* is that the events and energies of modernity have worked to undermine and finally destroy the "durability" and "tangibility" of the public world. Thus, an epoch that appears to usher in a new worldliness—and new opportunities for a "groundless" politics (see *On Revolution*)—in fact carries world *alienation* to its farthest possible extreme. In describing the *animal laborans* as "worldless," Arendt designates a creature bereft of the specific reality necessary for a "truly human life."[101]

What is modern world alienation and what connection, if any, does it have to Heidegger's thesis concerning the subjectification of the real?

In the last chapter of *The Human Condition* Arendt cites "three great events" that "stand at the threshold of the modern age and determine its character": the discovery of America, the Reformation, and (most peculiarly) the invention of the telescope.[102] The fear that one is in for a World Civilization lesson is dispelled when Arendt describes what gives *these* events their emblematic significance. The discovery of America is important not because it opens the New World, but rather because it signals the moment at which the earth, "the quintessence of the human condition," becomes subject to "the human surveying capacity." With this discovery, man's earthly surroundings are conceivable as object. The Reformation is significant not because of its contribution to secularization and loss of faith, but because with it began the process of expropriation through which millions ultimately lost their property, their "place in the world," and became subject to an unlimited, socialized accumulation of wealth. Finally, Galileo's invention of the telescope looms large because it "confirmed" the Copernican theory and demonstrated that man had indeed been deceived by his senses. With this confirmation the traditional concept of truth was destroyed.[103]

From Arendt's perspective, each of these events figures as an origin of modern world alienation. As a constellation, they mark a fundamental transformation in Western man's relation to his surroundings, his "being-in-the-world." Thus, the discovery of America begins the process of shrinkage by which the vastness of the earth is reduced to objectifiable dimensions—a process recently completed: "Only now has man taken full possession of his mortal dwelling place and gathered the infinite horizons into a globe whose majestic outlines and detailed surface he knows as the lines in the palm of his hand."[104] With the discovery of America, in other words, the earth becomes a representable object. Henceforth, man can alienate himself from his "immediate earthly surroundings" in order to picture the world; this picturing, in turn, is the sine qua non of its conquest: "Before we knew how to circle the earth, how to circumscribe the sphere of human habitation in days and hours, we had brought the globe into our living room to be touched by our hands and swirled before our eyes."[105]

The Reformation presents us with an "altogether different event" from the shrinkage of the world, yet it "eventually confronts us with a similar phenomenon of alienation."[106] Arendt sees the innerworldly alienation analyzed by Weber as equally present in the expropriation of the peasantry, an event that was an "unforeseen consequence" of the expropriation of the church. This expropriation, through which "certain strata of the population" are deprived of their "privately owned share of a common world," sets the stage for further appropriation, and for a process of wealth accumulation that has become both social and endless:

> Expropriation, the deprivation for certain groups of their place in the world and their naked exposure to the exigencies of life, created both the original accumulation of wealth and the possibility of transforming this wealth into capital through labor. These together constituted the conditions for the rise of a capitalist economy. What distinguished this development at the beginning of the modern age from similar

occurrences in the past is that expropriation and wealth accumulation did not simply result in new property or lead to a new redistribution of wealth, but were fed back into the process to generate further expropriations, greater productivity, and more appropriation.[107]

The "self-expansion of value" under capitalism can continue only so long as no boundaries hem in the accumulation process. No "worldly durability and stability" can be permitted to interfere with the cyclical, expanding nature of this process.[108] In Arendt's terms, "the process of wealth accumulation, as we know it . . . is possible only if the world and the very worldliness of man are sacrificed."[109] Property, in the sense of a "privately owned share of the common world," must be largely abolished; things, use objects, must be replaced by consumer goods; the bulk of the population, finally, transformed into nomadic labor-power. Expropriation is thus the first step in the progressive undermining of the durability and tangibility of the world.[110]

The invention of the telescope stands for the last great origin of modern world alienation, the "universal" standpoint of modern science. What Galileo's invention did was to underline the necessity of taking up a position *outside* the world if one wanted to avoid being deceived by the senses. Copernicus had imaginatively attained such an Archimedean point: Galileo's confirmation makes the adoption of such a speculative standpoint imperative. Henceforth, knowledge must adopt the standpoint of the universe, and view the earth as but one more object within that frame. Arendt describes the ambivalent nature of this withdrawal into the universe:

> Both despair and triumph are inherent in the same event . . . it is as if Galileo's discovery proved in demonstrable fact that both the worst fear and most presumptuous hope of human speculation, the ancient fear that our senses, our very organs for the reception of reality, might betray us, and the Archimedean wish for a point outside the earth from which to unhinge the world, could only come true together, as though the wish would be granted only provided that we lost reality and the fear was to be consummated only if compensated by the acquisition of supermundane powers.[111]

The "despair and triumph" manifest in this withdrawal has faded as the universal standpoint is increasingly taken for granted. As Arendt remarks, "Whatever we do today in physics . . . we always handle nature from a point in the universe outside the earth."[112] To be sure, we have not found an actual Archimedean point; yet it is clear that we "have found a way to act on earth and within terrestrial nature as though we dispose of it from outside."[113] The modern scientific project is "Archimedean" in essence: as knowers and manipulators of natural processes, we are "universal," rather than worldly, beings. Our knowledge and power arise out of a rigorously maintained alienation from the world, the necessity and utility of which first announced itself with Galileo.

In modern science, as with the conquest of the globe, we encounter world alienation in its triumphal form. There is, however, a crucial difference between the two. The world picture of modern science places the representing subject at an infinitely vaster imaginary distance from the earth. Thus, according to Arendt, "earth alienation," rather than mere world alienation, is the "hallmark of modern science."[114] Indeed, "compared with the earth alienation underlying the whole development of natural science in the modern age, the withdrawal from terrestrial proximity contained in the discovery of the globe as a whole and the world alienation produced in the twofold process of expropriation and wealth accumulation are of minor significance."[115] Only the withdrawal into the universe by modern sciences fully accomplishes the objectification of the earth, allowing it to appear as a fit candidate for "completion" (Kant), alteration, or destruction. As Kateb observes, the fruit of the Archimedean project—of the desire to dispose of the earth from the outside—is nuclear weapons.[116]

Each of Arendt's "three great events," then, illuminate a dimension of the modern withdrawal from the world. But what does this withdrawal, this alienation, have to do with the "subjectification of the real"? Once more, the answer is everything. The threshold traced by these events marks nothing less than a fundamental transformation in our "comprehension of Being" and our mode of comportment toward the real. The "twofold flight from the earth into the universe and from the world into the self" is a reactive move, but it is also the precondition for the "becoming picture of the world" (a fact driven home by Arendt's theme of the "Archimedean point"). And, as with Heidegger, this "becoming picture" is prelude to the conquest of the world by *homo faber*, whom Arendt refers to throughout *The Human Condition* as "lord and master." Like Heidegger, Arendt sees the will to ground underlying this retreat as inseparable from the will to power. Modernity's relentless subjectification of the real—its reduction of the world of appearances to (on the one hand) subjective experience and (on the other) the "objective" constructions of modern science—terminates in a world, a nature, and a universe in which man again and again "only encounters himself."[117] Like Heidegger, Arendt sees this total humanization of reality as the most extreme form of alienation.

There are, of course, differences. Heidegger concentrates on the "fundamental metaphysical position" of the modern age, on the way the figure of the subject swallows the entire horizon of the real. Arendt is concerned with the same general phenomenon, but from the point of view of its implications for the *vita activa*. Thus she concentrates on the modern reduction of freedom to will, property to the laboring subject, and the phenomenal world to the constructs of the knowing subject.[118] Throughout, her emphasis is upon the way the theory and self-understanding of the modern age have consistently worked to undermine the durability and tangibility—the *worldliness*—of these phenomena. Hence, for the modern mind, "freedom is never understood as an objective state of human existence"; nor is property understood to have any other ground than the living, laboring individual; nor, finally, is the "objectivity" of the world, its common character, understood to have any other ground than the patterns of the human mind itself.[119] Science, philosophy, economic and political theory: all conspire to cover over both the phenomenon of world and the worldliness of phenomena.

The effects of this pervasive subjectification cannot be undone by a revised self-understanding: for Arendt, it is hardly a question of theorizing ourselves into a more "worldly" form of existence. Modern *theory's* reduction of freedom, property, and the phenomenal realm to subjective structures or capacities is not the problem so much as a symptom. The real problem, for Heidegger as well as for Arendt, is the existential resentment that drives modern humanity to take itself so far out of the world, to ascribe to itself a position from which the world might be disposed of. The "radical novelty" of modernity consists in the fact that "now, for the first time is there any such thing as a 'position' of man." Now, "for the first time," there is a distance, an alienation, that encourages and makes plausible the Archimedean project of utterly transforming the conditions of human existence.[120]

From Homo Faber *to the* Animal Laborans: Instrumentality, Technology, *and the "Destruction of the Common World"*

Arendt sees the two sides of modernity's "flight" from the world as intimately connected. The universal standpoint of modern science demands the transcendence of the limits imposed by earthbound experience and the evidence of the senses. This transcendence is achieved, according to Arendt, by the mathematization of science and the real, and by the deployment of the experiment.[121] The former reduces terrestrial sense data and movements to mathematical symbols; the latter assertively subjects nature to conditions imposed by the human mind, eschewing what Kant called "accidental observation."[122] The result of the modern *reductio scientiae ad mathematicam* is the translation of "all that man is not" into "patterns that are identical with human, mental structures."[123] Echoing Heidegger's insight in "The Age of the World Picture," Arendt emphasizes how the projection of such a mathematical "ground plan" of nature guarantees that man could "risk himself into space and be certain that he would not encounter anything but himself, nothing that could not be reduced to patterns present in him."[124]

Thus, the "condition of remoteness" demanded by the Archimedean point is attained by purely mental means. But this trick, if we can call it that, carries its own dangers. On the one hand, it frees humanity from the "shackles of finitude" and earthbound experience; on the other, it seems to deprive humanity of any possible certainty, of any firm ground for knowledge of or action upon the world. The thoroughgoing reduction of appearances by mathematical and experimental means achieves a standpoint that is at once everywhere and nowhere, unmoored and apparently arbitrary. The relativity built into modernity's "flight" to a universal standpoint is an aspect of the Copernican revolution and the discovery of the Archimedean point that has only recently come to widespread consciousness.[125] The result is that we are haunted by the arbitrariness of our projections, and by the suspicion that a mathematical order can be "discovered" for even the most clearly haphazard array of elements. This suspicion, and the "outrage and despair" that accompany it, are unavoidable consequences of Galileo's discovery, a discovery that demonstrates, through its "confirmation" of the Copernican hypothesis, that Being and Appearance have parted company for good.[126] In Arendt's view, the world we live in is determined by this event—by the disappearance of a truth that reveals itself and by the "radical change of mind" this disappearance entails. The suspected groundlessness of the "universal standpoint"—which has become today a "politically demonstrable reality"—first yielded its existential significance to Descartes.[127]

Descartes's philosophy is "haunted by two nightmares which in a sense became the nightmares of the whole modern age": first, the fear that "everything is a dream and there is no reality"; second, that "not God but an evil spirit rules the world and mocks man," specifically by giving him a notion of truth but not the capacities necessary to attain it.[128] Descartes realized, according to Arendt, that the twin nightmares of the loss of the world and a permanent distrust of our faculties could be escaped only by *completing* the Archimedean withdrawal with a retreat to the self. The genius of Descartes resides in his explicit articulation of the epistemological assumption underlying modern science; namely, that "even if there is no truth, man can be truthful, and even if there is no reliable certainty, man can be reliable."[129] Whatever salvation there was could "only lie in man himself, and if there was a solution to doubting, it had to come from doubting."[130] The *cogito* draws the apparently inescapable conclusion: only the firm ground of the self, of introspection, can substitute for the lost certainty of a world fitted to our senses.

The *cogito* saves reality by shifting inwards, by making the representations of the subject the benchmark of the real: "Man . . . carries his certainty, the certainty of his existence, within himself; the sheer functioning of consciousness, though it cannot possibly assure a worldly reality given to the senses and to reason, confirms beyond doubt the reality of sensations and of reasoning, that is, the reality of processes which go on in the mind."[131]

The ingenuity of Cartesian introspection is manifest in the way it uses "the nightmare of nonreality" as a means to submerge "all worldly objects into the stream of consciousness and its processes."[132] This reduction of the real to representation (Heidegger) not only secures reality; it reopens the possibility of truth and genuine knowledge, now as an "objective" ordering of representations. In making this move (the basis for Kant's famous "Copernican revolution" in philosophy), Descartes explicitly articulates what Arendt calls "the most obvious conclusion to be drawn from the new physical science: though one cannot know truth as something given and disclosed, man can at least know what he makes himself," namely, the clear and distinct ideas of mathematical science.[133]

Arendt views the Cartesian subjectification of the real as a sign of "common sense in retreat": "what men have in common is not the world but the structure of their minds."[134] Where our senses are no longer adequate to fit us into the world, where the reality they reveal is felt to be insufficiently genuine, only a "shared" faculty of formal/mathematical reasoning can provide the simulacrum of a common world. The career of this transcendental supplement, from Kant to Habermas, has been a long (and, for Arendt, unpersuasive) one.[135] Nevertheless, it is precisely because Descartes presumes the eclipse of common sense, of our feeling for the world, that he is able to "solve" what Arendt calls "the perplexity inherent in the discovery of the Archimedean point." It is only by "removing the Archimedean point into the mind of man" that the disorientation experienced by an "earth-bound creature" who has severed its cognitive standpoint from any worldly referent is rendered bearable.[136] The Cartesian retreat to the self poses the "patterns of the human mind" as the "ultimate point of reference." The will to power manifest in the triumphal earth alienation of modern science (the objectification of the real) is grounded by modern philosophy's internalization of the Archimedean point. As Heidegger noted, for modernity, self-assertion and self-grounding go hand in hand.[137]

•

The Cartesian "removal" of the Archimedean point into "the mind of man" ameliorates the "disastrous blow to human confidence" dealt by Galileo's discovery. Yet this removal, while helping to free man "from given reality altogether," is finally less convincing than "the universal doubt from which it sprang and which it was supposed to dispel."[138] Cartesian doubt persists throughout the modern age—not, it is true, in the form of a lack of confidence, but rather as the unshakable suspicion that the mathematization performed by modern science and philosophy in order to "save" the real has, in fact, merely created a "dream world," one that has the character of reality "only as long as the dream lasts."[139] The very success of the Cartesian schematization of the real in terms of a *mathesis universalis* comes at a price: "wherever we search for that which we are not, we encounter only the patterns of our own minds."[140] Such is the cost of ensuring that we encounter, in Heidegger's words, only that for which we are prepared.

For many, this residual Cartesian doubt is assuaged by the tremendous increase in manipulative power born of modern science's renunciation of the senses and experimental/mathematical approach to the real. Surely, such people reason, this increase in power demonstrates the essential truth or correctness of "modern science's most abstract concepts." The enormous technical accomplishments of modern science, it is presumed, could have been achieved only if experimental science indeed revealed the "authentic order" of nature.[141] Yet, according to Arendt, this presumption is wishful, and unwarranted. It flows from the unfulfillable desire to break out of the "vicious circle" installed by the conditions man lays down for the presencing of nature in the experiment:

> The world of the experiment seems always capable of becoming a man-made reality, and this, while it may increase man's power of making and acting, even of creating a world, for beyond what any previous age dared to imagine . . . unfortunately puts man back once more—and now even more forcefully—into the prison of his own mind, into the limitations of patterns he himself has created.[142]

This entrapment, of course, is an inescapable consequence of the "constructivist" approach to knowledge made imperative by the demise of a truth that reveals itself. As Arendt writes, "after being and appearance parted company . . . there arose a veritable necessity to hunt for truth behind deceptive appearances . . . in order to know one had to do."[143] Foremost among the "spiritual consequences" of Galileo's discovery, then, is a *reversal* of the traditional hierarchy between contemplation and action, since certain knowledge could concern only what man had done himself, and this knowledge in turn could be tested only through more doing.[144]

Strictly speaking, the "reversal of contemplation and action" is no reversal at all, since with the rise of a constructivist/experimental approach to knowledge *contemplation*, the "beholding" of truth, is rendered "altogether meaningless."[145] In fact, the reversal characteristic of the modern age concerns the relationship between thinking and doing: after Galileo, the latter takes an undeniable precedence. If man can know or be certain only of that which he, as representing subject, "produces and arranges," then it follows that *fabrication* provides the new paradigm for securing truth. Thus, "first among the activities within the *vita activa* to rise to the position formerly occupied by contemplation were the activities of making and fabricating—the prerogatives of *homo faber*."[146] The ascendency of these productionist prerogatives is manifest not only in experimental science's reliance upon the toolmaker for its instruments, but also—and more profoundly—in the way the experiment itself tacitly posits a homology between the fabrication of the Creator and the natural processes "reproduced" in the laboratory:

> The experiment repeats the natural process as though man himself were about to make nature's objects, and although in the early stages of the modern age no responsible scientist would have dreamt of the extent to which man actually is capable of "making" nature, he nevertheless from the onset approached it from the standpoint of the one who made it.[147]

The early modern predominance of a metaphorics of fabrication in science and philosophy (what Arendt calls "the modern blending of making and knowing") is a direct result of the "shock" of Galileo's discovery, as underlined by Descartes. Vico's principle—that we can truly know only what we ourselves have made—becomes indisputable.

The constructivist epistemological stance of modern science and philosophy presumes not only a different approach to the real (the "reversal"), but also a different concept of reality. Arendt follows Heidegger in stressing how modern epistemology is ontology carried on by other means, and how the "victory of *homo faber*" in the modern age depends, ultimately, upon a transformation in the understanding of that which is underlying the forms of human knowledge:

> Nature, because it could be known only in processes which human ingenuity, the ingeniousness of *homo faber*, could repeat and remake in the experiment, became a process, and all particular natural things derived their significance and meaning solely from their functions in the overall process. *In the place of the concept of Being we now find the concept of Process.* And whereas it is the nature of Being to appear and to disclose itself, it is the nature of Process to remain invisible, to be something whose existence can only be inferred from the presence of certain phenomena. *This*

process was originally the fabrication process which "disappears in the product," and it was based on the experience of *homo faber*, who knew that a production process necessarily precedes the actual existence of every object.[148]

It is through this fundamental shift in the characterization of the real—a shift effected by the tacit installation of a fabrication metaphorics at the deepest levels—that modern science and philosophy give new life to the productionist prejudices of the tradition. Galileo's discovery may have destroyed the anthropocentric comfort of a teleological world order, but it also created the opening for a radically instrumentalist anthropocentrism, one that inscribes the entire horizon of the real (both "natural" and "social") in terms of concept of process. According to Arendt, the modern understanding of the real (which informs modern science, philosophy, economics, and political theory) elevates an aspect of the fabrication process to the status of a comprehensive ontological principle. The result is the "limitless instrumentalization of everything that exists." The difference between this modern reification of the fabrication experience and the ancient is that the former shifts the focus away from the *telos*, the end or product, to the "means," that is, the natural or human process of production itself. "From the standpoint of *homo faber*," Arendt writes, "it is as though the means, the production process or development, was more important than the end, the finished product."[149]

Paradoxically, it is the postteleological quality of the modern appropriation of the metaphorics of fabrication that both guarantees the "victory of *homo faber*" and ensures his eventual defeat. The "victory" is apparent in the mechanistic political philosophies of the seventeenth century, which attempted to invent the means by which (in Hobbes's words) to "make an artificial animal . . . called a Commonwealth, or State."[150] But it is more generally manifest in the hegemony of a broad set of attitudes arising from the reversal of contemplation and fabrication:

> Among the outstanding characteristics of the modern age from its beginning to our own time we find the typical attitudes of *homo faber*: his instrumentalization of the world, his confidence in tools and in the productivity of the maker of artificial objects; his trust in the all-comprehensive range of the means-end category, his conviction that every issue can be solved and every human motivation reduced to the principle of utility; his sovereignty, which regards everything given as material and thinks of the whole of nature as of "an immense fabric from which we can cut out whatever we want to resew it however we like"; his equation of intelligence with ingenuity . . .; finally, his matter-of-course identification of fabrication with action.[151]

What are the implications for politics, for our "attitude towards the world," when the productionist prejudices of the tradition are stripped of their contemplative character and concretized in a totally instrumentalized reality? And what is the impact of the fact that, in the modern age, "the oldest conviction of *homo faber*—that 'man is the measure of all things'—advanced to the rank of a universally accepted commonplace?"[152]

I have already discussed how Arendt thinks that it has become impossible for us to think about politics in terms *other* than means and ends. This impossibility flows, in part, from the antipolitical conceptualization of action, freedom, and agency performed by the tradition. Its stronger and more immediate ground, however, is this modern "victory of *homo faber*." In the modern age, the mentality of *homo faber* ceases to be merely the source of a persuasive antidemocratic metaphorics (as it was for Plato) and becomes—as the passage cited above suggests—an encompassing horizon for the presencing of things. This event (the "victory") has two chief effects. The first concerns the relation between ethics and politics. Arendt thinks that the hegemony of the means/end category creates a situation in which the credo "the end justifies the means" retains a permanent plausibility as the first maxim of politics.[153] The instrumentalization of politics narrows the moral syntax of politics along consequentialist lines, with predictably dire results.

The second effect of this "victory" flows from the internal logic of instrumentalization, and concerns our attitude toward the world. According to Arendt, the advent of an instrumentalist "world view" creates an endless chain of means and ends, in which "all ends are bound to be of short duration and to be transformed into means for some further end."[154] As we have seen, this promotes a confusion of utility and meaningfulness. Utilitarianism—for Arendt, *the* philosophy of the modern age—makes the "in order to" the *content* of the "for the sake of," and this establishment of utility as meaning generates meaninglessness.[155] Moreover, the utilitarianism of a victorious *homo faber* is haunted by the "perplexity" that it is unable to offer a convincing justification of either the means/end category or the principle of utility. This perplexity is exacerbated by the fact that "within the category of means and end . . . there is no way to end the chain of means and ends and prevent all ends from eventually being viewed again as means, except to declare that one thing or another is 'an end in itself.'"[156]

The colonizing and nihilistic logic of instrumentalism demands that the user—man—be elevated to the position of "end in himself," lest humanity fall under the rubric of "means." Yet it is precisely this elevation of man (most famously performed by Kant) that, according to Arendt, issues in a corresponding degradation of the world:

> The only way out of the dilemma of meaninglessness in all strictly utilitarian philosophy is to turn away from the objective world of use things and fall back upon the subjectivity of use itself. Only in a strictly anthropocentric world, where the user, that is, man himself, becomes the ultimate end which puts a stop to the unending chain of means and ends, can utility as such acquire the dignity of meaningfulness. Yet the tragedy is that in the moment *homo faber* seems to have found fulfillment in terms of his own activity, he begins to degrade the world of things, the end and end product of his own mind and hands; if man the user is the highest end, "the measure of all things," then not only nature . . . but the "valuable" things themselves have become mere means, losing thereby their own intrinsic "value."[157]

Arendt's description of the "victory of *homo faber*" draws out the political consequences of Heidegger's subjectification thesis through a radical shift in perspective. The "tragedy" referred to in the passage above is not the "oblivion of Being" but the degradation of the worldly in-between that accompanies any consistently anthropocentric outlook.[158] Arendt's quarrel with modernity is not that it deepens *Seinsvergessenheit* (forgetfulness of Being), but that its energies and outlook withdraw humanity from a worldly existence. Modernity's "world picture" and instrumentalism have the effect of taking man out of the world. In terms of world alienation, modernity excels both the contemplative tradition and Christianity. Its worldlessness is greater because its existential resentment is active, transformative, empowered.

Of course, it is not instrumentality per se that is the root of this degradation of the world. As Arendt is careful to note, "the instrumentalization of the whole world and earth, this limitless devaluation of everything given," does not "directly arise out of the fabrication process."[159] The problem, rather, lies in "the generalization of the fabrication experience in which usefulness and utility are established as the ultimate standards for life and the world of men."[160] For such a generalization to occur, the inherent limits of the means/end category must be overcome. Theoretically, the suspension of the *telos* is prepared by the introduction of process into making at the conceptual level. Practically, it is achieved by a transformation of the production process itself. The transition from "the limited instrumentality of *homo faber*" to the "limitless instrumentalization of everything that exists"—and thence to the "fixing" of humanity as *animal laborans*—occurs, as with Heidegger, through the medium of technology.

•

In Section 20 of *The Human Condition* Arendt critically engages the Marxian/Weberian theme of reification, noting "the frequent complaints we hear about the perversion of ends and means in modern society, about men becoming servants of the machines they themselves invented." The problem with such complaints is not so much that they are wrong as that they are superficial. By focusing on the issue of control, they obscure a deeper and more troubling phenomenon, namely, that we are losing the capacity to "distinguish clearly between means and ends."[161] The loss of this faculty is one result of the modern assimilation of work to labor, and to the performance of all work in the mode of laboring. For where "production consists primarily in preparation for consumption," as it does in laboring, there "the very distinction between means and ends . . . simply does not make sense."[162]

How does work come to be "absorbed" by labor, and instrumentality thereby transformed through the "life process"? The mechanization of labor plays a key role, in Arendt's view, insofar as it amplifies and extends the natural rhythms of man's "metabolism with nature," drawing fabrication into the repetitive cycles of production and consumption and stripping tools of their craft character (as implements or instruments rather than material or inputs). Indeed, according to Arendt, "nothing can be mechanized more easily and less artificially than the rhythm of the labor process, which in turn corresponds to the equally automatic repetitive rhythm of the life process and its metabolism with nature."[163] Nature's automatism is enhanced by the machine.

Arendt identifies technology with the "replacement" of tools by machines, noting that the full implications of this replacement come to light only with the "latest stage" of technological development, the advent of automation.[164] For Arendt, this "event" is "no less threatening" than the degradation of speech encouraged by the mathematization of the sciences.[165] The tendency of modern science is to render speech superfluous; the tendency of technological automatism is to render humanity, *qua* laborers, superfluous. This tendency, however, is not the only, or even the primary, danger posed by technological automatism. Nor, for that matter, is the creation of an utterly mechanized/technologized world:

> The danger of future automation is less the much deplored mechanization and artificialization of natural life than that, its artificiality notwithstanding, all human productivity would be sucked into an enormously intensified life process and would follow automatically, without pain or effort, its ever-recurrent natural cycle. The rhythm of machines would magnify and intensify the natural rhythm of life enormously, but it would not change, only make more deadly, life's chief character with respect to the world, which is to wear down durability.[166]

Even before modern technology becomes capable of "channeling the universal forces of the cosmos around us into the nature of the earth," it radically undermines "the very worldliness of the human artifice" by shattering what Arendt refers to as "the very purposefulness of the world."[167] Technological automatism ushers in a mode of production in which "the distinction between operation and products as well as the product's precedence over the operation . . ., no longer make sense and have become obsolete."[168] In other words, this automatism extends the "instrumentalization" of the world by *eliding* the distinction between end and means. The hallmark of the late modern technological real is precisely this dis-essencing of the "categories of *homo faber*." Of course, this does not mean that we cease to *apply* these categories. Like Heidegger, Arendt believes that the late modern consciousness is irreducibly instrumentalist; but, also like Heidegger, she believes that the reality "brought to presence" by technology has rendered instrumental categories more or less anachronisms.

For Arendt, then, the "question concerning technology" is not, finally, about the famous "reversal" of ends and means. Nor is it an issue of regaining control over an instrumentality which, like "The Sorcerer's Apprentice," has taken on a life of its own. Along with Heidegger, Arendt believes that such an instrumental/anthropocentric framing of the problem conceals more than it reveals:

> The discussion of the whole problem of technology, that is, of the transformation of life and the world through the introduction of the machine, has been strangely led astray through an all-too-exclusive concentration upon the service or disservice the machines render to men. . . . The question . . . is not so much whether we are the masters or slaves of our machines, but whether machines still serve the world and its things, or if, on the contrary, they and the automatic motion of their processes have begun to rule and even destroy world and things.[169]

With this passage we see both Arendt's proximity to and distance from Heidegger. On the one hand, her identification of technology with mechanization and automation clearly commits what is for Heidegger the category mistake of thinking of the *essence* of technology as "something technological." On the other hand, she clearly regards technology as something more than an instrument—as disclosive in the broad Heideggerian sense. Technology opens or "clears" a world, but it does so by dimming down, indeed *destroying*, the equipmental or reified character of "the human artifice." What we are left with, according to Arendt, is something closer to an *environment*. Technology, culminating what had been initiated by capitalist expropriation, swamps the human artifice in a process reality, renaturalizing human existence by assimilating it, in all its aspects, to the rhythm of cycles of production and consumption. The "defeat" of *homo faber* and the victory of the *animal laborans* is guaranteed by the technological destruction of reification (in the sense of thinghood).[170]

In the final analysis, then, Arendt's critique of technology is motivated by the fact that it makes artifice impossible, and thereby deprives humanity of a "proper space" for the exercise of its capacity for action. "Without a world between man and nature," she writes, "there is external movement, but no objectivity."[171] The parallel between the *un*reified, unarticulated character of a technologized process reality and what Heidegger calls the "objectlessness" of the standing reserve is clear. Similarly, Arendt also sees humanity as thereby "fixed" *qua animal laborans* in that all human activities come to be performed in the mode of *laboring*. The difference between Arendt and Heidegger here is that, whereas for Heidegger we are "at the brink of a precipitous fall," for Arendt we are clearly *fallen*:

> Even now, laboring is too lofty, too ambitious a word for what we are doing, or think we are doing, in the world we have come to live in. The last stage of the laboring society, the society of jobholders, demands of its members a sheer automatic functioning, as though individual life had actually been submerged in the overall life process of the species and the only active decision still required of the individual were to let go, so to speak, to abandon his individuality, the still individually sensed pain and trouble of living, and acquiesce in a dazed, "tranquillized," functional type of behavior.[172]

Through its destruction of the world and its "naturalization" of human existence, technological automatism promotes the mass behavior of the "worldless" *animal laborans*. We return here to the Heideggerian theme of fallenness (*Verfallenheit*), albeit in radicalized form. For Arendt, technological automatism and the "rise of the social" combine to create a set of existential conditions that bode ill indeed for human beings as disclosive agents.[173] Within the framework of a technologized "national household," the capacity for spontaneous action shrinks, reducing the human status to that of "the most important raw material." Hence the great irony of the modern age: the very "means" that help guarantee "the survival of the species . . . on a world-wide scale" can "at the same time threaten *humanity* with extinction."[174]

IV. A "REJECTIONIST CRITIQUE"? THINKING THE PRESENT FROM AN ARENDTIAN PERSPECTIVE

Arendt's appropriation of Heidegger's subjectification thesis illuminates the decline of public reality and the withering of our capacity for action throughout the modern age. Admittedly, she qualifies her conclusions. In *The Human Condition*, for example, we are told that "the instrumentalization of action and the degradation of politics into a means for something else has of course never really succeeded in eliminating action, in preventing its being one of the decisive human experiences, or in destroying the realm of human affairs altogether."[175] Moreover, as her interpretation of modern political action in *On Revolution* makes clear, Arendt thought that authentic political action was manifest in select moments of revolutionary upheaval and resistance. Yet these qualifications do little to mitigate the apprehensiveness and pessimism that colors her approach to late modernity. In *The Origins of Totalitarianism* she emphasized how totalitarian domination (itself an incarnation of the modernist credo "everything is possible") attempted a refabrication of man that threatened his very humanity.[176] What is unexpected, even shocking, is how this nightmare haunts her thinking about modernity at large. Arendt's analysis of the destruction of the common world, the rise of technological automatism, and the "victory" of the *animal laborans* implies that, one way or another, existential resentment will triumph. Modernity will attain its goal of not only remaking the world, but man also.

This line of thought, which gives concrete shape to what in Heidegger remains a vague and somewhat opaque danger, leads Kateb and others to question the validity of Arendt's critique. From Kateb's perspective, Arendt's critique of modernity is totalizing in the worst way: it leads to a rejection of the energies of the modern age on the basis of an essentially *religious* conviction that humanity exists to be at home in the world.[177] Arendt's emphasis upon the redemptive character of genuine political action hinges, Kateb observes, on the possibility (and desirability) of a nonalienated existence. Thus, "groups of people must be at home in the world first if the frame of memorable deeds, the frame of political action, is to be secured and strengthened."[178] Modernity, however, cultivates human capacities that produce world and earth alienation, and effectively prevent us from being at home and (thus) inhabiting such a frame. Arendt condemns modernity because it destroys the conditions that enable the existential achievement of political action: "The hope is that humanity could be at home rightly. The hope is dashed by modernity."[179]

Kateb is right to emphasize the redemptive role political action plays for Arendt. Her desire for reconciliation flows from the tragic sensibility she shares with the Greeks, and it colors her entire approach to modernity. Yet I would suggest that Kateb's exclusive focus upon the "existential achievement" of political action yields a distorted view of Arendt's critique of modernity. For while Arendt, like Hegel, idealizes the Greeks as being uniquely at home in the world, she also shares Hegel's conviction that there is no going back: diremption cannot be undone (this, I take it, is one of the reasons for her fondness for René Char's aphorism: "Our inheritance was left to us by no testament"; and Tocqueville's epigram: "Since the past has ceased to turn its light upon the Future, the mind of man wanders in obscurity"). Moreover, Arendt knows that no "rainbow bridge of concepts" will succeed in recovering such wholeness.[180]

Without the prospect of reconciliation, however, modernity looks like a downward spiral of increasing alienation. Arendt's political theory, then, would simply be another expression of the "unhappy consciousness" that, as Judith Shklar pointed out long ago,[181] followed the implosion of utopian hopes. In fact, it is difficult to avoid this conclusion so long as we, like Kateb, insist upon seeing Arendt driven by the desire to overcome alienation (a desire that transmutes into theoretical mournfulness with the demonstration of the impossibility of reconciliation). Kateb's story is complicated, however, once we balance the "religious" hope for reconciliation with the weight Arendt gives to the "pagan" value of worldliness. For Arendt, modern existential resentment is bad *not* because it blocks reconciliation, but because it undermines worldliness. To be sure, "at home-ness" is one of the qualities Arendt attributes to a "worldly" (in Kateb's terms, unalienated) existence. Yet it is precisely the *artificiality*, the *reified* quality, of this "home" that both Arendt's liberal critics and her communitarian admirers must ignore. Full humanity does not require the *absence* of alienation, the availability of a homey *Gemeinschaft* in which one's group identity provides a form of metaphysical comfort. The "frame" Kateb speaks of, as I have emphasized, is essentially a *stage*, and the worldly form of existence Arendt champions reserves an especially high place for *theatricality*. Kateb would have us elide the distinction between theatricality and community, the better to locate Arendt's antimodernism in terms of familiar categories. However, the history of political theory, from Plato to Rousseau and beyond (one could include Heidegger in this regard), warns us against the apparent ease of this move. From the beginning, theatricality has been singled out as the enemy of community, artifice as the source of alienation.

Any assessment of Arendt's critique of modernity, then, must first consider the implications of her performance model of political action. As a crucial dimension of worldliness, theatricality exceeds—indeed, often stands in opposition to—the yearning for community, and for an unalienated existence. This, in turn, reminds us of the specificity of Arendt's complaint: it is not alienation per se that she combats, but *world* alienation. One could go even further and say that to be *worldly* in Arendt's sense is to inscribe a certain modality of alienation at the heart of one's existence, and to give this alienation an extremely positive valorization. Arendt's emphasis upon agonism, performance, virtuosity, persona, and "alienated" representative thinking renders Kateb's identification of worldliness with the *absence* of alienation problematic, to say the least. To be at home in the world in Arendt's sense means to be at home with the estrangement that permeates both the performative conception of action and the notion of "disinterested" judgment. Thus, Arendt is, in her own way, as much a champion of "moderate alienation" as the liberal modernist.[182]

This puts the "destruction of the common world" and the loss of the *sensus communis* in a different light. What the modern subjectification of the real and the instrumentalization of politics have done is to render a certain kind of distance, a certain kind of estrangement, supremely problematic. Where the instrumentalist considerations of *homo faber* or the needs of life dominate, the serious play of politics devolves into administration, coercion, or violence. Our capacity for spontaneous action and judgment resides, ultimately, upon a worldly form of estrangement (by no means the same as estrangement *from* the world), one that the "extremist exertions" of modernity have radically undermined. One can speak, in this regard, not only of our loss of feeling *for* the world, but *of* the world itself. For modernity's will to will overwhelms the dimension of artifice that "frames" genuine action, destroying mediation and contributing to the growing "naturalization" of human existence.

Arendt's antimodernism, then, is not totalizing, at least not in the sense of the cultural conservative who abhors the alienation of modern life and yearns for the rootedness of a premodern existence (for example, Heidegger at his most simplistic and loathsome, or Pope John Paul II). But if Arendt's critique of modernity is not "rejectionist" in this sense, is it perhaps immanent in nature? This is the view taken by many of her admirers who, given their own political agendas, wish to give the widest possible currency to certain aspects of her thought. What are we to make of the claims of Habermasians, communitarians, and participatory democrats in light of the ontological implications of Arendt's critique of modernity?

Speaking broadly, the members of each of these three schools of thought wish to enlist Arendt in the project of recovering a robust, comprehensive, and unitary public sphere. The explanations offered for how this sphere has been denatured, fragmented, or lost vary. For Habermas, the prerogatives of the public sphere have largely been usurped by the technocratic assertion of the "steering imperatives" of a complex political economy. For the communitarians, the fact that the public world has lost its power to "gather us together" is traceable to an undernourished sense of membership and the absence of animating, shared public purposes (hence the view of the liberal public sphere as a proceduralist shell). For participatory democrats, the framework of liberal constitutionalism combined with late capitalism and the rise of the national security state conspire to undercut democracy and render the title of citizen meaningless. The different diagnoses ought not conceal the fact that all are agreed that the *res publica* is in dire condition, and that each sees Arendt as providing support for its particular programs. Hence Habermas's appeal to her "intersubjective" concept of political action, the communitarian appeal to her worldly, "rooted" conception of membership, and the participatory democrat's appeal to the echoes of civic republicanism in her text. Each school hopes that the pursuit of one of these "Arendtian" avenues will bring us noticeably closer to a genuine—more democratic, just, and meaningful—public sphere.

The notion of a unitary or comprehensive public sphere has recently come in for a good deal of criticism, as scholars working from Foucauldian, feminist, or neo-Gramscian perspectives draw attention to the irreducibility of mechanisms of exclusion in the constitution of any discursive community.[183] Arendt's Greek, hypermasculinist conception of the public sphere would appear to mark her as an extreme example of public-realm theory's general insensitivity to such concerns. The fact that her work inspires Habermas, the communitarians, and participatory democrats has done little to endear her to champions of difference who wish to expose the disciplinary techniques by which "virtuous" (read: docile) citizens are made, or the power relations implicit in the most resolutely intersubjective accounts of discursive rationality.

Interestingly, what binds Arendt's contemporary critics and admirers together is the unquestioned assumption that she stands for the recovery of a single, institutionalized public sphere. Of course, Arendt's work—with its idealization of the public realm of the *polis* and its invocation of the "lost treasure" of the revolutionary tradition—more or less invites this reading. But, it seems to me, the admirers and critics are a little too fixated upon the "models" of the public sphere they find in Arendt's text, models they decontextualize and treat as (laudatory or suffocating) normative ideals. One result of this fixation is a general disregard for the central argument of *The Human Condition*. As we have seen, this argument concerns the de-worlding of the public world manifest in modernity's relentless subjectification of the real. The upshot of this argument is that, in late modernity, Being cannot possibly equal appearance. Modern world alienation dissolves the *sensus communis*, with the result that the only things "seen and heard by all" are the false appearances (Heidegger's "semblances") offered up under the single aspect of mass culture.[184] The mistake of the Habermasians, the communitarians, and the participatory democrats is to assume that there may be a late-modern substitute for this feeling for the world. Arendt is under no such illusion.

In other words, we must take Arendt's various pronouncements about the "end of the common world" seriously. After this event—for Arendt the defining event of the modern age—the prospects for an authentic, comprehensive, and relatively permanent public sphere fall to just about zero. This is not to say she gives up on action, politics, or "publicity" in the Kantian sense. Rather, it is to say that she is keenly aware of how the energies of modernity, which initially open the possibility of a groundless politics, wind up intensifying the paradox inherent in every revolutionary founding or spontaneous political action; namely, that the moment of "clearing" in which a space of freedom emerges is also the beginning of its disappearance.[185] The combination of modern world alienation with the late-modern escalation of the automatism present in life itself renders the appearance of these "islands of freedom" an even more "miraculous" event.[186] Late modernity heightens their evanescence; such spaces lead a "fugitive" existence (to use Sheldon Wolin's phrase).[187]

It is not a question, therefore, of pretending that we can resurrect the *agora* or some approximation thereof by appealing to deliberation, intersubjectivity, or "acting in concert." What matters is our ability to resist the demand for "functionalized behavior" and to preserve, as far as possible, our capacity for initiatory, agonistic action and spontaneous, independent judgment. This project of preservation occurs in a "world" where, as Arendt constantly reminds us, the supports for these activities have been radically undermined.

It is here that Arendt's concerns intersect most sharply with those of certain "postmodern" theorists. An unlikely constellation appears when we view Arendt's emphasis upon agonism, plurality, and performance against the backdrop of her more Heideggerian thoughts concerning the destruction of the common world. Seen through this lens, Arendt's theory of political action, so clearly at odds with a Foucauldian politics of everyday life, links up with Foucault's concept of resistance. For where the space of action is usurped (as both Arendt and Foucault argue it is), action in the strict sense is no longer possible. *Resistance* becomes the primary vehicle of spontaneity and agonistic subjectivity, a kind of successor concept to action.[188] Similarly, where the public sphere is fragmented and the *sensus communis* a thing of the past, the autonomy of judgment is preserved by efforts such as Arendt's and Lyotard's, which resist the temptation to ground this faculty in a theoretical discourse, and which struggle to provide a phenomenology of judgment "outside of the concept and outside of habit."[189] Finally, in an age that has witnessed the withdrawal of the political, and its dispersion throughout the social body, Arendt's tenacious effort to think the specificity of the political is hardly an anachronism, as Lacoue-Labarthe and Nancy have recognized.[190] For where everything is political, nothing is.

Arendt's critique of modernity, like her theory of political action, eludes easy classification. Too antinostalgic to be "rejectionist," yet too radical to qualify as "immanent," it fully displays Arendt's uncanny ability to combine an Olympian perspective on an epoch with a phenomenology of contemporary existence. Among recent theorists, only Foucault can be said to match her Nietzschean capacity to distance herself from the unquestioned assumptions of the age. This ability is the source of equal embarrassment and frustration for those theorists who believe, with Michael Walzer, that the first duty of social or political critics is to identify with the hopes, fears, and basic values of their community.[191] It also clashes with the current prejudice, ironically perpetuated by Foucault, which insists upon viewing theory as a kind of "toolbox," to be judged and deployed according to strategic considerations.

It is possible, of course, to appropriate Arendt in this way, and to view her deconstruction of the traditional concept of action and her analysis of the "destruction of the common world" as somehow beside the point, as not *political* enough. The irony of this stance is that it reproduces the "technical" configuration of acting and thinking that she and Heidegger devoted so much energy to questioning. Moreover, it is extraordinarily shortsighted. Arendt's central theoretical works are of value not because they offer an edifying affirmation of human agency in an age of ideology, or even a vehement repudiation of docility.[192] What Arendt learned from the experience of totalitarianism is that all human capacities—and particularly the capacity for action and judgment—crucially depend upon the conditions of their exercise, and that it is indeed possible to uproot capacities that may appear to be part of our "nature." The urgency of her attempt to "think what we are doing" in *The Human Condition* flows from this insight. For what Arendt suggests is that the existential resentment underlying much of the modern project may yet succeed where totalitarian ideologies could claim an only temporary victory. The extirpation of the human capacity for action by "peaceful" means is the danger that looms "after Auschwitz." The light of the public can be extinguished by means other than terror.

PART III

The Critique of Heidegger's
Philosophical Politics

Arendt, Heidegger, and the Oblivion of *Praxis*

... thinking is a deed. But a deed that also surpasses all *praxis*.
Thinking towers above action and production.

—*Heidegger, "Letter on Humanism"*

If philosophers, despite their necessary estrangement from the everyday life
of human affairs, were ever to arrive at a true political philosophy they
would have to make the plurality of men, out of which arises the
whole realm of human affairs—in its grandeur and misery—
the object of their *thaumadzein*.

—*Arendt, "Philosophy and Politics"*

I. Introduction

My description of Arendt's project and Heidegger's influence upon it will strike
some as controversial, not to say perverse. For from the perspective I have offered, Heidegger's work appears as a kind of prolegomenon to Arendt's recovery
of *praxis*. But, it will be objected, has not Heidegger's philosophy itself contributed in no small degree to the oblivion of *praxis* in our time? Does not Heidegger consistently devalue the public realm (the arena of *praxis*), seeing it first
as the domain of inauthenticity, and later as the expression of the "dominance of
subjectivity"?

The confrontation of Arendt's work with Heidegger's is bound to raise such
questions. They have been forcefully put by such Arendt-inspired critics of Heidegger as Habermas and Richard Bernstein. And it must be admitted, Arendt, for
her part, hardly underlined the importance of Heidegger to her rethinking of
political action. Indeed, in the Heidegger critique composed toward the end of
her life and included in *The Life of the Mind*, she stressed Heidegger's avoidance
of the question of action throughout his work.[1]

In this chapter and the next, I address the nature of this avoidance with an eye
to its implications for political theory. Viewed from an Arendtian perspective,
this avoidance has been interpreted as the symptom of two very different impulses. Arendt herself sees it as reflecting the fundamentally unpolitical nature of
Heidegger's thought, which she presents as unworldly in the extreme. Habermas
and Bernstein, on the other hand, view the suppression of *praxis* as the sign of
something more dangerous, the outgrowth of a deeply antipolitical impulse. According to this reading, Heidegger's philosophy offers ample evidence of a quasi-

Platonist desire to overcome plurality, deny human freedom, and secure a cosmically grounded authority. Heidegger appears in one of two garbs: as an irrationalist voluntarist whose existentialism leads to a politics of will, or (in the later thought) as a kind of ascetic priest who denies the efficacy of human action.

Unpolitical or antipolitical? Both characterizations capture a part of the truth, and the criticisms they stand for must be taken into account in any assessment of Heidegger's relevance to political theory (on the one hand) and the relationship of his philosophy to his politics (on the other). Problems arise when one attempts to deduce the answer to the first question from the answer to the second. The failure to keep these questions at least analytically distinct is, I think, the root of a tendency to essentialize Heidegger, to present his thought as either absolutely remote from the realm of human affairs or as political in an all too predictable (authoritarian) sense. Such readings, as I show in Chapter 8, are dubious on interpretive and textual grounds; moreover, they make it all but impossible to see how Heidegger's thought can be a resource in the rethinking of the political. The present chapter explores both characterizations, in order to more fully articulate the nexus of Arendt's political theory and Heidegger's philosophy. The overarching question concerns the availability of Heidegger's thought for politics, a question that returns us to one of Arendt's primary themes: the conflict between philosophy and politics.

II. Heidegger's Concept of the Political

The Devaluation of Communicative Action and the Public Sphere in Being and Time

In the rehearsing of the central themes of *Being and Time* in Chapter 4, I stressed how Heidegger's notion of authentic disclosedness does not isolate *Dasein* from its world. Far from advocating a Kierkegaardian withdrawal from the world, Heidegger insists that "*authentic* existence is not something which floats above falling everydayness."[2] Authenticity is a mode of Being-in-the-world, and as such is both a way of acting and a mode of Being-with-others. Thus, the "transcendence" of fallen everydayness aims not at an individual purified of his ties to the world, but can imply the achievement of a more authentic form of community life. The possibility of an *authentic mitsein* (being with) opens the way to a political reading of *Being and Time*, a possibility seized upon by critics of Heidegger as well as those eager to escape a subject-centered political theory.[3]

From a political point of view, the Heideggerian notion of authenticity indicates a preference for those forms of community life that are most conducive to "striving activity," and that increase the opportunity for events of authentic disclosedness. Indeed, following Taminiaux's suggestion, it is possible to read the distinction between *Eigentlichkeit* (authenticity) and *Uneigentlichkeit* (inauthenticity) as an appropriation of the distinction between *praxis* (as authentic action) and *poiēsis* (as concernful absorption).[4] This reading helps to create a bridge to the Arendtian conception of an agonistic public sphere in which the *bios politikos* is the chief vehicle for such striving activity, in the form of genuine political action that achieves authentically disclosive effects.

Given these links, the question is whether the Heidegger of *Being and Time* can be said to share Arendt's enthusiasm for the public realm as the space in which the extraordinary becomes "an ordinary occurrence of everyday life." As any reader of *Being and Time* can attest, the answer would seem to be clearly and decisively negative. The antipublic rhetoric of sections 27 and 38 is overwhelming; the identification of "publicness" (*Öffentlichkeit*) with fallenness, inauthenticity, and the "they-self" is undeniable.

According to Heidegger, publicness is the mode of understanding characteristic of the "they," the readily accessible interpretation to which *Dasein*—as thrown Being-in-the-world—is always already given over to. Expressing the "distantiality, averageness, and leveling down" in which the "they" is, publicness, according to Heidegger, "proximally controls every way in which the world and *Dasein* get interpreted. . . . By publicness everything gets obscured, and what has thus been covered up gets passed on as something familiar and accessible to everyone."[5] Lost in the publicness of the "they," *Dasein* understands and expresses itself as "one" understands and expresses oneself.[6] It is through the "idle chatter" of fallen *Dasein* that the "public interpretation of the world" manifests and reifies itself.[7] Insofar as *Dasein* remains caught in the web of such public talk, insofar as it unthinkingly accepts the "way in which things have been publicly interpreted," it is "held fast" in its fallenness."[8]

In *The Philosophical Discourse of Modernity*, Habermas thinks through the consequences of what he calls Heidegger's denigration of "the communicative practice of everyday life."[9] Given Heidegger's emphasis upon the worldliness of *Dasein* and its Being-with-others, the disdain for the structures of "linguistic intersubjectivity" comes as a bit of a surprise. After all, one of the main thrusts of *Being and Time*, as Habermas notes, is to "dissolve the concept of transcendental subjectivity dominant since Kant" and thereby overcome the philosophy of the subject.[10] The concept of "world" goes a long way toward achieving this end, decentering the subject by thematizing the "meaning-disclosing horizon" in terms of which entities appear and upon which all being-toward-entities—all subject/object relations—are founded.

This decentering of the subject receives further impetus from Heidegger's insistence that being-in-the-world is always a being-with-others. The existential analytic, then, achieves a radical change in perspective, one in which the pretheoretical lifeworld established by social interaction becomes, for the first time in Western philosophy, the focus of attention. Hence, what Habermas calls the "promise" of *Being and Time*, the promise "to illuminate the very processes of mutual understanding . . . that keep present the world as an intersubjectively shared lifeworld background."[11] Yet the promise goes unfulfilled, and the paradigm shift it implies (from the philosophy of the subject to the "paradigm of mutual understanding" or communicative action) fails to occur. Heidegger emphasizes, instead, the constitutive, world-projecting performances of *Dasein* as well as the "mineness" of *Dasein*. In the end, fundamental ontology returns to what Habermas calls "the blind alley of the philosophy of the subject."[12]

Why does Heidegger's attempt to "tear away from the enchanted circle of the philosophy of the subject" break down? In part, Habermas suggests (following Michael Theunissen), because fundamental ontology is "still tinged with the solipsism of Husserlian phenomenology," and is therefore unable to accord the intersubjective lifeworld its full priority.[13] But the real reason has less to do with this theoretical taint than with a simple prejudice. From the beginning, Habermas states, Heidegger "degrades the background structures of the lifeworld that reach beyond the isolated *Dasein*," casting them as "structures of an average everyday existence, that is of inauthentic *Dasein*."[14] With the prejudice against "the communicative practice of everyday life" firmly in place, it is not surprising that Heidegger loses sight of the priority of the lifeworld's intersubjectivity and concentrates instead upon "the existential efforts of a *Dasein* that has tacitly assumed the place of transcendental subjectivity."[15] The denigration of communicative action so evident in the descriptions of "publicness" and the "they" thus not only shapes the fundamental theoretical choices of *Being and Time*, but it also guarantees that *praxis* will be ignored through the focus on a heroically projecting *Dasein*, manfully affirming its finitude.[16] The residual subjectivism of *Being and Time* is so strong that the political possibilities it opens are either nil or alarmingly predictable (in 1933, Habermas argues, Heidegger "substitutes for this 'in-each-case-mine' *Dasein*, the collective *Dasein* of a fatefully existing and 'in-each-case-our people'").[17] All of this stands in the starkest opposition to Arendt, who (as Habermas writes elsewhere) attempts to "read off the general structures of unimpaired intersubjectivity [from] the formal properties of communicative action."[18]

The denigration of communicative action also apparently yields what Richard Wolin has called a "radically dichotomous social ontology," one that splits the social world between authentic *Dasein* and the "they."[19] Once authenticity is defined in opposition to "the nefarious sphere of everydayness," it can only emerge as essentially nonrelational. As Habermas puts it, "the 'they' now serves as a foil before which a Kierkegaardian existence, radically isolated in the face of death . . . can now be identified as the 'who' of *Dasein*."[20] Such a polar opposition seems to open an "unbridgeable gulf" between the authentic and the inauthentic, a gap that can be interpreted in one of two ways: either as "a total repudiation of the public world and its projects," or as an "antihumanist philosophical anthropology" upholding an order of rank where the inauthentic (the "human, all too human") submit to those made of sterner (more authentic) stuff.[21]

What are we to make of Habermas's reading? Is the "subjectivism" of the early Heidegger so pervasive that not only is *praxis* ignored, but the entire space for political life is either closed off or rendered rigidly hierarchical and collectivist?

As the reading of *Being and Time* in Chapter 4 indicates, I do not think this is the case. It is tempting to read Heidegger's *Being and Time* in light of the *Rektoratsrede* (Rectoral Address) and texts from his middle period like *An Introduction*

to *Metaphysics*. Indeed, the thematic links are undeniable.[22] But Habermas's reading goes too far in suggesting a categorial predetermination of the *nature* of Heidegger's politics. The trope of "substitution" employed by Habermas (and originated by Karl Löwith) suggests that National Socialism is somehow the flip side
of fundamental ontology, a simple matter of plugging in the *Volk* for a "radically
isolated" *Dasein*. The problematic opened by *Being and Time* certainly makes such
a move possible; as I shall show below, Chapter 5, Division II, to some extent
prefigures it. Yet the politics of *Being and Time*—the kind of political space it
opens—are by no means reducible to the either/or Habermas suggests.

Another problem with Habermas's analysis is that it suggests a simple opposition between Arendt and Heidegger on the question of the public sphere. The
condescending descriptions of *Öffentlichkeit* (publicity or publicness) certainly
seem to warrant Habermas's placement of Arendt and Heidegger in two radically
different paradigms. "Following" Arendt, Habermas equates the public sphere
with communicative action, and tacitly presumes that Heidegger's *Öffentlichkeit*
has the same referent. If this were so—if Heidegger's contempt for publicness were
tantamount simply to a repudiation of the "public sphere"—then the politics of
Being and Time would be either nonexistent *or* a cryptototalitarian antipolitics, a
form of politics predicated upon the effacement of plurality and the public realm.
While Heidegger can scarcely be called a champion of plurality in Arendt's sense
(for reasons I will discuss below), the conclusion is nevertheless unjustified. The
relation between "publicness" and "the public sphere" is complex: Arendt is extremely rigorous about what constitutes a *genuine* (agonistic, world-illuminating)
public sphere. She fears, moreover, that the world alienation of modernity has
robbed the public realm of "the power of illumination which was originally part
of its very nature."[23] Under such historical conditions, the Heideggerian description of an existence "assaulted by the overwhelming power of 'mere talk' that
irresistibly arises out of the public realm" is, in fact, a phenomenologically accu-
rate description of a "world" in which public life has been reduced to show or
spectacle.[24] Anyone who would detect in Heidegger's descriptions of *Öffentlichkeit* a "total repudiation of the public world," or see in Arendt an undifferenti-
ated endorsement of publicity in all its forms, must come to grips with Arendt's
statement that, where public talk is manipulative and hypocritical, "the sarcastic,
perverse-sounding statement *Das Licht der Öffentlichkeit verdunkelt olles*" (The
light of the public obscures everything) goes "to the very heart of the matter."[25]

We can, then, bracket the conclusion that fundamental ontology entails a
kind of *a priori* repudiation of the public sphere, in order to focus upon the consequences for political speech and action that flow from Heidegger's devaluation of
communicative action. What role emerges for politics in the early Heidegger,
once we get past the impression that he simply relegates all Being-with-others to
"the sphere of inauthentic dealings"? How might politics contribute to the realization of a "more authentic form" of community life, and what sort of speech will
be conducive to this end?

In the most general of terms, it can be said that *Being and Time* reserves a
twofold role for politics. The first would be to shatter the tranquillity of everyday

Dasein, to perform for the community the role that anxiety performs for the individual.[26] Anxiety brings *Dasein* back from its absorption in the world of everyday concerns by bringing it face to face with its finitude, by confronting it with its thrown Being-in-the-world.[27] Once *mitsein* is fully recognized as a constitutive structure of *Dasein*, and once *Dasein*'s historizing is recognized as always a cohistorizing, it follows that the community of which *Dasein* is irreducibly a part stands in need of a similarly sharp reminder of *its* radical historicality and finitude, of the abysslike nature of its ground.[28] Such a reminder—presumably performed by authentic political speech and leadership—is necessary if the community is to be called back from its absorption in everyday life and politics, and made ready for a recommitment to its "ownmost distinctive possibility," a possibility opened at the founding of the community but long since covered over.[29]

The second role follows from the first. Simply calling the community back from its "lostness" to a sense of its finitude and, thus, to resoluteness is not enough. An authentic politics must do more. As Karsten Harries notes, the categorial structure of "resolve" in Heidegger threatens to collapse into arbitrariness: knowing the groundlessness of all pregiven measures for action, yet impelled to grasp *some* concrete possibilities, resolute *Dasein* faces a choice—a decision that seems, in a very real sense, criterionless.[30] The existential freedom of *Dasein* appears to be indistinguishable from spontaneity: *Dasein* will fall into what Habermas calls "the decisionism of an empty resoluteness" unless there is some authority to give it both *direction* and *content*.[31] Thus the second role reserved for authentic politics and political speech: to provide the *authority* needed to guide *Dasein*'s choice, an authority that can be reconciled with the demands of resolve, an authority that is neither metaphysical nor traditional.

There is, then, a clear role for politics and political speech in the space opened by *Being and Time*. One could even say that *Being and Time* implies a notion of an authentic public space. It already appears doubtful, however, that the agonistic yet deliberative politics advanced by Arendt could fulfill what for Heidegger are the two chief tasks of an "authentic politics." Arendtian speech and action can hardly be reduced to "the communicative practice of everyday life"; nevertheless, they remain, from a Heideggerian standpoint, far too mired in the everyday to achieve the kind of "shattering" effect authenticity demands. Because fallenness is a structurally built-in tendency of *Dasein*, even the most "fiercely agonal" deliberation by diverse equals will fail to do the trick.[32] (In this sense, the charge that Heidegger relegates "communicative action" to the sphere of inauthenticity hits home.) What *kind* of political speech could achieve the desired effect? What speech breaks through the alienation of everyday life and makes possible a transformative appropriation of the *essence* of the community?

Answering this question demands a return to *Entschlossenheit*: what speech serves as a spur to resolve? *Doxa* (opinion) is evidently excluded, since the plurality of perspectives it expresses yield nothing "essential": opinion takes its place as part of the "idle chatter" of the "they." As Taminiaux points out, there are clear resonances with Plato here.[33] Yet Heidegger's denigration of opinion in no way attributes the required tranquillity-shattering power to *epistēmē* (scientific or theoretical knowledge). To presume that the devaluation of opinion implies the privileging of a discourse of Truth is to fall back upon the most traditional of philosophical moves, the derivation of prescriptive statements from descriptive or cognitive discourse.[34] For Heidegger as much as Weber, the idea that any theoretical understanding of the world could provide us with a standard for how we ought to act is the height of bad faith.[35] If political speech as *doxa* stands for absorption in the way things are publicly interpreted, political speech as *epistēmē* represents that yearning for a ground beyond its own finitude that authentic *Dasein* knows it cannot have.

Neither *doxa* nor *epistēmē*, then, contribute to the cultivation of resoluteness in a community. Nor can authentic Being-in-the-world be spurred by the appeal to tradition or the status quo.[36] The last place a speech that seeks to shatter the numbing tranquillity of everyday life can turn to is that very life or its historical rootedness. To do so would be to cover over the moment of "pure" choice that, as many critics have noted, is implicit in Heidegger's concepts of resolve and authenticity. *Dasein must* crystallize its resolve in particular actions with others or remain trapped in fallenness. The "criterionlessness" of this choice will overwhelm it unless *some* agency provides the requisite direction-giving authority.

Thus the paradox alluded to: in order for the community to be called back to itself, a peculiar, nonfoundational authority must be exercised; one that directs without making *Dasein*'s commitment any easier; one that provides content without perpetuating the status quo or the comforting illusion of some higher, transcendental authority, such as God, Reason, Nature, or even History. The question of an "authentic politics" in Heidegger boils down to the question of the viability of such authority. What form can this authority possibly take? What kind of political speech is capable of conveying it? *Whose* speech is capable of reconciling *resolve* with *authority*?

Heidegger's answer to these questions, or at least the beginnings of an answer, can be found in Chapter 5, Division II ("Temporality and Historicality"), of *Being and Time* and in the notorious Rectoral Address of 1933 ("The Self-Assertion of the German University").[37] In *Being and Time*, the required authority is sought for in the past of concrete historical *Dasein*; that is, in the *heritage* of the particular historical community.[38] If thrown *Dasein* is to "come back to itself" from its dispersion in the "public way of interpreting existence" and uncover "current practical possibilities of authentic existing," then it must do so "in terms of that heritage which that resoluteness, as thrown, *takes over*."[39] The only authority commensurable with resolve (the "sole possible authority which a free existing can have," as Heidegger says) derives from the "repeatable possibilities of existence" buried in this mostly forgotten heritage.[40] In this understanding, authentic action—which is at the same time resolved but not arbitrary—can only be a kind of *repetition*, a repetition that "does not abandon itself to that which is past," but which willfully appropriates a heritage in light of *Dasein*'s essentially futural orientation.[41]

The authority that makes authentic action understood as repetition (*Wiederholung*) possible is, then, an *interpetation* of the *destiny* (*Geschick*) of the community.[42] Through such interpretation, authentic political leaders (those capable of what the Rectoral Address calls "spiritual legislation") enable citizens to "take over" their thrownness through the recognition of a shared destiny.[43] The interpretation of the "leader" itself repeats the moment of vision in which the world of the community "sprang into being."[44] As repetition, this interpretation brings into the present a sense of the greatness and uncanniness that attended the community's origin. The past now appears as an "abysslike" ground that draws the community back from its fallenness and makes possible a recommitment to the community's "ownmost distinctive possibility," its historical essence.[45]

Wresting a destiny from history through creative, even violent, interpretation, genuine political speech provides a way out of the "decisionism of an empty resoluteness." Resolute *Dasein* comes to see its fate as primordially linked to the destiny of the community, and to understand its "essence" in terms of the community.[46] The need for authority, Heidegger would persuade us, is met in a nonmetaphysical, nontraditionalist way, through interpretation permeated by a sense of finitude and the inevitability of ambiguity. It is clear that the kind of hermeneutic authority so exercised is *limited*: the categories of "resolve" and "authenticity" rule out anything like a blind or unquestioning obedience (although Heidegger's idea of an "authentic following" remains problematic).[47] The fact remains that the leader's interpretation stands above the deliberative judgment of the citizens, having, so to speak, a fuller ontological ground. Suspicious of the *bios politikos* (the sharing of word and deeds amongst equals) if not politics per se, Heidegger grounds the authority of authentic political speech in a "moment of vision" that transcends, in the manner of Plato, the deliberative speech of the many.

It is here that Heidegger's devaluation of the "communicative practice of everyday life" comes back to haunt us. Heidegger's supposed entrapment in the philosophy of the subject does not really answer the question of what a politics extrapolated from *Being and Time* would look like. Yet Habermas's focus upon the Heideggerian prejudice against intersubjectivity and "publicness" does help to illuminate Heidegger's preference for a species of authority that trumps the judgment (or "communicative rationality") exercised by deliberating equals. The problem here is not that *any* interpretation will do, so long as it stirs the masses; nor is it that all interpretations are equal (Heidegger is very clear about the difference between an authentic and inauthentic "historizing"). The problem instead involves the criteria for judging the authenticity or "rootedness" of a given interpretation. When genuine political speech is juxtaposed, even implicitly, to the deliberative speech of the many, *phronēsis* and hermeneutic judgment are torn apart, and the criterionlessness that had so plagued the notion of resolve returns. The authority envisaged by Heidegger produces interpretation, not truth; yet it might as well claim for itself the status of *epistēmē* insofar as Heidegger provides no answer to Harries's persistent question: "What enables us to distinguish the genuine leader from his false counterpart?"[48]

The seriousness of this lack, of course, is driven home by Heidegger's own experience in 1933. Unwilling or unable to subject such hermeneutic authority to the kind of judgment exercised in the public realm and oblivious to the minimal conditions necessary to preserve such judgment, Heidegger falls prey to a kind of intuitionism all too capable of seeing in National Socialism the disclosure of "the spiritual world" of the German people.[49] The antideliberative stance implied by the polarity of authentic and everyday speech yields a vision of authentically disclosive politics in which plurality, while not totally effaced, is neutered by an authority whose basis remains problematic.

The Poetic Model of Disclosure in the Work of the Thirties

As Karsten Harries (following Alexander Schwan) has observed, any attempt to understand Heidegger's thinking of the political in the thirties "has to begin with his analysis of the work of the artist and poet."[50] This is so because in his works of this period (*An Introduction to Metaphysics*, "The Origin of the Work of Art," "Hölderlin and the Essence of Poetry," the first volume of the Nietzsche lectures), Heidegger not only extends his thoughts on the political role of the creative leader, but also develops an explicitly poetic model of disclosure, one that comes to dominate his thinking of politics and the space of the political. The work of the thirties attempts nothing less than the radical rethinking of the notion of *poiēsis*, a rethinking that will bear its first fruit in the concept of the world-disclosing "work" in "The Origin of the Work of Art." This concept, in which the new, poetic model of disclosure is crystallized, emerges in the context of Heidegger's ruminations on art, but it is quickly generalized to include the work of all "genuine creators," including poets, thinkers, and statesmen as well as artists in the more limited sense.[51] It is through the work of such creators, Heidegger argues, that the historicity of a community is established, its "destiny" defined, and the possibility of an authentic relation to Being opened.[52]

Heidegger's political thinking of this period can be characterized as the attempt to subsume *praxis* under a new and postmetaphysical conception of authentic art (*technē*) or poetry (*poiēsis*). Driven by the need to overcome the subjectivism that had characterized aesthetics since Kant, Heidegger incessantly returns to the question of the ontological status of the work of art and its truth-revealing or world-disclosing capacity. In order to understand the political ramifications of Heidegger's notion of a "radical *poiēsis*"—a *poiēsis* liberated from the Aristotelian delimitation in terms of substance and causality—we need to answer two broad questions.[53] First, what, according to Heidegger, is the nature of art? What accounts for its singular ontological status? Second, in what does the "work-being" of the work consist? What is the "ontological vocation" of the work and how does it fulfill it?[54]

"All art," Heidegger writes in "The Origin of the Work of Art," ". . . is essentially poetry."[55] By this, Heidegger means that all genuine art is characterized by the poetic capacity to bring into being something that is *radically* new, that was not somehow contained, in *potentia*, in that which already is. Poetic in the sense of a radical (non-Aristotelian) *poiēsis*, art is a kind of "illuminating projection" that "first brings beings to word and appearance," that "nominates beings *to* their *being from out of* their being."[56] Because art is, in essence, poetic, it can be described as a "becoming and happening of truth," as a distinctive and privileged event of disclosure.[57]

A genuine work of art, then, neither represents nor expresses. What it does do, first and foremost, is to "open" or "set up" a *world*: the work establishes or clears that primordial space of truth in which "the world of [an] historical people" first comes to stand. The work-being of the work consists, according to Heidegger, in this world-disclosing or world-opening capacity: "To be a work means to set up a world."[58] Heidegger famously illustrates the ontological "opening up" performed by the work of art by the example of a Greek temple, which, though it "portrays nothing," nevertheless

> fits together and at the same time gathers around itself the unity of those paths and relations in which birth and death, disaster and blessing, victory and disgrace, endurance and decline acquire the shape of destiny for human being. The all-governing expanse of this open relational context is the world of this historical people. Only from and in this expanse does the nation first return to itself for the fulfillment of its vocation.[59]

"Towering up within itself," the temple-work "opens up a *world* and keeps it abidingly in being."[60] But what, Heidegger asks, *is* a world? Moreover, how is it that a work such as the temple not only "sets up" a world, but holds its openness open, thereby facilitating what Richard Wolin calls "the epochal encounter between Being and beings"?[61]

I have already described how the notions of "world" and "clearing" figure in Heidegger's thought (see Chapter 4). In OWA Heidegger amplifies his reference to the "open relational context" by explaining that "The world is not the mere collection of the countable or uncountable, familiar or unfamiliar things that are just there. But neither is it a merely imagined framework added by our representation to the sum of such given things. The *world worlds*, and is more fully in being than the tangible and perceptible realm in which we believe ourselves to be at home. . . . World is the ever non-objective to which we are subject as long as the paths of birth and death, blessing and curse keep us transported into Being."[62] It is the "vocation" of the work of art to accomplish the worlding of the world, to "hold open the open of the world" and prevent it from decaying into a taken for granted status quo, cut off from a sense of its partiality and finitude.

The work-being of the work fulfills this ontological task by being the site of *conflict* between the openness of the world and the concealedness of what Heidegger calls "earth." "Earth" stands for that more primordial darkness or concealment that every "clearing" for beings presupposes. As *work*, art clears a world while simultaneously "setting forth" the earth; that is, preserving that which conceals and shelters.[63] But the crucial ontological function of the work is not to mediate or reconcile world and earth; rather, the work-being of the work consists in "setting up a world" and "setting forth the earth" in a relation of strife or *striving*. The work, according to Heidegger, both "instigates" and "accomplishes" this striving, allowing the strife "to remain a strife."[64] By bringing world and earth into a relation in which the former constantly strives to surmount the latter, the work becomes the site of that primordial struggle for disclosure—the appropriation of Being—to which Heidegger's thought ceaselessly returns. And here we have an essential specification of the work-being of the work: "The work-being of the work consists in the fighting of the battle between world and earth."[65]

Neither the "setting up" of the world, nor the "setting forth" of the earth, let alone the establishment of the conflict between the two, could occur without the work. "Truth" (in the Heideggerian sense of the disclosure of Being) could not happen without the work, since "truth establishes itself *in the work*. Truth is present only as the conflict between lighting and concealing in the opposition of world and earth."[66] The work-being of the work (the "fighting of the battle between world and earth") is thus the vehicle through which Being is disclosed, the vehicle through which truth happens as a historical occurrence. Indeed, Heidegger claims that the *nature* of truth is such that "it has to happen in such a thing as something created."[67] There is an "impulse toward the work" in the nature of truth, an impulse toward occurrence in something whose essence involves *createdness*.[68] Truth "wills" to be established in the createdness of a work whose "bringing forth" clears "the openness of the Open into which it comes forth."[69] The happening of truth as a historical-ontological event is, for Heidegger, identical with what he refers to as the "setting-itself-into-work" of truth.

We have only to ask what counts as such a world-opening work to see the connection to the political. In OWA Heidegger observes that "one essential way in which truth establishes itself in the beings it has opened up is truth setting itself into work. Another way in which truth occurs is the act that founds a political state."[70] The apparent dichotomy between works and states as sites for the historical happening of truth is removed in a passage from An Introduction to Metaphysics: "Unconcealment," Heidegger states, "occurs only when it is achieved by work: the work of the word in poetry, the work of stone in temple and statue, the work of the word in thought; the work of the *polis* as the historical place in which all this is grounded and preserved."[71] Not only is the *polis* grouped with other artworks as an example of the "setting-into-work" of truth, but it is accorded a clear historical-ontological *priority*.

The works of "creators, poets, thinkers, statesmen" are precisely the works through which truth happens, through which worlds are "opened" or "founded." It is the nature of such works to embody the conflict or struggle through which "a world comes into being."[72] Glossing a fragment from Heraclitus—"Conflict is for all the creator that causes to emerge, but [also] the dominant preserver. For it makes some appear as gods, others as men; it creates [shows] some as slaves, others as freemen"—Heidegger comments upon the essential *agon* made manifest in such works:

> The struggle meant here is the original struggle, for it gives rise to the contenders as such; it is not a mere assault on something already here. It is this conflict that first projects and develops what had hitherto been unheard of, unsaid and unthought. The battle is then sustained by the creators, poets, thinkers, statesmen. Against the

overwhelming chaos they set up the barrier of their work, and in their work they capture the world thus opened up. It is with these works that the elemental power, the *physis* first comes to stand. Only now does the essent become essent as such. This world-building is history in the authentic sense. . . . When struggle ceases, the essent [beings] does not vanish, but the world turns away.[73]

The essential *agon* between world and earth comes to stand in or is accomplished by the originary struggle of "creators, poets, thinkers, statesmen." Through their works, which act as "barriers" against an "overwhelming chaos," the world of a historical people is founded and that people is *given* a history. This is what Heidegger means when he says "this world-building is history in the authentic sense." Art, which encompasses various kinds of radical *poiēsis*, *grounds* history; it is the origin of a "people's historical existence."[74] The artwork founds or begins a world; through the strife it opens the creators and preservers of this work and world have their origin.[75]

Two important themes emerge out of Heidegger's view of the process by which truth sets itself into work. The first is that this setting-into-work, by Heidegger's own admission, is *violent*. The "thrust" into history performed by the work, the beginning or the founding it accomplishes, is a "violent act" (*Gemalttat*), an act of originary violence through which new "paths" are created and old ones left behind.[76] The world-building work, whether it be words, thoughts, or a state, forms the openness of the world.[77] Such forming, despite its radical and primordial nature, is linked to more mundane examples of *poiēsis* by the unavoidable violence that attends all making.[78] Heidegger confirms this Arendtian/Aristotelian point even as he attempts to prevent such ontological violence from being confused with ontic violence, the violence born of human aggression and will: "The violence of poetic speech, of thinking projection, of building configuration, of the action that creates states is not a sanction of faculties man has, but a taming and ordering of powers by virtue of which the essent opens up as such when man moves into it."[79]

The second theme concerns the priority or primordiality of the work of the statesman amongst all such history-producing, world-disclosing works. The act of radical *poiēsis*, of originary violence, performed by the statesman creates the ground for all subsequent disclosure: the *polis*, according to Heidegger, is "the place, the *there*, wherein and as which historical being-there is. The *polis* is the historical place, the there *in* which, *out* of which, and *for* which history happens."[80] Commenting on Sophocles in *An Introduction to Metaphysics*, Heidegger elaborates the ontological primordiality of the political space, emphasizing the way in which this space "gathers" the essential aspects of Greek life. In the process, he gives a truly remarkable picture of those "artists with the look of bronze" (Nietzsche) whose work *is* this space:

To this place and scene of history belong the gods, the temples, the priests, the festivals, the games, the poets, the thinkers, the ruler, the council of elders, the assembly of the people, the army and the fleet. All this does not first belong to the *polis*, does not become political by entering into a relation with a statesman and a general and the business of state. No, it is political, i.e., at the site of history, provided there be (for example) poets *alone*, but then really poets, priests *alone*, but then really priests, rulers *alone*, but then really rulers. *Be*; but this means: as violent men to use power, to become pre-eminent in historical being as creators, as men of action. Pre-eminent in the historical place, they become at the same time *apolis*, without city and place, lonely, strange, and alien, without issue amid the essert as a whole, at the same time without statute and limit, without structure and order, because they themselves *as* creators must first create all this.[81]

The state or, to be more precise, the *polis*, emerges here as what Harries calls the "violent setting-itself-into-work of truth."[82] And while it is too easy to extrapolate a "statist conception of politics" from such passages, the distorting effects of Heidegger's identification of the political and the poetic can scarcely be denied.[83] Throughout the works of the thirties, the figure of the state as artwork intrudes violently, underscoring what Arendt calls the "conflict between art and politics," a conflict to which Heidegger appears oblivious.

How does the adoption of a poetic model of disclosure distort Heidegger's conception of the political and contribute to the oblivion of *praxis*? First, by perpetuating an organic notion of community, one that follows from framing the state as a harmonious or authentic artwork. Such a community/work, while the locus of a primordial ontological striving, is nevertheless devoid of genuine plurality and the agonism that goes with it. Second, the poetic model restricts authentic political action to *founding* and *preserving* the work/state.

Heidegger's emphasis upon founding is a direct result of his defining art as poetry. If "the nature of art is poetry" or projective saying, the "nature of poetry, in turn, is the founding of truth."[84] Through his originary violence, the creator sets truth into work in a way that "thrusts up the unfamiliar and extraordinary and at the same time thrusts down the ordinary and what we believe to be such."[85] Such founding is a "bestowing," "grounding," and "beginning."[86] In "setting up the barrier of their work against overwhelming chaos," the "lonely, strange and alien" founders of states simultaneously establish a world and instigate a strife, giving to a people through their world-founding work a place, a destiny, and an *ethos*.[87]

As a world-opening work or "field of strife," the state stands in need of preservers as well as founders. Indeed, this is so much the case that Heidegger claims that "the preservers of a work belong to its createdness with an essentiality equal to that of the creators . . . it is the work that makes creators possible in their nature, and that by its nature is in need of preservers."[88] The work-being of the work—the state—demands those who will "begin" and "bestow," but it also demands those who will ensure that the strife will remain a strife, whose creative intervention will preserve this "playing field of openness," preventing it from degenerating into "a rigid stage with a permanently raised curtain on which the play of beings runs its course."[89] Choosing a theatrical metaphorics to convey a sense of ontological/historical petrification, Heidegger's insists upon the importance of preservers, stressing the poetic nature of their vocation. The implication is that the work-character of *this* work—the state—can be brought into being and pre-served only by a poetic speech, a projective saying, of founders or leaders. The state remains a *work* so long as there are leaders of the sort *Being and Time* had gestured toward, leaders whose vision and speech pierces the fallenness of the public realm and reappropriates the original strife between world and earth.

Heidegger's framing of the political as work in need of creators and preservers shifts the agon of the political realm to an ontological level untouched by the political speech of deliberating equals. The agon that occurs here (in the public realm, as Arendt understands it) is a nonessential one. The *essential* striving is that which occurs between world and earth, between the political life of a com-munity and the unmastered depths of its past, the sheer uncanniness of its found-ing.[90] This agon is brought to language only by the poetic speech of those who, as founders and preservers, derive their being from the work.

Heidegger's work of the thirties is remarkable for the way it poeticizes the disclosiveness of political action—for the line it draws between the world-dis-closive speech of "founders and preservers" and the public, ontic speech of the many. The devaluation of communicative action is taken to new extremes, as authentic *praxis* is identified with a poetic saying whose sole concern and accom-plishment is to "nominate beings *to* their being *from out of* their being."[91] In "The Origin of the Works of Art," Heidegger insists upon seeing communicative and world-disclosive speech as antithetical: on the one hand, language "serves for verbal exchange and agreement, and in general for communicating"; on the other, there is poetic language that "brings what is, as something that is, into the open for the first time."[92]

The reification of world-disclosive, poetic speech goes hand in hand with Hei-degger's contempt for public talk. Such speech, Heidegger remarks in *An Intro-duction to Metaphysics*, is "worn out and used up," drained of all world-illuminat-ing capacity; it is an "indispensable but masterless means of communication that may be used as one pleases, as indifferent as a means of public transport, as a streetcar which everyone rides in."[93] The polarity of *Eigentlichkeit/Uneigentlichkeit* has hardened into a rigid dichotomy between ontic and ontological speech. The irony is that Heidegger's idea of a "happening of truth"—so obviously anti-Pla-tonic in intent—issues in a hierarchy parallel to the Platonic ranking of *doxa* and *epistēmē*. Like Plato, Heidegger is convinced that *doxa* is excluded from the "truth of Being." And while his concept of historicity prevents him from resurrecting a "true world" in opposition to appearance, it nevertheless inclines him to think of *praxis* in terms of *poiēsis*. Anxious to preserve the revelatory dimension of *praxis* from the taint of the "sharing of words and deeds," Heidegger rethinks it as a form of radical *poiēsis*.[94]

The "Oblivion of Praxis" in Heidegger's Later Work

Habermas's critique underlines the difference between Arendt's model of authen-tic disclosedness and Heidegger's. For Arendt, the "sharing of words and deeds," genuine political action, is simultaneously communicative and disclosive, intersubjective and "poetic," in the broad Heideggerian sense. The distinctions Heidegger draws between authentic (ontological) and inauthentic (ontic) speech, between "poetry" and communication, serve to obsure the disclosive potential—the ontological dimensions—of an agonistic, deliberative politics à la Arendt.[95]

From the Habermasian perspective, the devaluation of communicative action found in Heidegger's early and middle work is taken to new extremes after the "turning," or *Kehre*. The primary difference is that while the pre-*Kehre* work at least reserved a space for the political, the later work made it disappear: the perspective of *Seinsgeschichte* (the history of Being) deprives the realm of human affairs of any interest. As we shall see, the primary weight of this evaluation is echoed in Arendt's own Heidegger critique, which emphasizes Heidegger's unconcern with action in general.

The general import of Heidegger's "turning" is well known. Increasingly convinced that the technological goals of "planetary domination" and a total organization of the lacks inherent in human existence represented the culmination of the metaphysical project begun by the Greeks, Heidegger comes to see the "will to power" as the subterranean drive that animates the West from its inception. With modernity—that is, from Descartes to Nietzsche—this drive reveals itself in the subjectification of the world and the celebration of the "will to will" as the source of meaning after the death of God.[96] The "truth of Being"—the presencing process by which a particular historical world is "cleared" or "lighted"—is thrust farther into oblivion as our power to manipulate beings becomes limitless. In the technological age, our "fallenness" is extreme because the lacks that might call us back to our finitude are increasingly dominated and secured. Hence, the apocalyptic tone adopted by Heidegger in the notes entitled "Overcoming Metaphysics" (1936):

> The decline of the truth of beings occurs necessarily, and indeed as the completion of metaphysics.
>
> The decline occurs through the collapse of the world characterized by metaphysics, and at the same time through the desolation of the earth stemming from metaphysics.
>
> Collapse and desolation find their adequate occurrence in the fact that metaphysical man, the *animal rationale*, gets fixed as the laboring animal.
>
> This rigidification confirms the most extreme blindness to the oblivion of Being. But man wills *himself* as the volunteer of the will to will. . . .
>
> Before Being can occur in its primal truth, Being as the will must be broken, the world must be forced to collapse and the earth must be driven to desolation, and man to mere labor.[97]

While Heidegger will somewhat modify the apocalypticism of this passage, the direction of his later thought is clearly indicated. If, as this passage suggests, the reification of Being into a detemporalized, stable ground finds completion in an absorption of Being by the subject—in an anthropologism from which alterity, finitude, and historicality in the Heideggerian sense have been largely expunged—*then* a radical change of both mood and perspective is necessary to escape the coming technological world-night.[98] From Heidegger's post-*Kehre* perspective, the "will to will" represents the apogee of the "oblivion of Being," and the *Dasein*-oriented perspective of *Being and Time* (in which the meaning of Being is interpreted through the structures of human existence) appears intolerably anthropocentric. In *Being and Time*, Heidegger had written that "only as long as *Dasein* is (that is, only as long as an understanding of Being is ontically possible) 'is there' Being."[99] Heidegger's point after the *Kehre* is not that Being exists apart and above *Dasein*, as some sort of "cosmic ground" (although both Habermas and Arendt see *Seinsgeschichte* as implying precisely this); rather, he simply wants to avoid the impression that Being is, somehow, the "product" of man.[100] In a world characterized by the will to will, by the "struggle for dominion over the earth" and the unconditional objectification of all that is, the metaphors of "striving" and "violent co-creation" badly express the essential finitude of *Dasein*—its thrownness into the "destining" of a presencing process of which it is by no means the author.[101]

The *Kehre*, then, is Heidegger's attempt to complete the decentering of the subject begun in *Being and Time*. Responding to the "insurrection" of man in the form of an all-consuming subjectivity, Heidegger urges the cultivation of a sense of human inessentiality and "thankfulness for Being." The unconditional domination of subjectivity in the will to power has resulted in our essential *estrangement*, a "homelessness" that "is coming to be the destiny of the world."[102] "Homelessness," according to Heidegger in the "Letter on Humanism" (in *Basic Writings*), "consists in the abandonment of Being by beings"; it is "the symptom of oblivion of Being."[103] Such homelessness can be overcome only if man abandons the posture of "unconditional self-assertion" and "learns to exist in the nameless."[104] For Heidegger, "man is not the lord of beings. Man is the shepherd of Being,"[105] of the temporalized presencing process by which ontological preunderstandings are "sent" to man from nowhere. Thus, the later Heidegger's talk of the "destiny of Being" (*Seinsgeschick*), a figure of speech designed to underline the fact that "man does not decide whether and how beings *appear*, whether and how God and the gods or history and nature come forward into the lighting of Being, come to presence and depart."[106] That man does not control this "dispensation," anymore than he controls the history of modes of production (Marx) or the history of practices by which he is made a subject (Nietzsche), does not, in Heidegger's eyes, in any way lessen human dignity. For although "the advent of beings lies in the destiny of Being," it is through *Dasein* alone that the "lighting of Being" occurs, since only *Dasein* "has" language.[107]

Language, Heidegger famously declares in the "Letter on Humanism," is "at once the house of Being and the home of human beings."[108] It is through language that the "lighting" which is Being occurs, that beings first come to presence and *are*, that the *Da* of *Dasein* is cleared for the first time. The "homelessness of contemporary man" is a function of the dis-essencing of language, of the reduction of language to a means for communication employed by an all-dominating subjectivity. Such a reduction conceals "the word's primordial belongingness to Being": "Only because language is the home of the essence of man can historical mankind and human beings not be at home in their language, so that for them language becomes a mere container for sundry preoccupations."[109]

Here we return to a by now familiar Heideggerian theme, namely, the denaturing effects of communicative speech on the world-disclosive (poetic) essence of language. For Heidegger, the "word's primordial relationship to Being"—the fact that Being comes to presence in language—is obscured by the public realm. The reason for this (to draw an analogy with Wittgenstein) is that in this realm we play established, familiar language games, with evolving but fairly strict rules about what counts as an acceptable move or a meaningful utterance. The sum of a culture's language games constitutes a particular historical form of life—an understanding of Being or "clearing," as Heidegger would say—the contingency of which is obscured by its apparent self-evidence and our own absorption in playing these games.[110] So viewed, the public realm epitomizes "the widely and rapidly spreading devastation of language"; here, the "dominance of subjectivity" makes itself felt as "language surrenders itself to our mere willing and trafficking as an instrument of domination over beings."[111] Under the "peculiar dictatorship of the public realm," language is codified in a way "which decides in advance what is intelligible and what must be rejected as unintelligible."[112] Heidegger suggests, in a manner reminiscent of Nietzsche as well as Wittgenstein, that this sort of reification of language can be overcome only by a particular form of therapy, which dissolves the taken-for-granted and calcified and which opens us to the historicity and contingency of the vocabularies that make up *our* world.

The name Heidegger gives to this therapy is "thinking." Thinking brackets the willful attempts to regulate and secure and adopts a meditative, responsive attitude toward what is. This attitude—*Gelassenheit*, or "releasement"—achieves a poetic comportment toward Being by "letting beings be." Thinking "accomplishes" the relation of Being to man by giving up the metaphysical struggle for power inherent in the will to truth and *accepting* the contingency and partiality of the understanding of Being in which it finds itself. Withdrawing from "the peculiar dictatorship of the public realm," eschewing all willing and trafficking, thinking *listens* to language, and thereby allows language to slip back into its element (Being). Learning to "exist in the nameless," the thinker allows language to open out, to provide spaces of silence around those words and practices that seem literally unquestionable from our everyday standpoint—the standpoint of doing and acting.[113] Adopting an attitude of releasement, thinking allows language to resonate beyond the understanding of Being that gives our form of life both its coherence and its self-evidence. Thus, in its saying, thinking does not grasp, manipulate, or facilitate anything; thinking "merely brings the unspoken word of Being to language."[114]

On the face of it, this may seem an unusual way to lead the fly out of the fly bottle. Heidegger's response to the reification of language, and to the pathologies of modernity born of a consummated metaphysics, seems to be a retreat to the most traditional sort of philosophical contemplation. But this is hardly what Heidegger means by "thinking." As the "Letter on Humanism" emphasizes, the technical interpretation of action—action as causing an effect, as the achievement of an end—goes hand in hand with an interpretation of thinking as essentially calculative. Heidegger views *theoria*, as conceived by Plato and Aristotle, as the prototype of such calculative thinking: Plato and Aristotle "take thinking itself to be a *technē*, a process of reflection in the service to doing and working . . . here reflection is already seen from the perspective of *praxis* and *poiēsis*."[115] Moreover, the "characterization of thinking as *theoria* and the determination of knowing as 'theoretical' behavior occur already within the 'technical' interpretation of thinking. Such characterization is a reactive attempt to rescue thinking and preserve its autonomy over acting and doing."[116] But while Arendt chooses to rethink *praxis* against this constellation, Heidegger aims at the deeper, "more primordial" experience of genuine thinking. "Thinking," in his sense, is always the thinking of what metaphysics leaves unthought: Being, "the lighting," itself. The stakes of such thinking become clear when Heidegger asks, "In what relation does the thinking of Being stand to theoretical and practical behavior?" His answer deserves quoting in full:

> It exceeds all contemplation because it cares for the light in which a seeing, a *theoria*, can first live and move. Thinking attends to the lighting of Being in that it puts saying of Being into language as the home of existence. Thus thinking is a deed. But a deed that also surpasses all *praxis*. Thinking towers above action and production, not through the grandeur of its achievement and not as a consequence of its effect, but through the humbleness of its inconsequential accomplishment.[117]

It is at this point that even reasonably sympathetic readers, such as Richard Bernstein, balk. Heidegger's account, by emphasizing the mutual belonging together of *theoria* and *praxis* within the broader, metaphysical-technologizing interpretation of Being, evidently renders the distinctions between *praxis* and *poiēsis*, *phronēsis* and *technē*, superfluous.[118] Heidegger was intimately familiar with these distinctions, as the famous Marburg Seminar on Plato's *Sophist* (attended by Hans-Georg Gadamer and Arendt) makes clear.[119] Nevertheless, he chooses, in his later work, to "pass over these distinctions in silence." The reason for this, Bernstein argues, is that the later Heidegger's exclusive focus upon the question of Being and the ontological difference between beings and Being—the difference unthought, or not thought deeply enough, by metaphysics—results in a "relentless, inductable drive toward making manifest the concealed technical thrust implicit in the history of metaphysics."[120] If one views philosophy/metaphysics/humanism as culminating in the technological nihilism of enframing, and if one sees "the seeds of the technical sense of action and calculative thinking already implicit in Plato and Aristotle," then the conclusion that "all human activity . . . reduces itself—flattens out—into *Gestell*, manipulation, control, will to will, nihilism" will seem inescapable.[121] The *only* human activity that can possibly escape this all-encompassing technical horizon is the *thinking* Heidegger describes—a thinking that "accomplishes" the relation of Being to man by "unfolding" it, whose "inconsequential accomplishment" (the bringing of Being to language) mark it as the "simplest" yet "highest" form of *action*; indeed, as the only genuine action.[122]

Bernstein, then, suggests that the later Heidegger's primary contribution to the "oblivion of *praxis*" is the adoption of a perspective that renders reflection on the modern assimilation of *praxis* to a technical mentality redundant, since *praxis*, like *theoria*, was always already on the way toward *Gestell*. He argues that Heidegger further obscures things by identifying *thinking* with genuine action, by seeing the "thought of Being" as the only real deed.[123] Habermas goes Bernstein one better, suggesting that *Seinsgeschichte* constitutes an attack on the most basic categories of Western political thought, an attack in which the human faculties of reason, will, and freedom are denigrated as "subjectivist," as part and parcel of the "oblivion of Being."

According to Habermas, the *Kehre* signifies the switch from a radical voluntarism to an equally radical *fatalism*: Heidegger's later philosophy has "the illocutionary sense of demanding resignation to fate [in the form of *Seinsgeschick*]. Its practical-political side consists in the perlocationary effect of a diffuse readiness to obey in relation to an auratic but indeterminate authority [Being]."[124] Heidegger's later philosophy does not merely cover over the category of *praxis*, as Bernstein suggests; rather, the perspective of *Seinsgeschichte* (the history of Being) and *Seinsgeschick* (destiny of Being) is tantamount to a denial of the responsibility to act, and to act rationally and justly. By subjecting human will and reason to a radical critique, Heidegger contributes to a destruction of the conceptual resources within our tradition that make *praxis* conceivable in the first place, and that could potentially lead to a renewal of both practical philosophy and a democratic politics. This side of Habermas's critique is pushed very hard by Richard Wolin, who claims that the later Heidegger purveys a "philosophy of heteronomy," one that celebrates mysterious, fateful powers, while denigrating the human capacity for action; one that actually regresses behind the "inherited ethico-political foundations of the Western tradition."[125] Through his "uncritical celebration of a superordinate, nameless destiny," Heidegger supposedly negates "the central category of Western political thought"—freedom.[126]

As with the devaluation of intersubjectivity in *Being and Time*, what starts out as a plausible and helpful critique by Habermas and his followers rapidly degenerates into a fairly crude campaign to place Heidegger's thought outside the boundaries of the Western tradition. Whether willful (early) or nonwillful (later), Heidegger's thought is presented as ineluctably leading to a worship of authority and a celebration of obedience. The problem with this interpretation is that it so fully hinges upon the binary of voluntarism and fatalism, evils one supposedly slides into the moment reason's power to comprehensively adjudicate competing ends, or the subject's power to act autonomously, is questioned.[127] Thus, while the proponents of communicative rationality employ Arendt to expose a very real blind spot in Heidegger's thought, their desire to exclude him from any conversation about what postmetaphysical conceptions of action, freedom, and agency might look like produces a caricature. This, I suggest, is a function of two factors: first, a reifying, metaphysical interpretation of the ontological difference, which enables the view that Being is "an all-powerful metasubject"; second, a failure to penetrate the surface of Heidegger's thought in order to see how his critique of productionist metaphysics and the "technical interpretation of action" might be appropriated precisely to aide in the recovery of *praxis*. These themes will be explored further below, but first I wish to turn to the matter of Arendt's own Heidegger critique.

III. ARENDT'S HEIDEGGER CRITIQUE: THE UNWORLDLINESS OF THE PHILOSOPHER

Whatever problems Habermas's Arendt-inspired critique of Heidegger may present, its goal is clear. By focusing on Heidegger's disregard for intersubjectivity and his contempt for (merely) communicative speech, Habermas reveals a deeply antipolitical strain in Heidegger, which he hopes will compel a reconsideration of the totalizing tendencies of the Heideggerian critique of modernity and rationality. While Habermas may fall short of demonstrating that Heidegger's thought is, in Adorno's words, "fascist down to its most intimate components," he does succeed in presenting Heidegger as a dubious resource for the theoretical consideration of politics.

Arendt's critique of Heidegger, while elucidating some of the same themes, is very different. Her goal is not to reveal a profoundly *anti*political Heidegger; rather, she wishes to see Heidegger's contribution to the oblivion of *praxis* as the effect of the deeply *un*political nature of his thought.[128] Thus, while her earlier readings of Heidegger did not shy away from considering the political ramifications of his thought, the Heidegger critique she offers in *The Life of the Mind* is surprisingly unconcerned with such "direct" links. Ignoring, for the most part, the way Heidegger's devaluation of communicative speech determines his concept of the political, Arendt attempts something much more difficult. She constructs what is, in effect, a metacritique, which argues that, strictly speaking, there is no space for the political in Heidegger's thought, early or late. The oblivion of *praxis* follows from Heidegger's reification of *thought* as the only geniune action.

The unpolitical nature of Heidegger's thought is a function of its *unworldly* character, a feature of all genuine thinking, as Arendt defines it.[129] Thinking— which is distinct not only from the activities that constitute the *vita activa*, but from contemplation, cognition, and judgment as well—is an activity predicated upon withdrawal from the world.[130] It is a solitary and restless activity that can begin, according to Arendt, only when the commonsense world of appearances is left behind. Questing after meaning, thinking disdains particulars; by nature, it "clings to the absent," that which is obscured by particulars. It is only by drawing what is most distant into the nearness of its "sequestered stillness" that thinking truly engages its matter.[131] Considered as an activity, thinking, to use Heidegger's phrase, is "out of order": it produces no results and "does not endow us directly with the power to act."[132] Its essential unworldliness makes thinking notoriously ill-suited for the consideration of the realm of human affairs; its attempts to overcome its remoteness from this realm lead to comic misapprehensions (Arendt cites Aristotle's warning to his fellow philosophers not to yield to the Platonic temptation to consider this realm *sub specie aeternatatis*—under the aspect of eternity).[133]

What impulse motivates this reading, which goes out of its way to deny the relevance of Heidegger's thought to political theory and which ignores all those "worldly" aspects that would taint the picture Arendt wants to present? The stakes come into view in Arendt's tribute to Heidegger, "Martin Heidegger at Eighty." In addition to providing a compelling portrait of Heidegger's "passionate thinking," Arendt presents his brief but notorious entry into the realm of human affairs as a tragic episode resulting from the thinker's abandonment of his genuine (unworldly) abode. Leaving his "place of stillness," Heidegger plunges or falls into the world, becoming victim to the blindness and disorientation that accompany the philosopher's return to the cave.[134] Egregious errors of political judgment result. Arendt's controversial point is that these errors, inexcusable in themselves, are less the result of some kind of affinity between Heidegger's thought and National Socialism than a function of the purity of Heidegger's philosophical temperament (the "attraction to the tyrannical," she notes, is a kind of *deformation professionelle* among philosophers, one that "can be demonstrated theoretically in many of the great thinkers").[135] According to Arendt's extremely charitable reading, the "shock of the collision" of 1933 was enough to drive the thinker "back to his residence," where he would "settle in his thinking what he had experienced."[136] What emerged from all this was Heidegger's "discovery of the will as the 'will to will' and hence as the 'will to power.'"[137]

This discovery, made in the course of Heidegger's "confrontation" with Nietzsche between 1936 and 1940, led Heidegger to repudiate the will and, according to Arendt, the realm of human affairs. As an expression of the will to will, this realm is seen by the later Heidegger as a function of the self-withdrawal or self-concealment of Being.[138] It was Heidegger's desire to annul this withdrawal, and to draw closer to Being, that led to the "reversal" and the post-*Kehre* attitude of *Gelassenheit* (what Arendt calls his "will-not-to-will"). The change in mood after the *Kehre* is conveyed by Heidegger's identification of thinking as the only genuine (nonwillful) form of action. For Arendt, as for Bernstein, the subsumption of acting by thinking goes hand in hand with Heidegger's characterization of politics and human history as the realm of "erring," as functions of a predestined and unalterable oblivion of Being.

This picture provides the background of Arendt's extended Heidegger critique in *LM*. There, she takes Heidegger's own reinterpretation of the *Kehre* seriously, pointing to a fundamental continuity in his thought, which is revealed only in light of the opposition between willing and thinking. According to Arendt, Heidegger radicalizes this opposition, and it is this radicalization that allows us to see that what unites the two phases of his thought (all superficial differences aside) is an emphasis upon the "inner action" of thinking as the sole route to either the recovery of Self (*Being and Time*) or the retrieval of Being.[139] Minimizing the willfulness and worldliness of the early work as mere signs of the time, Arendt focuses upon the meditative kernel that she sees as linking the "call of conscience" to the "Thought of Being." By drawing out the mediative unity at the root of Heidegger's thought, Arendt finds support for her earlier characterization of Heidegger's "error" as a misstep analogous to Thales tumbling into the well.[140] This tack enables her to salvage Heidegger's philosophical reputation from the questions raised by his political involvements, while attacking his contributions to the oblivion of *praxis* (a contribution born of his denunciation of will and the realm of human affairs, on the one hand, and his deification of thought and Being, on the other).

While Arendt always drew attention to a certain "worldlessness" in Heidegger, she did not always shy away from a more directly political reading of his work. Before turning to her mature Heidegger critique, it is perhaps appropriate to trace the development of her later metacritical perspective out of earlier, more political, readings.

In her first published consideration of Heidegger in "What Is *Existenz* Philosophy?" (1946), Arendt unfavorably compares the early Heidegger to Karl Jaspers. Prefiguring much of Habermas's critique, she focuses upon the subjectivist tendencies of Heidegger's *Being and Time*. Her argument is that Heidegger's characterization of *existenz* as Being-in-the-world did not prevent him from promoting an ideal of the self that measured authenticity in terms of a *withdrawal* from social relations. "The most essential characteristic of this [Heideggerian] self," she writes, "is its absolute egoism, its radical separation from all of its fellows."[141] Heidegger's "Self," according to Arendt, absorbs the figure of "Man," which had previously usurped the place of God. Radically isolated through its anticipation of death, this Self absorbs and ultimately negates the humanity of Man via its fixation on the experience of "guilty nothingness."[142] "Heidegger's Self," Arendt suggests, "is an ideal which has been working mischief in German philosophy and literature since Romanticism."[143] Such romantic subjectivism stands in sharp contrast to Jasper's *Existenz-philosophie*, with its emphasis on "the togetherness of men in the common given world" and its concept of communication that contains, an embryo, "a new concept of humanity."[144]

Aside from its remarkable hostility, the notable feature of this early assessment of Heidegger is its direct confrontation with the political implications of Heidegger's "romantic subjectivism." Arendt's reading emphasizes how an ostensibly "this-worldly philosophy" winds up depriving the world of any significance other than providing the (fallen) context in which the Self strives for authenticity. From this perspective, the early Heidegger emerges as the twentieth-century culmination of the subjectification of the world initiated by Descartes and as an inheritor of the politics of authenticity promoted by Rousseau. His existentialism is a clear expression of the worldlessness of modernity. Insofar as the Heideggerian self is an extension of the romantic/Rousseauian ideal, it is destructive of the notions of a public world and self that Arendt later identifies as the sine qua non of a world-preserving politics.[145]

Arendt's next public consideration of Heidegger came in 1954, in the form of an only recently published address to the American Political Science Association (APSA).[146] Her stance here is critical, yet she is quite optimistic about Heidegger's potential contribution to political theory. Heidegger's approach, she suggests, while not being specifically geared to political phenomena, opens up an exit from the alien metaphorics Western philosophy has imposed upon them.

Arendt focuses her remarks upon the concept of "historicity" (*Geschichlichkeit*). Seen from the perspective of politics, this concept is double-edged. On the one hand, it serves as the basis for the development of Heidegger's "history of Being," a history that reveals the logic at work behind human history, much in the manner of Hegel's presupposition of the unfolding of *Geist* (spirit). To the extent that Heidegger's notion of historicity falls into the Hegelian pattern, it denies both the freedom and meaning of action; it is, as a result, antipolitical. However, on the other hand, the notion of historicity underlines the irreducibly partial nature of every presencing or understanding of Being. It therefore leads Heidegger to reject the Hegelian/Platonic presumption that *theoria* occupies a standpoint from which the whole can be grasped, a standpoint that provides the theorist with insight denied to the historical actors themselves. The concept of historicity points, *contra* Hegel, to an inescapable finitude of understanding and a notion of truth that is historical "all the way down." For this reason Heidegger can claim—quite rightly in Arendt's view—to have left "the arrogance of all Absolute behind us."[147]

From Arendt's perspective, the implications of Heidegger's concept of historicity are nothing less than revolutionary. With this notion "the philosopher left behind him the claim to being 'wise' and knowing eternal standards for the perishable affairs of the City of man," a claim that had force so long as the philosopher was understood to "dwell in the proximity of the Absolute."[148] With the advent of the concept of historicity, it becomes impossible to conjure away the contingency and haphazardness of politics by the appeal to *theoria* or History: the realm of human affairs no longer appears as an object for philosophical comprehension and domination. More to the point, and most exciting for Arendt, is the way that Heidegger's "rejection of the claim to wisdom" opens the way to a "reexamination of the whole realm of politics in light of elementary human experiences within this realm itself, and demands implicitly concepts and judgments which have their roots in altogether different kinds of human experience."[149]

This is as close as Arendt ever comes to acknowledging Heidegger's work's decisive importance for illuminating the distortion that results from philosophical conceptualization in the realm of human affairs. As argued above, Heidegger's critique of productionist metaphysics reveals the predominance of the metaphorics of fabrication within the Western tradition. This insight provides the cornerstone for the entire analysis given by Arendt in *The Human Condition*, an analysis devoted to showing how long we have been thinking of acting in terms of making and the resulting deformation of our understanding of the political.[150] The hint contained in Arendt's APSA address is made even more tantalizing by her judgment that Heidegger failed to exploit the opening created by his concept of historicity. This failure indicated that a questioning of the West's productionist ontological prejudices was, in itself, insufficient for "the reexamination of the whole realm of politics in the light of . . . experiences within this realm itself." What was needed was a theorist who would put action itself at the center. This Heidegger manifestly failed to do; for although he abandoned the philosopher's claim to wisdom, he was unable to divest himself entirely of philosophy's contemplative prejudices. These prejudices assert themselves in the concept of historicity that, despite its obvious closeness to the political realm, "never reaches its center—man as acting being."[151]

Because it is geared toward the "coincidence of thought and event" rather than the nexus of action and judgment, the concept of historicity can "throw new light on history rather than politics, on happenings rather than action."[152] Heidegger's ability to elucidate such world-historical trends as the "technicalization of the world, the emergence of One World on a planetary scale, the increasing pressure of society upon the individual and the concomitant atomization of society" is a function of thought tuned to historicity rather than action.[153] Ironically, it is this very historical insight, born of the abandonment of Platonic pretensions, that leads to a forgetfulness concerning what Arendt calls "the more permanent questions of political science"; namely, "What is politics? Who is man as a political being? What is freedom?"[154]

Arendt develops the critical themes of the APSA lecture and her "*Existenz* Philosophy" essay in the Heidegger critique *The Life of the Mind*; however, she situates them in an entirely new context. The goal is no longer to explore Heidegger's possible contribution to political theory, but to trace the disjunction between thinking and acting, ontology and politics, to the core of his thought.

She begins by considering the *Kehre* independently of Heidegger's subsequent reinterpretation. Bracketing, for the moment, the claim of continuity, Arendt presents the "reversal" in terms of the thematization of the opposition between willing and thinking, a thematization that culminates in Heidegger's contention (contra Nietzsche) that the will is essentially destructive, not creative.[155] Heidegger's "reversal," according to Arendt, pits itself against this destructiveness, which is manifest in technology's desire to "subject the whole world to its domination and rulership."[156] Heidegger's alternative to such rulership (characteristic of the will to will) is, of course, "letting-be" or releasement, a mode of ontological comportment opposed to the "mood of purposiveness" dominant in willing. Thus, the Nietzsche lectures produce the insight that "thinking and willing are not just two different faculties," but in fact are "opposite," engaged in "deadly conflict." The reversal signifies Heidegger's repudiation of willing in favor of the kind of comportment toward entities enabled by thinking. However—and for Arendt this is decisive—Heidegger makes it clear that it is the History of Being— and not the mind of man—that "determines whether men respond to Being in terms of willing or in terms of thinking."[157]

With the theme of *Seinsgeschichte*, of a separate and determining history of Being, we approach what is for Arendt the most radical of Heidegger's claims: that Being itself, "*forever changing*, manifests itself in the thinking of the actor so that *acting and thinking* coincide."[158] The idea of such a "merging" is enough to distinguish Heidegger from philosophies of history such as Hegel's, in which human actors are the unconscious vehicles of Spirit. Moreover, it highlights the most "startling consequences" of the reversal, consequences that flow directly from Heidegger's repudiation of the will and that are obscured by the later claim of an inner continuity. For Arendt, these consequences are "first, the notion that solitary thinking in itself constitutes the only relevant action in the factual record of history, and second, that thinking is the same as thanking."[159]

These consequences certainly lend support to Arendt's thesis that Heidegger is an essentially unworldly philosopher, one who denies a priori any relation between the disclosure of Being and politics. But they also stand in stark contrast to the positions staked out in Heidegger's Being and Time and his writings up to Nietzsche, in which authentic disclosedness appeared as something worldly, active, willful, and poetic. This very real difference would seem to throw the later Heidegger's claim of a profound inner unity in doubt, and it certainly places Arendt's claim—that the experience of thinking is determinative for the whole of Heidegger's philosophy—in question.

For her part, Arendt is aware of the discrepancy between the later Heidegger's view of thinking as the only genuine form of action and his earlier conception of authentic disclosedness. She makes no attempt to deny the similarity between Being and Time's futurally oriented care structure and the will (man's "organ for the future").[160] Nor does she deny Heidegger's tendency to define the authentic individual in terms of a spontaneous and resolved willing, which liberates this self from the social and linguistic bonds of the "they-self." In this regard, Arendt notes the affinity between the early Heidegger's view of a spontaneously disclosive self and Nietzsche's emphasis upon the priority of "artistic willing" over thought. Heidegger appears to confirm this link when he writes in the first volume of Nietzsche, "To will means: to bring oneself to one's self. . . . Willing, we encounter ourselves as who we are authentically."[161]

Yet despite these affinities, Arendt maintains that Heidegger never really intended the notion of authenticity or authentic disclosedness to be read in terms of an artistic or poetic creativity, much less in a political mode. (She dismisses the former possibility by noting that "nowhere in Being and Time . . . is artistic creativity mentioned.")[162] What distinguishes the authentic individual from his fallen peers is neither spontaneity nor creativity, according to Arendt, but that individual's response to the call of conscience, which "calls man back from his everyday entanglement in the 'they'."[163] Emphasizing conscience's role in revealing Dasein's guilt to itself, Arendt frames an opposition between an authentic Dasein withdrawn into thought and the worldliness (and alienation) of public existence. Conscience calls the self to an acceptance of its indebtedness or thrownness, to "a kind of 'acting' (handeln) which is polemically understood as the opposite of the 'loud' and visible actions of public life—the mere froth of what truly is."[164] Authentic Dasein hardly seizes upon possibilities latent in its everyday existence. In Arendt's interpretation, the "taking up" that Heidegger speaks of is, in fact, a meditative reconciliation with what is. The movement of reconciliation born of the call of conscience is achieved through an "entirely inner 'action' in which man opens himself to the authentic actuality of being thrown." Such action "can exist only in the activity of thinking."[165]

It is through thinking that Dasein effects reconciliation with its essential finitude. Authenticity, then, is not really a mode of Being-in-the-world at all, for "what the call of conscience actually achieves is the recovery of the individual-ized self from involvement in the events that determine man's everyday activities as well as the course of recorded history—*l'écume des choses* (the foam of things)."[166] The authentic self, in other words, is not essentially with others, but apart from them; it does not strive for a more authentic form of community life, it gives thanks for individual existence in all its contingency. Turned away from everything public and everyday, the authentic Heideggerian self, according to Arendt, is turned toward "a thinking that expresses gratitude that the 'naked That' has been given at all."[167]

Arendt's reading of *Being and Time* makes it a relatively small step from the "inner activity" of such a self to the later Heidegger's conception of the thinker who listens attentively for the call of Being. Noting how Heideggerian *Seinsge-schichte* differs from German Idealism while extending its basic speculative thrust, Arendt observes that, in Heidegger, "there is a Somebody who *acts out* the hidden meaning of Being and thus provides the disastrous course of events [of human history] with a counter-current of wholesomeness."[168] This Somebody (the thinker who "has weaned himself from willing to 'letting be'") is, according to Arendt, "actually the 'authentic Self' of *Being and Time*, who now listens to the call of Being instead of the call of conscience."[169]

Thus, from Arendt's perspective, the later Heidegger is distinguished not by a renunciation of worldly activity (this, in her account, is nothing new), nor by a rethinking of the "poetic" nature of disclosure (which was not really artistic in inspiration anyway). What marks Heidegger after the *Kehre* is a new self-con-sciousness concerning the meditative core of authentic disclosedness (the disclo-sure of Being). For the later Heidegger, the "inner activity" of the thinker is not willed: unlike the authentic self of *Being and Time*, the thinker does not initiate, he *responds*. He is not "summoned by himself to his Self," but is rather summoned by Being *to* Being.[170] Hence, Heidegger's famous characterization of thinking as *thanking*, as an expression of gratefulness to Being that could not exist without the "generosity" of Being. So viewed, the activity of thinking is radically desubjecti-fied; as Arendt puts it, "the Self no longer acts in itself but, obedient to Being, enacts by sheer thinking the counter-current of Being underlying the 'foam' of beings—the mere appearances whose current is steered by the will to power."[171] Necessarily withdrawn from the public world and everydayness, thinking, it turns out, must also be withdrawn from the Self if it is to engage the absent, if it is to bring the silent word of Being to language. It is only by severing its ties to both the world *and* the Self that thinking responds to the call of Being.[172]

By focusing upon the meditative thread that she sees running through all of Heidegger's work, Arendt is able to present a novel, even surprising, picture of his philosophy. Her claim, roughly, is that Heidegger's ontological concern, obscured by the existential motifs of *Being and Time*, realizes itself after the *Kehre* in thought's communion with Being, in a thinking that stands in radical opposition to the entire realm of beings/appearances.[173] Heidegger, who claimed to be more genuinely anti-Platonist than Nietzsche, turns out to be more Platonist than

Plato, insofar as the ontological difference between Being and beings is not seen as something to be overcome (by recourse to the Idea of the Good, God, mind, dialectic, etc.), but rather as the sine qua non of thought. The "philosophical" withdrawal of the later Heidegger is pure and complete: the *Kehre* does not lead the thinker back into the cave as does the Platonic turning, or *periogoge*. Quite the contrary; it is the *total* character of Heidegger's withdrawal from the world of appearances, his "taking up residence" in an abode where even the most renowned of philosophers only sojourned, that makes him, even more than Plato (though perhaps less than Socrates), the "philosopher's philosopher." It is this total withdrawal that also makes his "error" both more grotesque and more tragic than Plato's misguided attempt to transform a run of the mill tyrant into a philosopher-king.[174] And, Arendt would add, it also makes Heidegger's actions more demanding, and perhaps more worthy, of forgiveness.

Arendt was no doubt aware of the objections that her interpretation of Heidegger's philosophy (which locates its gravitational center in the experience of thinking) would elicit. By presenting the *Kehre* as the radicalization of thinking's essential unworldliness, she opens herself to the charge that she effaces the very dimensions of the early Heidegger's thought that were conducive to (if not a sufficient cause of) the commitment of 1933. We can read the conclusion of her Heidegger critique as the attempt to forestall objections from those who take issue with her portrait of a deeply unpolitical philosophy, a philosophy whose fidelity to the activity of thinking made it all the more opposed (or oblivious) to the realm of action.

Arendt devotes the last pages of her critique to a consideration of an "interruption" in Heidegger's life and thought even more radical than the "reversal"—namely, the "point zero" (Jünger) of Germany's defeat.[175] With this interruption, according to Arendt, there came a brief but dramatic change of mood in Heidegger's thought, a change of outlook captured in the rather obscure ontological speculations of "*Der Spruch des Anaximander*" ("The Anaximander Fragment," 1946). The mood here, distinct from earlier willfulness and *Gelassenheit* (releasement) is one of despair tempered by the anticipation of an epochal transformation, a "transitional moment" in the history of Being that follows "the most monstrous transformation our planet has ever undergone."[176] According to Arendt, this change in mood produced "an altogether new and unexpected outlook on the whole posing of the problem of Being," a radical change in perspective on the *Seinsfrage* (question of Being) that affords a telling glimpse into the core of Heidegger's ontological vision.[177]

The object of Heidegger's commentary in "The Anaximander Fragment" is the following text: "But that from which things arise also gives rise to their passing away, according to what is necessary; for things render justice and pay penalty to one another for their injustice, according to the ordinance of time."[178]

This fragment, as Arendt notes, concerns "the coming-to-be and passing-away of everything that is."[179] Heidegger extrapolates from Anaximander in order to identify the being of entities with a "lingering awhile is presence" between a "twofold absence." All that is emerges from an original concealment to "linger awhile" in the world of appearances, ultimately departing and withdrawing once again into concealment.[180]

From Arendt's perspective, the Heideggerian gloss on Anaximander is noteworthy for its stark departure from his usual teaching on *aletheia* (the disclosure of Being) and the ontological difference. Normally, Heidegger places disclosure or unconcealment "on the side of Being," identifying, for example, the attentive response of the thinker with the revelation of Being in the world of appearances.[181] However, as Arendt observes, in "The Anaximander Fragment," "unconcealment is not truth; it belongs to the beings that arrive and depart into a hidden Being."[182] The relation of disclosure previously implied by the ontological difference between Being and beings has been reversed. Once the presencing of beings is seen as belonging to beings, it follows that "the unconcealment of beings, the brightness granted them, obscures the light of Being."[183] Hence, Heidegger's central thesis: "as it reveals itself in beings, Being withdraws."[184]

This new view of disclosure, in which truth by nature remains concealed, covered over by the unconcealment of beings, leads Heidegger (according to Arendt) to reconfigure the relationship between Being and Becoming. Whereas before and after "The Anaximander Fragment" the realm of Becoming appears as an arena for the disclosure of Being through the poetic/thinking activity of man, in the essay it is viewed as "the opposite of Being."[185] Becoming—the process of emergence into the light of presence—is the "law that rules beings"; but this law also dictates that things will pass away, that the entire realm of Becoming "changes again into that Being from whose sheltering, concealing darkness it had originally emerged."[186] Instead of a disclosure in which Being is illuminated through the presencing of beings, we now find, according to Arendt, an opposition between Being "in the strong durative sense" and a Becoming that conceals but does not disclose Being.

In the Anaximander essay, Arendt maintains, Heidegger has inscribed Becoming in an eternally recurring economy of presence and absence. The unconcealment of beings now depends upon the self-concealment or withdrawal of Being. This is not only a reversal with respect to disclosure, but it is also a new way of posing the *Seinsfrage*. For with the position Heidegger takes in the Anaximander essay, it is "no longer genuine inauthenticity or any particularity of human existence that causes man to 'forget' Being . . . nor does he do it because he is distracted by the sheer superabundance of mere entities."[187] Rather, Heidegger's new position is that "oblivion of Being belongs to the self-veiling essence of Being . . . the history of Being begins with the oblivion of Being, since Being . . . keeps to itself."[188]

One crucial result of this reversal, according to Arendt, is that there is no longer a link between the history of Being and human history actualized through some form of human activity (for example, "thinking" as the only real action). Being's initial withdrawal sets in motion a double movement that radicalizes the "categorical separation of Being and beings" by placing the two in an alternating, mutually exclusive temporal sequence. Thus, Arendt can say that the ontological difference acquires "a kind of history with a beginning and an end": Being discloses itself in beings, simultaneously withdrawing into itself as beings are "set adrift" to constitute what Heidegger calls "the realm of error"; that is, the sphere of common human history.[189] The only time the "*Da*" draws closer to Being is when it ceases to exist.

The difference between the history of Being outlined in "The Anaximander Fragment" (in which Being "keeps to itself") and *Seinsgeschichte* proper is that the former does not allow a "secret" ontological history to be enacted "behind the backs of acting men" by philosophers who say the word of Being.[190] The thinker, no less than any other man, is cast adrift in the realm of erring. So long as Being remains "sheltered in its concealment," it has, strictly speaking, no history, and thinking cannot lay claim to responding to and actualizing Being in the midst of human history.[191] At most, the thinker can hope to respond to those "transitional moments" between epochs of erring. At such moments, "Being *qua* Truth breaks into the continuum of error," not to disclose itself, but to withdraw itself once again.[192] It is the trace of this withdrawal manifest in such moments that the thinker must content himself with.

Arendt's reading of the Anaximander essay reveals a step beyond the radicalization of the opposition between thinking and willing found in the *Kehre*. If the change of mood manifest in Heidegger's "reversal" signaled his desire to strip thinking of its willful and self-centered elements, the Anaximander essay contains a recognition of the irreducible willfulness of life or existence itself. No "purified" thinking can annul Being's withdrawal through its disclosive action, for all action—even thinking—is erring. Insofar as thinking desires to overcome this withdrawal and make Being manifest in the realm of beings, it remains tied to the will to persist, to self-preservation. From this perspective, *Gelassenheit* affords no escape from errancy, since all comportment toward beings—all "lingering awhile in presence"—is tainted by the "craving to persist." The ontological difference—which, at other moments, Heidegger felt could be bridged by the disclosive action of the thinker—is here an unbridgeable abyss. Trapped by virtue of his sheer existence in the realm of erring; knowing full well that "to act is to err, to go astray," the thinker ceases to view his activity as "the only genuine form of action" and sees it, rather, as an activity that allows him to join with, however fleetingly, that which lies beyond life—the absent in its enduring withdrawal.[193]

"The Anaximander Fragment," then, expresses a mood of truly radical unworldliness, a mood that is extreme even by the standards of the Western tradition. Heidegger expresses no gratitude for existence here: thinking is not a thanking. But neither does Heidegger give vent to the resentment against the human condition that both he and Arendt see at the root of the Western tradition and modernity's self-assertion. If anything, the tone is closest to the wisdom of Silenus, to the deeply tragic view of existence that Arendt and Nietzsche also (provisionally) accept. The difference, of course, is that for Nietzsche art, and for Arendt political action, could redeem human existence. For Heidegger in the Anaximander essay, no such redemptive powers exist: there is only "erring," estrangement, homelessness.

What, then, does the Anaximander essay reveal about Heidegger's thought?

From Arendt's point of view, the essay dramatically confirms the trajectory away from all willing and acting manifest throughout the Heideggerian corpus. Embodying the unworldly (one might almost say contemplative) impulse behind all genuine philosophy in a pure, even exaggerated, form, the Anaximander essay reveals a philosopher every bit as much in love with death as Plato in the *Phaedo*.[194] And with this insight a new level of depth and irony is added to Arendt's claim that Heidegger is the "philosopher's philosopher."

While the philosophical urge to overcome the will to life, to have done with this world in order to draw closer to Being, is something that, in Arendt's view, unites Heidegger and Plato, an important difference remains. It is marked by the lines Arendt cites from Goethe at the conclusion of her Heidegger critique:

> The Eternal works and stirs in all
> For all must into Nothing fall,
> If it is to persist in Being.[195]

For Plato, the contemplative metaphysician par excellence, the Eternal (Being) was constant presence as "embodied" in the forms. Two thousand years later, after all the "monstrous transformations" enabled by Plato's interpretation of Being have been played out, the philosopher (Heidegger) remains steadfast in his unworldly commitment to the Eternal. However, at the end of metaphysics "the Eternal" can signify only one thing: an enduring Nothing.

Heidegger, *Poiēsis*, and Politics

To be a work means to set up a world. . . . The work as work,
in its presencing, is a setting forth, a making.

—Heidegger, *"The Origin of the Work of Art"*

Enframing conceals that revealing which, in the sense of *poiēsis*, lets what
presences come forth into appearance. . . . Enframing . . . blocks *poiēsis*.

—Heidegger, *"The Question Concerning Technology"*

Since all acting contains an element of virtuosity, and because virtuosity is
the excellence we ascribe to the performing arts, politics has often been
defined as an art. This, of course, is not a definition but a metaphor, and
the metaphor becomes completely false if one falls into the common error
of regarding the state or government as a work of art, as a kind of collective
masterpiece. In the sense of the creative arts, which bring forth something tangible and reify human thought to such an extent that the
produced thing possesses an existence of its own, politics is
the exact opposite of an art.

—Arendt, *"What Is Freedom?"*

I. The Ambiguity of Heidegger's Contribution to the Oblivion of *Praxis*

The criticisms leveled at Heidegger by Arendt and Habermas confront us
squarely with the issue of Heidegger's contribution to the oblivion of *praxis* in the
post-Nietzschean, technological age. Generally speaking, the critiques are persuasive, revealing fundamental reasons for the underdevelopment of the concept
of action in Heidegger. Thus, even those who would argue that the concept of
praxis plays a key role in the articulation of fundamental ontology endorse the
Habermasian conclusion that Heidegger's dismissal of communicative action
leads to a radically foreshortened understanding of "authentic" action, one that
neglects entirely the doxastic and plural dimensions Arendt highlights.[1] That
this neglect colors Heidegger's (largely implicit) concept of the political is, as the
above analysis shows, also beyond doubt. Attacking the problem from a somewhat different angle, Arendt demonstrates how the Heideggerian "avoidance" of
action flows from his preoccupation with the experience of thinking, an activity
that is, in crucial respects, the "opposite" of action. Withdrawn from the world,

obsessed with the *Seinsfrage*, Heidegger is clearly an "apolitical" thinker in the broad sense suggested by Dominique Janicaud.[2]

Yet while they illuminate the same broad tendency in Heidegger, Arendt's and Habermas's critiques sit uneasily with one another. This tension is the result of the radically opposed ways they view the relationship between Heidegger's philosophy and his politics. For Habermas, there is an integral relationship: the denigration of communicative action, the reification of great or world-disclosing speech, the swing from decisionism to fatalism—all point to a latent authoritarianism. In contrast, Arendt sees Heidegger's decision to support the regime in 1933 as having little if any direct relation to the content of his philosophy. For Arendt, Heidegger's politics can be said to follow from his philosophy only in the sense that his single-minded pursuit of the "meaning of Being" left him ill-equipped when it came to making judgments in the realm of human affairs (here, her "defense" of Heidegger comes in conflict with her effort to portray thinking as a moral force, one of the few real bars against complicity with the radical evil produced by the twentieth century).[3] From Arendt's perspective, the devaluation of action and the failure to appreciate either plurality or the everyday are less distinguishing characteristics of Heidegger's thought than they are generic attributes of philosophy—as is, of course, the attraction to the tyrannical.[4]

One could leave the consideration of Arendt's and Habermas's critiques at this, were it not for the fact that they both desire to do more than catalog "the theoretical flaws in Heidegger's understanding of interaction and intersubjectivity."[5] Their responses to the question of the place of action and the political in Heidegger are overdetermined by 1933; by the question, which will not go away, of the relation between the philosophy and the politics. It is scarcely exaggeration to state that the desire to forgive and the need to condemn stand behind Arendt's and Habermas's respective readings. Thus, Arendt attempts to preserve Heidegger's rightful place in the history of thought by isolating his philosophy from his politics, while Habermas questions the critique of metaphysics and Western *ratio* by (in effect) reading the politics back into the philosophy. The logical result is a tendency to absolutize the characterization of Heidegger as essentially unpolitical or antipolitical. The interpretive consequences are predictably distorting; moreover, they block access to whatever resources Heidegger may hold for the "recovery" of *praxis*.

The essentializing interpretations offered by Arendt and Habermas are strategic. By elevating Heidegger to a realm beyond that of human affairs (Kant's "land of thought"), Arendt can contain the effects of a political reading of his philosophy. Likewise, by demonstrating that the philosophy and the politics work together to form one antipolitical, authoritarian whole, Habermas hopes to inoculate contemporary theory against a Heideggerian skepticism toward communicative rationality as the escape hatch from the universalization of technical reason. Both critiques strive to provide us with a clearly decidable text, one purged of all ambiguity and reduced to its fundamental kernel. The construction of such a text is accomplished largely through the application of certain key oppositions; for instance, between thinking and acting, philosophy and politics, world-disclosive and communicative speech. These oppositions do the work of effacing precisely those aspects of Heidegger that are most suggestive for the rethinking of action. The irony, in the case of Arendt, is clear, for her political theory demonstrates how important Heidegger is for thinking of action as freed from the domination of teleology, first principles, and the autonomous subject—*despite* its clear inattention to the "interactive" dimension of politics.[6]

In their quest to drain Heidegger's contribution to the "oblivion of *praxis*" of ambiguity, Arendt and Habermas relegate the notions of disclosedness, being-in-the-world, being-together (*mitsein*), and freedom to the extreme margins of his thought. Nowhere is this interpretive violence more in evidence than in the reifying interpretations of the ontological difference upon which they build their critiques. It is no coincidence that Arendt and Habermas "metaphysicalize" this difference, reading it back into a traditional philosophical framework, one structured by the distinctions between Being and appearance, essence and existence, universal and particular.[7] By reading the ontological difference in this way, Arendt is able to effectively short-circuit any relation between the "thought of Being" and the realm of human affairs. An ontological abyss is seen to separate the "object" of Heidegger's thought (Being) from the (merely obscuring) realm of beings. Likewise, Habermas does his best to segregate the ontological difference into its polar components, the better to argue for the radically nonrelational nature of authentic *Dasein*, on the one hand, and the mystifying presentation of Being as the impenetrable ground of history, on the other. As Habermas characteristically states in *The Philosophical Discourse of Modernity*, "only Being, as distinguished from beings by way of hypostatization, can take over the role of Dionysus."[8] Not insignificantly, the characterization of Heidegger as radically unpolitical or antipolitical turns on the suppression of his deconstruction of the ontotheological tradition and the questionable postulation of a "Heideggerian metaphysics."[9]

The distortions present in Arendt's and Habermas's readings suggest that Heidegger's attitude toward *praxis*, and the relation between his philosophy and his politics, are more complex than the "unpolitical" or "antipolitical" characterizations allow. As Lacoue-Labarthe observes, with more or less direct reference to Arendt, "the engagement of 1933 is neither an accident or an error."[10] Nor is it, as Habermas suggests, a foregone conclusion. There is a clear relation between Heidegger's sublimation of *praxis* and his predisposition to grotesquely misread National Socialism as the advent of a more authentic revealing—as the enactment of the global encounter between technology and modern man.[11] However, while it is tempting to view the fate of *praxis* in Heidegger's thought as either total avoidance or total effacement (the better to explain his commitment as "error," or as consistent with his antipolitical, authoritarian stance), we must resist the simplicity of such a solution. Heidegger's effect on *praxis*—on the thinking of action—is, like his legacy for political thought, ambiguous. It is precisely this ambiguity that Arendt and Habermas, for their very different reasons, wish to dispel. However, once we see how Heidegger's thought constantly moves against the background of the *praxis/poiēsis* distinction—reappropriating it in *Being and*

Time, attempting to overcome it in the middle work, returning to it once again in his critique of technology—we see the need of speaking, with Taminiaux, of a simultaneous "radicalization and obliteration" of *praxis* in Heidegger.[12] It is because Heidegger radicalizes as well as obliterates *praxis* that his thought remains essential to its recovery and to the rethinking of the political.

The complexity of this issue—of Heidegger's simultaneous contributions to the oblivion and the recovery of *praxis*—is underlined if we return to Bernstein's critique. Bernstein emphasizes how the later Heidegger's view of all action as essentially technical effaces the very distinctions needed to articulate the deformation of *praxis* in the late modern age. The reductive and "dangerous" nature of Heidegger's genealogy of the technical understanding of action, according to Bernstein, is manifest in his view that "the seeds of the technical sense of action and calculative thinking are already implicit in Plato and Aristotle."[13] Intent on uncovering the "concealed technical thrust" implicit in the history of metaphysics, Heidegger renders the distinctions between *praxis* and *poiēsis, technē* and *phronēsis,* superfluous. He thereby blocks access to the very tradition of political philosophy that might help save us. Prevented by Heidegger's "leveling gaze" from distinguishing between a practical and a technical horizon, we are all the more susceptible to Heidegger's siren song that "no mere action will change the world."[14] Bernstein starkly juxtaposes this view to "Gadamer, Arendt, Habermas and the pragmatists," all of whom concern themselves with the "practical questions Heidegger does not directly confront."[15]

Bernstein's critique reduplicates the dichotomy advanced by Habermas in *The Philosophical Discourse of Modernity*—the opposition between theorists of *praxis,* dialogue, or communicative understanding, on the one hand, and totalizing critics of Western reason, on the other. But what this dichotomy obscures, and what Bernstein neglects, is Arendt's fundamental agreement with Heidegger on how deeply the roots of the technical understanding of acting and thinking penetrate our tradition. Arendt's theory of political action departs from the conviction that the current "oblivion of *praxis*" is, in fact, firmly rooted in the Platonic-Aristotelian conceptualization of action.[16] This conceptualization submits *praxis* to the dominance of *poiēsis* (overtly in Plato, more insidiously in Aristotle), the better to curtail plurality, drain action of ambiguity, and assert the supremacy of *theoria.* The bottom line is that the (philosophic) constitution of "the political" in the West coincides with the erection of a teleocratic concept of action, a concept that submits action to the rule of a goal-representing reason and a commanding, sovereign will.[17]

Arendt's fundamental argument is that this conception, while not yet overtly technical, nevertheless obscures the prephilosophic experience of action in the public realm, and thus paves the way for our own instrumental, plurality-hostile view of politics. Indeed, an important part of Arendt's argument is that this first "forgetting" of action leads to a reification of the teleocratic, sovereign model of action by the tradition, to the point where this model becomes almost impossible to question: "the whole terminology of political theory and political thought" works to limit the discussion of action to "the categories of ends and means and

thinking in terms of instrumentality."[18] With the collapse of the traditional relationship between ontology and politics, between first and practical philosophy,
this reification grips us ever more firmly. The loss of transcendent principles and
the withering of ultimate grounds for action (the "death of God") leaves action
determined *qua* effecting suspended in a void. It is then that the technical essence
of the teleological model comes to the fore, revealing its full antipolitical feroc-
ity.[19] Such, at any rate, is the lesson that emerges from Arendt's tracing of the
historical movement from the ascendancy of *homo faber*'s aggressive instrumentalism to the "worldlessness" of contemporary man, the *animal laborans*.

My recapitulation is intended to show how Heidegger's "reductive" and obscuring account, which supposedly shoves *praxis* into "the shadows of the background," in fact informs Arendt's "recovery" of *praxis* at every step. Moreover,
Heidegger's genealogy determines the form or method of this recovery. For what
Heidegger's relentless drive to reveal the "concealed technical thrust" at work in
our tradition reminds Arendt—and ourselves—is that the contemporary oblivion of *praxis* in technocratic politics is no simple forgetting. As with the
Seinsfrage, one must speak, instead, of a "forgetting of the forgetting."[20] The hope
that this oblivion can be overcome by hermeneutic remembrance or the renewal
of key Aristotelian distinctions in a theory of communicative action is a naive
and false one. What Heidegger's genealogy of the technical understanding of
action suggests, and what Arendt's deconstruction of the teleocratic model in her
own "disclosive" theory of political action demonstrates, is that this oblivion is
already inscribed in the distinctions that philosophical hermeneutics and critical
theory take at face value.[21] This is not to say that these distinctions (between
praxis and *poiēsis*, *technē* and *phronēsis*) are irrelevant to the critique of contemporary politics. To the contrary, it is to insist upon their importance and upon the
need to interrogate them at their origin, with an eye toward the ontological
preunderstanding that informs their articulation. Yet this is something neither
Habermas nor Gadamer attempt. Arendt's project differs fundamentally from
theirs insofar as it takes this double forgetting seriously and adopts the Heideggerian strategy of deconstruction (*Abbau*) to deal with it.[22] It is not enough to
return to the origins of practical philosophy; rather, one must drill through the
husks of action's original philosophic conceptualization if the phenomenon itself
(like the manifold meaning of Being) is to be revealed.[23]

Arendt's appropriation of Heidegger's genealogy of the technical understanding of action reveals the essential ambiguity of Heidegger for the problem of
action and the thinking of the political. On the one hand, his "leveling gaze"
tends to obliterate *praxis* in the manner described by Bernstein; on the other, his
linkage of the technical sense of action to the productionist ontological prejudices of Plato and Aristotle enables us to see the problem of action in its full
depth for the first time. Heidegger's history of metaphysics reveals a teleocratic
paradigm for action that stretches from Aristotle to the present. Once the implications of this continuity are absorbed, it is no longer possible to simply juxtapose
action with technique, or communicative with strategic rationality. With Heidegger, it is the philosophical delimitation of politics that becomes the prob-

lem.[24] The Platonic-Aristotelian articulation of the theory/practice relationship in grounding, deductive terms imposes an entirely alien metaphorics upon the phenomenon of action, a fact both Arendt and Schürmann emphasize.[25] Hence the necessity of penetrating this articulation, of deconstructing this origin, of putting into question this determination of action and the political. Only then can the antipolitical consequences of thinking of acting in terms of making, or of subjecting *praxis* to an end-representing reason, be fully appreciated.

It is here that Heidegger makes his most profound contribution to the recovery of *praxis*, and it is here that he also goes astray in the manner noted by both Bernstein and Taminiaux. Having raised the problem of the origin of the technical understanding of action in the philosophical, Heidegger abandons his concern with "authentic action," preferring instead to rethink *poiēsis* and action as a "poetic revealing."[26] *This*, I shall argue, is Heidegger's greatest contribution to the oblivion of *praxis*, exceeding both his inattention to intersubjectivity and his obsession with thinking. Strangely enough, it is Arendt's radicalization of the *praxis/poiēsis* distinction along lines originally suggested by *Being and Time* that enables us to draw out the political implications of this abandonment.

II. POLITICS AS PLASTIC ART: THE PRODUCTIONIST PARADIGM AND THE PROBLEM OF HEIDEGGER'S AESTHETICISM

Arendt appropriates Heidegger's genealogy of the technical sense of action in order to highlight the tradition's persistent attempt to overcome plurality, the politically most relevant expression of the finitude of the human condition. Subjecting *praxis* to the rule of an end-representing reason makes it possible to exchange the nonsovereign freedom of plural political actors for the command and control exercised by the artisan. The Platonic "translation" of acting into the idiom of making established the pattern for deriving action from first philosophy or theory, a pattern that offered an escape from the irreducible relativity which besets the realm of human affairs. The substitution of making for acting initiates a paradigm of correspondence that, as Lyotard notes, delimits the Western tradition of political philosophy. Within the tropological space opened by this substitution, politics is viewed as the means or *technē* by which "the 'fashioning' of a people according to the idea or ideal of a just being-together" is accomplished.[27]

So long as political philosophy sees its task as the articulation of first principles with which actions, peoples, and institutions must be brought into accord, it reiterates the Platonic schema; moreover, it perpetuates the idea that politics resembles a plastic art. Arendt's critique of the "Platonic" tradition reveals the drive to conflate political and artistic categories at the core of Western political theory, underlining the stubborn persistence of the state as artwork/politics as *technē* tropes. The strength of these figures is measured by the fact that the closure of the tradition barely shakes the logic of justification institutionalized by the Platonic separation of theory and practice. Western political theory, as Schürmann points out, has always demanded that action be grounded in some extrapolitical first (the cosmic order, natural or divine hierarchy, Reason and natural right, History, the greatest good for the greatest number, the emancipatory interest of the discursive community).[28] As a result, it never really abandons the view that politics is a kind of plastic art, the "fashioning," more or less violent, of a people in conformity with an ideal. The persistence of this trope is explained by its efficacy for reducing plurality and difference, and by its ability to represent violence and coercive power as "right."[29]

Arendt's theory of nonsovereign, agonistic action smashes this figure, breaking the circuit of justification through the liberation of action from the rule of grounding principles and pregiven ends.[30] The essentially normative function of political theory—that is, the theoretical specification of the conditions for the legitimate exercise of power—is suspended.[31] In its place Arendt develops a phenomenology of action and a narrative approach to the closure of the public realm in modernity, an approach designed to keep the memory of an agonistic public sphere alive. With this bracketing of the legitimation problematic, a new appreciation of spaces and practices not typically viewed as political becomes possible.[32] Moreover, the Arendtian liberation of action throws the antipolitical, not to say the *inhuman*, consequences of the tradition's conflation of artistic and political categories into sharp relief.

The teleocratic concept of action may be seen as the primary and most enduring expression of this conflation. With the collapse of transcendental grounds for the political, the logic of correspondence and justification built into this concept turns inward. The result is that the fashioning or "fictioning" of the community in conformity with an ideal of Justice is transformed into an exercise in self-production.[33] And with this transformation, the threshold of modernity is traced. We can see this transformation at work in the emergence of the Hobbesian problematic: the construction of the "Leviathan" needed to overawe its subjects is the work of those very subjects, in their "natural," presubjected, and radically dissociated state.[34] The example of Hobbes clearly demonstrates how, once the "art" of politics is deprived of its natural ground (once *technē* can no longer be seen as the completion or accomplishment of *physis*), a paradoxical and impossible logic asserts itself. The conundrum is simply put: the people, who do not yet exist *as a people*, must somehow always already be enough of a subject in order to author or fashion themselves *qua* community. The answers to this riddle proposed by the social contract tradition—Hobbes's pact of association, which is simultaneously a transfer of power to a designated sovereign; Locke's presupposition of what Laslett has called "natural political virtue"; the Rousseauian mechanism of the total alienation of individual rights and powers by which a communal, sovereign power is formed—have all been unconvincing, to say the least.[35]

Romanticism can be seen as the attempt to escape this paradox by radicalizing it. Instituting what Jean-Luc Nancy has called an "immanentist" logic of communal self-formation, romanticism elides the distinction between process and end: the subject is redefined as work in the double sense of self-formative activity *and* product.[36] As Philippe Lacoue-Labarthe notes, in the romantic vision the community at work creates and works *itself*, thereby accomplishing the "subjective process *par excellence*, the process of self-formation and self-production."[37] The aim of the community of beings becomes "in essence to produce their own essence as community."[38]

With this move, a peculiarly *modern* version of the traditional conflation of art and politics is created. The *organicity* of the political, originally laid down by Plato's *Republic*, takes a new and extreme form: the figure of the subject who is simultaneously artist *and* work absorbs that of the aesthetically integrated state. This subjectivization of the state as artwork trope culminates in the totalitarian will to self-effectuation: the will to the self-creation of a people characterized by full actualization, complete self-presence.[39] The only community capable of achieving such self-presence is one from which plurality, difference, mediation, and alienation have been expunged: a community, in other words, that is not a *political* community at all.

That the will to immediacy leads, in politics, to the suicide of the self-fashioning community is something that has been clear at least since Hegel. Yet, however "impossible" the totalitarian project is, it can succeed (for a time) by infinitizing the very process of self-formation: the romantic emphasis upon the expression of a culture's particular genius gives way to an endless process of organization, discipline, and control, a process that becomes an end in itself. Eliding the distinction between process and product even more radically than romanticism, totalitarianism yields a supremely novel version of politics as making. *This* version succeeds by default: its suppression of plurality by means of ideology and terror creates the political community as *subject*, as that "One man of gigantic dimensions" dreamt of by Hobbes at the dawn of modernity and identified by Arendt as the late modern antithesis of politics.[40]

The totalitarian fulfillment of politics as "the plastic art of the State" (Goebbels) underlines the stakes of Arendt's attempt to escape the conflation of art and politics (the "substitution of making for acting") performed by the tradition from Plato to Nietzsche. Heidegger's "destruction of the history of ontology" is, as I have suggested, crucial to the identification of the antipolitical, finitude-suppressing metaphorics Arendt targets. But while Heidegger reveals the profound and shaping influence the production experience has upon the Western understanding of Being and the articulation of theory and practice, *he, too, remains caught within the productionist paradigm*. This entrapment is most clearly displayed in the discourse on *technē* (art) during the thirties, which was characterized by the explicit embrace of a poetic model of disclosure and the view that the state is a "setting-into-work" (*ins-Werk-setzen*) of truth. Heidegger, it should be pointed out, intended this discourse as a contribution to the "surmounting" (*Verwindung*) of Platonism and nihilism. He equated this project with the destiny of the West, and initially construed National Socialism as making an important contribution to it.[41] Yet it is precisely this discourse that expresses, in no uncertain terms, what Christopher Norris (paraphrasing Lacoue-Labarthe) has called "the deepest, most persistent drive" of Western metaphysics: the drive to substitute artistic for political terms of judgment.[42]

How does Heidegger's discourse on *technē* contribute to this drive? Why does

Heidegger succumb to a thinking of the political grounded in the desire to suppress finitude/plurality? Finally, what does Heidegger's entrapment in the productionist paradigm reveal about the "essence of the political" in the West, and about the relation of National Socialism to this essence?

By presenting the state as a privileged instance of the historical "happening of truth" in the work, Heidegger's discourse on art broadens and deepens the aestheticist impulse of the tradition. The idea that the state is a work through which the unconcealment of Being "occurs" is, as I have indicated, clearly directed *against* Plato. However, the anti-Platonic thrust of this historicizing move is undercut by the fact that the political community continues to be thought of under the sign of *poiēsis*. Heidegger liberates *poiēsis* from the closure in which it had been inscribed by substantialist metaphysics—the closure of *idea* and *telos*. Nevertheless, his idea of a postmetaphysical *poiēsis*, which emphasizes the radical newness of that which is poetically disclosed, remains in extreme tension with the essential plurality of *praxis*. This opposition comes to the fore in Heidegger's identification of the strife between world and earth as the *essential* agon. Authentic politics, as the work that must bring this agon to stand, can only happen in the poetic, world-disclosing speech of founders and preservers. The result, as we have seen, is the ironic reinscription of the quasi-Platonic hierarchy of authentic poetic speech and inauthentic (merely communicative) speech.

With the restriction of authentic *praxis* to the poetic functions of founding and preserving, the raison d'être of the political community ceases to be the articulation of plurality. Instead, its chief mission is the creation and preservation of a particular historical *world*. It comes as no surprise that Heidegger's identification of politics, world building, and history "in the authentic sense" yields an implicit emphasis upon the organic character of the authentic political-historical community. Only a rounded, aesthetically integrated, and culturally homogenous community such as the Greek *polis* is capable of creating an *ethos* distinctive enough to make the world "world."[43] Thus, while Heidegger's anti-Platonism leads him to think of the political in terms of temporal differentiation (the political as *historial*), he is incapable of making difference the synchronic principle of the political community. Historicizing and ontologizing *poiēsis*, Heidegger, like Hegel before him, comes to focus on the people (*Volk*) as the carrier of historical truth.[44]

Why does Heidegger adopt a metaphorics that, as he well knew, originated with the metaphysical quest to suppress finitude and contingency? The answer, I would suggest, derives from the immanent nature of his "destruction" of Western ontology. As Robert Bernasconi points out, Heidegger did not view the thematization of the productionist prejudices of Greek ontology as a pretext for the abstract negation of the understanding of Being expressed by that ontology.[45] On the contrary, "The destruction of the traditional content of ancient ontology is not so much directed against that ontology as against its standard interpretation, which has come to provide an obstacle to its appreciation, blocking our access to the original experiences in which the first ways of determining the nature of Being were achieved."[46]

Heidegger, in other words, does not attempt to escape the predominance of

poiēsis in Greek ontology; rather, he "destroys" its reified (latinized) interpretation, the better to uncover the phenomenological experience of presence
(*Anwesenheit*) at the root of the tradition. It is because Heidegger's "destruction"
of the history of ontology takes the form of a repetition of a "first beginning," in
which the experience of presence derives from the production process, that his
thought remains curiously blind to plurality and intersubjectivity. For, as Arendt
helps us to see, the phenomenological field that gives rise to the Western understanding of Being *qua* presence is one that obsures the constitutive dimensions of
human plurality.[47] Thus, while Heidegger questions the reification of presence as
constant presence, reasserting its finitude through the temporalization of Being,
the "recovery" of Being as *physis*-like presencing remains oblivious to the experience of finitude found in *praxis* and in the realm of human affairs generally.

Arendt's interrogation and reappropriation of the distinction between *praxis*
and *poiēsis* is thus absolutely essential for thinking about the "ubiquity of the
finite" in a *political* way, and for sounding the depths of Heidegger's entrapment
in the productionist paradigm.[48] A renewed emphasis upon intersubjectivity is
not, by itself, adequate to this task. It is only when we view Heidegger through
the prism of Arendt's radicalized and reinforced distinction between acting and
making that his underlying aestheticism emerges fully. By offering an antiteleological concept of action, Arendt's theory of action overturns the teleocratic
paradigm *and* reveals the limits of Heidegger's radical rethinking of *poiēsis*. Neither of these tasks could be accomplished simply by relying upon the *philosophical*
distinction between acting and making.

The isolation of Heidegger's aestheticism is crucial to providing insight into
the "truth" of National Socialism and into the "nonpolitical essence of the political" in the West that is simultaneously revealed and concealed by this
"truth."[49] Yet this point of entry into the critique of Heidegger, so clearly marked
by Arendt's analysis of the tradition, is one Arendt chose to ignore. Lacoue-
Labarthe, however, has provided the outline of an Arendtian critique of Heidegger that abandons the distorting apologetics of her portrayal of a meta-ascetic.
Showing how Heidegger's discourse on *technē* participates in the conflation of
artistic and political categories, Lacoue-Labarthe demonstrates how his *Verwindung* (surmounting) of Platonism/nihilism produces an antitraditional aestheticism that nevertheless expresses the basic impulse of the tradition.[50]

Lacoue-Labarthe's analysis places the question of art (and, by implication, poetry) at the very center of Heidegger's philosophical politics. His primary thesis
is that this politics is not to be found in the texts of 1933, but rather in those
following the break with National Socialism.[51] In these texts Heidegger transforms the character of his discourse on *technē*. The *Rektoratsrede* had pointed to
the necessity of reintegrating knowledge (*technē*) in accordance with its Greek
roots in order to achieve spiritual regeneration; in the texts after 1933, however,
science gives way to art, which is now seen as harboring the capacity for grounding the world of historial *Dasein*.[52] This shift is of the greatest importance: in
developing his notions of the world-founding work and a poetic speech that
"grants" or "bestows" the people's historical existence, Heidegger places himself

in direct opposition to a regime whose nihilistic character could no longer be ignored. However, as Lacoue-Labarthe points out, this opposition to the *reality* of National Socialism is framed in terms of an appeal to its "truth." Heidegger opposes the regime in the name of a possibility contained in, yet ultimately betrayed by, the National Socialist movement.[53] This truth—the unique historical destiny of the German people in the face of the nihilism of modernity, a destiny articulated by the poet Friedrich Hölderlin—grows out of the romantic vision of the state as artwork. Appealing to Hölderlin, Heidegger poeticizes this vision, bringing the romantic conception of the aesthetic state to fulfillment in his conception of the political community as vehicle for the disclosure of Being.

Heidegger's "romantic" conception of the state as artwork (or poetry in the strong, ontological sense) throws a precise light upon what Lacoue-Labarthe calls the "real, or profound, nature of Nazism."[54] It enables us to see National Socialism as a vulgarized version of the aesthetic state; as, essentially, a *national aestheticism* in which the "plastic art of the state" refers to the process through which the German people form themselves in accordance with the Aryan myth (their "essence"). Heidegger's mid-thirties discourse on *technē* throws this dimension of Nazism into sharp relief, at once revealing and exemplifying the complicity between a movement whose political model was the *Gesamtkunstwerk* (total artwork) and a discourse (running from Schiller through Hegel to Nietzsche, Wagner, and, finally, Heidegger) that espoused an overtly aesthetic ideal of the political community.

Now this "romantic" aestheticism is hardly the "cause" of National Socialism; nor can it be confused with what Arendt called a "gutter-born ideology." But it is important to see the way in which the "high" and "low" versions of this aestheticism reinforce each other, particularly in moments of extreme tension. Thus, Heidegger's infamous 1935 appeal to the "inner truth and greatness" of the National Socialist movement—an appeal directed *against* the ideologues of the party—refers to the unactualized possibilities of a poetic politics strong enough to preserve European culture from the twin evils of Bolshevism and Americanism (which, "from a metaphysical point of view," are the same).[55] In such a politics, Hölderlin would take the place of Homer, bestowing upon the embattled center of European culture a sense of its unique historical mission through the "hymning of what is German." This poetic politics shrinks back in horror when confronted with its hideous ape—the Nazi appeal to race, myth, and the "total artwork" to be achieved through a hygienic sculpting of the "body" of the *Volk*. Yet while Heidegger's appeal to Hölderlin is clearly opposed to Nazism's "will to will," it hardly questions the conflation of art and politics performed by National Socialism.

Viewing National Socialism as a national aestheticism enables us to make sense of Heidegger's "mistake" and his feeling of betrayal (which was to last a good ten years after 1933).[56] The "high" and "low" versions of the aesthetic ideology propounded by Heidegger and Nazism, respectively, have as their common ground the idea of politics as art, a *poiēsis* or *technē* whose job is to bestow or fashion a people's historical identity according to the primordiality of language or myth.[57] The range of possibilities opened by this figure is vast, and runs from the brutality and kitsch of the Reich's attempt to "beautify" the body of the *Volk* to the philosopher's appeal to the people to listen to the poet's hymning of what is German. Yet both extremes of this aestheticism refer us to the dream that has inspired the Western tradition of political philosophy from its inception, the "dream of the City as a work of art," of a political community whose organicity would give full expression to the specific genius of a historical people.[58]

The essential aestheticism of National Socialism, then, is thematized by the nature of Heidegger's opposition. His discourse on art thus provides a privileged insight into the idea of the political that lay behind Nazism. This idea—the political as the truth of art, politics as the "plastic art" of the state—is one that, as we have seen, has deep roots in the tradition. These roots are, in Lacoue-Labarthe's phrase, "simultaneously veiled and unveiled by National Socialism."[59] The movement's appeal to myth, to the self-production of the Aryan myth through the auto-*poiēsis* of the German people, disguises what is, in essence, a Platonic trope.[60] The isolation of Heidegger's aestheticism by Arendtian means becomes doubly important, in that it shows us how the *Verwindung* (surmounting) of Platonism is, in fact, merely an *inversion*, a conflation of art and politics in the figure of "poetry," inscribed in the field opened by "the traditional substitution of making for acting." Nazism obscures this filiation insofar as the mimetic logic governing the production of the Aryan myth twists the Platonic logic of correspondence into a paradoxical, unrecognizable form: the Germans can "become who they are" only by imitating themselves, by willing the Aryan type from myth to fully formed subjectivity.[61] The "death of God" dictates that the "self-formation" of the people not appeal to anything outside itself; "the people" must search for their "type" not in the realm of universal truth, but in its fictionalized mythic origins.[62]

Heidegger's aestheticism enlightens us as to the "real, or profound, nature of Nazism" precisely because it reveals this "ideology" as the immanentist version of politics as *technē*: national aestheticism perversely fulfills the logic instituted by the Platonic trope. Moreover, Heidegger's thinking of politics in terms of a post-metaphysical *poiēsis* illuminates not only the "essence" of Nazism, but what Lacoue-Labarthe calls "the non-political essence of the political" in the West as well.[63] We cannot imagine the will to pure, unmediated identity manifest in the Nazi aestheticization of politics apart from the aestheticization of the political that occurs with the philosophic delimitation of *ta politika* (the political). In our tradition, as Arendt points out, the substitution of making for acting *founds* the political: politics is always already art (*technē*).

The importance of Lacoue-Labarthe's analysis is that it brings to light the subterranean connections between Heidegger's poetic model of disclosure, Nazi aestheticism, and the fundamental impulse of the tradition (the conflation of political and artistic categories in the pursuit of a univocal concept of action). If, as Lacoue-Labarthe argues (and Arendt would agree), the political has, from the beginning, been seen as the truth of art, then the attempts of Heidegger and National Socialism to surmount the tradition fall back within the range of possibilities opened by its founding. Indeed, borrowing a figure from Arendt, nowhere does the nonpolitical essence of the political (as thought of by the West) reveal itself so fully as at the beginning and the end of our tradition.[64]

Lacoue-Labarthe's Arendtian/deconstructive perspective enables us to see how the most deeply antipolitical aspects of Heidegger's thought indicate a profound continuity between his "poetic" politics and the traditional substitution of making for acting. The Heideggerian attempt to preserve the disclosive dimensions of *praxis* by assimilating it to a radicalized *poiēsis* repeats Plato's initiating gesture, albeit in the name of an anti-Platonic notion of truth (truth as revealing, as *aletheia*). The resulting hierarchy of disclosive political speech and mere opinion underlines not only the danger of applying a poetic model of disclosure to the realm of human affairs (a "category mistake" from Arendt's perspective), but also the antipolitical consequences of conflating truth and meaning.[65] Arendt's suspicion of Truth as antipolitical in its univocity is borne out by the example of a poetic politics that privileges the *event* of truth manifest in the world-founding work over the meaning that arises from the plural realm of opinion. Conflating truth and meaning, art and politics, in a way that excels even Plato, Heidegger effaces plurality through the figure of poetry.

III. Art, Technology, and Totalitarianism

Heidegger's attempt to rehabilitate *poiēsis* in the thirties in effect reversed his reappropriation of the Aristotelian distinction between acting and making in *Being and Time*. In that work, the disclosive dimensions of "poetic" or productive activity were limited to the kind of "sight" presupposed by the concernful absorption of everyday life: *poiēsis*, considered as production, *reveals*; however, the world it reveals (the world of *zuhandenheit*) is fallen and inauthentic. With the radical rethinking of *poiēsis* in "The Origin of the Work of Art," art or poetic activity is juxtaposed to "mere" making, and is elevated to a position of clear disclosive superiority over action. The transsubjective status of the work of art enables it to bring the original struggle (*polemos*) between world and earth to stand. The result, as Taminiaux notes, is that the disclosive action of *Dasein* (*praxis*) is relegated to an ancillary role—a clear measure of the revaluation performed by the work of the thirties.[66]

That Heidegger came, after the *Kehre*, to see to the complicity between this revaluation and the willful aestheticism of Nazism is clear. This awareness is manifest in the transformation his discourse on *technē* undergoes: Heidegger shifts his focus from a concern with the ontological vocation of the artwork to the question of the technological organization of the lacks inherent in human existence. It is also apparent in the self-criticism Heidegger offers concerning the willful or metaphysical character of the project of *Überwindung* (overcoming).[67] From the midpoint of the Nietzsche lectures on (as Arendt notes), Heidegger's suspicion of all such projects grows, culminating in the counsel offered in *On Time and Being*: we must learn to "cease all overcoming" if we wish to avoid becoming any more deeply entangled in the web of metaphysics.[68]

Such insight was not exactly quick in coming to Heidegger. It required not only that he recognize the inherent willfulness of his own attempt to surmount the tradition, but that he recognize the "technical" character of his rehabilitation of *poiēsis*. This, in turn, presupposed the foregrounding of the "concealed technical thrust" at the heart of Western metaphysics/humanism. With this foregrounding—achieved by Heidegger in 1953 with "The Question Concerning Technology," although foreshadowed in *Nietzsche* and the *Beiträge*—the way was opened for Heidegger to see his "higher" aestheticism of the thirties as the flip side of Nazism's national aestheticism, and to see both as variations upon the "traditional substitution of making for acting." Thus, as Lacoue-Labarthe points out,

> It was not until ten years after the collapse of the Third Reich that Heidegger had the definitive revelation that National Socialism (national aestheticism) was the truth of the inversion of Platonism or the restoration of what Plato had fought against—though not without yielding to tyranny himself—in other words, the thinking of the technical or the political as fiction: the last attempt at "mythicizing" the West. Though not, probably, the last aestheticization of the political.[69]

It is, then, only with the completed transformation of his discourse on *technē* that Heidegger is capable of seeing how deeply implicated his earlier aestheticism was with both National Socialism and the fundamental impulse of the tradition. This impulse—the conflation of political and artistic categories—was capable of taking "rationalist" (Platonic/theoreticist) or "irrationalist" (poeticizing, mythicizing) forms without ever breaching the broad paradigm of correspondence opened by Plato. The concept of technology framed in 1953 enables Heidegger, finally, to see his earlier rehabilitation of *poiēsis* as an aestheticism, which mirrors, albeit in inverted form, philosophy's founding aestheticization of the political.

Lacoue-Labarthe claims that Heidegger's mature concept of technology enables Heidegger (and ourselves) to see the "aestheticization of the political" as a figure that encompasses the tradition. Heidegger's autocritique reveals the "nonpolitical essence of the political" in our tradition and converges remarkably with Arendt's critique of Western political philosophy's defining "substitution of making for acting." In addition, Heidegger's transformed discourse on *technē* helps us to make sense of the novel political forms that arise once the old sources of authority—the grounding "firsts" for the plastic art of the state—dry up. The historical juncture at which totalitarianism arises is one in which the tradition, though tottering, has not yet collapsed (as Arendt notes, it will receive its death blow with the advent of such regimes).[70] It is one in which the withdrawal of traditional sources of authority threatens the "essential" organicity of the political. This threat—the dispersion and pluralization of the "ground" of the political—elicits the immanentist response of totalitarianism: the utterly novel attempt to fashion the political community as a vehicle for the *direct* expression of the "laws" of Nature or History. The will to immediacy, an immediacy to be achieved through technological means, is the last resort of an organic conception of the political faced with a permanent loss of ground.

We can say, following Arendt, that totalitarianism responds to "the more or less general, more or less dramatic breakdown of all traditional authorities" in the twentieth century by attempting to eliminate the gap between the "external" ground of authority and the organicity of the community.[71] The promise of total-itarianism is that it can overcome this crisis in authority by subjecting mankind *directly* to the suprahuman forces of Nature or History. As Arendt points out in "Ideology and Terror," no previous regime entertained the idea of identifying the transhuman source of authority *directly* with the political order: all had seen the need for mediating, artificial structures of authority—for example, positive law—as the necessary "translation" of the immutable *ius naturale*, without which this law would be irrelevant to the realm of human affairs.[72] The resulting distinction between justice and legality is overcome by a totalitarian regime that clears away the rubble of traditional authorities and pretends "to establish the direct reign of justice on earth":

> Totalitarian lawfulness . . . executes the law of History or of Nature without translat-ing it into standards of right and wrong for individual behavior. It applies the law directly to mankind without bothering with the behavior of men. The law of Nature or of History, if properly executed, is expected to produce mankind as its end prod-uct. . . . Totalitarian policy claims to transform the human species into an active and unfailing carrier of a law to which human beings otherwise would only passively and reluctantly be subjected.[73]

In Arendt's formulation, totalitarianism appears as anything but an exagger-ated form of tyrannical *lawlessness*. On the contrary, the *nature* of totalitarianism is revealed precisely in the attempt "to make mankind itself the embodiment of the law" by identifying the political order with the law of movement of Nature or History.[74] Once these laws are established as the principles of motion of the political body, the self-formative activity of the community becomes one with the forces of Nature or History. Under totalitarianism, the "plastic art" of politics consists in the production of a collective subject whose movement is directly determined by these laws. This art necessarily entails the *elimination*, as waste or impediment, of those classes, races, and individuals whose existence retards the production of the collective subject that (so the ideology claims) Nature or His-tory will ultimately create. The totalitarian project of "fabricating mankind" pre-sumes there is a human material, the malleability of which is limited only by the presence of anachronistic, underdeveloped, or "inorganic" elements. The totali-tarian art of the political is distinguished from its classical counterpart in that it immanentizes the superhuman source of authority; it is, however, akin to this model in that it sees the art or *technē* of politics as the completion or accomplish-ment of *physis*. Totalitarian teleology yields a kind of perverse Aristotelianism.

There is, of course, an important difference between these two "natural" arts. The totalitarian art of the political proceeds by naturalizing the fabrication pro-cess; that is, by dissolving the idea of a guiding *telos* that represents the perfection of the process of development, a final end. Naturalizing the fabrication process means eliding the distinction between process and product in such a way that the human "material" becomes a living embodiment of suprahuman laws of motion.

The result is that the process of self-formation becomes identical with life itself. Thus, the totalitarian naturalization of the fabrication process transforms it into a never-ending cycle, a process as necessary, repetitive, and ceaseless as that of production and consumption. The "art" of totalitarian politics—the fabrication of mankind—is, in principle, as uncompletable as the laws of motion of Nature or History themselves:

> Totalitarian politics . . . has unmasked the true nature of these movements [of natural and historical "laws"] insofar as it clearly showed there could be no end to this process. If it is a law of nature to eliminate everything that is harmful and unfit to live, it would mean the end of nature itself if new categories of the harmful and unfit-to-live could not be found; if it is the law of history that in class struggle certain classes "wither away," it would mean the end of human history itself if new classes did not form, so that they in turn could "wither away" at the hands of totalitarian rulers. In other words, the law of killing by which totalitarian movements seize and exercise power would remain a law of movement even if they ever succeeded in making all humanity subject to their rule.[75]

The idea of an art of the political that strictly obeys natural or historical laws of motion in its continual, never-ending fabrication of the human species flows from what Arendt calls the "fundamental belief of totalitarianism"; namely, that everything is possible.[76] This belief—the purest possible expression of the resentment of the human condition, which Arendt sees as driving modernity—illuminates a fundamental precondition of the totalitarian project. In order for mankind to become a "walking embodiment" of natural or historical laws of motion, it is not only necessary to embark on a ceaseless program of elimination of anachronistic or substandard materials, but it is also necessary for totalitarianism to first destroy those artificial, reified boundaries (rights, positive laws, etc.) that map out the man-made world and articulate public and private spaces. The relative permanence of the "human artifice" must itself be dissolved into process if human society is to become an adequate conductor of natural or historical forces. Allowing such boundaries to remain means that the channels of communication between men also remain open. And where such channels exist—where they have not been eliminated by means of total terror—freedom and action remain realities: the political order has yet to transform the community into a vehicle of (suprahuman) necessity.[77]

It is here that Arendt's analysis of the novelty of the totalitarian "plastic art" of politics intersects most sharply with Heidegger's later discourse on *technē*. The totalitarian attempt to naturalize this art by immanentizing the suprahuman ground of authority becomes possible only within the horizon of technology as described by Heidegger. The project of fabricating mankind—the sine qua non of totalitarian ideology—could scarcely be conceived without the prior framing of the world (and the beings within it) as "standing reserve," as so much graspable, manipulable stuff. The "destining" of such a "revealing" allows humanity to appear, for the first time, as raw material waiting to be reordered or remade. This "ordering-revealing" of human beings as manipulable stock is by no means a sufficient cause of totalitarianism; nor is it necessarily limited to totalitarian regimes. Nevertheless, the "challenging revealing" that Heidegger identifies as the essence of technology remains the unsurpassable horizon within which the project of "fabricating mankind" takes shape.[78]

Technology, then, is not merely a crucial instrumentality of totalitarian domination. It is, of course, extraordinarily difficult to conceive such domination stripped of its enormous technological apparatus. From the dissemination of ideology to the bureaucratically efficient murder of millions, totalitarianism relies upon technology. Yet the employment of technological means to achieve a wide variety of political ends should not blind us to the deeper sense in which totalitarianism is technological. Totalitarianism is, in fact, *the specifically technological form of politics as plastic art*. It is true that the internal limits of the West's organic/artistic conception of the political are destabilized by the withdrawal of traditional authorities in the twentieth century. However, it is only with the crossing of the ontological threshold marked out by Heidegger in "The Question Concerning Technology" that these limits disappear completely. Within the frame (*Gestell*) of technology, everything that is appears as orderable and (potentially) controllable. This presencing of everything as orderable and controllable is the *conditio sine qua non* for everything appearing to be possible—for the totalitarian project as such.

The thesis that totalitarianism is the specifically technological form of politics as art or making is, I believe, implicit in Arendt's analysis in "Ideology and Terror." The essay demonstrates how totalitarianism appropriates by naturalizing what is, in fact, a very traditional metaphorics. This approach allows Arendt to underline both the startling novelty of totalitarianism and its deep roots within the "traditional substitution of making for acting." In showing how totalitarianism infinitizes the process of self-formation, Arendt reveals the paradox at the heart of the Western/organic conception of the political community: the "product" must somehow always already be the foundation of the project of "making," especially where this product can no longer be an ideal revealed by reason. Such making, in other words, never really creates anything new; its job is to make manifest the essential unity that was always already there. The immanentist/totalitarian recourse to mythic origins—to "fictioning" the political community—appears with the closure of substantialist metaphysics in upon itself.

Once we see totalitarianism as the specifically technological form of politics as making, we are able to see the kernel of truth contained within Heidegger's otherwise scandalous equation of the extermination camps with the advent of a mechanized food industry or the production of hydrogen bombs.[79] This remark, made at Bremen in 1949, is the ultimate example of the "leveling gaze of *Seinsgeschichte*": it denies the apocalyptic nature of the Extermination, reducing it to but one manifestation of the advent of the reign of technology. Nevertheless, while there is an "incommensurable difference" between this event and "any other technical phenomenon whatever," the extermination of the Jews was, as Lacoue-Labarthe points out, an eminently technological affair.[80] The "systematic production of corpses" at Auschwitz and elsewhere was the technological actualization of an essential possibility implied by the "nonpolitical essence of the political" in the West. The Extermination was the seizure of the possibility of expunging all traces of originary difference—of a plural, multiple origin—in the name of a primordial self-identity of the West. Thus, the logic behind the Extermination is one of a "pure metaphysical decision": it is the decision to eliminate, "without trace or residence," that "stain" upon the Greco-Roman origins of the West (the model for modern European republicanism as well as fascism). Hence, the purely hygienic or sanitary nature of this operation, which, as Lacoue-Labarthe remarks, "has no parallel in history."[81]

Nazism's attempt to fabricate mankind can thus be seen as the twisted attempt to realize what had long been the dream of the Western tradition: the dream of the City as a work of art. Within the space delimited by the closure of this tradition and the "frame" of technological revealing, this dream produces an event—the Extermination—the logic of which cannot be reduced to either technology or totalitarianism. For while the Extermination is irreducibly technological and totalitarian, the decision to eliminate *the Jews* flows from a much more specific logic, a logic that exceeds the totalitarian attempt to speed up the natural law of evolution by technological means. The decision to exterminate the Jews—to eliminate, once and for all, those witnesses to the plural origins of the Greco-Judeo-Latin West itself—follows, as Lacoue-Labarthe emphasizes, from a logic that is, strictly speaking, spiritual or metaphysical.[82] It is the decision to identify heterogeneity with one people—to see the Jews as the heterogeneous element par excellence—and to "eliminate" the threat posed by this heterogeneity by exterminating its externalized embodiment. The difference that precedes and haunts identity, and that destabilizes all attempts at institutionalizing identity, produces a violent will to immediacy in that "people"—the Germans—who are most threatened by the artificiality of their own national identity.[83] How else to understand Hitler's paradoxical statement, "The jew is in each of us," a statement that at once acknowledges the primordial "contamination" of identity and demands the annihilation of an externalized, substantialized otherness?

It is the spiritual or metaphysical nature of this decision that marks the Extermination of the Jews as a unique event in Western history—a history drenched in mass-scale political and religious murder. Lacoue-Labarthe calls Auschwitz the "caesura of our times," and it is so precisely because the logic that gave birth to it exceeds that of a culture or political system, and reaches into the essence of the West itself. It is because the chosen victims of the Extermination—this most systematic elimination—were *the Jews* that *this* event of totalitarian/technological mass murder penetrates more deeply into the roots of the West than any other (equally miserable, equally tragic) example of totalitarian evil. As Lacoue-Labarthe puts it:

We knew that there existed a centuries old anti-semitism (with an essentially religious base). We knew that Western man was a killer (in fact he is not the only one, but he succeeded in equipping himself with unrivalled means to kill). We even know—or could guess—that the West had always hated something in the Jew. Could we guess that Western man was going to fulfill himself in what he proclaimed to be his truth, in himself and for himself, in the calculation and planning of the murder of those whom he had decreed, with contempt for the most elementary evidence, did not belong to the West, or were sapping it from within?[84]

The world-historical significance of this event—which Lacoue-Labarthe calls the "terrible revelation" of the essence of the West to itself—is only partially illuminated by the Arendtian reflection on the *nature* of totalitarianism. Likewise, no philosophy of history can pretend to wrest meaning from this event by placing it within a positive or negative dialectic: it is an abyss that swallows all theodocies and critiques, whether rooted in faith or reason. Yet—and this is Lacoue-Labarthe's central claim—the Heideggerian reflection on history as the deployment of metaphysics contributes to our ability to see this event in its unique, history-splitting significance.[85] To use Walter Benjamin's phrase, it does so not by reducing this event to a "bead on a rosary"; rather, the illuminating value of the Heideggerian reflection on history resides in its capacity to reveal the *metaphysical significance* of the Extermination of the Jews.[86] It is this significance that distinguishes *this* massacre from all others, for it is here that the "useless residue" of the Western idea of art wreaks a technological revenge on those whose sheer existence testifies to the impossibility of recovering a univocal origin, a primordial unity devoid of plurality, finitude, otherness. The Heideggerian reflection on history and technology illuminates the way the "concealed technical thrust" of the tradition attempts to replace difference with identity, finitude with mastery; and, in this way, it helps to highlight the "pure metaphysical decision . . . inscribed at the very heart of National Socialism."[87]

It is the illuminative capacity of the Heideggerian reflection on history—its potential ability to show how the Extermination was the "terrible revelation" of the essence of the West to itself—that makes Heidegger's *silence* on the massacre of the Jews all the more intolerable.[88] If the other side of "the leveling gaze of *Seinsgeschichte*" is, as Arendt argues, the "coincidence of thought and event" manifest in the concept of historicity, then the failure of thought to respond to *this* event stands, even more than the acceptance of the rectorate, as Heidegger's "greatest act of stupidity" (*die grösste Dummheit*). Precisely because of the transformation wrought by his "collision" with National Socialism, and the way this new thinking of *technē* colored his view of the "destining" of the West, Heidegger's silence concerning the Jews testifies to the most profound blindness of thinking—a capacity for thoughtlessness against which even the most passionate thinking is not immunized.

Heidegger's thundering silence on the question of the Extermination—his blindness to its implications for the "destining of the West"—is clearly a function of his earlier complicity with a regime whose racism he found vulgar, yet which he nevertheless tolerated. But it is also partly explained by the fact that his historical reflection on the destining of the West *qua* technology was prophylactically circumscribed in terms of a Greek *philosophical* origin, whose priority he never questioned. One result of this privileging is that the Platonic rage against plurality—the driving force behind the traditional substitution of making for acting and the view of politics as plastic art—is deprived of its political context.[89] The Platonic reification of truth as correspondence and presence as constant presence are thereby isolated; they are seen as attesting less to a will to self-identity and sovereignty than to a generalized fear of finitude and otherness. From this perspective, the "concealed technical thrust" of the tradition appears as a will to the domination of all that is as such, rather than as a response to the finitude and contingency born of plurality. This imposes limits upon the political significance of Heidegger's genealogy of the technical understanding of action. A potentially powerful tool for revealing the antipolitical consequences of thinking of politics as making, this genealogy nevertheless remains blind to the essence of National Socialist aestheticism: the elimination of plurality through the creation of the *Volk* as subject, a process of self-fashioning that demands the expulsion and elimination of those who are decreed to represent absolute, irreducible heterogeneity.

This symptomatic failure leads us to ask, with renewed urgency, whether Heidegger's later thought provides adequate resources for a postmetaphysical concept of action. Even if we grant Lacoue-Labarthe his essential point—namely, that the blindness of the *Überwindung* (overcoming) of the thirties is replaced by the insight of a transformed, self-reflexive discourse on *technē*—the question of whether Heidegger has sufficiently freed himself from his earlier productionist prejudices remains. And while it provides no litmus test in this regard, Heidegger's postwar silence on the Extermination occasions renewed suspicion and distrust.

IV. Questions Concerning Technology—and the Rethinking of Action

Can it really be said that the later Heidegger succeeds in radicalizing *praxis* without obliterating it? Reiner Schürmann's work provides a strong affirmative answer to this question.[90] Reading Heidegger from back to front, Schürmann argues that a broad postmetaphysical concept of action is implied by the notion of *Gelassenheit* (releasement or letting be). The way of "facing the world" this notion conveys stands in direct contrast to the grasping, technologizing attitude Heidegger describes in the "Letter on Humanism" and "The Question Concerning Technology." Moreover, *Gelassenheit* points toward a mode of conduct or a way of being-in-the-world in which action is no longer legislated by a reason bent on mastery. Glossing Heidegger's appeal to Master Eckhart's concept of existence in *Der Satz vom Grund*, Schürmann identifies a "life without why" as the "practical *a priori*" both for understanding Being as releasement and for action liberated from the compulsions of *Gestell* (enframing).[91] By resisting the imperative to structure one's life in accordance with the demand for ultimate grounds or final (preapproved) goals, the actor opens the possibility of a mode of action that, strictly speaking, is goalless or unteleological. Such action affirms the free play, spontaneity, and flux of *praxis*—precisely those dimensions crushed by the teleocratic conception. Thus, the "turn beyond metaphysics" indicated by the later Heidegger—a turn that is made manifest "practically" in the "life without why" and "theoretically" in the understanding of Being as releasement—reveals what Schürmann calls "the essence of *praxis*: exchange deprived of a principle."[92] Far from offering evidence of a latent authoritarianism, Heidegger's later thought emerges, in Schürmann's reading, as politically *subversive* in the extreme.[93]

Richard Bernstein has also emphasized the political implications of Heidegger's later thought.[94] However, while he is sensitive to what he sees as the ultimately Socratic concerns of this thought (with *ethos* and "dwelling"), his assessment of the "ethical-political consequences" of Heidegger's later thought is a good deal less sanguine than Schürmann's. Extending his critique of the Heideggerian attack on "metaphysical humanism," Bernstein attempts to show how Heidegger's silence on the Extermination of the Jews is a "necessary consequence" of his view of the essence of technology as *Gestell*.[95] Heidegger's description of the technological mode of revealing as the "supreme danger" that "drives out every other possibility of revealing" denigrates *praxis* as a possible response to *Gestell*, identifying the possible "upsurgence of the saving power" exclusively with the attainment of a meditative relation to the essence of technology *qua* revealing.[96] This exclusive focus on the need to meditatively preserve man's disclosive essence in the face of *Gestell* helps shape a perspective from which the range of human activity (from *praxis* to fabrication, agriculture to genocide) appears as variations on "enframing."

From Bernstein's perspective, then, Heidegger's thought concerning technology scarcely provides the resources necessary for a genuine rethinking of action. It is, rather, one, if not the central, component in the "oblivion of *praxis*" performed by Heidegger's post-*Kehre* thought. The silence concerning action promoted by this discourse, moreover, is seen as directly linked to Heidegger's silence concerning the fate of the Jews: it is the *manner* of Heidegger's "questioning concerning technology" that, Bernstein argues, explains both silences. The reason Heidegger conflates "the manufacturing of corpses in gas chambers and extermination camps" with such phenomena as the "motorized food industry" and the "manufacture of hydrogen bombs" is also the reason why he reduces *praxis* to technicity and the will to will. In both instances, Heidegger's only concern is to reveal the *essence* of technology. From *this* angle, the differences between types of human activity, as well as between the Extermination and the transformation of agriculture, fade away. Indeed, as Bernstein notes, "the manufacturing of corpses in gas chambers more fully reveals [from Heidegger's perspective] the essence of technology."[97] Such is the thrust of Heidegger's thinking—a thinking whose desire to place the critique of technology within the ontological context of *Seinsgeschichte* leads it to reduce, without embarrassment or shame, the Extermination—the *Shoah*—to the status of an *example*.

The diametrically opposed evaluations Schürmann and Bernstein offer on the later Heidegger's thought illustrate the difficulty—and the stakes—of assessing the proportion of his blindness and insight. Insofar as Bernstein responds to Heidegger's more or less arbitrary "forgetting" of the revelatory or aletheic dimensions of *praxis* by insisting upon the need to preserve the distinction between *praxis* and *poiēsis*, I think he (like Taminiaux) is on the right track.[98] Indeed, there is no compelling reason why the contrast between technological "challenging-forth" and poetic "bringing-forth" should be regarded as exhaustive or ultimate. However, I think Bernstein goes astray when he suggests that Heidegger's silence on the Extermination reduces to more pervasive "silences" concerning *phronēsis* and *praxis*. Conflating these two silences—tracing them back to the same source—allows Bernstein to attack, once again, what he sees as the totalizing or reductive nature of Heidegger's category of the "technical interpretation of action." This category subsumes all human activity, with the exception of meditative thinking and poetic dwelling. The Habermasian point Bernstein wishes to press is that *praxis*, or communicative action, stands, *by its very nature*, in opposition to *Gestell*. Had Heidegger been more sensitive to this tension, Bernstein argues, he would have been less quick to see the "will to will" behind *all* action; moreover, he would have been less Olympian in his contempt for the realm of human affairs, and less indifferent to its victims.[99]

This schematization is far too simple. The lesson of Heidegger's later discourse on *technē* for the thinking of action is *not* that all human activity reduces to *Gestell*; it is, rather, that *praxis* and *phronēsis* (action and what Habermas calls "communicative rationality") are not exempt from the dynamics of the "ordering-revealing" that holds sway in modernity. What Heidegger's questioning concerning technology can help us to see is how *praxis* is always endangered by this ordering, even where "communicative action" has been preserved from the more blatant forms of technocratic usurpation. The analyses of Arendt, Foucault, and Lyotard have, I take it, all served to sharpen our appreciation of this point: the normalization of subjects and the denaturing of action are not phenomena limited to the extension of subsystems of purposive rationality.[100] To be sure, the growth of what Weber called the "iron cage" is a not insignificant part of *Gestell*, but it fails to illuminate the rise of the social, the extension of disciplinary techniques, and the "terroristic" effects of a consensus-driven politics. Moreover, the fact that Heidegger (in *QCT*, *LH*, and elsewhere) focuses our attention on the more subterranean deformations of *praxis* in the technological age by no means compels us to conclude with him that action per se is futile or that the only *genuine* action is thinking or poetic dwelling.[101]

Thus, while Heidegger's silence on the Extermination rightly leads us to question the adequacy of his later philosophy for rethinking action, we need to guard against the suggestion that he simply suspends the discussion. How, then, do we characterize the inadequacy of this reflection, if not as a "necessary consequence" of a "monolithic" conception of technology?

It is desirable, I think, to steer a middle course between Schürmann and Bernstein on this issue. I agree with Schürmann that the later Heidegger radicalizes the question of action by interrogating the metaphysical construction of *praxis*; but I also agree with Bernstein that the discourse on technology proves insufficient, finally, for a genuine rethinking of action. I view this inadequacy not as the result of the reductive or totalizing nature of Heidegger's notion of *Gestell*, but rather as a consequence of the fact that the later discourse on *technē* remains totally inscribed within the broad project of rehabilitating *poiēsis*. The link between the Heidegger of the fifties and the Heidegger of the thirties is to be found in his unwavering conviction that poetic modes of disclosure possess the capacity to liberate us from the technonihilism of the will-to-will. To be sure, the *content* of "poetic revealing" undergoes a sea change: the emphasis upon "violent co-creation" so typical of the earlier attempt gives way to the notion of "co-responsibility" and letting be. The crucial point, however, is that the later Heidegger does not abandon the general project of rehabilitating *poiēsis*; rather, he explicitly sets out a second, posthumanist version of this project. This can be seen by returning, briefly, to QCT.

As noted above, "The Question concerning Technology" and the "Letter on Humanism" mark Heidegger's repudiation of his earlier (aestheticist) rehabilitation of *poiēsis*. The later discourse on *technē* frames the earlier as willful, as technological-metaphysical. The attempt to think the essence of technology, however, hardly signals a break with the *topos* of poetic revealing. Indeed, as Bernstein notes, the entire rhetorical construction of QCT is based upon the contrast Heidegger draws between the "bringing-forth" mode of revealing manifest in the Greek experience of *poiēsis* and the "challenging-forth" revealing characteristic of modern technology.[102]

Poiēsis, however, is not resurrected merely as a contrasting pole to *Gestell*. In QCT it clearly figures as a normative—more primordial or authentic—model of unconcealment. Thus, the worst thing Heidegger can bring himself to say about the mode of revealing found in technology is that it "blocks *poiēsis*": "where this ordering holds sway, it drives out every other possibility of revealing. Above all, enframing conceals that revealing which, in the sense of *poiēsis*, lets what presences come forth into appearance."[103] Whereas the "bringing-forth" of poetic revealing is permeated by a sense of its co-responsibility in bringing things to presence, the "challenging-forth" of enframing conceals the fact of revealing as such: the presencing of the real is covered over by the wish to regulate and secure. Thus, as Bernstein notes, "the supreme danger of *Gestell* is that it conceals revealing itself."[104] This concealment sets the stage for a radical forgetting of man's essence as disclosive being, and thus for a "precipitous fall."

Heidegger, of course, does not leave matters here; rather, he focuses upon what he calls the "ambiguous essence" of technology in order to show that even *this* revealing is a "granting," one that harbors within itself "the possible upsurgence of the saving power."[105] Heidegger implies that, by giving up the metaphysical/anthropocentric interpretation of technology as a neutral instrument, it becomes possible to achieve a meditative relationship to the essence of technology. Through such a meditative reorientation, we begin to see that "challenging-forth" and "bringing-forth," though fundamentally different, are nevertheless related.[106] For *our* mode of revealing in fact has its roots in the Greek notion of *technē*, which, according to Heidegger, meant "a bringing forth of the beautiful": "Once there was a time when the bringing-forth of the true into the beautiful was called *technē*."[107] The essence of enframing, or *Gestell*, thus points us—both despite and because of it "blocking" character—to the "more primally granted revealing" of *poiēsis* and *technē*. Which is to say that the thoughtful appropriation of *Gestell* points to a possible return to "poetic dwelling."[108]

The remarkable thing about this argument, as Bernstein emphasizes, is the way it frames *poiēsis* and art (*technē*) as the only possible alternatives to *Gestell*: it "excludes and conceals the possible response of *phronēsis* and *praxis*."[109] Bernstein would have us see this exclusion as a *necessary consequence* of Heidegger's concept of technology. What I want to suggest, however, is that there is no *necessity* here: the notion of *Gestell*, in and of itself, does not simply efface *praxis*. The fact that Heidegger limits us to the choice between *poiēsis* and enframing is itself a matter of choice and emphasis. It is determined, in large part, by Heidegger's *decision* to pursue the rehabilitation of *poiēsis* after the *Kehre*. This decision not only shapes the entire later discourse on *technē*, but it accounts for the otherwise arbitrary restriction of Heidegger's consideration of alternatives to *Gestell*. Heidegger's decision to pursue one avenue—namely, the rehabilitation of *poiēsis* as a way out of technonihilism—is "necessary" *only* in the sense that Heidegger was "always already" predisposed to think of revealing as *poiēsis* or *technē*. This predisposition can be seen as a "necessary consequence" of his subservience to the productionist ontological prejudices of the Greeks—a subservience that accounts, in no small measure, for the vast differences between his project and Arendt's.[110]

There are two ways of viewing this attempt to come to terms with metaphysics and technology through *poiēsis*. The first, suggested by Schürmann's account, is to see Heidegger's second attempt at rehabilitation as *successful*, as clearing the way for a genuine rethinking of action. The second is to see this return to the project of rehabilitation as evidence of his continued investment in the productionist paradigm.[111] Thus, Bernasconi and Taminiaux take great pains to show, contra Bernstein, how Heidegger does not *simply* ignore or efface the *praxis/poiēsis* distinction; rather, it provides a constant background for his evolving thought. But they also demonstrate how Heidegger, while uncovering the predominance of production in metaphysical thought, nevertheless continues to follow the lead of the Greeks by himself privileging *poiēsis*. As Bernasconi puts it: "Having recognized the decisive role of *poiēsis* within metaphysics, Heidegger does not turn his back on it, but attempts to come to terms with metaphysics *through poiēsis*."[112]

The conclusion that follows from Bernasconi's and Taminiaux's analyses is that Heidegger's deconstruction of the *metaphysical* articulation of the distinction between *praxis* and *poiēsis* is *insufficiently radical*. His destruction of the history of ontology, while thematizing and problematizing the tradition's naive reliance upon the notion of presence derived from the production experience, nevertheless has as its goal a return to the phenomenal bases of Greek ontology *in that experience*. Hence the "immanent" character of this "destruction," as noted by Bernasconi. In contrast, Arendt's phenomenology of action and the public realm effects what Taminiaux calls "a destruction of metaphysics *more* radical than that of fundamental ontology."[113] Arendt "places Heidegger and Plato back to back," and questions "the phenomenological pertinence of the Greeks' [philosophical] analysis of the *vita activa* (in which human affairs arise altogether from *poiēsis*)."[114]

In the present context, the province of these remarks by Taminiaux can be extended: the later Heidegger's sublimation of *praxis* follows not from the logic of *Gestell* or from theoretical antihumanism alone, but rather—at a deeper level—from his lifelong faithfulness to the experience of Being/presence embedded in Greek ontology. If we wish to be clear about the nature of Heidegger's "blind spot" concerning action and human affairs, we would do well to ponder the root of his propensity to think of disclosure or unconcealment along poetic lines of one sort or another. Doing so enables a more nuanced appreciation of the way Heidegger's later discourse on *technē* both opens and closes—radicalizes and obliterates—the discussion concerning action.

Three important facts emerge when we see the later discourse on *technē* as a continuation of the attempt to rehabilitate *poiēsis*. First, this perspective on the later Heidegger's thought reveals the extent to which Arendt's project remains *irreducible* to Heidegger's. In this regard, Taminiaux is absolutely right to take issue with those (for example, Luc Ferry) who would dismiss Arendt as a mere "disciple" of Heidegger's.[115] The phenomenology of action displaces the *topos* of disclosure in a way that Heidegger, given his philosophical/productionist prejudices, would never have contemplated.

Second, the thematization of Heidegger's "Greek" ontological prejudices helps us to see how a reading like Schürmann's depends not only upon a novel "theory of texts" (that is, reading Heidegger from "back" to "front," late to early), but also upon the availability of Arendt's theory of action. Heidegger's later discourse on *technē*—and his later thinking generally—*can* be seen as holding adequate resources for the rethinking of action, but, I would contend, only after one had digested the antiteleological implications of *Arendt's* theory of action. Reading the later Heidegger, as it were, through the lens of Arendt is a precondition for the emergence of "action without a principle" from his text.[116]

Third, and most significant from the point of view of the argument I have been making, the critical perspective on the later Heidegger suggested by Taminiaux and Bernasconi enables us to grasp the full significance of Arendt's problematic insistence upon the self-containedness of *praxis*. This insistence, of course, has been the source of much misunderstanding, and it figures as the chief stumbling block to the assimilation of her theory of political action. From the point of view of many critics, it appears as arbitrary, formalist, even reactionary. Such judgments are to be expected so long as the *context* for this insistence is forgotten. However, once we locate Arendt's insistence upon the self-containedness of *praxis* not only in terms of a tradition of political philosophy that has accepted the translation of acting into the idiom of making as *foundational*, but also in terms of an originary privileging of *poiēsis* over *praxis* in the ontological preunderstanding of Greek metaphysics, her "willfulness" becomes more comprehensible. Reversing the predominance of *poiēsis* over *praxis*, a predominance installed at the very deepest levels of the Western tradition, is no small task. The fact that the chief "overcomers" of the tradition, Nietzsche and Heidegger, also read action back into *poiēsis* testifies to the need for an unbending resolve on the question of action's *distinctness*.

With regard to this last point, I have argued—against Habermas and Bernstein—that a simple reassertion of the Aristotelian distinction between acting and making hardly avoids the same "productionist" trap. As Bernasconi notes, "simply to ignore the distinction between *praxis* and *poiēsis* is to succumb to the metaphysical dominance of *poiēsis*. But to insist upon *praxis* in contradistinction to *poiēsis* is still to remain in the orbit of metaphysics."[117] The distinction that our tradition of political philosophy does its best to efface (through the substitution of making for acting) is itself drawn within a broadly technical (teleological) understanding of action.[118] Arendt's idiosyncratic theory of action "goes through" Nietzsche and Heidegger in the manner I have described in order to reach a place from which action can be thought *qua* action—which is to say, a place apart from the alien metaphorics imposed upon it by philosophical conceptualization. This "place" is *not* a return to the political philosophy of Aristotle.[119] One arrives at it, instead, only via the overcoming of the tradition performed by the Nietzschean/ Heideggerian critique of metaphysics.

As I argued in Chapters 2 and 3, it is the necessity of escaping these alien metaphorics that leads Arendt to "aestheticize" action by appealing to its performative character. However, we must be very precise here: Arendt's "aestheticization" of action, while paralleling the Nietzschean attack on Platonism, stands *diametrically opposed* to the kind of aestheticization of the political performed by the central trope of the *Republic* and reiterated in Nietzsche and Heidegger's appeal to the state as artwork. The *difference* between Arendt's "aesthetic" approach to action (viewing action in its self-containedness) and the tradition's aestheticization of politics (which links Platonism's appeal to Truth to National Socialism's appeal to myth) is the difference between action viewed as openended, nonviolent performance in a context of plurality and action viewed as a kind of plastic art. As Arendt puts it in "What Is Freedom?" politics is "the exact opposite of an art," if by "art" one has in mind the plastic art of making.[120]

The critical perspective I have proposed on Heidegger's later discourse on *technē* has, I think, one additional virtue: it enables us to distinguish Arendt's "pearl fishing" from Heidegger's "destruction" and "repetition." The latter, to borrow Theodor Adorno's phrase, accompanies metaphysics in the moment of its fall. Its sine qua non is the thesis concerning the closure of metaphysical rationality, which at once makes possible the delimitation of an "epoch" of metaphysics and prevents escape to anything like a "beyond" of metaphysics.[121]

Arendt's critique of the tradition takes its bearings from Heidegger's deconstruction, and from the thesis of closure that informs it. Her argument in "Tradition and the Modern Age" (in *Between Past and Future*) is that our tradition has played out its structural possibilities and lies in ruins; nevertheless, these ruins exercise a persistent hold on our thinking. Her "phenomenology of action," on the other hand, takes as its point of departure that which precedes and exceeds this closure: the "miracle" of spontaneous initiatory action. In Arendt, the notion of "natality" stands for that which perpetually escapes even the most reified order of presence. And, in fact, it is this focus upon a pervasive initiatory power that enables her to distance herself from the history of substantialist metaphysics in a way that would have been unthinkable for Heidegger. His attempt to think the radically new remains circumscribed by the possibilities opened by poiēsis and Seinsgeschichte (the history of Being).[122] This is not to say that Arendt, in "retrieving" that which precedes and exceeds metaphysics, falls into the familiar trap of positing a "beyond" of metaphysics, a realm of pure spontaneity untainted by the conceptualizations instituted by the tradition. Rather, what I am suggesting is that her view of history, ultimately, has more in common with Walter Benjamin's "fragmentary history" than with Seinsgeschichte. It is the spirit of Benjamin, not Heidegger, that informs her search for hidden treasures—moments of pure initiatory action—covered in wreckage by the "angel of history."

What allows us, at the end of the day, to juxtapose Arendt and Benjamin to Seinsgeschichte in this way? It has often been pointed out how Heidegger's linear history of Being comes uncomfortably close to reinscribing the substantialist patterns he seeks to deconstruct.[123] Arendt's critique of the tradition—framed in terms of Plato's "originary" substitution of making for acting—can be said to mirror this dubious linearity. However, we cannot make this critique of her story about the fate of political action itself, for this is a story not of structural possibilities or unfolding inner logics but of moments and events; of spontaneous resistance, revolution, and disobedience; of heroic yet failed causes. It is, in short, a very un-Heideggerian history, in which every moment is "the strait gate through which the Messiah might enter."[124] Such a history repudiates the Hegelian standard of historical success as a criterion of significance; it eschews, moreover, the notion of process that enabled the nineteenth century to locate meaning in history. This repudiation is summed up in one of Arendt's favorite maxims, from Cato, which she was to use as the epigraph to the never completed third volume of The Life of the Mind (on judging): "The victorious cause pleased the gods, but the defeated one pleases Cato."[125]

From Arendt's perspective, as Bernstein suggests, praxis, rather than poetic bringing-forth, emerges as "the saving power." But what marks it as such power is not, as Bernstein would have it, that it represents a clear and accessible alternative to Gestell. Arendt asks much of political action, yet she does not presuppose a world easily divided into spheres of technical and communicative rationality. For her, the "ordering revealing" is a primary and irreducible fact of our existence. Yet even the all-encompassing force of this revealing cannot extinguish the moments of initiatory action that occur at its interstices.

V. HEIDEGGER, ARENDT, AND THE QUESTION OF "FAITH" IN HUMAN ACTION

Many readers of Arendt have noted her hostility toward philosophies of history, toward determining "inner logics" in the manner of Hegel or of Heidegger at his worst or most careless. Arendt's hostility, these readers point out, flows from a strong faith in the possibilities of human action, a faith at odds with the contemplative stance of philosophy (e.g., Hegel's) and the quiescence—the "will not to will"—of the later Heidegger. The contrast between Arendt and Heidegger in this regard is indeed striking. However, it is extremely important not to reduce the later Heidegger's suspicion of action to a self-effacing *fatalism*. As Bernstein emphasizes, critics like Wolin and Habermas are simply *wrong* on this score: destining is *not* fate; it is a "starting upon a way" that holds open alternative responses.[126] Heidegger's suspicion concerning action can be traced, as I have suggested, to a certain Platonic (philosophical) bias. But two additional factors—neither reducible to fatalism—also inform this suspicion. They are (1) Heidegger's own previous overestimation of the potentialities of human action (thought as *poiēsis*, as violent cocreating); and (2) the depth and world-historical sweep of *Gestell*.

The role played by the first factor has been widely noted—not only by Arendt, but by critics as disparate as Habermas and Lacoue-Labarthe. With regard to the second factor, I should like to suggest, contra Bernstein and other critics, that wherever Heidegger's conception of the essence of technology as an "ordering revealing" is seriously attended to, the thesis that human action is unlikely to liberate us from this revealing is not particularly controversial. Indeed, the correctness of Heidegger's characterization of our "destiny" is attested to by those critical projects devoted to slowing the colonization of the lifeworld by the system (Habermas) or resisting the further penetration of disciplinary technologies into everyday life (Foucault). To be sure, these projects, unlike Heidegger's, take an activist stance; but neither questions the validity of the Heideggerian thesis that, within enframing, everything that is appears as standing reserve.

The reason why Heidegger does not think that human action can "directly confront the danger of *Gestell*" is, simply, that a new economy of presence is not something brought about by human intention, effort, and will. Heidegger's appeal to thinking as the "only genuine action" displays his Platonic bias; however, it also alerts us to the fact that all attempts to "directly confront" the danger of *Gestell* take the shape of projects to reestablish *control* over the regime of instrumentalization that has seized us. From Marx to Habermas, the hope has been to place human creations back under the will of their authors, and so to curtail the process of reification by which means become ends.[127] Heidegger, like Weber, is skeptical of the naive Prometheanism at the heart of this vision; he believes that the attempt to assert control will, ironically, produce more of the same.[128] Where Habermas urges that the Weberian "negative dialectic" of modernity fails to adequately distinguish between system and communicative rationalization, Heidegger injects a skeptical note concerning the "saving power" of this difference. The legacy of Heidegger's "questioning concerning technology," taken up by postmodern critics, has been to subject the self-evidence of this distinction to renewed interrogation. Is it really the case that discursive rationalization is formed in an essential tension with system rationalization? Might not the former impose its own regime of "regulating and securing," of ordering through exclusion, homologous to the latter? Such questions, most sharply put by Lyotard, lead us to wonder whether other strategies of "direct confrontation" with *Gestell* might not be recuperated in equally insidious ways.

Insofar as Heidegger's questioning concerning technology tends to "seduce" us into believing that "no mere action can change the world," Bernstein is right to urge us to resist it. But once we stop reading this questioning as a withdrawal into fatalism, the Arendtian faith in action so often opposed to it takes on a different cast. Clearly, her "activism" is not grounded in a humanism of the Marxian sort: she does not view action as a vehicle through which man might regain control and assume, once again, his rightful place as "lord of beings." The exclusion of this misreading, however, has led some to view the Arendtian faith in action as essentially *religious*: a "natality" posited by faith is seen as the guarantee that humanity will survive the world and action-undermining forces unleashed by modernity. Increasingly—and, I think, unfortunately—Arendt has been read along these lines.[129] I believe, however, that there is another way of viewing her faith in action, one that avoids both the reiteration of Enlightenment clichés and the appeal to an amorphous religiosity.[130]

Arendt was profoundly pessimistic about the prospects for a genuine public sphere in our time. Our epoch is one in which "Heidegger's perverse sounding statement" that "the light of the public obscures everything" goes, in fact, "to the heart of the matter."[131] Indeed, from the standpoint of her critique of modernity, action in the strict sense is no longer possible. Those who see her analysis of totalitarianism as implying that liberal democracy or "republican government" are adequate responses to the world-destroying forces of modernity would do well to consider the following words of warning from "Ideology and Terror" (in *The Origins of Totalitarianism*): "It may even be that the true predicaments of our time will assume their authentic form—though not necessarily the cruelest—only when totalitarianism has become a thing of the past."[132] There is in Arendt's thought none of the confidence of Heidegger's recent critics, a confidence in the resources of liberal democracy to deal with the advent of an increasingly technological world (in this regard, it is possible, as Schürmann points out, to read the doubts Heidegger expresses in the *Spiegel* interview about whether democracy can be "adequately coordinated with the technological age" as indicative of something other than authoritarianism).[133] Of course, Arendt was committed to constitutional government in a way that Heidegger, the philosopher and cultural conservative, never was. However, this commitment did not stop her from worrying about liberalism's complicity in the instrumentalization of politics, the closure of a public space for action, and the creation of an increasingly undemocratic world. If anything, her commitment stimulated her anxiety.

We should not be surprised, then, that Arendt makes no attempt to escape "the true predicaments of our time" by appealing to platitudes concerning reason, will, and the institutions of representative democracy.[134] Alive to the dangers of a posttotalitarian, technological world in a way many recent converts to liberalism are not, she stressed the profound and irrevocable consequences of the public realm's loss of reality. This loss is wrought by the emerging structure of modernity itself (the "rise of the social"), and it makes any direct appeal to *praxis*, or "the public sphere," infinitely problematic, if not downright ironic. It is precisely the impossibility of a genuine public sphere in postmodernity (the impossibility, as

Lyotard notes, of a *sensus communis*) that leads Arendt to stress agonism over consensus, resistance over docility, and the "defeated causes" of the "revolutionary spirit" over the normalizing politics of representative democracy. Her point as a critic of liberalism (and modernity) is similar to Foucault's: it is not that everything is bad, but that everything is dangerous. This includes those modern political innovations for which she—and we—are necessarily grateful. Arendt's theoretical work demonstrates how the champion of the *bios politikos* must also refuse the "blackmail of Enlightenment."[135]

We must not, then, view Arendt's "faith in action" as the legacy of Rousseau or of Kant in the second *Critique*; nor should we see it as a semireligious worship of the human capacity for initiation. Least of all does it flow from an obstinate, peculiarly German, nostalgia for Greece. Those readers who see her using the *polis* as a "stick to beat modernity with" stay at the surface of her thought. By focusing our attention on the nature and conditions of political action before the "traditional substitution of making for acting" took hold, Arendt keeps alive an appreciation of the spontaneous, plural, doxastic, and agonistic dimensions of politics. Her "faith in action" does not rest on the futile desire to resurrect the *agora* in contemporary society; rather, it reflects a continuing wonder at the fact that political action persists in the various "defeated causes" our political historians relegate to the dustbin of history. Public spaces continue to be "cleared," and "islands" of freedom continue to pop up, only to submerge once again. For some, this state of affairs may be a source of untempered regret; for Hannah Arendt, however, it signifies both loss *and* hope.

INTRODUCTION

1. See, among others, George Kateb, *Hannah Arendt: Politics, Conscience, Evil*, p. 39; N. K. O'Sullivan, "Hannah Arendt: Hellenic Nostalgia and Industrial Society"; Hanna Pitkin, "Justice: On Relating Private and Public"; Mildred Bakan, "Hannah Arendt's Concepts of Labor and Work," in Melvyn Hill, ed., *Hannah Arendt: The Recovery of the Public World*, p. 59.

2. Jürgen Habermas, "Hannah Arendt: On the Concept of Power," in *Philosophical-Political Profiles*, p. 174.

3. Friedrich Nietzsche, *The Gay Science*, Section 228.

4. See Sheldon Wolin, *Politics and Vision*, and Benjamin Barber, *Strong Democracy*. The influence of Arendt is strongly felt in both books; e.g., Barber's focus on political action as "the ultimate political problem," p. 121ff.

5. Hannah Arendt, *The Human Condition*, chapter 2 (hereafter cited as HC); Aristotle, *The Politics*, books III and VII.

6. Barber, *Strong Democracy*, pp. 2, 13.

7. Ibid., p. 120.

8. See Jürgen Habermas, *Theory and Practice*, and *The Theory of Communicative Action*; Seyla Benhabib, *Critique, Norm, and Utopia*; Richard Bernstein, *Beyond Objectivism and Relativism*, part four.

9. Theodor Adorno and Max Horkheimer, "The Concept of Enlightenment," in *Dialectic of Enlightenment*.

10. Habermas's most recent articulation of this position can be found in his *Philosophical Discourse of Modernity*, chapters 11 and 12.

11. Ibid., chapter 11.

12. Habermas, "Hannah Arendt," in *Philosophical-Political Profiles*, and *Theory and Practice*, pp. 42, 286. Benhabib is particularly good at drawing out the indebtedness of Habermas to Arendt's distinctions and her concept of plurality. See Benhabib, *Critique, Norm, and Utopia*, pp. 243–245.

13. For Habermas's initial formulation of this distinction, see "Science and Technology as Ideology," in *Toward a Rational Society*, p. 96.

14. Habermas, "Hannah Arendt," pp. 174–175.

15. See Michael Sandel, *Liberalism and the Limits of Justice*; Charles Taylor, "Cross-Purposes: The Liberal-Communitarian Debate"; Alasdair MacIntyre, *After Virtue*.

16. Michael Sandel, "The Procedural Republic and the Unencumbered Self," in *Political Theory*, p. 82.

17. Ibid., p. 91.

18. Ibid., p. 89.

19. Sandel, *Liberalism*, p. 183.

20. Arendt, HC, pp. 200–201; also "Ideology and Terror," in *The Origins of Totalitarianism*, p. 474; and, finally, "On Violence," in *Crises of the Republic*, pp. 142–143 (hereafter cited as CR).

21. See the analysis of legality in Arendt, "Ideology and Terror," in *Origins of Totalitarianism*, p. 465, and the critique of constitutionalism in Arendt, *On Revolution*, chapter 3 (hereafter cited as OR).

22. Sandel, *Liberalism*, p. 183.

23. Hannah Arendt, Preface to *Between Past and Future*, p. 7 (hereafter cited as *BPF*).

24. S. Wolin, *Politics and Vision*, p. v.

25. Ernst Vollrath, "Hannah Arendt and the Method of Political Thinking," p. 163.

26. Arendt, Preface, *BPF*, p. 14. See also "Tradition and the Modern Age," in the same volume, p. 28, and Stan Draenos's essay, "Thinking without a Ground: Hannah Arendt and the Contemporary Situation of Understanding," in Hill, ed., 1979.

27. Arendt, "Tradition and the Modern Age," in *BPF*, p. 26.

28. Ibid., p. 15.

29. Walter Benjamin, "Theses on the Philosophy of History," in *Illuminations*, p. 261.

30. Hannah Arendt, *Men in Dark Times*, pp. 193, 197, 199 (hereafter cited as *MDT*).

31. Ibid., pp. 205–206.

32. Ibid., "Walter Benjamin," p. 201.

33. Martin Heidegger, *Being and Time*, pp. 41–49 (hereafter cited as *BT*).

34. Ibid., p. 43.

35. Friedrich Nietzsche, *The Use and Abuse of History*, p. 40 (translation altered).

36. Arendt, Preface to *BPF*.

37. Ibid.

38. Arendt, *MDT*, pp. 201, 205.

39. Rootlessness is a persistant theme in Arendt, as Kateb points out in chapter 5 of his *Hannah Arendt*. See in particular Arendt, part VI of *HC*, and "Ideology and Terror," in *The Origins of Totalitarianism*, in which the connection between rootlessness and totalitarianism is directly made.

40. Arendt, "Ideology and Terror," p. 475.

41. Kateb, *Hannah Arendt*, p. 7.

42. This phrase is borrowed from Kateb.

43. Arendt, OR, p. 281.

44. This phrase is borrowed from Stephen K. White's fine piece, "Heidegger and the Difficulties of a Postmodern Ethics and Politics," p. 85.

45. See especially the objections raised by Arendt's interlocutors at a conference devoted to her work in Toronto, 1972, excerpts of which are contained in Hill, ed., pp. 301–339.

46. Habermas, "Hannah Arendt," in *Philosophical-Political Profiles*, pp. 178–179.

47. Philippe Lacoue-Labarthe and Jean-Luc Nancy, *Le Retrait du Politique*. For a discussion of the importance of this theme to contemporary French thought, see Nancy Fraser, "The French Derrideans: Politicizing Deconstruction or Deconstructing the Political," in *Unruly Practices*.

48. For the notion of "an-archic" action, of action ungrounded by first principles, see Reiner Schürmann, *Heidegger on Being and Acting: From Principles to Anarchy*, Introduction and pp. 82–93. See also White's discussion in "Heidegger and the Difficulties of a Postmodern Ethics and Politics."

49. The "revolutionary conservative" charge is made by Pierre Bourdieu in *The Political Ontology of Martin Heidegger*, and by Luc Ferry and Alain Renaut in *Heidegger and Modernity*, chapter 2. It is reiterated at length by Richard Wolin in *The Politics of Being: The Political Thought of Martin Heidegger*, chapters 1–3. For a good discussion of the intellectual background to this interpretation, particularly Heidegger's debt to Ernst Jünger, see Michael E. Zimmerman, *Heidegger's Confrontation with Modernity*.

50. Schürmann and Lacoue-Labarthe have emphasized the ambition of Arendt's project in this regard. See Reiner Schürmann, *Heidegger on Being and Acting*, and Philippe Lacoue-Labarthe, *Heidegger, Art and Politics*.

CHAPTER 1

1. Arendt, *HC*, p. 17; also p. 85.
2. Ibid.; cf. Arendt, "Tradition and the Modern Age," in *BPF*.
3. Arendt, *HC*, p. 86.
4. Ibid., pp. 4–5, 321.
5. Habermas, Bernstein, Bakan, and numerous others criticize Arendt on this score.
6. Aristotle, *The Politics*, I.2, p. 28.
7. Arendt, *HC*, p. 30; also *BPF*, p. 116.
8. Aristotle, *Politics*, I.3, p. 30.
9. Ibid., I.1, III.9; also Aristotle, *Nicomachean Ethics*, I.7, 1098a.
10. Aristotle, *Politics*, I.2, p. 28.
11. Ibid.
12. Ibid.
13. Aristotle, *Physics*, in *Basic Works of Aristotle*, VIII.7.
14. Aristotle, *Politics*, I.2, p. 29; also *Ethics*, VIII.8, 116a, 25.
15. Arendt, *HC*, chapter 2.
16. Ibid., p. 30.
17. Ibid., pp. 30–31; also Arendt, *BPF*, pp. 116–117.
18. Arendt, *HC*, p. 37.
19. Ibid., p. 28; also Chapter 2, Section VI.
20. Ibid., p. 47.
21. Ibid., p. 28.
22. Ibid., p. 40.
23. Ibid., p. 6.
24. Habermas is particularly adamant on this score. See Chapter 1, Section III, of this book.
25. Aristotle, *Politics*, I.2, p. 28.
26. My opting for "self-containedness" will become clear when, in Chapters 2 and 3, I examine the aesthetic dimension of Arendt's theory of action.
27. Aristotle, *Ethics*, 1097a.
28. Ibid., 1097b.
29. Ibid., 1094a.
30. See, for example, Aristotle, *Ethics*, X.6 and X.7. In *Physics*, Aristotle cites sense activity (e.g., seeing) as a kind of activity that contains its own end.
31. Aristotle, *Ethics*, 1140b.
32. Ibid., 1098a; also 1139b.
33. Ibid., 1139b.
34. Ibid., 1140b.
35. Ibid., 1140a.
36. Aristotle, *Politics*, I.4, p. 32; cf. VII.14, pp. 287–288, for his distinction between those activities that have moral worth and those that, while necessary, do not.
37. Aristotle, *Ethics*, 1099a.
38. Aristotle, *Politics*, III.5 and VII.9. Cf. also Arendt's note, in Arendt, *HC*, p. 82.
39. Arendt, *HC*, p. 207.
40. Arendt, *BPF*, pp. 215–216.
41. Arendt, *HC*, pp. 305, 153–154.
42. Ibid., p. 156.
43. Ibid., p. 154.

44. Ibid., p. 305.

45. Ibid., p. 154.

46. Ibid.

47. Arendt, *BPF*, p. 217.

48. Arendt, *HC*, p. 45.

49. Ibid.

50. Ibid., p. 46.

51. Ibid., p. 47.

52. Ibid., p. 40.

53. Ibid.

54. Ibid.

55. Ibid.

56. Ibid., p. 46.

57. Ibid.

58. See Bhikhu Parekh, "Hannah Arendt's Critique of Marx," in Hill, ed., p. 72.

59. Arendt, *HC*, p. 84.

60. See, most famously, the description of the self-formation of the human species through work in the 1844 *Manuscripts* (spelled out most specifically in the section entitled "Critique of the Hegelian Dialectic and Philosophy as a Whole"), in Karl Marx and Friedrich Engels, *The Marx-Engels Reader*, p. 112.

61. Arendt, *HC*, p. 99 (note 34).

62. Ibid.

63. Ibid., p. 87.

64. Ibid., p. 98.

65. Ibid., p. 88.

66. Ibid., p. 79.

67. Ibid., p. 143.

68. Ibid.

69. Ibid., pp. 143–144.

70. Aristotle, *Ethics*, 1140a.

71. Arendt, *HC*, p. 139.

72. Ibid., p. 134.

73. G.W.F. Hegel, Introduction to *The Philosophy of Right*, p. 20.

74. Arendt, *HC*, p. 137.

75. Ibid., p. 143.

76. Ibid., p. 206.

77. Ibid., p. 176.

78. Aristotle, *Politics*, books I and III.

79. This is a basic theme in Arendt's political theory, one made much of by Habermas and others for whom the distinction between communicative and strategic action is paramount. For its classic formulation, see Arendt, "On Violence," in *CR*, p. 142ff. She cites Weber's famous definition of the state on p. 134.

80. Cf. Arendt's remarks on tyranny, *HC*, pp. 202–203.

81. Arendt, *OR*, pp. 29–35.

82. Ibid., p. 249ff; also pp. 256–257.

83. *Ibid.*, p. 60.

84. Ibid.

85. Hence Arendt's distinction between "freedom" and "liberation." Cf. Arendt, *OR*, p. 29. Also Arendt, *BPF*, p. 148.

86. Arendt, OR, chapter 2, section 2. See Marx's famous formulation from volume 3 of *Capital*, in Marx and Engels, *The Marx-Engels Reader*, pp. 439–441.

87. The parallel between Arendt's analysis and Hegel's critique of the French Revolution is striking. Both think that striving to achieve "universal" (as opposed to political) freedom accomplishes but "one work and deed," death. Social revolution is not the essence of politics and political action, but its abstract negation: action and speech are deprived of all significance by the "most cold-blooded and meaningless death of all," the catastrophic, undiscriminating violence of political terror. See the section entitled "Absolute Freedom and Terror," in G.W.F. Hegel, *Phenomenology of Spirit*.

88. Max Weber, "Politics as a Vocation," in *From Max Weber*, p. 80–88.

89. Arendt, OR, p. 272.

90. Arendt, BPF, p. 155.

91. Arendt, OR, p. 268.

92. Ibid., p. 269.

93. Ibid., p. 272.

94. Ibid., p. 237.

95. Ibid., p. 269.

96. See Arendt, HC, pp. 154–155.

97. Aristotle, *Politics*, I.2, pp. 28–29.

98. Arendt, HC, p. 3.

99. Arendt, "On Humanity in Dark Times," in *MDT*, p. 24.

100. Arendt, HC, pp. 26–27. Cf. OR, p. 35.

101. Arendt, HC, p. 27.

102. Ibid., p. 207.

103. Arendt, OR, p. 86.

104. Ibid., p. 34.

105. It is not political, because it has become solely concerned with the question of the most efficient *means*.

106. Aristotle, *Ethics*, VI.9, 1142b, 30.

107. Ibid., VI.5, 1140a, 25.

108. Ibid., VI.9, 1142b, 20.

109. Ibid., VI.5, 1140b, 5.

110. Arendt, BPF, p. 241.

111. Arendt, HC pp. 57, 50.

112. Arendt, OR, pp. 31, 124, 246.

113. Arendt, HC, p. 7.

114. Ibid., p. 58.

115. Ibid., p. 7. As with her emphasis on deliberation, Arendt's focus on plurality is, apparently, derived from Aristotle, notably his critique, in book II of *The Politics*, of the "Socratic" idea that "the state should be as much of a unity as possible."

116. Arendt, OR, p. 31.

117. Ibid., p. 237.

118. Arendt, HC, p. 52.

119. Ibid., p. 53.

120. Arendt, MDT, p. 24.

121. Aristotle, *Ethics*, IX.6. Arendt's appeal to a friendship that "is not intimately personal but makes political demands and preserves reference to the world," and that is born of a "community sense" and actualized in debate, rethematizes the distinctive commonality Aristotle attributed to the *polis*. However, as I shall argue in Chapter 3,

Arendt's appeal to the *sensus communis* in fact distinguishes her from Aristotle and the communitarians.

122. Arendt, OR, pp. 275, 279.

123. Ibid., p. 277.

124. Ibid., p. 274.

125. See Aristotle's discussion of distributive justice in Aristotle, *Politics*, III.9 and *Ethics*, V.3.

126. Kateb, *Hannah Arendt*, p. 15.

127. Richard Bernstein, "Judging: The Actor and the Spectator," in *Philosophical Profiles*, pp. 220–232.

128. Beiner, *Political Judgment*; Pitkin, "Justice: On Relating Private and Public."

129. For as good a formulation as any of this criticism, see Richard Bernstein, "Rethinking the Social and the Political," in *Philosophical Profiles*, pp. 238–259.

130. Pitkin, "Justice," p. 336. See Mary McCarthy's comment in Hill, ed., p. 315.

131. Wellmer is quoted in Hill, ed., p. 318.

132. The motive behind this greater consistency will become apparent in Chapter 2, and it will be totally clear only in light of Heidegger's critique of productionist metaphysics. Suffice it to note here that Arendt's paradoxical and occasionally maddening insistence upon "self-contained" *praxis* is intended to break free of the domination of *poiēsis* within the tradition of Western philosophy and political thought. See Chapter 8 of this book.

133. Kateb, *Hannah Arendt*, p. 17.

134. Ibid., p. 16; cf. Margaret Canovan, "Politics as Culture: Hannah Arendt and the Public Realm."

135. Kateb, *Hannah Arendt*, p. 17.

136. Ibid.

137. Ibid.

138. Arendt, CR, p. 142ff. *Power*, according to Arendt, "corresponds to the human ability not just to act, but to act in concert. Power is never the property of an individual; it belongs to a group and remains in existence only so long as the group keeps together." Power is therefore distinct from strength, force, violence, and authority in that it is engendered by "the living together of people," by a community based on the principle of recognition rather than coercion or obedience. It "springs up between men when they act together and vanishes the moment they disperse." It is, finally, that which "keeps the public realm, the potential space of appearance between acting and speaking men, in existence." A constitution, understood as a system of power, is the institutional reification of the formal conditions of this acting together. It is the primary manifestation of the original power born of "sheer human togetherness," the foundation of the edifice in which freedom "finds a home" and becomes a "tangible, worldly reality."

139. Arendt, OR, p. 125.

140. Arendt, HC, p. 199.

141. Arendt, OR, p. 35.

142. Ibid., p. 255ff.

143. For Aristotle's definition of "constitution" in this extended sense, see *Politics*, IV.4 and IV.11.

144. Kateb, *Hannah Arendt*, p. 18.

145. Arendt, CR, pp. 88, 95.

146. Canovan, "Politics as Culture," p. 639.

147. James Knauer, "Motives and Goal in Hannah Arendt's Concept of Political Action," p. 730.

148. Kateb, *Hannah Arendt*, p. 19.

149. Habermas, "Hannah Arendt: On the Concept of Power," in *Philosophical-Political Profiles*, pp.172–173.

150. Ibid., p. 178.

151. James Knauer has mounted a powerful critique against those who would interpret Arendt's concept of action as predicated upon a denial of purposiveness or instrumentality. In Arendt, he points out, the instrumental dimension of action is not so much denied as relegated to a secondary status: action, to be genuine, must not be *essentially* instrumental or strategic in character, but this does not mean it must be devoid of purposiveness. Knauer is certainly correct, at this level of generality; however, the gist of Habermas's critique is not by any means refuted. Within Arendt's conceptual framework, it is simply impossible to see the content of political action as socioeconomic. To be sure, all action has goals, but this acknowledgment on the part of Arendt is not tantamount to the full-scale toleration of socioeconomic content Knauer ascribes to her. Political action, as she conceives it, is not "typically about" socioeconomic issues. Habermas, like Bernstein and Pitkin, is correct to see a structural link between Arendt's notion of a purified *praxis* and the rigorous distinction between the social and the political, the private and the public, the instrumental and the communicative or deliberative.

152. Bernstein, "Rethinking," in *Philosophical Profiles*, p. 249.

153. Martin Jay, "The Political Existentialism of Hannah Arendt," in *Permanent Exiles*, p. 242.

154. As indicated above (note 151), I think Knauer's recuparation of Arendt in this regard is *too* successful.

155. I shall return to this theme in Chapters 2, 3, and 6.

156. Bernstein, "Rethinking," in *Philosophical Profiles*, p. 249.

157. Arendt, HC, p. 182.

158. Ibid., pp. 50, 57.

159. Arendt, quoted in Hill, ed., p. 316.

160. Ibid., p. 318.

CHAPTER 2

1. Arendt, HC. p. 222.

2. Habermas, "Hannah Arendt: On the Concept of Power," in *Philosophical-Political Profiles*, p. 174. In "On the German-Jewish Heritage," in *Telos*, p. 128, Habermas distinguishes between Arendt's *systematic* renewal of the *concept of praxis* and a "philological" renewal of Aristotelian theory per se.

3. Habermas, "Hannah Arendt," p. 173. For a reading that develops this perspective on Arendt, see Bernstein's *Beyond Objectivism and Relativism*, part IV, pp. 207–223.

4. Habermas, "Hannah Arendt," p. 171.

5. Cf. Introduction.

6. Schürmann, *Heidegger*, p. 10. Cf. Habermas's characterization in "On the German-Jewish Heritage," p. 128, where he labels Arendt's project a "reconstruction of an Aristotelian concept of *praxis* for political theory."

7. Arendt, BPF, p. 15; MDT, p. 204.

8. Arendt, BPF, pp. 143–171; HC, chapter 5.

9. Ibid., p. 146.

10. Bernard Yack, *The Longing for Total Revolution*, pp. 71–72. Yack sees this as an inexplicable anachronism on the part of Arendt: she reads the modern idea of freedom back into the classics. Like Habermas, he presumes that Arendt's self-understanding is that of a neo-Aristotelian, albeit one who does not understand Aristotle very well (see Yack, *The Problems of a Political Animal*, for a repetition of this charge).

11. Aristotle, *Politics*, I.1, III.9, and VII.13–15. Cf. *Ethics*, I.9.

12. Arendt, HC, p. 177.

13. Arendt, BPF, p. 151; also HC, pp. 231, 234.

14. Arendt, HC, p. 247. Here Arendt states that the faculty of action is "ontologically rooted" in the "fact" of natality. Cf. HC, p. 9, and BPF, p. 167.

15. Arendt, HC, p. 178.

16. See Ernest Barker's Introduction to his translation of Aristotle's *Politics*, p. lxvii. The best examination of the "paradigm shift" required for "innovation" to take on a more radical connotation remains John Pocock's, in J.G.A. Pocock, *The Machiavellian Moment*; see especially chapters II, III, and VI.

17. Arendt, BPF, pp. 153–154.

18. Ibid., p. 153.

19. See Aristotle, *Ethics*, II.

20. Ibid., II.4, 1105a, 30.

21. The character of the "autonomy" Arendt attributes to action is absolutely crucial for comprehending her project.

22. Aristotle, *Ethics*, 1098a, 15.

23. See Arendt, HC, p. 206.

24. Ibid. Also 1176b.

25. Ibid.

26. Ibid., 1094a.

27. Arendt, HC, p. 207.

28. Aristotle, *Ethics*, I.7.

29. Ibid., 1099b.30. See also Aristotle, *Politics*, III.9.

30. Aristotle, *Ethics*, V.1 and *Politics*, I.1. See Ernest Barker, *The Political Thought of Plato and Aristotle*, p. 322.

31. Aristotle, *Politics*, III.12, p. 128.

32. See Aristotle's discussions of distributive justice in *Ethics*, V, and *Politics*, III.

33. Book VII of Aristotle's *Politics*, on the "ideal" *polis*, drives this point home.

34. W. D. Ross, for example, emphasizes this point. See his *Aristotle*, p. 188. It should be noted that more recent commentators (for example, David Wiggins) have questioned the degree to which a tension actually exists. See Wiggins's essay, "Deliberation and Practical Reason," in *Essays on Aristotle's Ethics*, pp. 221–240.

35. Arendt, LM, vol. 2., p. 15.

36. Arendt, HC, p. 196.

37. Aristotle, *Ethics*, 1168a.

38. Ibid., my emphasis.

39. Arendt, HC, p. 196.

40. Ibid.

41. Ibid.

42. Arendt, LM, vol. 2. p. 62.

43. Ibid. Cf. Aristotle, *Ethics*, 1113a14–15, 1113b3–4.

44. Aristotle, *Politics*, I.2.

45. Cf. Arendt, *OR*, p. 35; *HC*, p. 52.

46. Arendt, *LM*, vol. 2, p. 140.

47. Hegel, quoted in Arendt, *LM*, vol. 1, p. 139. Cf. Arendt, *OR*, p. 54, where Arendt deals directly with the Hegelian paradox that "freedom is the result of necessity."

48. G.W.F. Hegel, *Reason in History*, p. 24.

49. Arendt, *HC*, p. 195; also p. 301.

50. Aristotle, *Ethics*, 1177b.

51. Ibid., 1177a. See Arendt, *Lectures on Kant's Political Philosophy*, p. 21.

52. Arendt, *LM*, vol. 1, pp. 14–15.

53. Immanuel Kant, *Critique of Pure Reason*, B xx.

54. Ibid., A viii.

55. Ibid., B 476.

56. Arendt, *LM*, vol. 1, p. 15.

57. For Plato's position in the story Heidegger tells about Western metaphysics, see Martin Heidegger, "Plato's Doctrine of Truth," in *Philosophy in the Twentieth Century*.

58. This is not meant to imply that Plato plays a secondary role in Arendt's interpretation of the tradition. Like Nietzsche and Heidegger, Arendt can be described as a vehement anti-Platonist (see Chapter 3 of this book). Plato's formulations have a decisive effect on the understanding of action within the Western tradition of political philosophy; nevertheless, it is Aristotle who, by importing the fabrication experience into the "pure" concept of action (*praxis*), does most to institutionalize the teleocratic conception. See "What Is Authority?" in Arendt, *BPF*, pp. 104–114 and 115–120.

59. Arendt, *BPF*, p. 118.

60. Ibid.

61. Aristotle, *Politics*, 1328b, 35, quoted by Arendt in *BPF*, p. 116.

62. Aristotle, *Politics*, III.4. See also VII, 14: "every association of persons forming a state consists of rulers and ruled."

63. Arendt, *BPF*, p. 117.

64. Arendt, *HC*, p. 222.

65. Arendt, *BPF*, p. 118.

66. Ibid.

67. See Aristotle, *Ethics*, X.9, 1180a, 1–5. Richard Mulgan has a good discussion of Aristotle's "authoritarianism" in this regard; see his *Aristotle's Political Theory*, p. 79ff.

68. Beiner's characterization in his *Political Judgment* is, thus, somewhat misleading. Specific political goals may be rhetorically constituted according to the Aristotelian notion of deliberation, but not the broader ends of the community per se. These lie beyond the constitutive power of rhetorical speech.

69. Arendt, *CR*, p. 150.

70. See Arendt, "The Concept of History," in *BPF*, p. 76. Compare this perspective to that taken by Habermas in his essay "The Classical Doctrine of Politics in Relation to Social Philosophy," in *Theory and Practice*.

71. See Arendt, "What Is Authority?" in *BPF*, p. 119: "nothing is more questionable than the political relevance of examples drawn from the field of education."

72. See Arendt, *Lectures on Kant's Political Philosophy*, pp. 69–72.

73. See, for example, Ronald Beiner's comments in his "Interpretive Essay," in Arendt, *Lectures on Kant's Politcal Philosophy*, pp. 137–138, where he criticizes Arendt's Kantian turn from a neo-Aristotelian perspective.

74. Arendt, "On Humanity in Dark Times," in *MDT*, p. 30.

75. Arendt, *HC*, p. 206. Of course, all action has ends and motives. See Arendt, *OR*, p. 98: "To be sure, every deed has its motive as it has its goal and its principle."

76. Arendt, *HC*, p. 206.

77. For the technical sense, see Jean-François Lyotard's discussion in *The Postmodern Condition: A Report on Knowledge*, pp. 41–53.

78. Arendt, *BPF*, p. 153.

79. Arendt, *BPF*, p. 154.

80. Ibid., pp. 152–153.

81. Ibid., p. 153.

82. Ibid., p. 154. Cf. *HC*, p. 187.

83. Arendt, *BPF*, p. 154.

84. Ibid.

85. Arendt, *OR*, pp. 237–239.

86. Arendt, *HC*, pp. 198–199.

87. Ibid., p. 205.

88. Ibid., p. 206.

89. Ibid., pp. 41, 42.

90. Ibid., p. 41.

91. Ibid., pp. 25, 197.

92. See Arendt, *HC*, p. 74ff. A parallel discussion, focusing on compassion, occurs in Arendt, *OR* (chapter 2, section 3). Here, in a discussion of Rousseau and the French Revolution, Arendt presents compassion as a specifically antipolitical virtue (pp. 86–87). The logic of her argument is similar to that employed by Machiavelli in chapters XV to IXX of *The Prince*, where private virtues are revealed to have disastrous consequences when practiced by the political actor.

93. Arendt, *BPF*, p. 137.

94. Arendt, *HC*, p. 77.

95. See Kateb, *Hannah Arendt*, p. 32. Pitkin, Bakan, Jay, and O'Sullivan make similar points.

96. Machiavelli, *The Prince*, chapter VII.

97. Arendt is aware, of course, of the way a politics of appearance or opinion can be perverted into a politics of deception or image-making. See especially her essay "Truth and Politics," in *BPF*. Her invocation of Machiavellian *virtu* is not intended to *deny* Machiavelli's emphasis upon force and fraud, but rather to elucidate aspects of *virtu* that are lost in the usual "strategic" picture of his political theory. In another context ("What Is Authority?" in *BPF*, pp. 139–140), she cites Machiavelli as the "ancestor of modern revolutions," insofar as he, like Robespierre, justified *all* means in terms of a "supreme end" (namely, the founding of a republic). Cf. *OR*, pp. 37–39.

98. Habermas, *Theory and Practice*, p. 50. Wolin, Pitkin, and Pocock have also pointed to this as a central aspect of Machiavelli's "modernity."

99. Kateb, *Hannah Arendt*, p. 31.

100. Ibid., p. 33.

101. Ibid.

102. Arendt, *HC*, p. 77.

103. Ibid., p. 75.

104. Arendt, *OR*, chapter 2, section 3.

105. Ibid., pp. 86–87.

106. Ibid., pp. 97–98.

107. Ibid., p. 82.

108. Arendt, *HC*, p. 77.

109. See Machiavelli's consideration of Agathocles and Oliverotto in chapter VIII of *The Prince*. For further remarks concerning the incompatability of glory and wickedness or baseness, see Machiavelli, *The Discourses*, book I, chapter X. For Machiavelli's linkage of glory and the common good, see *The Discourses*, book I, chapter LVIII.

110. Machiavelli, *The Prince*, chapters XV to XVIII.

111. My discussion here is indebted to Sheldon Wolin, *Politics and Vision*, chapter 7.

112. See Weber, "Politics as a Vocation," in *From Max Weber*, pp. 117, 123.

113. Ibid., p. 129.

114. As Arendt's analysis of the Terror, in Arendt, *OR*, demonstrates, she is aware of this dynamic. However, she generally refuses to view the problem in the "cost/benefit" terms implied by Machiavelli and (to a lesser degree) Weber. Exceptions to this rule are found in "On Violence," in *CR* (p. 106), and in her essay on Broch (*MDT*, pp. 147–148). See also "Truth and Politics," in *BPF*, p. 245, where her position is closer to Machiavelli's notion of a specifically political ethic, and *Lectures on Kant's Political Philosophy*, pp. 50–51.

115. Arendt, "On Violence," in *CR*, p. 106.

116. Ibid.

117. Kateb, *Hannah Arendt*, p. 39.

118. To some degree, Arendt anticipates these objections to her "theatrical" conception of politics, appealing to "principles" as nonfoundational referents for action. According to Arendt, principles "are the legitimate guides to action," saving "the act of beginning from its own arbitrariness." Insofar as an action manifests a principle, that is, insofar as the appearance of action is inseparable from the appearance of a principle in the world, action ceases to be the sheer display of virtuosity and becomes something else: a meaningful, depersonalized, "objective" phenomenon. Arendt, *BPF*, p. 152. See also p. 243, where she speaks of "such political principles as freedom, justice, honor, and courage, all of which may inspire, and then become manifest in, human action."

119. See Seyla Benhabib, "Judgment and the Moral Foundations of Politics in Hannah Arendt's Thought," in *Situating the Self*, and Habermas, "Hannah Arendt: On the Concept of Power," in *Philosophical-Political Profiles*.

120. J. Glenn Gray, "The Abyss of Freedom—and Hannah Arendt," in *The Recovery of the Public World*.

121. James Miller, "The Pathos of Novelty: Hannah Arendt's Image of Freedom in the Modern World," in Hill, ed.

122. Ibid., p. 192.

123. Cf. Benhabib's characterization of Arendt as a "reluctant" modernist, in her forthcoming book of the same name.

124. Judith Shklar, "Rethinking the Past," p. 90.

125. Ibid.

126. Arendt, *Lectures on Kant's Political Philosophy*, p. 19.

127. Arendt, *BPF*, p. 164.

128. Ibid., p. 151.

129. Arendt, *BPF*, p. 155. See Chapter 4.

130. Ibid., pp. 157, 165.

131. Arendt, *Kant Lectures*, pp. 21–24, 27–30.

132. Ibid., p. 19.

133. Ibid., p. 75; also Arendt, "The Crisis in Culture," in *BPF*, p. 223. It is interesting

that Beiner, like the Habermasians, tends to make just such a reduction. See his "Interpretive Essay," Arendt, in *Kant Lectures*, p. 112.

134. Arendt, *Kant Lectures*, p. 61.

135. Ibid., pp. 20, 27.

136. Patrick Riley, "Hannah Arendt on Kant, Truth and Politics."

137. Ibid., p. 384.

138. See Arendt, "Crisis in Culture," *BPF*, p. 219

139. Arendt, *MDT*, p. 27.

140. See "What Is Authority?" in Arendt, *BPF*, and Chapters 3 and 4 in this book.

141. Arendt, *BPF*, p. 220.

142. G.W.F. Hegel, *Philosophy of Right*, Introduction, note to §29.

143. Plato, "Gorgias," in *Collected Dialogues*, p. 482. See Arendt, *BPF*, p. 220.

144. Arendt, *Kant Lectures*, p. 37.

145. Immanuel Kant, *Groundwork of the Metaphysics of Morals*, p. 114.

146. Hegel, *Philosophy of Right*, pp. 89–90.

147. Kant, *Groundwork*, p. 98.

148. See Kant, *Political Writings*, pp. 73–79.

149. Ibid., p. 125.

150. Ibid., pp. 55–59 ("What Is Enlightenment?"); also Arendt, *Kant Lectures*, pp. 38–41.

151. Arendt, *Kant Lectures*, pp. 15–16.

152. Kant, *Groundwork*, p. 61.

153. Kant, *Political Writings*, p. 41.

154. Ibid., p. 42.

155. Ibid., p. 88. See Arendt, *Kant Lectures*, pp. 50, 59.

156. Arendt, *BPF*, pp. 82, 83.

157. Arendt, *Kant Lectures*, p. 52.

158. Arendt, *BPF*, p. 78.

159. Ibid.

160. Ibid., p. 79. See also p. 243.

161. Arendt, *CR*, pp. 128–130. Compare Walter Benjamin, "Theses on the Philosophy of History," in *Illuminations*.

162. Arendt, *OR*, pp. 51–52.

163. See Hegel, *Reason in History*, p. 47.

164. Arendt, *OR*, pp. 54, 62–63; also *CR*, p. 132.

165. Arendt, *OR*, p. 58.

166. Hence Arendt's repeated citation of Cato's preference for "defeated causes."

167. Arendt, *BPF*, pp. 220–221.

168. Seyla Benhabib, "Moral Foundations," in *Situating the Self*, p. 132.

169. Ibid., pp. 121, 140.

170. Arendt, *Kant Lectures*, p. 15.

171. Benhabib, "Moral Foundations," in *Situating the Self*, p. 136.

172. Ibid., pp. 124, 139.

173. Ibid., pp. 141, 139.

174. Ibid., p. 121.

175. In this regard, I disagree with Benhabib's formulation in *Critique, Norm, and Utopia*, pp. 244–245.

176. Habermas, "Hannah Arendt on the Concept of Power," in *Philosophical-Political Profiles*, p. 172 (my emphasis).

177. Ibid.

178. See Habermas, *The Structural Transformation of the Public Sphere*, pp. 117–129, and Benhabib, *Critique, Norm, and Utopia*.

179. Arendt, *MDT*, p. 27. Cf. Habermas, "On the German-Jewish Heritage," p. 128, where he refers to the "unifying power of intersubjectivity." For Habermas, as for Rousseau, validity ultimately resides in generalizability, a fact that comes through quite clearly in his *Legitimation Crisis*.

180. See Thomas McCarthy's discussion in his *Critical Theory of Jürgen Habermas*, pp. 307–317.

181. See Lyotard, *Postmodern Condition*, pp. 60–67.

182. Richard Rorty, "Habermas and Lyotard on Postmodernity," in Bernstein, ed., *Habermas and Modernity*.

183. Habermas, "Hannah Arendt," in *Philosophical-Political Profiles*, p. 184.

184. Ibid., p. 185.

185. See Chapter 3.

186. Habermas, "Hannah Arendt," in *Philosophical-Political Profiles*, p. 184.

187. See Habermas, "German-Jewish Heritage," p. 129. Cf. Habermas, *Legitimation Crisis*, p. 108.

188. Arendt, *Kant Lectures*, pp. 38–39. I should note her hostility to "show trials" of any sort, to "political theater" as normally construed. See Arendt, *Eichmann in Jerusalem*, pp. 3–12.

189. Arendt, *Kant Lectures*, p. 37.

190. Arendt, *CR*, pp. 58–59. Cf. Gregory Vlastos, "Socrates on Political Obedience and Disobedience."

191. See Rousseau, *Social Contract*, book III, chapter XV, and Arendt, *OR*, chapter 6.

192. See Rousseau, *Social Contract*, book I, chapters I, V, and VIII. Cf. Canovan, "Arendt, Rousseau, and Human Plurality in Politics, pp. 287–289.

193. Arendt's reading here clashes with those, like Maurizio Viroli's, that emphasize Rousseau's indebtedness to civic republicanism. See Viroli, *Jean-Jacques Rousseau and the Well-Ordered Society*.

194. Arendt, *OR*, p. 77.

195. Rousseau, *Social Contract*, book I, chapter VI. See Hobbes, *Leviathan*, chapter 17, p. 227, for the contrasting view of the mechanics of the pact of association/creation of a sovereign power.

196. Rousseau, *Social Contract*, book I, chapter VI.

197. Ibid., book II, chapter III.

198. Ibid., book IV, chapter II.

199. Ibid., p. 114.

200. Arendt, *OR*, p. 78.

201. Ibid., pp. 78–79.

202. See Canovan, "Arendt, Rousseau, and Human Plurality," p. 201. Also Rousseau, *Social Contract*, p. 118, for Rousseau's account of voting on legislation.

203. Arendt, *OR*, p. 79.

204. Arendt, *BPF*, p. 164.

205. Miller, "The Pathos of Novelty," in Hill, ed., p. 191.

206. Ibid., p. 192.

207. See Arendt's reading of the Declaration of Independence, in *OR*, pp. 165–178.

208. Miller, "The Pathos of Novelty," in Hill, ed., p. 198.

209. Ibid., pp. 190–191.

210. Ibid., p. 194. See also, on p. 202, Miller's remarks, which reinforce his hostility to the "individualism" of social contract theory.

211. See Beiner, "The Moral Vocabulary of Liberalism."

212. Arendt, "On Humanity in Dark Times," in *MDT.*

213. Ibid., p. 16.

214. Ibid, p. 27.

CHAPTER 3

1. Beiner, "Interpretive Essay," in Arendt, *Kant Lectures,* p. 104.

2. This is a controversial claim, which would not readily win the assent of many Arendt scholars, who instead see a vast difference between the judgment exercised in deliberation and the redemptive, meaning-creative judgment of the spectator removed in time or place. For a summary of the issues involved, see Beiner's "Intepretive Essay," in Arendt, *Kant Lectures,* and Bernstein, "Judging—the Actor and the Spectator," in *Philosophical Profiles.*

3. Arendt, *HC,* p. 7.

4. Ibid., pp. 175, 182.

5. Arendt, *LM,* vol. 2, p. 200.

6. Arendt, *BPF,* p. 146.

7. Ibid. See also *LM,* vol. 2, p. 200, for the distinction Arendt draws between philosophical and political freedom, following Montesquieu.

8. Ibid., p. 153.

9. Arendt, *HC,* pp. 182–184.

10. Arendt, *BPF,* p. 151.

11. Arendt, *HC,* p. 176.

12. Ibid., p. 190.

13. Ibid. Arendt continues by stating that "To do and to suffer are like opposite sides of the same coin."

14. With regard to this point, see Arendt, "What Is Freedom?" in *BPF,* p. 164. Cf. Arendt, *Lectures on Kant's Political Philosophy,* p. 55, where she discusses the "non-autonomous" character of action viewed from the contemplative standpoint.

15. Arendt, *HC,* p. 195.

16. Ibid., p. 222.

17. Ibid., p. 234.

18. Ibid., p. 235.

19. Ibid., p. 220.

20. Ibid., p. 222.

21. Ibid., p. 225. See also Arendt, "What Is Authority?" in *BPF,* pp. 107–115, and *Lectures on Kant's Political Philosophy,* pp. 59–60.

22. Arendt, *HC,* p. 225.

23. Ibid., p. 229. Also p. 225.

24. Ibid., section 26.

25. Arendt, *BPF,* p. 137.

26. Ibid., p. 135.

27. Arendt, *HC,* p. 57. Also p. 199.

28. Ibid., pp. 184–186.

29. Arendt, *BPF,* p. 151.

30. Ibid.

31. Ibid.
32. Arendt, HC, pp. 190, 192.
33. Ibid., p. 184.
34. Ibid.
35. Kateb, *Hannah Arendt*, chapter 1.
36. Arendt, HC, p. 197.
37. Ibid., p. 198.
38. Ibid., pp. 197–198.
39. Ibid., pp. 198–199.
40. Nietzsche, *The Genealogy of Morals*, I, 13.
41. Ibid.
42. Ibid.
43. This formulation is from Gilles Deleuze, *Nietzsche et la Philosophie*.
44. Cf. Alexander Nehamas, *Nietzsche*, chapter 6.
45. Arendt, *Human Condition*, chapter 4.
46. Ibid. Nietzsche cites the "rude fetishism" of language as the source of the belief in the self as substance/subject, as a unity detached from and prior to its actions, effects and thoughts. See Nietzsche, *Twilight of the Idols*, p. 38.
47. Arendt, "Tradition and the Modern Age," in BPF; Nietzsche, *The Will To Power*, part I, "European Nihilism."
48. Deleuze, *Nietzsche et la philosophie*, pp. 137–139. Cf. also Nietzsche, *Genealogy*, I, 10.
49. Nietzsche, *Genealogy*, III, 18.
50. Nietzsche, *Genealogy* I, 13.
51. Ibid., III, 13. Nehamas calls this inducement of shame "the central purpose of slave morality." See Nehamas, *Nietzsche: Life as Literature*, p. 126.
52. As Nietzsche says in *The Birth of Tragedy*, "understanding kills action."
53. Nietzsche, *Genealogy*, II, 16.
54. Ibid., I, 12.
55. Nietzsche, *Beyond Good and Evil*, p. 199.
56. Arendt, HC, p. 194.
57. Ibid., p. 43.
58. See Nietzsche, *Beyond Good and Evil*, p. 225.
59. Arendt, HC, p. 179.
60. Ibid., p. 175.
61. Ibid., p. 176.
62. Ibid., p. 176 (my emphasis).
63. Ibid., p. 178.
64. Ibid.
65. Ibid., pp. 178–179.
66. Ibid., p. 179.
67. See, for example, Pitkin, "Justice," in *Political Theory*; Jay, "The Political Existentialism of Hannah Arendt," in *Permanent Exiles*; and O'Sullivan, "Hellenic Nostalgia."
68. For a good description of the expressivist conception, see Charles Taylor, *Hegel*, pp. 16–50.
69. See, Chapter 2, Section III.
70. Thus, the "worldlessness" of the *animal laborans* is also a literal selflessness. See, in this regard, Arendt's discussion of the split Rousseauian "authentic self" in ORJ pp. 96–98. Also Kateb, *Hannah Arendt*, pp. 8–13.
71. See Friedrich Nietzsche, *The Will to Power*, sections 490 and 488, for his conception

of the subject as multiplicity (also *Beyond Good and Evil*, section 12). Honig argues that Arendt shares Nietzsche's "political" conception of the self, citing a passage from *LM* in which Arendt affirms "the obvious plurality of men's faculties and abilities" against the "implicit monism" of the tradition (see "Arendt, Identity and Difference," p. 485). Unfortunately, the same claim could be made about Plato's model of the soul or Kant's conception of the faculties. I think Honig positively valorizes the "fragmented" or multiple self in a way Arendt would find dubious, despite her assertion of our inner plurality. See Arendt's discussion in "Thinking and Moral Considerations," in *Social Research*. An excellent discussion of Nietzsche's "political metaphor for the self" is contained in Alexander Nehamas, *Nietzsche: Life as Literature*, pp. 177–186.

72. Arendt, "Philosophy and Politics," p. 86.

73. Ibid.

74. Ibid., p. 88.

75. Arendt, *BPF*, p. 153.

76. Arendt, *OR*, pp. 106–107.

77. Arendt, *HC*, pp. 184–188.

78. Nietzsche, *Gay Science*, section 290.

79. Nehamas, *Nietzsche*, p. 186.

80. Arendt, *OR*, pp. 106–108.

81. Nehamas, *Nietzsche*, p. 186. This is, of course, only one side of the matter, at least in the case of Nietzsche, who emphasized his own lack of audience and his reliance upon self-given standards.

82. Arendt, *HC*, p. 184.

83. Ibid., p. 179.

84. Ibid., pp. 184–185.

85. Nietzsche, *Genealogy*, Preface, I.

86. Arendt, *HC*, p. 180.

87. Ibid., pp. 52–53; Arendt, *MDT*, pp. 4–11.

88. Arendt, *HC*, p. 52.

89. Ibid., p. 182.

90. Ibid., pp. 134, 137. See also Chapter 1, Section II, in this book.

91. Ibid., pp. 182–183.

92. Ibid., p. 51.

93. Ibid., p. 154.

94. Ibid.

95. Arendt, *BPF*, p. 218.

96. Arendt, *HC*, p. 199.

97. Arendt, *OR* p. 98.

98. Arendt, *BPF*, pp. 154–155.

99. Ibid., p. 154.

100. Arendt, *HC*, p. 199; *MDT*, p. 4.

101. Arendt, *HC*, p. 57.

102. Ibid.

103. Ibid.

104. Ibid.

105. Arendt, *OR*, pp. 268–269; *MDT*, pp. 26–27; "Philosophy and Politics," pp. 80–81; *BPF*, pp. 241–242.

106. Arendt, "Philosophy and Politics," p. 80.

107. Ibid.

108. Ibid.

109. Ibid., pp. 73–80; *BPF*, pp. 239–247. For a summary of Arendt's analysis of philosophy's "degradation of the realm of human affairs," see her *Lecture on Kant's Political Philosophy*, pp. 21–27. Arendt is at her most Nietzschean in these pages. The theme of philosophy's *resentment* of the human condition comes across quite clearly.

110. Arendt, *BPF*, p. 233.

111. Ibid., p. 241.

112. Arendt, "Philosophy and Politics," pp. 90–91; *BPF*, pp. 107–115.

113. Arendt, "Philosophy and Politics," p. 74.

114. Arendt, *BPF*, p. 233.

115. Arendt, *MDT*, p. 27.

116. Arendt, "Philosophy and Politics," p. 81.

117. Arendt, *BPF*, pp. 233–234; *MDT*, pp. 26–27.

118. Arendt, *BPF*, p. 238.

119. Ibid., pp. 252–259.

120. Ibid., pp. 246–247.

121. Ibid., p. 247.

122. Arendt, "On Violence," in *CR*, p. 140.

123. See Arendt, *CR*, p. 139. Also *BPF*, pp. 162–163.

124. Nietzsche, *Genealogy*, I, 13; also *Twilight of the Idols*, p. 38. See also Nehamas, *Nietzsche*, p. 121.

125. Nietzsche, *Genealogy*, III, 23.

126. Jean-François Lyotard, *Just Gaming*, pp. 23–25. Cf. Arendt, "What Is Authority?" in *BPF*, p. 115.

127. Deleuze, *Nietzsche*, pp. 19–34.

128. Nietzsche, *Genealogy*, III, 12.

129. Nietzsche, *The Will to Power*, pp. 3–4.

130. Michel Haar, "Nietzsche and Metaphysical Language," in *The New Nietzsche*, p. 14.

131. Alphonso Lingis, "The Will to Power," in *The New Nietzsche*, p. 38. Cf. Arendt's discussion of Kant's prejudice in favor of the thing in itself in her *Life of the Mind*, I, p. 24.

132. Nietzsche, *The Gay Science*, p. 125.

133. Tracy Strong, *Friedrich Nietzsche and the Politics of Transfiguration*, p. 77.

134. See Arendt, "Tradition and the Modern Age" and "What Is Authority?" in *BPF*.

135. Nietzsche, *Birth of Tragedy*, p. 29; Arendt, *OR*, p. 281. See also Arendt, *Lectures on Kant's Political Philosophy*, p. 23.

136. Arendt, *HC*, pp. 154–157.

137. Arendt, "Philosophy and Politics," p. 82.

138. For Habermas, Nietzsche's appeal to taste judgment is tantamount to sheer irrationalism. See Habermas, *The Philosophical Discourse of Modernity*, p. 127.

139. See Lyotard, *The Postmodern Condition*, p. 10; Michel Foucault, *Power/Knowledge*, pp. 93–108, 131–133; Gilles Deleuze, *Nietzsche et la Philosophie*, pp. 84–95.

140. Nietzsche, *Genealogy*, II, 3.

141. Theodor Adorno and Max Horkheimer, "The Concept of Enlightenment," in *Dialectic of Enlightenment*; Michel Foucault, *Discipline and Punish*.

142. In foreward to Peter Sloterdijk, *Thinker on Stage*, p. x.

143. This is Dews's formulation. See Peter Dews, *Logics of Disintegration*, p. 160.

144. Nietzsche, *Genealogy*, II, 2. Also, *Beyond Good and Evil*, p. 188.

145. Ibid. Cf. Deleuze, *Nietzsche*, p. 157.

146. Nietzsche, *Twilight*, p. 92. See also Nietzsche's famous description of Goethe, pp. 102–103.

147. Nietzsche, *Genealogy*, II, 12.

148. Ibid.

149. Ibid.

150. Nehamas emphasizes this aspect in his *Nietzsche: Life as Literature*.

151. Cf. Richard Rorty's notion of the "strong textualist" in *Consequences of Pragmatism*, pp. 151–154.

152. Nietzsche, *Twilight*, p. 40: "We have abolished the true world: what world is left? the apparent world perhaps? . . . But no! with the real world we have also abolished the apparent world!"

153. Arendt, *BPF*, p. 218.

154. Ibid., p. 219.

155. Nietzsche, *Beyond Good and Evil*, p. 24.

156. Arendt, *BPF*, p. 219.

157. Immanuel Kant, *Critique of Judgment*, p. 15.

158. Ibid. pp. 42, 43.

159. Nietzsche, *Twilight*, pp. 71, 72.

160. Arendt, *BPF*, p. 210.

161. Ibid.

162. Ibid.

163. Ibid.

164. Arendt, *BPF*, p. 210.

165. Ibid.

166. Ibid. p. 222.

167. Cf. Kateb, *Hannah Arendt*, chapter 1.

168. Arendt, *HC*, chapter 1. See also Arendt, *Lectures on Kant's Political Philosophy*, pp. 55–59.

169. Arendt, *BPF*, p. 241.

170. Ibid. Cf. Arendt, *Lectures on Kant's Political Philosophy*, p. 43.

171. Kant, *Critique*, p. 136.

172. Arendt, *BPF*, p. 241.

173. Nietzsche, *Genealogy*, III, 12. Cf. Arendt, *Lectures on Kant's Political Philosophy*, p. 43.

174. Foucault, "Nietzsche, Genealogy and History," in *The Foucault Reader*; also Jacques Derrida, "Structure, Sign and Play," in *Writing and Difference*, pp. 278–295.

175. Kant, *Critique of Judgment*, p. 136.

176. Nietzsche, *Genealogy*, III, 11; also "On Truth and Lie," in *Philosophy and Truth*, p. 79. See also Arendt, *Lectures on Kant's Political Philosophy*, pp. 65–72.

177. Max Weber, "Science as a Vocation," in *From Max Weber*, pp. 152–153.

178. Lyotard, *Postmodern Condition*, p. 26; also *Just Gaming*, p. 58.

179. Nietzsche, *Beyond Good and Evil*, p. 151.

180. Kant, *Critique of Judgment*, section 20.

181. Ibid., p. 74. Cf. Arendt, *Lectures on Kant's Political Philosophy*, pp. 63–64.

182. Kant, *Critique of Judgment*, section 40.

183. Arendt, *BPF*, p. 221.

184. Ibid. Cf. Beiner, "Interpretive Essay," in *Kant Lectures*, p. 119: "In matters of 'taste' I never judge only for myself, for the act of judging always implies a commitment to communicate my judgment."

185. Arendt, *BPF*, p. 221.

186. Ibid., p. 222.

187. Ibid., p. 221.

188. Ibid., p. 222.

189. Ibid.

190. Ibid. Cf. Arendt, *Lectures on Kant's Political Philosophy*, p. 72.

191. Arendt, *BPF*, pp. 221–222.

192. Lyotard, *Just Gaming*, p. 16; see, however, p. 14, where Lyotard denies the possibility of a *sensus communis* in what he calls "modernity," tying taste judgments to both the premodern and the universal.

193. Jürgen Habermas, *Legitimation Crisis*, p. 110.

194. Arendt, *BPF*, p. 241.

195. Ibid., p. 227.

196. Ibid., p. 218. In this regard, see Beiner's statements regarding the ontological significance of judgment in Arendt, *Kant Lectures*, pp. 151, 155.

197. Arendt, *BPF*, pp. 216–218.

198. Ibid., pp. 153–154. Cf. Nietzsche, *Genealogy* II, 17.

199. Lacoue-Labarthe, *Heidegger, Art and Politics*, p. 66.

200. Arendt, *BPF*, p. 217.

201. I shall return to this theme in Chapters 7 and 8, with particular reference to Heidegger.

202. See Arendt, "Tradition and the Modern Age," in *BPF*. Cf. Arendt, "Thinking and Moral Considerations," *Social Research*, p. 25: "a reversed Plato is still Plato."

203. Arendt, *BPF*, pp. 28–30.

CHAPTER 4

1. Arendt, *MDT*, p. 204.

2. Arendt, *OR*, p. 124.

3. See Jacques Taminiaux's "Arendt, disciple de Heidegger?"

4. See Arendt, *BPF*, p. 163.

5. Martin Jay, "Political Existentialism of Hannah Arendt," in *Permanent Exiles*; Luc Ferry and Alain Renaut, *Heidegger and Modernity*; Richard Wolin, *The Politics of Being*.

6. Leo Strauss, "An Introduction to Heideggerian Existentialism," in *The Rebirth of Classical Political Rationalism*.

7. Leo Strauss, "What Is Political Philosophy?" in *What Is Political Philosophy? and Other Studies*, pp. 26–27.

8. Jay, *Permanent Exiles*, pp. 240–242.

9. Schürmann, *Heidegger on Being and Acting*, p. 6.

10. Arendt, *BPF*, pp. 97, 104–105, 141.

11. Ibid., pp. 104–115.

12. Lacoue-Labarthe and Nancy, *Rejouer le Politique*, p. 14.

13. Richard Rorty, "The Priority of Democracy to Philosophy" and "Postmodern Bourgeois Liberalism," both in *Objectivity, Relativism, and Truth*,

14. Arendt, *HC*, p. 229.

15. Arendt, *BPF*, pp. 157–158.

16. Ibid., p. 148.

17. Ibid., pp. 162–165; see also Chapter 2 of this book.

18. Arendt, *BPF*, pp. 160–161; *LM* II, pp. 198–199.

19. Arendt, BPF, p. 169.

20. Arendt, LM, II, pp. 29, 205; Kant, *Critique of Pure Reason*, B 478.

21. Arendt, LM, II, p. 196.

22. Ibid., p. 207.

23. Ibid., p. 198.

24. Ibid., p. 216.

25. Arendt, LM, II, pp. 31, 135–141, 195; BPF, p. 167.

26. I borrow this formulation from Taminiaux's "Arendt, disciple de Heidegger?"

27. Martin Heidegger, *Schelling's Treatise on the Essence of Human Freedom*, p. 9 (translation altered).

28. Frederick Dallmayr, "Ontology of Freedom: Heidegger and Political Philosophy," pp. 220–224.

29. Heidegger, *Basic Writings*, p. 128.

30. See Chapters 2 and 3, and the discussions in Schürmann (1987) and White (1990).

31. Arendt, BPF, pp. 152, 151. It is important, in this context, to distinguish between the early and middle Heidegger's "ontological" approach to freedom and what Arendt refers to as the later Heidegger's "will not to will." See Chapter 7.

32. For a discussion of the views of *Being and Time* as "unpolitical" or "antipolitical," see Chapter 7.

33. Hannah Arendt, "What Is *Existenz* Philosophy?"

34. Hannah Arendt, "Concern with Politics in Recent European Philosophy," in *Essays in Understanding*, p. 432.

35. Ibid., p. 443, and LM II, p. 200.

36. Arendt, *Essays in Understanding*, p. 432.

37. Heidegger, *Being and Time*, §12, p. 78; *Sein und Zeit* (hereafter cited as SZ), p. 53.

38. Heidegger, *Being and Time*, §44.

39. Heidegger, *Being and Time*, §13, pp. 90, 67; SZ, pp. 62, 43. See also L. P. Hinchman and S. K. Hinchman, "In Heideggers's Shadow," p. 190.

40. Ibid., §14, p. 92; SZ, p. 64.

41. Ibid., §15, p. 97; SZ, p. 62.

42. Ibid., §15, p. 99; SZ, p. 69.

43. Ibid., §15, p. 98; SZ, p. 69.

44. This has become a widely accepted generality of interpretive social science. See Charles Taylor's essay, "Interpretation and the Sciences of Man," in his *Philosophy and the Human Sciences: Philosophical Papers*, vol. 2.

45. Karsten Harries, "Fundamental Ontology and the Search for Man's Place," in *Heidegger and Modern Philosophy*.

46. Heidegger, BT, §16, p. 103; SZ, p. 73.

47. Heidegger, BT, §16, p. 105.

48. Ibid., §25, p. 150; SZ, p. 114.

49. Heidegger, BT, §25, p. 150. Habermas emphasizes this point, seeing it as an expression of Heidegger's residual subjectivism. See Habermas, *The Philosophical Discourse of Modernity*, chapter VI, and Chapter 7 in this book.

50. Heidegger, BT, §25, p. 152; SZ, p. 116.

51. Ibid., §25, p. 155; SZ, p. 118. See also BT, p. 156, where Heidegger characterizes Being-alone as a deficient mode of Being-with.

52. Arendt, HC, pp. 9–10.

53. See Arendt, "Rejoinder to Eric Voegelin's Review of *The Origins of Totalitarianism*," pp. 68–76. Hinchman correctly gauges the extent of Voegelin's failure to comprehend

what Arendt is up to. See "In the Shadow of Heidegger: The Phenomenological Humanism of Hannah Arendt," pp. 184–185. See also Arendt, OT, pp. 458–459.

54. Arendt, HC, p. 7.

55. Heidegger, BT, §28, p. 170; SZ, p. 132.

56. Heidegger, BT, §28, p. 170.

57. Ibid. Also Harries, "Fundamental Ontology and the Search for Man's Place," p. 68,
and Arendt's preface to BPF.

58. Heidegger, BT, §28, p. 171; SZ, p. 132.

59. Ibid., §43, p. 245; SZ, p. 201.

60. Ibid., §28, p. 171; SZ, p. 133.

61. Ibid., §43, p. 255; SZ, p. 212. See also BT, pp. 269, 272 ("Being [not entities] is
something which 'there is' only in so far as truth is. And truth is only in so far and as long
as Dasein is").

62. See R. Wolin, The Politics of Being (hereafter cited as POB), p. 149.

63. My reading here takes its cue from R. Rorty's. See his Essays on Heidegger and
Others.

64. Heidegger, BT, §44, p. 263; SZ, p. 220.

65. Heidegger, BT, §44, p. 263.

66. Ibid., pp. 260–261; SZ, pp. 218–219. Thus, for example, one can hardly expect the
laws of Newtonian physics to be available on the basis of a Greek understanding of Being.
Heidegger wants us to stop thinking of Newton's laws as somehow correctly describing or
corresponding to Nature "as it is in itself," prior to all description. From a Heideggerian
standpoint, these laws figure as a new description, as a vocabulary that reconstitutes the
object realm we denote by "Nature" in a way more amenable to the pragmatic concerns of
the modern Western project. The domination of Nature stands at the center of this project
as formulated by Bacon, and Kant only drew the logical conclusion when, confronted by
the success of Newtonian science as measured by the Baconian criteria of utility and
power, he made man the "lawgiver to Nature." Heidegger's polemic against the correspondence theory of truth—and the idea of man as a being equipped with special faculties that
allow him to get in touch with a Truth untainted by the constitutive concerns of human
beings—can be seen as merely completing Kant's "Copernican revolution": truth is not
something "found," but "made," a point that has become a cliché of postempiricist philosophy of science.

67. Heidegger, "On the Essence of Truth," in Basic Writings, p. 132.

68. Ibid.

69. Again, the conflation of the Just and the True is a Platonic inheritance we have yet
to entirely shake off.

70. Heidegger, BT, §31, p. 183; SZ, p. 143.

71. Ibid., pp. 184–185; SZ, p. 145.

72. Heidegger, "What Is Metaphysics?" in Basic Writings, pp. 105–106.

73. Heidegger, BT, §31, p. 183; SZ, p. 143.

74. Ibid., p. 185; SZ, p. 145.

75. Dallmayr, "Ontology of Freedom," p. 216. Cf. Arendt's remarks on the derivative
character of freedom of the will in Arendt, "What Is Freedom?" in BPF.

76. Heidegger, "On the Essence of Truth," in Basic Writings, p. 128.

77. Heidegger BT, §44, p. 264; SZ, p. 221. See also §29, p. 174 (SZ, p. 135).

78. Heidegger, BT, §44, p. 264.

79. See, for example, W. R. Newell's essay, "Heidegger: Some Political Implications of
His Early Thought."

80. Heidegger, *BT*, §7, p. 63; *SZ*, p. 38.

81. Arendt, *HC*, p. 10.

82. Arendt, *LM*, II, ch. 13.

83. Arendt, *HC*, p. 9 (my emphasis).

84. Heidegger, *BT*, p. 210; *SZ*, p. 167.

85. Ibid., §38, p. 222; *SZ*, p. 177.

86. Ibid., §38, p. 220; *SZ*, p. 176.

87. There is an apparent shift in Heidegger's later work on this point.

88. Heidegger, *BT*, §38, p. 224; *SZ*, p. 179.

89. Heidegger, "On the Essence of Truth," in *BW*, p. 121.

90. Thomas Kuhn, *The Structure of Scientific Revolutions*, chapters II and IX.

91. Heidegger, *BT*, §44, p. 264; *SZ*, p. 222.

92. This formulation is borrowed from Taminiaux, *Heidegger and the Project of Fundamental Ontology*, p. 117.

93. See this chapter, Section V.

94. Taminiaux, *Heidegger and the Project of Fundamental Ontology*, p. 122.

95. Heidegger, quoted in Taminiaux, *Heidegger and the Project of Fundamental Ontology*, p. 124.

96. Heidegger, *BT*, §44, p. 265; *SZ*, p. 222.

97. Heidegger, *BT*, §44, p. 265.

98. The best overview of the evolution of Heidegger's thought on the relation between Being and man is in Werner Marx, *Heidegger and the Tradition*.

99. Heidegger, "The Origin of the Work of Art," in *Poetry, Language, Thought*. See especially pp. 46–47, 60–63.

100. See R. Rorty, *Philosophy and the Mirror of Nature*; also Nietzsche, "On Truth and Lie in an Extramoral Sense," in *Philosophy and Truth*, and J. S. Mill, *On Liberty*.

101. See K. Harries, "Heidegger as a Political Thinker," p. 309; R. Wolin, *The Politics of Being*, pp. 37–39; Leo Strauss, "Philosophy as Rigorous Science," in *Studies in Platonic Political Philosophy*.

102. Heidegger, *BT*, §40, p. 232; *SZ*, p. 188.

103. Heidegger, *BT*, §40, pp. 232–233.

104. Karsten Harries, "Fundamental Ontology and the Search for Man's Place," pp. 77.

105. Heidegger, *BT*, §57, p. 319.

106. Ibid., §58; see Arendt's critique of the notion of "guilt" in Arendt, *LM*.

107. Heidegger, *BT*, §58, p. 330. See also Harries, "Heidegger as a Political Thinker," p. 308.

108. Heidegger, *BT*, §58, p. 330.

109. Ibid., pp. 330–331.

110. Harries, "Heidegger as a Political Thinker," p. 308.

111. Heidegger, *BT*, §60, p. 344; *SZ*, p. 298.

112. Ibid., §60, p. 345; *SZ*, p. 298.

113. Heidegger, *BT*, §60, p. 345.

114. Strauss, "Philosophy as a Rigorous Science," in *Studies in Platonic Political Philosophy*, p. 30.

115. R. Wolin, *Politics of Being*, pp. 38–39.

116. Ibid.

117. Wolin is aware of the "inadvisability" of his reading in light of Heidegger's questioning of the will and critique of philosophical subjectivism. He forestalls objections by claiming that the early Heidegger's relation to philosophical subjectivism is "aporetic," a

characterization that allows him to pursue his depiction of Heidegger's *BT* as "Nietz-schean" in its reliance upon a value-creating subjectivity.

118. This issue is discussed in Section I of ch. 5.

119. Heidegger, *BT*, §44, p. 365. Cf. Mill, *On Liberty*, ch. 2.

120. This, according to Arendt, is precisely what Heidegger did with his rereading of Greek philosophy in the twenties. See her description in "Martin Heidegger at Eighty," in *Heidegger and Modern Philosophy*.

121. Heidegger, *BT*, §38, p. 224. In this regard, authenticity or resoluteness can be seen as deepening the effect Kant was after when he asked us to ponder the possibility of our maxims for action becoming "natural" or universal laws. The thrust of this "thought experiment," I take it, is to place our everyday rules of guidance in a radically different light, forcing us to own up to their ethical (or unethical) import by stressing our vocation as moral legislators. As "making one's own," authenticity/resoluteness likewise demands that we take the familiar and everyday with renewed seriousness; not as something "they" do, but that *we* do and bear responsibility for. This dimension, of course, was emphasized by Sartre, albeit to laughable extremes. See his *L'Existentialisme est un humanisme*.

122. Arendt, *LM*, I, p. 15 (notwithstanding what Arendt views as the conflation of meaning and truth built into Heidegger's account).

123. Taminiaux, "Reappropriation," in *Heidegger and the Project of Fundamental Ontology*, p. 124.

124. Arendt, *HC*, §20, p. 73.

125. Ibid., pp. 115, 118.

126. Ibid.

127. Ibid., p. 84. Compare Heidegger, "Letter on Humanism," in *BW*, p. 203.

128. Arendt, *HC*, pp. 134–135 and "Crisis in Culture," in *BPF*, pp. 209–210.

129. Arendt, *HC*, §19, 20.

130. Ibid., pp. 143, 153.

131. Ibid., p. 154.

132. Ibid.

133. Ibid., p. 155.

134. Ibid., pp. 156–158.

135. Ibid., p. 157.

136. Ibid., p. 41.

137. See Chapter 3, and Taminiaux, "Reappropriation," in *Heidegger and the Project of Fundamental Ontology*.

138. Heidegger, *BT*, p. 265.

139. Arendt, *HC*, pp. 182–183.

140. Ibid., p. 197.

141. Ibid., p. 168.

142. Ibid., §23.

143. Arendt, *HC*, p. 73.

144. See Chapter 2 and Arendt, *OR*. For an Arendt-inspired genealogy and critique of the politics of authenticity, see Richard Sennett, *The Fall of Public Man*.

145. Needless to say, this transposition opens Arendt up to a deconstructive reading parallel to that Derrida gives of Heidegger in *Of Grammatology* and elsewhere. This is, perhaps, a worthwhile task; yet, in my view, it is a far too obvious strategy. Insofar as Arendt's text proceeds by making sharp distinctions, it begs to be deconstructed; yet the more we undo her various "binary oppositions," the more likely we are to miss her primary point, which is that ubiquitous functionalization dissolves everything into process, making

it all but impossible to preserve the essential articulations of our lifeworld. For Arendt, the boundaries have always already been blurred beyond recognition.

146. See Chapter 6.

147. Arendt, HC, p. 9.

148. Arendt, HC, pp. 186, 35–36.

149. See Arendt, "On Violence," in CR, and "Concern for Politics," in *Essays in Understanding*.

150. See Chapter 7 for a discussion of this point.

151. Heidegger, *An Introduction to Metaphysics*, pp. 62–63, 152; "The Origin of the Work of Art," in *Poetry, Language, Thought*, pp. 43, 48–49, 61–63.

152. See Taminiaux, "Reappropriation," in *Heidegger and the Project of Fundamental Ontology*, pp. 133–135. Both elements are clearly evident in a passage taken from Heidegger's 1942 seminar, *Parmenides*:

> What is the *polis*? The word itself directs us toward the answer, provided we commit ourselves to acquiring an essential understanding of the Greek experience of Being and truth. *Polis* is the *polos*, the pivot, the place around which gravitates, in its specific manner, everything that for the Greeks is disclosed amidst beings. As this location, the pivot lets beings appear in their Being subject to the totality of their involvement. The pivot neither makes nor creates beings in their Being, but as the pivot, it is the site of the unconcealedness of beings as whole. The *polis* is the essence of a location, so we speak of the regional location of the historical dwelling of Greek humanity. Because the *polis*, in one way or another, always lets the totality of beings come forth in the unconcealedness of their involvement, it is essentially related to the Being of beings. Between *polis* and Being, a relation of the same origin rules.

153. Taminiaux, "Reappropriation," in *Heidegger and the Project of Fundamental Ontology*, p. 116.

154. Ibid., pp. 117–127.

155. Heidegger, *The Metaphysical Foundations of Logic*, p. 183. This passage is cited by both Taminiaux and Bernasconi.

156. Taminiaux, "Reappropriation," in *Heidegger and the Project of Fundamental Ontology*, p. 126.

CHAPTER 5

1. Heidegger, QCT, p. 61. See also pp. 65 and 69.

2. Arendt, LM, I, p. 10. See also Arendt, "Thinking and Moral Considerations," pp. 10–11. Arendt here adds the necessary but obvious clarification that it is not a question of God's death in a literal sense—a clearly absurd notion. Arendt's personal faith in God is an irrelevant issue, although she *did* believe.

3. Sheldon Wolin, "Hannah Arendt: Democracy and the Political"; Pitkin, "Justice: On Relating Private and Public."

4. See Chapter 3.

5. There is, of course, some question as to whether "rank order" in Nietzsche can be so easily (and simply) interpreted. Wolin, for one, does not doubt it. See R. Wolin, *The Politics of Being*, chapter 2.

6. R. Wolin, *Politics of Being*, pp. 123–130.

7. See Chapter 7.

8. See Heidegger, "On the Essence of Truth," in BW.

9. Arendt, BPF, Preface.

10. Heidegger, BW, pp. 119–220.

11. Ibid., p. 132.

12. Ibid., p. 134.

13. Ibid. p. 135.

14. See Heidegger, *Letter on Humanism*, in *BW*, p. 239.

15. Arendt, *HC*, p. 71 (my emphasis).

16. Ibid., pp. 62–63.

17. Ibid., p. 64. There is a resonance here with Heidegger's interpretation of *physis* in the "Anaximander Fragment" as a "lingering awhile in presence." Nevertheless, Arendt sees Heidegger's interpretation as the symptom of a deeply unworldly, unpolitical yearning. See my discussion in Chapter 7.

18. Arendt, *HC*, p. 157.

19. Ibid.

20. Ibid., p. 45.

21. Arendt, *MDT*, preface.

22. Arendt, *HC*, p. 43.

23. Ibid., p. 46. One does not get much more Heideggerian; see Chapter 6 of this book.

24. Arendt, *OR*, p. 21.

25. Ibid., chapter 2.

26. Ibid., chapter 4.

27. Ibid., chapter 3.

28. Ibid., p. 135.

29. Ibid., p. 232.

30. Ibid., pp. 48–49.

31. Ibid., p. 272.

32. Arendt, *BPF*, p. 5.

33. Ibid., pp. 168–169.

34. Nowhere has the acceleration of this fate become more apparent than the recent revolutions in Eastern Europe, whose newly born public spheres shone brightly for the briefest of moments before being overtaken by "household concerns" and the problems of moving from a command to a market economy.

35. Sheldon Wolin, *Politics and Vision*, chapter 7.

36. See Chapter 3 and Chapter 5, Section V.

37. See, for example, Schürmann's definition of postmodern politics in *Heidegger on Being and Acting*, p. 18.

38. Arendt, *HC*, p. 55.

39. One can, however, read Nietzsche as an "institutional" theorist, as does B. Honig, in *Political Theory and the Displacement of Politics*.

40. See Chapter 3; and Arendt, "Tradition and the Modern Age," in *BPF*. The interpretation of Nietzsche as "invertor" comes from Heidegger. See Heidegger, "Nietzsche's Word: God is Dead," in *QCT*.

41. Again, this phrase is Heidegger's. See Heidegger, "Anaximander Fragment," in *Early Greek Thinking*.

42. Heidegger, *IM*, p. 199.

43. Ibid., pp. 37, 45.

44. Ibid., p. 36.

45. Ibid.

46. Ibid.

47. Ibid., ch. 4.

48. See Chapter 5, Section V.

49. Heidegger, *IM*, p. 105.

50. Ibid., p. 100.
51. Ibid.
52. Ibid.
53. Ibid., p. 14.
54. Ibid.
55. Ibid., pp. 100–101.
56. Ibid., p. 101.
57. Arendt, *LM*, I, pp. 19–39; *HC*, p. 50; *OR*, p. 98.
58. Arendt, *LM*, I, p. 27.
59. Heidegger, *IM*, p. 103.
60. Ibid., p. 104.
61. Ibid., p. 106.
62. Ibid., p. 109.
63. Ibid.
64. Ibid., p. 107–108.
65. Ibid.
66. Ibid., p. 62; see Chapter 6.
67. Ibid., pp. 62, 152.
68. See, in this regard, Heidegger's slighting remarks concerning Thucydides in comparison to Plato and Aristotle in the Introduction to *BT*.
69. Arendt, "What Is Authority?" in *BPF*, note 16.
70. Jay, *Permanent Exiles*, pp. 242, 252.
71. R. Wolin, *POB*, p. 191 (note 3).
72. See Chapter 7, and R. Wolin, *POB*, pp. 35–40.
73. See, in this regard, Richard Rorty's comments on Habermas in "Habermas and Lyotard on Postmodernity," in R. Bernstein, ed., *Habermas and Modernity*.
74. See Villa, "Postmodernism and the Public Sphere."
75. Jay, *Permanent Exiles*, p. 243.
76. Arendt, *OR*, pp. 76–81, 94–98.
77. Ibid., p. 229.
78. Jay, *Permanent Exiles*, pp. 249, 251–252.
79. Arendt, *OR*, p. 20.
80. Arendt "On Violence," in *CR*.
81. Arendt, *OR*, p. 215.
82. Arendt, *BPF*, p. 93.
83. See Habermas, "Hannah Arendt: On the Concept of Power," in *Philosophical-Political Profiles*.
84. See Jaspers's revealing remark in Hannah Arendt and Karl Jaspers, *Correspondence 1926–1969*, p. 284.
85. Arendt, *BPF*, p. 95.
86. Ibid., pp. 94–95.
87. Ibid., p. 93.
88. Ibid.
89. Ibid.
90. Ibid.
91. Ibid.
92. Needless to say, Arendt's opposition to authority in the political sphere does not rule out her favoring it in other fields, e.g., education. See Arendt, "The Crisis in Education," in *BPF*.
93. Arendt, *BPF*, p. 92 (hence Jaspers's comment).

94. Ibid., p. 95.

95. Ibid.

96. Ibid., p. 91.

97. Ibid., p. 141.

98. Ibid., p. 93.

99. Ibid., p. 97.

100. Ibid., p. 115.

101. Ibid., p. 104.

102. Ibid.

103. Ibid.

104. Ibid., p. 106.

105. Ibid., p. 105.

106. Ibid., p. 107.

107. Ibid. See Arendt, *Kant Lectures*, pp. 33–46.

108. Plato, *Republic*, books VI and VII.

109. Schürmann, *Heidegger on Being and Acting*, p. 1.

110. Arendt, *BPF*, p. 115.

111. Heidegger, "Letter on Humanism," in *BW*, p. 194.

112. Schürmann, *Heidegger*, pp. 1, 4, 82–83.

113. Arendt, *BPF*, p. 115.

114. The phrase is from Lacoue-Labarthe and Nancy, *Rejouer le Politique*.

115. Arendt, *BPF*, p. 108.

116. Ibid.; Plato, *Republic*, book X.

117. Arendt, *BPF*, pp. 127, 132.

118. Ibid., pp. 124–125.

119. Ibid., p. 124.

120. Arendt, *LM*, I, p. 11 (my emphasis); see also p. 212.

121. See Nietzsche, *Will to Power*, part I, "European Nihilism"; Heidegger, "Nietzsche's Word," in *QCT*, and vol. IV of his *Nietzsche*.

122. Hill, ed., *Hannah Arendt: The Recovery of the Public World*, pp. 313–314.

123. Ibid.

124. Ibid., p. 314. See also Arendt, "Thinking and Moral Considerations," *Social Research*, pp. 26–27.

125. Arendt, "Organized Guilt and Universal Responsibility," in *The Jew as Pariah: Jewish Identity and Politics in the Modern Age*, pp. 231–232.

126. Arendt, *BPF*, p. 210. Also Arendt, "Understanding and Politics," *Partisan Review*, pp. 383, 379.

127. See Nietzsche's remarks on the "ascetic priest," in *Genealogy of Morals*, essay III.

128. Arendt, *BPF*, p. 141.

129. Schürmann, *Heidegger*, pp. 5, 86–89. See also Heidegger, *QCT*, p. 65, and R. Rorty's discussion in *Essays on Heidegger and Others*, p. 20.

130. Arendt, *LM*, I, p. 212.

131. Arendt, "Understanding and Politics," p. 379.

132. Ibid., p. 383.

133. Nietzsche, *Will to Power*.

134. Arendt, "Understanding and Politics," p. 384.

135. Ibid., p. 388.

136. Ibid., p. 391.

137. Arendt, *Eichmann in Jerusalem*, pp. 257, 267.

138. Ibid., pp. 252–258 (Menthon, p. 257).

139. Arendt, "Thinking and Moral Considerations," *Social Research*, p. 7.

140. Ibid., p. 9.

141. Beiner, "Interpretive Essay," in Arendt, *Kant Lectures*, p. 96.

142. In a recent article Martin Jay is much more sympathetic to Arendt's peculiar attempt to link the aesthetic and the political. See Jay, "The 'Aesthetic Ideology' as Ideology; or, What Does It Mean to Aestheticize Politics?"

143. Beiner, in Arendt, *Kant Lectures*, p. 112.

144. Arendt, *Eichmann in Jerusalem*, p. 296.

145. See Lacoue-Labarthe and Nancy *Rejouer le Politique*; also Fraser, "French Derrideans," in *Unruly Practices*.

146. Heidegger, "Overcoming Metaphysics," in *The End of Philosophy*, p. 90.

147. Heidegger, *Nietzsche*, IV, pp. 214–215, 224–225; also "Metaphysics as a History of Being," in *End of Philosophy*, pp. 1–46.

148. See Arendt's discussion in *LM*, II, chapter 15.

149. Heidegger, *IM*, p. 205.

150. Heidegger, "The Question Concerning Technology," in *QCT*; also *Nietzsche*, IV.

151. Heidegger, *IM*, p. 14, and Chapter 5, Section III, of this book.

152. Heidegger, *IM*, pp. 184–185.

153. See Chapter 8 of this book.

154. Heidegger, *IM*, pp. 193, 202.

155. Heidegger, *End of Philosophy*, p. 4.

156. Otto Pöggeler, *Martin Heidegger's Path of Thinking*, p. 121.

157. Heidegger, *BW*, p. 109.

158. Heidegger, *End of Philosophy*, pp. 90–94.

159. Heidegger, "End of Philosophy and the Task for Thinking," in *BW*, p. 374.

160. Heidegger, *The Basic Problems of Phenomenology*, pp. 100–117.

161. Ibid.; see also Taminiaux, "Reappropriation," in *Heidegger and the Project of Fundamental Ontology*.

162. See, for example, Heidegger, "The Origin of the Work of Art," in *Poetry, Language, Thought*, pp. 28–33; *On Time and Being*, pp. 46–47; and Michael Zimmerman, *Heidegger's Confrontation With Modernity*, chapter 11.

163. Taminiaux, "Reappropriation," in *Heidegger and the Project of Fundamental Ontology*, p. 119.

164. Heidegger, *End of Philosophy*, p. 9.

165. Heidegger, *IM*, pp. 193–194.

166. Heidegger, "Age of the World-Picture," in *QCT*.

167. Heidegger, "Nietzsche's Word," in *QCT*.

168. See Heidegger, "Plato's Doctrine of Truth," in *Philosophy in the Twentieth Century*, pp. 269–270.

169. Heidegger, "The Question Concerning Technology," in *QCT*.

170. See Chapters 7 and 8.

CHAPTER 6

1. Arendt, *HC*, p. 254.

2. Ibid., p. 6.

3. Ibid., p. 157.

4. Ibid., p. 204.

5. Arendt, *MDT*, p. 13; Heidegger, *BW*, p. 219. Also Heidegger, *Nietzsche*, vol. IV, p. 248.

6. Arendt, *HC*, p. 57.

7. Adorno and Horkheimer, *Dialectic of Enlightenment*, p. 54.

8. Arendt, *HC*, pp. 2, 3.

9. Ibid., p. 3.

10. Heidegger, "The Word of Nietzsche," in *QCT*, p. 100; Arendt, *HC*, p. 3.

11. Heidegger, "The Age of the World Picture," in *QCT*, p. 128.

12. Heidegger, "The Question Concerning Technology," in *QCT*, p. 27.

13. Ibid.

14. Arendt, *HC*, p. 52.

15. Ibid., p. 46.

16. Ibid., p. 322.

17. See Benhabib, *The Reluctant Modernism of Hannah Arendt*, forthcoming.

18. Kateb, *Hannah Arendt*, p. 183.

19. Ibid., chapter 5.

20. For example, that of Habermas.

21. Arendt, *HC*, p. 10.

22. Arendt, "Rejoinder to Eric Voegelin," pp. 68–76.

23. Heidegger, *The End of Philosophy*, p. 86.

24. Heidegger, "The Word of Nietzsche," in *QCT*, pp. 84, 107. Also Heidegger, *Nietzsche*, vol. IV, p. 99.

25. Heidegger, "The Age of the World Picture," in *QCT*, p. 126.

26. Ibid., p. 128; also Heidegger, *Nietzsche*, vol. IV, p. 96.

27. Heidegger of course follows in Hegel's footsteps here. See G.W.F. Hegel, *Hegel's Lectures on the History of Philosophy*, vol. III. Heidegger's characterization occurs in vol. IV of *Nietzsche*, p. 100. See also Heidegger, "The Word of Nietzsche," in *QCT*, p. 82.

28. Heidegger, "The Age of the World Picture," in *QCT*, p. 149. Compare Heidegger, *Nietzsche*, vol. IV, p. 97.

29. Heidegger, "The Age of the World Picture," in *QCT*, p. 149.

30. Ibid; also Heidegger, *Nietzsche*, vol. IV, p. 97.

31. Heidegger, "The Word of Nietzsche," in *QCT*, p. 83.

32. Heidegger, *Nietzsche*, vol. IV, p. 114.

33. Ibid., p. 116. Cf. Heidegger, "The Word of Nietzsche," in *QCT*, p. 89.

34. See Heidegger, "Overcoming Metaphysics," in *The End of Philosophy*, p. 88.

35. Heidegger, "The Age of the World Picture," in *QCT*, p. 127.

36. Ibid., p. 133.

37. Heidegger, *Kant and the Problem of Metaphysics*, §38.

38. Heidegger, *What Is a Thing?* p. 181.

39. Heidegger, "Overcoming Metaphysics," in *The End of Philosophy*, p. 88.

40. Heidegger, *What Is a Thing?* p. 121.

41. Heidegger, "The Word of Nietzsche," in *QCT*, p. 84.

42. Ibid., pp. 83–84.

43. Ibid.

44. See Heidegger, "Who Is Nietzsche's Zarathustra?" in *The New Nietzsche*. Heidegger's reading has been questioned, most prominently, by Derrida, Deleuze, and Foucault.

45. Heidegger, "The Age of the World Picture," in *QCT*, p. 115.

46. Heidegger, "The Word of Nietzsche," in *QCT*, p. 100; cf. p. 107.

47. See Heidegger, "Plato's Doctrine of Truth"; also "The Word of Nietzsche," in *QCT*, p. 84.

48. For a account of the former, see Taylor, *Hegel*, part I. Cf. Michael Zimmerman, *Heidegger's Confrontation with Modernity*, p. xiii.

49. Heidegger, "The Age of the World Picture," in QCT, pp. 116–117.

50. Ibid., p. 128.

51. Heidegger, "The Age of the World Picture," in QCT, p. 117.

52. Ibid.

53. Ibid., p. 118.

54. Ibid.

55. Ibid., p. 127.

56. Ibid.

57. Ibid.

58. Ibid.

59. Ibid., p. 128. See Hans Blumenberg, *The Legitimacy of the Modern Age*, and Manfred Riedel, "Nature and Freedom in Hegel's 'Philosophy of Right.'"

60. Heidegger, "The Age of the World Picture," in QCT, p. 128.

61. Ibid.

62. Ibid.

63. Ibid.

64. Ibid., pp. 128–129.

65. Ibid., Appendix 5.

66. Ibid., pp. 129–130.

67. Ibid., p. 130.

68. Ibid., p. 131.

69. Ibid., p. 132.

70. Ibid., pp. 129, 130. Also Appendix 6.

71. Ibid., p. 132.

72. Ibid., pp. 130–131.

73. Ibid., p. 132.

74. Ibid.

75. Ibid., p. 129.

76. Ibid., pp. 129–130.

77. Ibid., p. 116. Cf. Gadamer, *Truth and Method*, part 1.

78. Heidegger, "The Age of the World Picture," in QCT, p. 134.

79. Ibid., pp. 134–135.

80. See Zimmerman, *Heidegger's Conformatation with Modernity*, chapter 10.

81. Heidegger, "What Are Poets For?" in *Poetry, Language, Thought*, p. 116.

82. The text was originally delivered as a lecture in 1949.

83. Heidegger, QCT, p. 17.

84. Ibid., p. 27.

85. Ibid., p. 28.

86. See, again, "What Are Poets For?" in *Poetry, Language, Thought*, p. 116.

87. Heidegger, BW, p. 229.

88. Kateb, *Hannah Arendt*, p. 172.

89. Heidegger, BW, p. 225.

90. Heidegger, "Overcoming Metaphysics," in *The End of Philosophy*, p. 104.

91. Heidegger, *Poetry, Language, Thought*, p. 116.

92. See Karl Löwith, *Max Weber and Karl Marx*.

93. Heidegger, "Overcoming Metaphysics," in *The End of Philosophy*, p. 110.

94. See, for example, Arendt's statement in HC, p. 252.

95. Arendt, *HC*, pp. 55, 59, 60.
96. Ibid., p. 257.
97. Ibid., p. 55.
98. Ibid., p. 58.
99. Ibid. See also Arendt, *MDT*, preface.
100. See Chapter 4.
101. Arendt, *HC*, p. 58.
102. Ibid., p. 248.
103. Ibid., pp. 248–262.
104. Ibid., p. 250.
105. Ibid., p. 251.
106. Ibid.
107. Ibid., pp. 254–255.
108. Ibid., p. 256.
109. Ibid.
110. See Arendt, "The Crisis in Culture," in *BPF*.
111. Arendt, *HC*, p. 262.
112. Ibid.
113. Ibid.
114. Ibid., p. 264.
115. Ibid.
116. Kateb, *Hannah Arendt*, p. 152. See also Arendt, *HC*, pp. 268–269.
117. Arendt, *HC*, p. 261.
118. Arendt, *HC*, pp. 70–71, 284. Also Arendt, "What Is Freedom?" in *BPF*.
119. Arendt, *HC*, pp. 70–71, 283–284.
120. Heidegger, "Age of the World Picture," in *QCT*, p. 132; Arendt, *HC*, p. 3.
121. Arendt, *HC*, p. 265.
122. Kant, *Critique of Pure Reason*, B xiii.
123. Arendt, *HC*, p. 266.
124. Ibid.
125. Ibid., pp. 267–268.
126. Ibid., p. 275.
127. Ibid., pp. 268–271.
128. Ibid., p. 277.
129. Ibid., p. 279.
130. Ibid.
131. Ibid., p. 280.
132. Ibid., p. 282. Cf. Arendt, *The Life of the Mind*, vol. I, pp. 46–49.
133. Ibid.
134. Ibid., p. 293.
135. See, for example, Arendt, *BPF*, p. 96.
136. Arendt, *HC*, p. 284.
137. Hans Blumenberg disagrees. See his analysis in *The Legitimacy of the Modern Age*, part 1.
138. Arendt, *HC*, p. 285.
139. Ibid., p. 286.
140. Ibid., p. 287.
141. Ibid.
142. Ibid., p. 288.

143. Ibid., p. 290.
144. Ibid.
145. Ibid., pp. 290–291.
146. Ibid., p. 294.
147. Ibid., p. 295.
148. Ibid., pp. 296–297 (emphasis mine).
149. Arendt, *HC*, p. 297.
150. Ibid., p. 299.
151. Ibid., pp. 305–306.
152. Ibid., p. 306.
153. Arendt, "On Violence," in *CR*, p. 106.
154. Arendt, *HC*, p. 154.
155. Ibid.
156. Ibid.
157. Ibid., p. 155.
158. Thus, for example, Arendt concentrates on the *continuity* between Protagoras' position and that of the moderns, in contrast to Heidegger, who emphasizes the difference. See Arendt, *HC*, pp. 157–158, and Heidegger, "The Age of the World Picture," in *QCT*, Appendix 8 (pp. 143–147).
159. Arendt, *HC*, p. 157.
160. Ibid.
161. Ibid., p. 145.
162. Ibid. See chapter 1 of this book.
163. Ibid., p. 146.
164. Ibid., p. 147.
165. Ibid., p. 4.
166. Ibid., p. 132.
167. Ibid., p. 150.
168. Ibid., p. 151.
169. Ibid.
170. See *HC*, §12 and §19.
171. Ibid., p. 137.
172. Arendt, *HC*, p. 322. The Heidegger reference ought not to obscure the equally strong Nietzsche allusion (Nietzsche, *The Genealogy of Morals*).
173. Arendt, *HC*, pp. 40–41.
174. Ibid., p. 246 [emphasis mine].
175. Ibid., p. 230; cf. also p. 10.
176. Arendt, *OT*, pp. 458–459.
177. Kateb, *Hannah Arendt*, p. 158.
178. Ibid.
179. Ibid.
180. Arendt, *LM*, vol. II, pp. 157–158.
181. Judith Shklar, *After Utopia*.
182. See Kateb, *Hannah Arendt*, p. 178.
183. For an overview of these criticisms, see Nancy Fraser, "Rethinking the Public Sphere," in Craig Calhoun, ed., *Habermas and the Public Sphere*.
184. Arendt, *HC*, p. 58.
185. Arendt, *OR*, p. 232.
186. Arendt, *BPF*, p. 168.

187. See Sheldon Wolin, "Fugitive Democracy."

188. See Villa, "Postmodernism and the Public Sphere." Cf. Foucault, "The Subject and Power," in Hubert Dreyfus and Paul Rabinow, *Michel Foucault.*

189. Lyotard, *Just Gaming*, p. 82. See Chapters 3 and 4 of this book.

190. Lacoue-Labarthe and Nancy, "Ouverture," in *Rejouer le Politique.*

191. Michael Walzer, *Interpretation and Social Criticism.*

192. The former is J. Isaac's position, in *Arendt, Camus and Modern Rebellion*; the latter is B. Honig's, in *Political Theory and the Displacement of Politics.*

CHAPTER 7

1. Arendt, *LM*, vol. II, pp. 172–194.

2. Heidegger, *Being and Time*, p. 224. See Harries, "Heidegger as a Political Thinker," p. 310; and Newell, "Heidegger: Some Political Implications of His Early Thought," p. 778.

3. See, for example, Ferry and Renaut, *Heidegger and Modernity*, pp. 38–39; for a more sympathetic treatment, see Dallmayr, "Ontology of Freedom: Heidegger and Political Philosophy."

4. See Taminiaux, "Reappropriation," in *Heidegger and the Project of Fundamental Ontology*, p. 124.

5. Ibid., p. 165.

6. Ibid., p. 220.

7. Ibid., §35 and p. 221.

8. Ibid., pp. 220, 221.

9. Habermas, *The Philosophical Discourse of Modernity*, p. 150.

10. Ibid., p. 142.

11. Ibid., p. 149.

12. Ibid., p. 151.

13. Ibid., p. 149.

14. Ibid.

15. Ibid.

16. Ibid., p. 180.

17. Ibid., p. 157.

18. Habermas, *Political-Philosophical Profiles*, p. 75.

19. R. Wolin, *The Politics of Being*, pp. 45, 49.

20. Habermas, *PDM*, p. 150.

21. Wolin, *POB*, pp. 45, 46.

22. See K. Harries, "Heidegger as Political Thinker," and W. R. Newell, "Heidegger: Some Political Implications of His Early Thought."

23. Arendt, *MDT*, p. 4.

24. I am thinking, for example, of the work of Jean Baudrillard and Guy Debord.

25. Arendt, *MDT*, p. 5.

26. Heidegger, *BT*, pp. 222, 223; §40.

27. Ibid., pp. 233–234.

28. Ibid., p. 436.

29. Newell, "Heidegger," p. 779. See also Heidegger, *BT*, p. 384. There is a resonance here with Machiavelli's prescription, in the *Discourses*, for jolting a declining community back to its founding principles. See Machiavelli, *Discourses*, book III, chapter 1.

30. K. Harries "Heidegger as Political Thinker," p. 308.

31. Ibid., p. 313; Habermas, *PDM*, p. 141.

32. This characterization comes from Kateb, *Hannah Arendt*, p. 15.

33. Taminiaux, "Reappropriation," in *Heidegger and the Project of Fundamental Ontology*, p. 130. Cf. also Dominique Janicaud, "Heidegger's Politics," p. 832.

34. Lyotard, *Just Gaming*, pp. 20–22.

35. See Weber, "Science as a Vocation," in *From Max Weber*.

36. Newell, "Heidegger," p. 781.

37. Heidegger, "The Self-Assertion of the German University" (Rectoral Address), in *Martin Heidegger and National Socialism*, pp. 5–13.

38. Heidegger, *BT*, p. 435.

39. Ibid.

40. Ibid., p. 443.

41. Ibid., p. 438. My treatment here owes a substantial debt to K. Harries, "Heidegger as Political Thinker," p. 311, and W. R. Newell, "Heidegger: Some Political Implications of His Early Thought," p. 781. See Heidegger, *IM*, pp. 38–39, for a highly charged rendition of what it means for the German people to recapture or repeat [*wieder-holen*] the beginnings of their "spiritual existence."

42. Heidegger, *BT*, pp. 436, 437. Heidegger, "The Self-Assertion of the German University" (Rectoral Address), pp. 6, 8–9; K. Harries emphasizes the *interpretive* quality of authority.

43. Heidegger, *BT*, p. 436; Rectoral Address, p. 6; K. Harries, "Heidegger as Political Thinker," p. 313.

44. Heidegger, *BT*, p. 437; Newell, "Heidegger: Some Political Implications of His Early Thought," p. 781.

45. Heidegger, "The Self-Assertion of the German University" (Rectoral Address), p. 10.

46. Heidegger, *BT*, pp. 435–436; Harries, "Heidegger as Political Thinker," p. 313.

47. See, in this regard, Heidegger's description of the "battle" between leaders and followers in the Rectoral Address, p. 12.

48. Harries, "Heidegger as Political Thinker," pp. 318, 319, 320.

49. Heidegger, "The Self-Assertion of the German University," p. 9. Habermas views this intuition as grounded in Heidegger's loyalty to Husserl's phenomenological method. See Habermas, *PDM*, p. 138.

50. K. Harries, "Heidegger as Political Thinker," p. 316.

51. Heidegger, *IM*, p. 62.

52. Heidegger, *OWA*, p. 77; cf. also R. Wolin *POB*, p. 102.

53. I adopt the phrase "radical *poiēsis*" from Werner Marx. Heidegger's "Origin of the Work of Art," in *Poetry, Language, Thought*, gives brief but helpful characterizations of the tradition's entrapment in productionist categories (pp. 29–30, 32), while his "Question Concerning Technology," in *QCT*, is the source of the essential Heideggerian distinction between *poiēsis* as production and *poiēsis* as "bringing forth."

54. The phrase "ontological vocation" is borrowed from R. Wolin, *POB*, p. 100.

55. Heidegger, *OWA*, in *Poetry, Language, Thought*, p. 72.

56. Ibid., p. 73.

57. Ibid., p. 71.

58. Ibid., p. 44.

59. Ibid., p. 42.

60. Ibid., p. 44.

61. R. Wolin, *POB*, p. 101.

62. Heidegger, OWA, *Poetry, Language, Thought*, p. 44.

63. Ibid., p. 46.

64. Ibid., p. 49.

65. Ibid.

66. Ibid., p. 62.

67. Ibid., p. 60.

68. Ibid., pp. 60, 58.

69. Ibid., p. 62.

70. Ibid.

71. Heidegger, *IM*, p. 191.

72. Ibid., p. 62.

73. Ibid; cf. also OWA, *Poetry, Language, Thought*, p. 63.

74. Heidegger, OWA, pp. 77–78.

75. Ibid., p. 78.

76. Ibid., p. 77; also Heidegger, *IM*, p. 157.

77. W. Marx, *Heidegger and the Tradition*, p. 151.

78. See Chapter 1 on Arendt's agreement with Aristotle as to the *violence* of making.

79. Heidegger, *IM*, p. 157. R. Wolin makes a great deal of this in *POB*, pp. 124–126.

80. Heidegger, *IM*, p. 152.

81. Ibid., pp. 152–153.

82. K. Harries, "Heidegger as Political Thinker," p. 318.

83. See R. Wolin, *POB*, pp. 114–115. Wolin's criticisms here remind one of the criticisms liberals used to make of Hegel's political theory. In both cases, a lot hinges upon the word "state" and its deployment, and one has to be fairly specific about the connotations. The model for Heidegger's "state" is the *polis*, and in order to effectively criticize this conception one has to do more than point to the "world-opening" function of the political space in Heidegger. Claiming that any attribution of ontological significance to the *political* realm leads, inevitably, to "statism" is highly dubious, as Arendt's work points out.

84. Heidegger, OWA, in *Poetry, Language, Thought*, p. 75.

85. Ibid.

86. Ibid.

87. Heidegger, "Letter on Humanism," in *BW*, p. 233.

88. Heidegger, OWA, in *Poetry, Language, Thought*, p. 71.

89. Ibid., p. 54.

90. Heidegger, *IM*, p. 157.

91. Heidegger, OWA, in *Poetry, Language, Thought*, p. 73.

92. Ibid. There is an important irony here in that Habermas reproduces this dichotomy in his critique of Heidegger. See Habermas, *PDM*, chapters 6 and 10. R. Wolin similarly dichotomizes *ontology* and *interaction*, in rhetoric intended to make the attribution of any disclosive dimension to politics appear latently totalitarian. See R. Wolin, *POB*, p. 117.

93. Heidegger, *IM*, p. 51.

94. With respect to *doxa* in Heidegger, see the very important discussion in Heidegger, *IM*, p. 103ff. The continuities and discontinuities with Arendt here are fascinating. See Chapter 5 of this book.

95. This, of course, is not *Habermas*'s point: the primary thrust of his critique is that the Heideggerian dichotomy between poetic and communicative or political speech in the usual sense is well founded, and that Heidegger's attempts to frame a conception of the political in poetic terms only underlines the untenable nature of a political theory with ontological stakes. For an account of the way Habermas deploys the opposition between

"action coordinating" and "world-disclosive" language, see S. White, *Political Theory and Postmodernism*, chapter 2.

96. See Chapter 6 of this book.

97. Heidegger, "Overcoming Metaphysics," in *The End of Philosophy*, p. 86.

98. For the characterization of Western metaphysics as a "power trip" ending in pragmatism/technology, see Richard Rorty, "Heidegger, Contingency and Pragmatism," in *Essays on Heidegger and Others*, p. 31.

99. Heidegger, *BT*, p. 255.

100. Heidegger, "Letter on Humanism," in *BW*, p. 216.

101. Heidegger, "Nietzsche's Word," in *The Question Concerning Technology*, pp. 69, 100, 107.

102. Heidegger, *LH*, in *BW*, p. 219.

103. Ibid., p. 218.

104. Ibid., p. 199.

105. Ibid., pp. 221, 210.

106. Ibid., p. 210.

107. See, in this regard, Schürmann, *Heidegger on Being and Acting*, pp. 47–50, 60. See also Heidegger, "Poetically man dwells . . . ," in *Poetry, Language, Thought*, pp. 215–216.

108. Heidegger, *LH*, in *BW*, p. 239.

109. Ibid.

110. See R. Rorty, "Heidegger, Contingency and Pragmatism," in *Essays on Heidegger and Others*.

111. Heidegger, *LH*, in *BW*, pp. 198, 197.

112. Ibid., p. 199, 197.

113. I am drawing here on R. Rorty, "Heidegger, Contingency and Pragmatism," in *Essays on Heidegger and Others*, p. 46, and T. Strong, *Friedrich Nietzsche*.

114. Heidegger, *LH*, in *BW*, p. 239 and 193.

115. Ibid., p. 194.

116. Ibid.

117. Heidegger, *LH*, in *BW*, p. 239.

118. Bernstein, "Heidegger on Humanism," in *Philosophical Profiles*, p. 208.

119. See Taminiaux, *Heidegger and the Project of Fundamental Ontology*, pp. 139–143, for a summary of some of Heidegger's main points in the Marburg course.

120. Bernstein, "Heidegger on Humanism," in *Philosophical Profiles*, p. 207.

121. Ibid., pp. 206, 208.

122. Ibid., pp. 208, 219. For a similar critique, see R. Rorty's essay, "Heidegger, Kundera and Dickens," in *Essays on Heidegger and Others*, p. 70.

123. Bernstein, "Heidegger on Humanism," pp. 152–153. See also R. Wolin, *POB*, p. 149.

124. Bernstein, "Heidegger on Humanism," p. 140.

125. R. Wolin, *POB*, p. 155.

126. Ibid., p. 154.

127. Ibid. R. Wolin's critique ends by insisting that "any plausible conception of practical reason" and action presupposes "an understanding of human beings . . . as autonomously acting subjects" (*POB*, pp. 152–153). See also Ferry and Renaut, *Heidegger and Modernity*, pp. 104–110.

128. A similar strategy has been followed by Janicaud in response to Farias. See Janicaud, "Heidegger's Politics: Determinable or Not?"

129. See, for example, Arendt, *LM*, I, pp. 13, 180–92, 200–201.

130. Thinking's withdrawal from the world, it should be noted, is of a different order than the withdrawal of *judgment*. See Arendt, *LM*, I, pp. 92–94. I should also note, in this regard, that it is misleading to say that Arendt criticized "from beginning to end" Heidegger's "isolation from the world of human affairs." This claim, made by L. P. and S. K. Hinchman in their otherwise illuminating essay, "In Heidegger's Shadow: Hannah Arendt's Phenomenological Humanism," ignores the fact that, for Arendt, the activity of thinking is necessarily solitary, withdrawn, and "isolated." This isolation may lead to tragic misjudgments, as in the case of Heidegger, but Arendt is clear that the greatness of Heidegger's thought is, in fact, partially a function of its splendid isolation.

131. Arendt, "Martin Heidegger at Eighty," p. 300.

132. Arendt, *LM*, I, p. 71; "Heidegger at Eighty," p. 297.

133. Arendt, "Heidegger at Eighty," p. 300.

134. Ibid., pp. 301–302.

135. Ibid., p. 303.

136. Ibid.

137. Ibid.

138. Arendt, *LM*, II, pp. 188–192.

139. Ibid., pp. 185, 187.

140. Arendt, "Heidegger at Eighty," p. 301.

141. Arendt, "What Is *Existenz* Philosophy?" p. 50.

142. Ibid., p. 51.

143. Ibid., p. 50.

144. Ibid., pp. 55–56.

145. See Arendt's discussion of the Rousseauian Self in *OR*, pp. 97–109.

146. Arendt, "Concern with Politics in Recent European Philosophical Thought," in *Essays in Understanding*.

147. Heidegger quoted by Arendt, in "Concern with Politics." See Young-Bruehl, *Hannah Arendt: For Love of the World*, p. 303.

148. Young-Bruehl, *Hannah Arendt*, p. 303.

149. Ibid.

150. See Schürmann, *Heidegger On Being and Acting*; Bernasconi, "The Fate of the Distinction between *Praxis* and *Poiēsis* in Heidegger."

151. Young-Bruehl, *Hannah Arendt*, p. 303.

152. Ibid.

153. Ibid.

154. Ibid., p. 304.

155. Arendt, *LM*, II, p. 178.

156. Ibid.

157. Ibid., p. 179.

158. Ibid., p. 180.

159. Ibid., p. 181.

160. Ibid., p. 183.

161. Heidegger quoted in Arendt, *LM* II, p. 183.

162. Arendt, *LM*, II, p. 194.

163. Ibid.

164. Ibid.

165. Ibid., p. 185.

166. Ibid.

167. Ibid.

168. Ibid., p. 187.
169. Ibid.
170. Ibid.
171. Ibid.
172. Arendt, "Heidegger at Eighty," p. 298.
173. See Rorty's similar critique, "Heidegger, Kundera, Dickens," p. 70.
174. Arendt, "Heidegger at Eighty," pp. 299, 303.
175. Arendt, LM, II, pp. 188–189.
176. Ibid., p. 188.
177. Arendt, LM, II, p. 189.
178. Ibid. See also Heidegger, "The Anaximander Fragment," in Early Greek Thinking, p. 13.
179. Ibid.
180. Heidegger, "Anaximander Fragment," in Early Greek Thinking, p. 37.
181. Arendt, LM, II, p. 190.
182. Ibid.
183. Ibid. Heidegger, "Anaximander Fragment," in Early Greek Thinking, p. 26.
184. "Das Sein entzieht sich indem es sich in das Seiende entbirgt."
185. Arendt, LM, II, p. 191.
186. Ibid.
187. Ibid.
188. Ibid. Heidegger, "Anaximander Fragment," Early Greek Thinking, p. 50.
189. Ibid., pp. 191–192.
190. Ibid., p. 192.
191. Ibid.
192. Ibid.
193. Ibid., p. 194.
194. Ibid., p. 193. The obvious contrast is Arendt's own preoccupation with the category of natality.
195. Ibid., p. 194.

CHAPTER 8

1. Taminiaux, Heidegger and the Project of Fundamental Ontology, pp. 129–32.
2. Janicaud, "Heidegger's Politics."
3. See Robert Bernasconi, "Habermas and Arendt on the Philosopher's 'Error': Tracking the Diabolical in Heidegger."
4. Arendt, "Martin Heidegger at Eighty."
5. S. White, Political Theory and Postmodernism, p. 33.
6. Ibid., p. 37. Cf. Taminiaux, "Heidegger and Praxis," in The Heidegger Case.
7. F. Dallmayr, Margins of Political Discourse, p. 62.
8. Habermas, The Philosophical Discourse of Modernity, p. 135.
9. See Derrida, "Différance," in Margins of Philosophy.
10. Lacoue-Labarthe, Heidegger, Art and Politics, p. 18.
11. Heidegger, IM, p. 192.
12. See Chapter 4 and Taminiaux, Heidegger and the Project of Fundamental Ontology, p. 130. See also Bernasconi, "The Fate of the Distinction Between Praxis and Poiēsis."
13. Bernstein, "Heidegger on Humanism," in Philosophical Profiles, p. 206.
14. Heidegger, "Overcoming Metaphysics," in The End of Philosophy, p. 81. In this

regard, R. Wolin speaks of Heidegger's "campaign against practical reason," in *POB*, p. 147. The sense in which he is correct is that Heidegger puts in question the traditional deductive relationship between first and practical philosophy. See Schürmann, *Heidegger on Being and Acting*, pp. 4–7.

15. Bernstein, "Heidegger on Humanism," in *Philosophical Profiles*, p. 219.

16. See Chapters 2 and 3 of this book. Cf. Schürmann, *Heidegger on Being and Acting*, pp. 82–84; also White, *Postmodernism and Political Theory*, p. 48.

17. See Schürmann, *Heidegger on Being and Acting*, p. 83.

18. Arendt, *HC*, p. 229.

19. Schürmann, *Heidegger on Being and Acting*, pp. 5–7, 11, 83. Cf. Arendt, "Tradition and the Modern Age," and "What Is Authority?" in *BPF*.

20. Heidegger, *IM*, p. 19.

21. See Habermas, "Technology and Science as Ideology," in *Toward a Rational Society*; and Gadamer, *Reason in the Age of Science*, especially "Hermeneutics as Practical Philosophy" and "Hermeneutics as a Practical and Theoretical Task."

22. See John Caputo, *Radical Hermeneutics*, pp. 63–65.

23. Arendt, *MDT*, pp. 201–204.

24. Lacoue-Labarthe and Nancy, "Ouverture," in *Rejouer le Politique*, pp. 11–28.

25. Schürmann, *Heidegger on Being and Acting*, p. 83. Cf. pp. 101–105 and Bernasconi, "The Fate of the Distinction Between *Praxis* and *Poiēsis*," pp. 116–117.

26. Taminiaux, "Reappropriation," in *Heidegger and the Project of Fundamental Ontology*, p. 131ff; Bernstein, "Heidegger on Humanism," in *Philosophical Profiles*, p. 214.

27. Lyotard, *Heidegger and "the jews,"* p. 76.

28. Schürmann, *Heidegger on Being and Acting*, p. 5.

29. In this regard, see Arendt's discussion of the coercive force of logic in "Ideology and Terror," in *Origins of Totalitarianism*, p. 468–474.

30. See Schürmann, *Heidegger on Being and Acting*, pp. 90–91.

31. Like Foucault, Arendt also "brackets" the problematic of legitimacy. See Nancy Fraser, *Unruly Practices*, chapter 1.

32. See my article, "Postmodernism and the Public Sphere."

33. Lacoue-Labarthe, *Heidegger, Art and Politics*, p. 70.

34. See G. Shulman, "Metaphor and Modernization in the Political Thought of Thomas Hobbes."

35. See P. Laslett's Introduction in Locke, *Two Treatises of Government*.

36. Jean-Luc Nancy, *The Inoperative Community*, p. 2–15.

37. Lacoue-Labarthe, *HAP*, p. 70.

38. Nancy, *The Inoperative Community*, p. 3.

39. Lacoue-Labarthe, *HAP*, pp. 70, 75.

40. Arendt, "Ideology and Terror," in *OT*, pp. 465–466; see also pp. 139–143.

41. Lacoue-Labarthe, *HAP*, p. 18.

42. Cf. Christopher Norris, "Complicity and Resistance: Heidegger, de Man, and Lacoue-Labarthe," p. 132.

43. K. Harries, "Heidegger as a Political Thinker," p. 327.

44. Ibid.

45. Bernasconi, "The Fate of the Distinction Between *Praxis* and *Poiēsis*," p. 113. Taminiaux makes a similiar point in "Arendt, disciple de Heidegger?" pp. 123–124.

46. Ibid.

47. Arendt, *HC*, chapters 3 and 4.

48. D. Schmidt, *The Ubiquity of the Finite*.

49. Lacoue-Labarthe, *HAP*, p. 77.

50. Ibid.

51. Ibid., p. 53.

52. Ibid., p. 55.

53. Ibid., p. 57.

54. Ibid.

55. Heidegger, *IM*, p. 45.

56. Lacoue-Labarthe, *HAP*, p. 54.

57. Ibid., pp. 56, 79–82, 92–95.

58. Ibid., p. 66.

59. Ibid., p. 77.

60. Ibid.

61. Ibid., p. 94.

62. Lacoue-Labarthe, *Heidegger, Art and Politics*. As Lacoue-Labarthe puts it: "The awakening of the power of myth—the auto-poetic act—becomes a necessity once the inconsistency of the abstract universals of reason have been revealed and the beliefs of modern humanity (Christianity and the belief in humanity itself), which were at bottom only bloodless myths, have collapsed."

63. Ibid., p. 77.

64. Arendt, *BPF*, p. 18.

65. Arendt, *LM*, I, p. 15.

66. Taminiaux, "Reappropriation," in *Heidegger and the Project of Fundamental Ontology*, p. 129.

67. See Heidegger, *On Time and Being*, p. 24.

68. Arendt, *LM*, II, p. 173.

69. Lacoue-Labarthe, *HAP*, p. 86.

70. Arendt, *BPF*, Preface.

71. Arendt, "What Is Authority?", in *BPF*, p. 91.

72. Arendt, "Ideology and Terror," in *OT*, p. 464.

73. Ibid., p. 462.

74. Ibid. This view of the "essence" of totalitarianism directly contradicts the Straussian thesis that totalitarianism is a form of tyranny, best understood by reference to classical sources. See Leo Strauss, *On Tyranny*.

75. Arendt, "Ideology and Terror," in *OT*, p. 464.

76. Arendt, *Origins of Totalitarianism*, p. 437.

77. Arendt, "Ideology and Terror," in *OT*, pp. 465–466.

78. Ibid., pp. 462, 465.

79. Quoted in Bernstein, *New Constellation*, p. 130. See also Lacoue-Labarthe, *HAP*, pp. 33–34.

80. Lacoue-Labarthe, *HAP*, p. 34. Cf. Arendt's characterization in *Essays in Understanding*, pp. 13–14.

81. Lacoue-Labarthe, *HAP*, p. 37.

82. Ibid., p. 35.

83. Ibid., pp. 70, 94–95.

84. Ibid., p. 49.

85. Ibid., pp. 46, 48.

86. Ibid., p. 49.

87. Ibid., p. 48.

88. Ibid.

89. See Arendt's note to "What Is Authority?" in *BPF*, p. 291 (note 16).

90. Schürmann, *Heidegger on Being and Acting*; also "Political Thinking in Heidegger," p. 198.

91. Schürmann, *Heidegger on Being and Acting*, p. 18.

92. Ibid., p. 4.

93. Schürmann, "Political Thinking," p. 201ff.

94. Richard Bernstein, *The New Constellation: The Ethical-Political Horizons of Modernity/Postmodernity*, chapter 4: "Heidegger's Silence? *Ethos* and Technology."

95. Bernstein, *New Constellation*, p. 131.

96. Heidegger, *QCT*, pp. 27, 38.

97. Bernstein, *New Constellation*, p. 131.

98. Taminiaux, "Heidegger and *Praxis*," in *The Heidegger Case*, pp. 188–207; Bernstein, *New Constellation*, pp. 122–125.

99. Bernstein, *New Constellation*, pp. 134–135.

100. See my article "Postmodernism and the Public Sphere."

101. See Heidegger, "Letter on Humanism," in *BW*; also "Building, Dwelling, Thinking," and ". . . Poetically Man Dwells," in *Poetry, Language, Thought*.

102. Heidegger, *QCT*, pp. 14–15.

103. Ibid., pp. 30, 31.

104. Bernstein, *New Constellation*, p. 109.

105. Heidegger, *QCT*, p. 36.

106. Ibid., p. 24.

107. Ibid., p. 38.

108. Bernstein, *New Constellation*, p. 117.

109. Ibid., p. 122.

110. See Bernasconi, "The Fate of the Distinction Between *Praxis* and *Poiēsis*," p. 122.

111. Taminiaux, "Reappropriation," in *Heidegger and the Project of Fundamental Ontology*, and Bernasconi, "The Fate of the Distinction Between *Praxis* and *Poiēsis*."

112. Bernasconi, "The Fate of the Distinction Between *Praxis* and *Poiēsis*," p. 122; also pp. 129–30; Taminiaux, "Heidegger and *Praxis*," p. 206; Taminiaux, "Reappropriation," pp. 134–135; and Taminiaux, "Arendt, disciple de Heidegger?" p. 113.

113. Taminiaux, "Arendt, disciple de Heidegger?" p. 113.

114. Ibid.

115. Ibid, p. 111.

116. I am not sure that Schürmann would necessarily disagree with this.

117. Bernasconi, "The Fate of the Distinction Between *Praxis* and *Poiēsis*," p. 129.

118. See Chapter 2; also Bernasconi, "The Fate of the Distinction," pp. 116–117; Schürmann, *Heidegger on Being and Acting*, p. 84.

119. See Taminiaux, "Heidegger and *Praxis*," pp. 200–201. In this regard, I think Taminiaux is guilty of exaggerating the extent of Aristotle's anti-Platonism.

120. Arendt, *BPF*, p. 153.

121. See, in this regard, Heidegger, *The Question of Being*, and Derrida's essays in *Writing and Difference*.

122. See W. Marx, *Heidegger and the Tradition*.

123. It is important to avoid overstating this linearity, as R. Wolin does. For a contrasting view, see Bernasconi, *The Question of Language in Heidegger's History of Being* (New York: Humanities Press, 1990), chapter 1.

124. Walter Benjamin, "Theses on the Philosophy of History," in *Illuminations*. I deal with this similarity at greater length in an unpublished essay, "Tradition and Remembrance in Political Theory."

125. Arendt, *LM*, I, "Postscriptum," p. 216. Also Arendt, *Lectures on Kant's Political Philosophy*, p. 5.

126. Bernstein, *New Constellation*, p. 106.

127. See K. Löwith, *Max Weber and Karl Marx*.

128. Heidegger, *QCT*, p. 27.

129. See for example, the essays in James W. Bernauer, ed., *Amor Mundi*, and Patricia Bowen-Moore, *Hannah Arendt's Philosophy of Natality*.

130. See, for example, Ferry and Renaut, *Heidegger and Modernity*, and R. Wolin, *The Politics of Being*.

131. Arendt, *MDT*, p. 5.

132. Arendt, *Totalitarianism*, p. 158.

133. Heidegger, "Only a God Can Save Us," Heidegger interview with *Der Spiegel*.

134. Ferry and Renaut, *Heidegger and Modernity*, pp. 94–108; R. Wolin, *Politics of Being*, pp. 152–154.

135. Foucault, "What Is Enlightenment?" in *The Foucault Reader*, pp. 42–44.

Adorno, Theodor. *The Jargon of Authenticity*. Translated by Knut Tarnowski and Frederick Will. Evanston: Northwestern University Press, 1973.

———. *Minima Moralia*. Translated by E.F.N. Jephcott. London: Verso Editions, 1978.

Adorno, Theodor, and Horkheimer, Max. *Dialectic of Enlightenment*. Translated by John Cumming. New York: Seabury Press, 1972.

Arendt, Hannah. "What Is *Existenz* Philosophy?" *Partisan Review*, Vol. 13, No. 1 (Winter 1946): 34–56.

———. "Rejoinder to Eric Voegelin's Review of *The Origins of Totalitarianism*." *Review of Politics*, No. 15 (January 1953): 76–85.

———. "Understanding and Politics." *Partisan Review*, Vol. 20, No. 4 (July-August 1953): 377–392.

———. *The Human Condition*. Chicago: University of Chicago Press, 1958.

———. *On Revolution*. New York: Penguin Books, 1962.

———. *The Origins of Totalitarianism*. New York: Harcourt Brace Jovanovich, 1966.

———. *Between Past and Future*. New York: Penguin Books, 1968.

———. *Men in Dark Times*. New York: Harcourt Brace Jovanovich, 1968.

———. *Crises of the Republic*. New York: Harcourt Brace Jovanovich, 1972.

———. *Eichmann in Jerusalem: A Report on the Banality of Evil*. New York: Penguin Books, 1977.

———. *The Jew as Pariah: Jewish Identity and Politics in the Modern Age*. Edited and with an Introduction by Ron H. Feldman. New York: Grove Press, 1978.

———. *The Life of the Mind*. 2 vols. New York: Harcourt Brace Jovanovich, 1978.

———. "Martin Heidegger at Eighty," *Heidegger and Modern Philosophy*. Edited by Michael Murray. New Haven: Yale University Press, 1978.

———. *Lectures on Kant's Political Philosophy*. Edited by Ronald Beiner. Chicago: University of Chicago Press, 1982.

———. "Thinking and Moral Considerations." *Social Research*, Vol. 51, Nos. 1–2 (Spring/Summer 1984): 7–37.

———. "Philosophy and Politics." *Social Research*, Vol. 57, No. 1 (1990): 73–103.

———. *Essays in Understanding*. Edited by Jerome Kohn. New York: Harcourt Brace Jovanovich, 1994.

Arendt, Hannah, and Jaspers, Karl. *Correspondence: 1926–1969*. Edited by Lotte Kohler and Hans Saner. Translated by Robert Kimber and Rita Kimber. New York: Harcourt Brace Jovanovich, 1992.

Aristotle. *Basic Works of Aristotle*. Edited by Richard McKeon. New York: Random House, 1941.

———. *The Politics*. Translated by T. A. Sinclair. New York: Penguin Books, 1977.

———. *Nicomachean Ethics*. Translated by Martin Ostwald. Indianapolis: Bobbs-Merrill Educational Publishing, 1980.

Bakan, Mildred. "Hannah Arendt's Concepts of Labor and Work," in Hill, ed., 1979.

Barber, Benjamin. *Strong Democracy*. Berkeley: University of California Press, 1984.

Barker, Ernest. *The Political Thought of Plato and Aristotle*. New York: Dover Publications, 1959.

———. Introduction to Aristotle's *Politics*. New York: Oxford University Press, 1968.

Beiner, Ronald. *Political Judgment*. Chicago: University of Chicago Press, 1983.

———. "The Moral Vocabulary of Liberalism," in *Virtue*. Nomos XXXIV. Edited by

John W. Chapman and William A. Galston. New York: New York University Press, 1992.

Benhabib, Seyla. *Critique, Norm, and Utopia*. New York: Columbia University Press, 1987.

———. *Situating the Self: Gender, Community, and Postmodernism in Contemporary Ethics.* New York: Routledge, 1992.

———. *The Reluctant Modernism of Hannah Arendt.* Sage Publications. Forthcoming.

Benhabib, Seyla, and Dallmayr, Fred, eds. *The Communicative Ethics Controversy.* Cambridge: MIT Press, 1990.

Benjamin, Walter. *Illuminations.* Edited by Hannah Arendt. New York: Schocken Books, 1968.

Bernasconi, Robert. "The Fate of the Distinction Between *Praxis* and *Poiēsis*." *Heidegger Studies* 2 (1986).

———. "Habermas and Arendt on the Philosopher's 'Error': Tracking the Diabolical in Heidegger," in Brainard, ed., "Heidegger and the Political." Special Issue, *Graduate Faculty Philosophy Journal*, Vol. 14, No. 2–Vol. 15, No. 1 (1991).

Bernauer, James W., ed. *Amor Mundi: Explorations in the Faith and Thought of Hannah Arendt.* Boston: Martinus Nijhoff Publishers, 1987.

Bernstein, Richard. "Hannah Arendt: The Ambiguities of Theory and Practice," in *Theory and Practice: New Perspectives.* Edited by Terence Ball. Minneapolis: University of Minnesota Press, 1977.

———. *Beyond Objectivism and Relativism.* Philadelphia: University of Pennsylvania Press, 1984.

———. *Philosophical Profiles.* Philadelphia: University of Pennsylvania Press, 1986.

———. *The New Constellation: The Ethical-Political Horizons of Modernity/Postmodernity.* Cambridge: MIT Press, 1992.

Bernstein, Richard, ed. *Habermas and Modernity.* Cambridge: MIT Press, 1985.

Blumenberg, Hans. *The Legitimacy of the Modern Age.* Translated by Robert Wallace. Cambridge: MIT Press, 1982.

Bourdieu, Pierre. *The Political Ontology of Martin Heidegger.* Stanford: Stanford University Press, 1991.

Bowen-Moore, Patricia. *Hannah Arendt's Philosophy of Natality.* New York: St. Martin's Press, 1991.

Buci-Glucksmann, Christine, ed. *Ontologie et Politique: Actes du Colloque Hannah Arendt.* Paris: Editions Tiesce, 1989.

Calhoun, Craig, ed. *Habermas and the Public Sphere.* Cambridge: MIT Press, 1992.

Canovan, Margaret. "The Contradictions of Hannah Arendt's Political Thought." *Political Theory*, No. 6 (February 1978): 5–26.

———. "Arendt, Rousseau, and Human Plurality in Politics." *Journal of Politics*, No. 45 (1983): 286–302.

———. "Politics as Culture: Hannah Arendt and the Public Realm." *History of Political Thought*, Vol. 6, No. 3 (1985): 617–642.

———. "Socrates or Heidegger? Hannah Arendt's Reflections on Philosophy and Politics." *Social Research*, Vol. 57, No. 1 (1990): 135–165.

———. *Hannah Arendt: A Reinterpretation of Her Political Thought.* New York: Cambridge University Press, 1992.

Caputo, John. *Radical Hermeneutics: Repetition, Deconstruction, and the Hermeneutic Project.* Bloomington: Indiana University Press, 1987.

Chytry, Josef. *The Aesthetic State.* Berkeley: University of California Press, 1989.

Dallmayr, Fred. "Ontology of Freedom: Heidegger and Political Philosophy." *Political Theory*, No. 12 (1984): 204–234.

————. *Margins of Political Discourse*. Albany: State University of New York Press, 1989.

————. *The Other Heidegger*. Ithaca: Cornell University Press, 1993.

Deleuze, Gilles. *Nietzsche et la Philosophie*. Paris: Presses Universitaires de France, 1962.

Derrida, Jacques. *Of Grammatology*. Translated by Gayatri Spivak. Baltimore: Johns Hopkins University Press, 1976.

————. *Writing and Difference*. Translated by Alan Bass. Chicago: University of Chicago Press, 1982.

————. *Margins of Philosophy*. Translated by Alan Bass. Chicago: University of Chicago Press, 1982.

————. *Of Spirit*. Translated by Geoffry Bennington and Rachel Bowlby. Chicago: University of Chicago Press, 1989.

Dews, Peter. *Logics of Disintegration*. New York: Routledge, 1987.

Dostal, Robert. "Judging Human Action: Arendt's Appropriation of Kant." *Review of Metaphysics*, No. 37 (1984): 725–755.

Draenos, Stan. "Thinking without a Ground: Hannah Arendt and the Contemporary Situation of Understanding," in Hill, ed., 1979.

Dreyfus, Hubert, and Haugeland, John. "Husserl and Heidegger: Philosophy's Last Stand," in *Heidegger and Modern Philosophy*. Edited by Michael Murray. New Haven: Yale University Press, 1978.

Dreyfus, Hubert, and Rabinow, Paul. *Michel Foucault*. Chicago: University of Chicago Press, 1983.

Farias, Victor. *Heidegger et le Nazisme*. Paris: Editions Verdier, 1987.

Ferry, Luc, and Renaut, Alain. *Heidegger and Modernity*. Translated by Franklin Philip. Chicago: University of Chicago Press, 1990.

Fichte, Johann Gottlieb. *The Vocation of Man*. Translated by William Smith. Chicago: Open Court Publishing Company, 1925.

Foucault, Michel. *The Order of Things*. New York: Random House, 1970.

————. *Discipline and Punish*. Translated by Alan Sheridan. New York: Vintage Books, 1979.

————. *Power/Knowledge*. Edited by Colin Gordon. New York: Pantheon Books, 1980.

————. *The Foucault Reader*. Edited by Paul Rabinow. New York: Pantheon Books, 1984.

Fraser, Nancy. *Unruly Practices*. Minneapolis: University of Minnesota Press, 1989.

Friedlander, Paul. *Plato*. 3 vols. Translated by Hans Meyerhoff. Princeton: Princeton University Press, 1969.

Gadamer, Hans-Georg. *Truth and Method*. New York: Seabury Press, 1975.

————. *Philosophical Hermeneutics*. Edited and translated by David E. Ling. Berkeley: University of California Press, 1977.

————. *Reason in the Age of Science*. Translated by Frederick G. Lawrence. Cambridge: MIT Press, 1981.

Gray, J. Glenn. "The Abyss of Freedom—and Hannah Arendt," in *The Recovery of the Public World*. Edited by Melvyn A. Hill. New York: St. Martin's Press, 1979.

Gunnell, John. *Political Theory: Tradition and Interpretation*. Cambridge, Mass.: Winthrop Publishers, 1979.

Haar, Michel. "Nietzsche and Metaphysical Language," in *The New Nietzsche*. Edited by David B. Allison. New York: Dell Publishing Company, 1980.

Habermas, Jürgen. *Toward a Rational Society*. Translated by Jeremy J. Shapiro. Boston: Beacon Press, 1970.

————. *Theory and Practice*. Translated by John Viertel. Boston: Beacon Press, 1973.

————. *Legitimation Crisis*. Translated by Thomas McCarthy. Boston: Beacon Press. 1975.

Habermas, Jürgen. "On the German-Jewish Heritage." *Telos*, No. 44 (1980).

———. *Philosophical-Political Profiles*. Translated by Frederick Lawrence. Cambridge: MIT Press, 1983.

———. *The Theory of Communicative Action*. 2 vols. Translated by Thomas McCarthy. Boston: Beacon Press, 1984.

———. *The Philosophical Discourse of Modernity*. Translated by Frederick Lawrence. Cambridge: MIT Press, 1987.

———. *The New Conservatism*. Edited by Sherry Weber Nicholsen. Cambridge: MIT Press, 1989.

———. *The Structural Transformation of the Public Sphere*. Translated by Thomas Burger. Cambridge: MIT Press, 1989.

Harries, Karsten. "Fundamental Ontology and the Search for Man's Place," in *Heidegger and Modern Philosophy*. Edited by Michael Murray. New Haven: Yale University Press, 1978.

———. "Heidegger as Political Thinker," in *Heidegger and Modern Philosophy*. Edited by Michael Murray. New Haven: Yale University Press, 1978.

Hegel, G.W.F. *The Philosophy of Right*. Translated by T. M. Knox. New York: Oxford University Press, 1942.

———. *Hegel's Lectures on the History of Philosophy*. 3 vols. Translated by Elizabeth Haldane. New York: Humanities Press, 1968.

———. *Reason in History*. Translated by Robert S. Hartman. Indianapolis: Bobbs-Merrill Educational Publishing, 1978.

———. *Phenomenology of Spirit*. Translated by A. V. Miller. New York: Oxford University Press, 1979.

Heidegger, Martin. *The Question of Being*. Translated by Jean T. Wilde and William Kluback. New Haven: College and University Press, 1958.

———. *An Introduction to Metaphysics*. Translated by Ralph Manheim. New Haven: Yale University Press, 1959.

———. *Being and Time*. Translated by John Macquarrie and Edward Robinson. New York: Harper and Row, 1962.

———. *Kant and the Problem of Metaphysics*. Translated by James S. Churchill. Bloomington: Indiana University Press, 1962.

———. "Plato's Doctrine of Truth," in *Philosophy in the Twentieth Century*. Volume 3. Edited by William Barrett. New York: Random House, 1962.

———. *What Is a Thing?* Translated by W. B. Barton, Jr., and Vera Deutsch. Chicago: Henry Regnery Company, 1967.

———. *Identity and Difference*. Translated by Joan Stambaugh. New York: Harper and Row, 1969.

———. *Poetry, Language, Thought*. Translated by Albert Hofstader. New York: Harper and Row, 1971.

———. *On Time and Being*. Translated by Joan Stambaugh. New York: Harper and Row, 1972.

———. *Sein und Zeit*. Tübingen: Max Niemayer, 1972.

———. *The End of Philosophy*. Translated by Joan Stambaugh. New York: Harper and Row, 1973.

———. *Early Greek Thinking*. Translated by David Farrell Krell and Frank A. Capuzzi. New York: Harper and Row, 1975.

———. "Only a God Can Save Us." *Der Spiegel* Interview with Heidegger, September 23, 1966. Translated by Maria P. Alter and John D. Caputo. *Philosophy Today* (Winter 1976): 267–284.

————. *Basic Writings*. Edited by David Farrell Krell. New York: Harper and Row, 1977.

————. "Who Is Nietzsche's Zarathustra?" in *The New Nietzsche*. Edited by David B. Allison. New York: Dell Publishing Company, 1977.

————. *The Question Concerning Technology and Other Essays*. Translated by William Lovitt. New York: Harper and Row, 1977.

————. *Nietzsche*. 4 vols. Edited by David Farrell Krell. New York: Harper and Row, 1979.

————. *The Basic Problems of Phenomenology*. Translated by Albert Hofstadter. Bloomington: Indiana University Press, 1982.

————. *The Metaphysical Foundations of Logic*. Translated by Michael Heim. Bloomington: Indiana University Press, 1984.

————. *Schelling's Treatise on the Essence of Human Freedom*. Translated by Joan Stambaugh. Athens: Ohio University Press, 1985.

————. *Beiträge zur Philosophie*. Gesamtausgabe 65. Frankfurt: Vittorio Klostermann, 1989.

————. "The Self-Assertion of the German University," in *Martin Heidegger and National Socialism*. Edited by Gunther Nesler and Emil Kettering. Translated by Karsten Harries. New York: Paragon House, 1990.

————. *The Principle of Reason*. Translated by Reginald Lilly. Bloomington: Indiana University Press, 1991.

————. *Platon's Sophist*. Gesamtausgabe 19. Frankfurt: Vittoria Klosterman, 1992.

————. *Parmenides*. Translated by André Schuwer and Richard Rojcewicz. Bloomington: Indiana University Press, 1992.

Hill, Melvyn, ed. *Hannah Arendt: The Recovery of the Public World*. New York: St. Martin's Press, 1979.

Hinchman, L. P. and Hinchman, S. K. "In Heidegger's Shadow: Hannah Arendt's Phenomenological Humanism," *Review of Politics*, Vol. 46, No. 2 (1984): 183–211.

Hobbes, Thomas. *Leviathan*. Edited by C. B. MacPherson. New York: Penguin Books, 1968.

Honig, Bonnie. "Arendt, Identity, and Difference." *Political Theory*, Vol. 16, No. 1 (1988): 77–98.

————. *Political Theory and the Displacement of Politics*. Ithaca: Cornell University Press, 1993.

Ingram, David. "The Postmodern Kantianism of Arendt and Lyotard," in *Judging Lyotard*. Edited by Andrew Benjamin. New York: Routledge, 1992.

Isaac, Jeffrey C. *Arendt, Camus and Modern Rebellion*. New Haven: Yale University Press, 1992.

Janicaud, Dominique. "Heidegger's Politics: Determinable or Not?" *Social Research*, Vol. 56, No. 4 (1991): 819–847.

Jay, Martin. *Permanent Exiles*. New York: Columbia University Press, 1985.

————. "The 'Aesthetic Ideology' as Ideology; or, What Does It Mean to Aestheticize Politics?" *Cultural Critique*, No. 21 (Spring 1992): 41–61.

Kant, Immanuel. *Critique of Judgment*. Translated by J. H. Bernard. New York: Hafner Press, 1951.

————. *Groundwork of the Metaphysics of Morals*. Translated by H. J. Paton. New York: Harper and Row, 1956.

————. *Critique of Pure Reason*. Translated by Norman Kemp Smith. New York: St. Martin's Press, 1965.

————. *Political Writings*. Edited by Hans Riess. Translated by H. B. Nisbet. New York: Cambridge University Press, 1971.

————. *Critique of Practical Reason*. Translated by Lewis White Beck. Indianapolis: Bobbs-Merrill Educational Publishing, 1978.

Kateb, George. *Hannah Arendt: Politics, Conscience, Evil.* Totowa, N.J.: Rowman & Allanheld, 1983.

———. *The Inner Ocean.* Ithaca: Cornell University Press, 1991.

Kierkegaard, Soren. *The Present Age.* Translated by Alexander Dru. New York: Harper and Row, 1962.

Knauer, James T. "Motive and Goal in Hannah Arendt's Concept of Political Action." *American Political Science Review*, Vol. 74, No. 3 (1990): 721–733.

Kuhn, Thomas. *The Structure of Scientific Revolutions.* Chicago: University of Chicago Press, 1970.

Lacoue-Labarthe, Philippe. *Typography: Mimesis, Philosophy, Politics.* Edited by Christopher Fynsk. Cambridge: Harvard University Press, 1989.

———. *Heidegger, Art and Politics.* Translated by Chris Turner. Cambridge: Basil Blackwell, 1990.

Lacoue-Labarthe, Philippe, and Nancy, Jean-Luc. "Ouverture," in *Rejouer le Politique.* Paris: Editions Galilee, 1982.

———. *Le Retrait du Politique.* Paris: Editions Galilee, 1983.

Lingis, Alphonso. "The Will to Power," in *The New Nietzsche.* Edited by David B. Allison. New York: Dell Publishing Company, 1977.

Lobkowicz, Nicholas. *Theory and Practice: History of a Concept from Aristotle to Marx.* Lanham, Md.: University Press of America, 1967.

Locke, John. *Two Treatises of Government.* Edited by Peter Laslett. New York: Cambridge University Press, 1960.

Löwith, Karl. *Max Weber and Karl Marx.* Translated by H. Fontel. London: Allen & Unwin, 1982.

———. *Mein Leben in Deutschland vor und nach 1933.* Stuttgart: J. B. Melzer, 1986.

———. "The Political Implications of Heidegger's Existentialism." Translated by Richard Wolin and Melissa Cox. *New German Critique* (1988).

Lyotard, Jean-François. *The Postmodern Condition: A Report on Knowledge.* Translated by Geoff Bennington and Brian Massumi. Minneapolis: University of Minnesota Press, 1984.

———. *Just Gaming.* Minneapolis: University of Minnesota Press, 1985.

———. *The Differend: Phrases in Dispute.* Translated by George Van Den Abbeele. Minneapolis: University of Minnesota Press, 1988.

———. *Heidegger and "the jews."* Translated by Andeas Michel and Mark Roberts. Minneapolis: University of Minnesota Press, 1990.

MacComber, John. *The Anatomy of Disillusion.* Evanston: Northwestern University Press, 1967.

Machiavelli, Niccolò. *The Prince*, in *The Portable Machiavelli.* Edited by Peter Bondanella and Mark Musa. New York: Penguin Books, 1979.

———. *The Discourses*, in *The Portable Machiavelli.* Edited by Peter Bondanella and Mark Musa. New York: Penguin Books, 1979.

MacIntyre, Alasdair. *After Virtue.* Notre Dame: University of Notre Dame Press, 1981.

Marx, Karl, and Engels, Friedrich. *The Marx-Engels Reader.* Edited by Robert Tucker. New York: Norton, 1978.

Marx, Werner. *Heidegger and the Tradition.* Translated by Theodore Kisiel and Murray Greene. Evanston: Northwestern University Press, 1971.

McCarthy, Thomas. *The Critical Theory of Jürgen Habermas.* Cambridge: MIT Press, 1979.

Mill, J. S. *On Liberty.* Edited by David Spitz. New York: Norton, 1975.

Miller, James. "The Pathos of Novelty: Hannah Arendt's Image of Freedom in the Modern World," in Hill, ed., 1979.

————. *Rousseau: Dreamer of Democracy*. New Haven: Yale University Press, 1984.

Mulgan, Richard. *Aristotle's Political Theory*. New York: Oxford University Press. 1977.

Nancy, Jean-Luc. *The Inoperative Community*. Edited by Peter Connor. Minneapolis: University of Minnesota Press, 1991.

Nehamas, Alexander. *Nietzsche: Life as Literature*. Cambridge: Harvard University Press, 1985.

Neske, Gunther and Kettering, Emil, eds. *Martin Heigegger and National Socialism*. New York: Paragon House, 1990.

Newell, W. R. "Heidegger: Some Political Implications of His Early Thought." *American Political Science Review*, Vol. 78, No. 2 (1984): 775–784.

Nietzsche, Friedrich. *The Birth of Tragedy*. Translated by Francis Goffling. New York: Doubleday, 1956.

————. *The Use and Abuse of History*. Translated by Adrian Collins. Indianapolis: Bobbs-Merrill Educational Publishing, 1957.

————. *The Will to Power*. Translated by Walter Kaufmann and R. J. Hollingdale. New York: Vintage Books, 1968.

————. *Beyond Good and Evil*. Translated by Walter Kaufmann. New York: Random House, 1974.

————. *The Gay Science*. Translated by Walter Kaufmann. New York: Random House, 1974.

————. *The Genealogy of Morals*. Translated by Walter Kaufmann. New York: Random House, 1974.

————. *Philosophy and Truth: Selections from Nietzsche's Notebooks of the Early 1870s*. Translated and edited by Donald Brazeale. Atlantic Highlands, N.J.: Humanities Press International, 1979.

————. *Twilight of the Idols*. Translated by R. J. Hollingsdale. New York: Penguin Books, 1979.

Norris, Christopher. "Complicity and Resistance: Heidegger, de Man, and Lacoue-Labarthe." *Yale Journal of Criticism*, Vol. 4, No. 2 (1981): 129–161.

O'Sullivan N. K. "Hannah Arendt: Hellenic Nostalgia and Industrial Society," in *Contemporary Political Philosophers*. Edited by A. de Crespigny and K. Minogue. London: Methuen, 1976.

Panis, Daniel. "La Question de l'Etre Comme Fond Abyssal d'après Heidegger." *Etudes Philosophique*, No. 1 (1986): 59–78.

Parekh, Bhikhu. "Hannah Arendt's Critique of Marx," in Hill, ed., 1979.

————. *Hannah Arendt and the Search for a New Political Philosophy*. London: Macmillan, 1981.

Pippin, Robert B. *Modernism as a Philosophical Problem*. Cambridge: Basil Blackwell, 1991.

Pitkin, Hanna Fenichel. "Justice: On Relating Private and Public." *Political Theory*, Vol. 9, No. 3 (1981): 327–352.

————. *Fortune Is a Woman*. Berkeley: University of California Press, 1984.

Plato. *Collected Dialogues*. Edited by Edith Hamilton and Huntington Cairns. Princeton: Princeton University Press, 1982.

Pocock, J.G.A. *The Machiavellian Moment*. Princeton: Princeton University Press, 1975.

Pöggeler, Otto. *Martin Heidegger's Path of Thinking*. Translated by Daniel Magurshak and Sigmund Barber. Altantic Highlands, N.J.: Humanities Press International, 1987.

Rawls, John. *Political Liberalism*. New York: Columbia University Press, 1993.

Riedel, Manfred. "Nature and Freedom in Hegel's 'Philosophy of Right,'" in *Hegel's Political Philosophy*. Edited by Z. A. Pelczynski. New York: Cambridge University Press, 1971.

Riley, Patrick. *Will and Political Legitimacy*. Cambridge: Harvard University Press, 1982.

Riley, Patrick. "Hannah Arendt on Kant, Truth and Politics." *Political Studies*, Vol. 35, No. 3 (1987): 379–392.

Rorty, Amelie Oksenberg. "The Place of Contemplation in Aristotle's Nicomachean Ethics," in *Essays on Aristotle's Ethics*. Edited by Amelie Oksenberg Rorty. Berkeley: University of California Press, 1980.

Rorty, Richard. *Philosophy and the Mirror of Nature*. Princeton: Princeton University Press, 1979.

————. *Consequences of Pragmatism*. Minneapolis: University of Minnesota Press, 1982.

————. *Contingency, Irony and Solidarity*. New York: Cambridge University Press, 1989.

————. *Essays on Heidegger and Others*. New York: Cambridge University Press, 1991.

————. *Objectivity, Relativism, and Truth*. New York: Cambridge University Press, 1991.

Rosen, Stanley. *Nihilism: A Philosophical Essay*. New Haven: Yale University Press, 1969.

Ross, W. D. *Aristotle*. London: Methuen, 1971.

Rousseau, Jean-Jacques. *Discourses*. Edited and translated by Roger D. Masters. New York: St. Martin's Press, 1964.

————. *The Social Contract*, in *Political Writings*. Edited and translated by Frederick Watkins. Madison: University of Wisconsin Press, 1986.

Sandel, Michael. *Liberalism and the Limits of Justice*. New York: Cambridge University Press, 1982.

————. "The Procedural Republic and the Unencumbered Self." *Political Theory*, Vol. 12, No. 1 (February 1984): 81–97.

Sartre, Jean-Paul. *L'Existentialism est un humanisme*. Paris: Editions Nagel, 1960.

————. *Being and Nothingness*. Translated by Hazel E. Barnes. Secaucus, N.J.: Citadel Press, 1977.

Schmidt, Dennis. *The Uniquity of the Finite*. Cambridge: MIT Press, 1989.

Schmitt, Carl. *The Concept of the Political*. Translated by George Schwab. New Brunswick: Rutgers University Press, 1976.

Schürmann, Reiner. "Political Thinking in Heidegger." *Social Research*, No. 45 (1978): 191–221.

————. *Heidegger on Being and Acting: From Principles to Anarchy*. Translated by Christine-Marie Gros. Bloomington: Indiana University Press, 1987.

Schwan, Alexander. *Politische Philosophie im Denken Heideggers*. Opladen: Westdeutscher Verlag, 1988.

Sennett, Richard. *The Fall of Public Man*. New York: Pantheon Books, 1978.

Shklar, Judith. *After Utopia*. Princeton: Princeton University Press, 1957.

————. "Rethinking the Past." *Social Research*, No. 44 (Spring, 1977).

Shulman, George. "Metaphor and Modernization in the Political Thought of Thomas Hobbes." *Political Theory*, Vol. 17, No. 3 (1989): 392–416.

Silber, John. "The Copernican Revolution in Ethics," in *Kant: A Collection of Critical Essays*. Edited by Robert Paul Wolff. Notre Dame: University of Notre Dame Press, 1967.

Sloterdijk, Peter. *Thinker on Stage: Nietzsche's Materialism*. Translated by Jamie Owen Daniel. Minneapolis: University of Minnesota Press, 1989.

Strauss, Leo. *Studies in Platonic Political Philosophy*. Chicago: University of Chicago Press, 1983.

————. *What Is Political Philosophy? and Other Studies*. Chicago: University of Chicago Press, 1988.

————. *The Rebirth of Classical Political Rationalism*. Edited by Thomas L. Pangle. Chicago: University of Chicago Press, 1989.

————. *On Tyranny*. Edited by Victor Gourevitch and Michael S. Roth. New York: *Free Press*, 1991.

Strong, Tracy. *Friedrich Nietzsche and the Politics of Transfiguration*. Berkeley: University of California Press, 1975.

Taminiaux, Jacques. "Arendt, disciple de Heidegger?" *Etudes Phenomenologiques* No. 2 (1985): 111–136.

————. *Heidegger and the Project of Fundamental Ontology*. Translated by M. Gendre. Albany: State University of New York Press, 1991.

————. "Heidegger and *Praxis*," in *The Heidegger Case: On Philosophy and Politics*. Edited by Tom Rockmore and Joseph Margolis. Philadelphia: Temple University Press, 1992.

————. *La Fille de Thrace et le Penseur Professionel: Arendt et Heidegger*. Paris: Payot, 1992.

Taylor, Charles. *Hegel*. New York: Cambridge University Press, 1975.

————. *Philosophy and the Human Sciences: Philosophical Papers 2*. New York: Cambridge University Press, 1985.

————. "Cross Purposes: The Liberal-Communitarian Debate," in *Liberalism and the Moral Life*. Edited by Nancy Rosenblum. Cambridge: Harvard University Press, 1989.

————. *Sources of the Self*. Cambridge: Harvard University Press, 1989.

Theunissen, Michael. *The Other: Studies in the Social Ontology of Husserl, Heidegger, Sartre, and Buber*. Translated by Christopher Macann. Cambridge: MIT Press, 1978.

Villa, Dana R. "Beyond Good and Evil: Arendt, Nietzsche, and the Aestheticization of Political Action." *Political Theory*, Vol. 20, No. 2 (May 1992): 274–308.

————. "Postmodernism and the Public Sphere." *American Political Science Review*, Vol. 86, No. 3 (September 1992): 712–721.

Viroli, Maurizio. *Jean-Jacques Rousseau and the Well-Ordered Society*. New York: Cambridge University Press, 1988.

Vlastos, Gregory. "Socrates on Political Obedience and Disobedience." *Yale Review*, No. 63 (1974): 517–534.

Vollrath, Ernst. "Hannah Arendt and the Method of Political Thinking." *Social Research*, No. 44 (1977).

Walzer, Michael. *Interpretation and Social Criticism*. Cambridge: Harvard University Press, 1987.

Weber, Max. "Politics as a Vocation" and "Science as a Vocation," in *From Max Weber*. Edited by Hans H. Gerth and C. Wright Mills. New York: Oxford University Press, 1972.

White, Stephen K. "Heidegger and the Difficulties of a Postmodern Ethics and Politics." *Political Theory*, Vol. 18, No. 1 (February 1990): 80–103.

————. *Political Theory and Postmodernism*. New York: Cambridge University Press, 1991.

Wiggins, David. "Deliberation and Practical Reason," in *Essays on Aristotle's Ethics*. Edited by Amelie Oksenberg Rorty. Berkeley: University of California Press, 1980.

Wilkes, Kathleen V. "The Good Man and the Good for Man in Aristotle's Ethics," in *Essays on Aristotle's Ethics*. Edited by Amelie Oksenberg Rorty. Berkeley: University of California Press, 1980.

Wittgenstein, Ludwig. *Philosophical Investigations*. Translated by G.E.M. Anscombe. New York: Macmillan, 1958.

————. *Tractatus Logico-Philosophicus*. Translated by D. F. Pears and B. F. McGuinness. London: Routledge and Kegan Paul, 1961.

Wolin, Richard. *The Politics of Being: The Political Thought of Martin Heidegger*. New York: Columbia University Press, 1990.

Wolin, Sheldon. *Politics and Vision*. Boston: Little, Brown, 1960.

Wolin, Sheldon. "Hannah Arendt: Democracy and the Political." *Salmagundi* 60 (1983): 3–19.

———. "Fugitive Democracy," *Constellations*, Vol. 1, No. 1 (1994).

Yack, Bernard. *The Longing for Total Revolution*. Princeton: Princeton University Press, 1986.

———. *The Problems of a Political Animal*. Berkeley: University of California Press, 1993.

Young-Bruehl, Elizabeth. *Hannah Arendt: For Love of the World*. New Haven: Yale University Press, 1982.

Zimmerman, Michael E. *Heidegger's Confrontation with Modernity*. Bloomington: Indiana University Press, 1990.

Zuckert, Catherine. "Martin Heidegger: His Philosophy and His Politics." *Political Theory*, Vol. 18, No. 1 (February 1990): 51–79.

238; Arendt and Heidegger's models of, compared, 136, 224; Heidegger's poetic model of, 219–224, 248–253, 263, 265; as human capacity, threatened by technological revealing, 182–183, 187–188, 201, 261
Duns Scotus, John, 118–119

Eastern Europe, 295n.34
enframing (*Gestell*), 173, 182–183, 187–188, 228–229, 260–265, 267–268. *See also* Heidegger: on technology
equality, 33–34, 89
Eudemian Ethics, 48
everydayness, 114–115, 127–133, 136–139, 145–146, 148, 167, 170, 212; identified with publicness, 130. *See also* fallenness
Extermination of the Jews, 164–165, 257–262

fabrication, 23–24, 47–49; ascendancy of, in modernity, 196–199; metaphorics of, 156–157, 169, 196–200, 233, 279n.58; naturalized in totalitarianism, 255–258. *See also* action: subsumed by making
fallenness (*Verfallenheit*), 115, 126, 128, 130–133, 145–146, 148–149, 170, 188, 225. *See also* everydayness
Fanon, Frantz, 156
feminism, 72, 147, 204–205
Ferry, Luc, 13, 115, 265
Fichte, Johann Gottlieb, 127
finitude, 114, 127, 134, 141, 225, 249–250; of Being, 124
Foucault, Michel, 24, 99, 100, 174, 206, 262, 268, 270, 299n.44
freedom, 18, 25, 43–45, 54, 61–62, 117–120, 229; as action, 25, 82; and finitude, 134; Heidegger's ontological approach to, 114, 119–136, 187; modern grounding of, in the will, 64–65, 67, 73–76; and modern revolutions, 149, 275n.87; from motives and goals, 84, 120; and necessity, 19–20, 29–30, 115; political, as nonautonomous, 76, 80, 82–84; and resoluteness, 141; and sovereignty, 61–62, 76, 80, 82–85; and thrown projection, 125–126; as virtuosity, 45, 53–55, 84, 91
French Revolution, 29–30, 67, 149, 275n.87, 280n.92

Gadamer, Hans-Georg, 8, 10, 69, 228, 244, 245
Galileo, 190–191, 193, 195–196
Gay Science, The, 91
Gelassenheit (releasement), 13, 167, 189, 227, 231, 234, 237, 239, 260
Genealogy of Morals, The, 86–88, 92, 100

Goebbels, Joseph, 248
Goethe, Johann Wolfgang von, 240
Gray, J. Glenn, 60
Groundwork of the Metaphysics of Morals, 61

Haar, Michel, 98
Habermas, Jürgen, 3–6, 12, 23, 25, 39–40, 42–43, 59, 60, 70–72, 77–78, 99, 194, 204–205, 244–245, 262, 266, 274n.79, 277n.151, 283n.179; on Heidegger, 211, 213–216, 218, 224–226, 229–230, 232, 241–243, 268, 305nn. 92 and 95
Harries, Karsten, 121, 133, 216, 218–219, 223
Hegel, G.W.F. 10, 27–28, 49, 60–61, 65, 66–67, 108, 142, 202, 233, 234, 248, 249, 251, 267, 275n.87
Heidegger, Martin: aestheticism of, 249–254, 263–266; on anxiety, 133, 216; on art, 219–224, 249–254; attempted overcoming (*Uberwindung*) and surmounting (*Verwindung*) of Platonism/nihilism, 145, 151–154, 248–254, 260; on Being-in-the-world, 120–124; on care, 126; on concealment and unconcealment, 145–147, 154–155, 185–188, 221, 238–239; conception of the state, 142, 221–224, 248–249, 251–252, 266, 305n.83; critique of modernity, 172–173, 175–188, 225; deconstruction and repetition, xi, 9, 114, 151–155, 217–218, 243, 245–246, 248–250, 264, 266; on Descartes, 175–176, 178, 225; on dialectic of transcendence and everydayness, 128–129, 132–133, 136–138, 145–146, 148–149, 212–213; discourse on *techne*, 250–252, 254, 256, 260, 262–265; on epistemology, 121; and German Idealism, 127, 176, 236; on Kant, 176–178, 181, 219; *Kehre* (turning), 119, 166–167, 225–226, 229, 231, 234, 236–237, 239, 253, 264; on modern science, 179–180; and Nazism, 151, 219, 231, 243, 248–254, 259–260; and Nietzsche, 127, 132, 135, 169, 177–178, 225, 231, 235–236; on oblivion of Being (*Seinsvergessenheit*), 151, 166–167, 183, 198–199, 226, 238; philosophical prejudice against the realm of human affairs, 154–155, 211, 225, 231–240; on *poiēsis*, 132, 142, 185, 187, 219–224, 246, 249–254, 263–265, 267, 304n.53; and politics, 212–224, 241–243, 251–252; on *praxis*, 132, 142, 146, 154–155, 189, 211, 219, 223–224, 227–229, 243–246, 249–250, 253, 260–262, 264–265; on presence, 152, 155, 167–170, 238, 250, 264–265; privileging of thinking over action, 146–147, 211, 227–231, 234–241, 268, 307n.130; on productionist metaphysics,

ABOUT THE AUTHOR

DANA R. VILLA is Assistant Professor of Political Science at Amherst College.